Filmmaker's Dictionary
2nd Edition

Ralph S. Singleton
and James A. Conrad

Edited by Janna Wong Healy

FILMMAKER'S DICTIONARY
Second Edition
Copyright © 2000 by Ralph S. Singleton and Lone Eagle Publishing

LONE EAGLE PUBLISHING COMPANY™
1024 North Orange Drive
Hollywood, California 90038
Tel: 323-308-3400 or 800-FILMBKS
A division of IFILM Corp., www.ifilm.com

Printed in the United States of America

Cover design by Lindsay Albert
Book design by Carla Green

Library of Congress Cataloging-in-Publication Data

Singleton, Ralph S. (Ralph Stuart)
    Filmmaker's dictionary / Ralph S. Singleton and James Conrad; edited by
Janna Wong Healy. —2nd ed.
        p.   cm.
    ISBN 1-58065-022-8
    1. Motion pictures—Dictionaries. 2. Cinematography—Dictionaries.
3. Television—Dictionaries. I. Conrad, James A. II. Healy, Janna Wong. III. Title.

PN1993.45 .S56 2000
791.43'03—dc21   00-034900
                                                        CIP

Lone Eagle books may be purchased in bulk at special discounts for promotional or educational purposes. Special editions can be created to specifications. Inquiries for sales and distribution, textbook adoption, foreign language translation, editorial, and rights and permissions inquiries should be addressed to: Jeff Black, Lone Eagle Publishing, 1024 North Orange Drive, Hollywood, CA 90038 or send e-mail to: info@loneeagle.com

Distributed to the trade by National Book Network, 800-462-6420

A Abbreviation for "actor" used on union forms.

A and B cutting (aka A and B rolling) Negative cutting technique used in 16mm film to make invisible splices. The first shot is put onto the A roll, with black leader in the corresponding position on the B roll; the second shot is put onto the B roll, with black leader in the corresponding position on the A roll. All subsequent shots are checkerboarded (alternated) with black leader in the same manner. The two rolls are printed separately onto the stock of the next generation so that the shots touch each other with no splice in between. This is not necessary for 35mm film because the frame is large enough that the splice does not show. A and B cutting is used in both 16mm and 35mm to make fades and dissolves that are not done by an optical house. For a dissolve or superimosition, two shots are overlapped (aka lap dissolve) on the A and B rolls. More rolls (C, D, etc.) can be used for additional superimpositions, titles, etc.

A and B editing 1. Process, using a video mixer, of selecting and assembling images from two separate, video playback machines, identified as "A" and "B." The combined footage is placed onto a single master tape, which is part of a third machine. Some video mixers accept more than two input sources; e.g., A-B-C-D. Also called A and B roll editing. Related term: videotape editing. 2. Film editing process in which two rolls of film, "A" and "B," alternately contain lengths of black leader between shots or scenes so that dissolves, fades, invisible splices (for 16mm film) and other editing effects can be achieved. Related term: film editing.

A and B rolling See A and B cutting.

AA Abbreviation for a classification or rating of a theatrical film or video in which the words "Adult Accompaniment" appears. In Canada, the classification is "'14'—Adult Accompaniment Required Under Age 14." In Great Britain, "AA" was changed to the classification symbol "15" in 1982. Related term: rating.

A-B blood Theatrical blood produced when its two clear liquid parts are combined. Used in knife-cutting and flogging scenes. Part A is applied to the actor's skin, part B to the knife or whip. When the two solutions make contact, fake red blood dramatically appears. The active chemical ingredients in A-B blood are potassium thiocyanate and ferric chloride (both suspended in water). Two mail-order sources for A-B blood are the U.S.-based special-effects companies Burman Industries, Inc., of Van Nuys, California, and Tri-Ess Sciences, Inc., of Burbank, California. Related term: special blood effects.

A-B foam Two-part liquid foam mix that produces, for about 15 minutes, a frothy mass of fine bubbles similar to the foam on beer. A source for A-B foam, as well as other special-effects foam products, is Tri-Ess Sciences, Inc., of Burbank, California.

A-B smoke Simulated smoke produced when the vapors (fumes) of its two liquid parts are mixed in the air, one of the methods used to give food or drink the appearance of steam rising from it. Two sources for A-B smoke are Tri-Ess Sciences, Inc., of Burbank, California and Zeller International, Ltd., of Downsville, New York. Related terms: smoke effect, steam chips.

Abby Singer Shot Production jargon for the next-to-the-last shot of the day (e.g., "The next shot is the Abby Singer.") The term came into use when Mr. Singer was an assistant director.

about-face Act of turning one's body halfway to face the opposite direction; e.g., "When you get to that mark on the stage, do an about-face and walk back to your starting point." Related term: half-turn.

above the title credits Refers to the position of front credits that appear before the main title of the film. The order of credits is usually as follows: distributor, producer/production company, presenting a (director's name) film, followed by name(s) of principal star(s), then the film title. Recently, more credits appear above the title. In previous days, however, this space was carefully guarded, with only the name of the distributor, and perhaps a particularly powerful producer appearing (e.g., David O. Selznick, Samuel Goldwyn, Dino De Laurentiis). Frank Capra was the first director to have his name above the title. Related terms: billing, top billing.

above-the-line Production expenses relating to the purchase of rights to literary material and salaries for producers, writer, director, and principal cast. A film's budget is divided into two main sections: above-the-line costs and below-the-line costs. Above-the-line expenditures are usually negotiated on a run-of-show basis and, generally, are the most expensive individual items on the budget (e.g., costs for story and screenplay, producer, director and cast). Below-the-line costs consist of the technicians, materials and labor. (Labor costs are usually calculated on a daily basis.) Also included in below-the-line costs are: raw stock, processing, equipment, stage space, and all other production and post-production costs.

abrasions Damage to film caused by improper handling or winding. These usually are visible as cuts and scratches on the surface of processed film.

AC Television rating meaning "Adult Content."

Academy aperture Motion picture frame-mask size having a non-widescreen aspect ratio of 1.33:1 (4:3). In use since 1906 for silent movies, it was set by the Academy of Motion Picture Arts and Sciences as a Hollywood standard for 35mm soundtrack-on-film movies in 1932. Standardization was necessary because moviemakers, in the new era of the "talkies," were taking up too much space on the film for soundtrack purposes, which then squared-off the frame size. Today, all theatrical motion pictures are shot in various widescreen aspect ratios, with sufficient edge space for a time-code track or one or more magnetic or optical soundtracks. The 1.33:1 size is still important, however, because it is the same width-to-height ratio as the screen on a standard television set. Related terms: aperture, aspect ratio, safe action area, widescreen.

Academy Award® (aka Oscar®) Award bestowed yearly by the Academy of Motion Picture Arts and Sciences upon film actors, directors, producers, writers, cinematographers, composers, songwriters, art directors, editors, costume designers, makeup artists, visual-effects supervisors, engineers, chemists, etc., in recognition of achievement during the previous year, a lifetime of work or a contribution to the film industry; scientific or technical advancement in filmmaking is also awarded. The term "Academy Award®" can refer to the Award of Merit (Oscar® statuette), Special Achievement Award (Oscar® statuette; also called a special Oscar® or honorary Oscar®), Lifetime Achievement Award (Oscar® statuette; also called an honorary Oscar®), Irving Thalberg Memorial Award (a small golden bust of Thalberg mounted on a cubed base), Jean Hersholt Humanitarian Award (Oscar® statuette), Gordon E. Sawyer Award (Oscar® statuette; presented for long-term contributions to film-related science and technology), Medal of Commendation, Scientific and Engineering Award (a free-standing Academy Plaque with the front half of a small Oscar® statuette sculpted on it and an engraved metal plate on its base), or Technical Achievement Award (an Academy Certificate inscribed with the winner's name). In January, nominating ballots for the 24 film-production Oscars® are mailed to members of the Academy in their respective fields (actors nominate only actors, directors nominate only directors, etc.) for films released the previous calendar year. Final voting to select the winner from among the five nominees in each category takes place,

again by mail, in February and March. The five Best Picture nominees are chosen by the entire eligible membership. Nominating committees are formed for the categories of Foreign Language Film, Documentary (Feature and Short Subject), Makeup and Sound Effects Editing, since these categories have no corresponding branch of the Academy (subject to change). In the category of Visual Effects, a preliminary steering committee narrows the choice of nominees to seven films. Samples of the effects from those seven films are screened by visual-effects branch members, who then select the five nominees. In the final general voting, each Academy member is allowed to vote for winners in all categories, not just those in his professional branch; however, in the Documentary, Short Films, and Foreign Language categories, only members who have attended special screenings of the films may vote. The announcement of winners and the presentation of Oscars® takes place in late March on live television. The Scientific and Technical Awards are voted by the Academy's Board of Governors, based on recommendations submitted by the Scientific and Technical Awards Committee, and are bestowed in a separate ceremony held in advance of the internationally televised Oscars® ceremony. The Academy's official list of winners dates each Academy Award® according to the year of nominating eligibility (the year the work took place), not the following year in March when the Award is actually presented. When presented, the Oscar® statuette has only a serial number displayed on it. Later, the name "Academy Award®," the award category, winner's name, the Academy's full name and the year for which it was won are engraved by machine on a metal plate that is affixed to its base. The Scientific and Engineering Award (Academy Plaque) and Technical Achievement Award (Academy Certificate) are physically inscribed with the year of presentation; e.g., "Presented March [year]," even though both awards are officially listed with all the Oscar® winners for the previous year of nominating eligibility. The first awards were presented in 1927. The names "Academy Award®" and "Oscar®" are registered trademarks and service marks of the Academy of Motion Picture Arts and Sciences (AMPAS), which also owns the copyright for the image of the Oscar® statuette. Internet addresses: http://www.oscars.org, http://www.oscars.com, http://www.ampas.org. Related terms: Academy of Motion Picture Arts and Sciences, Oscar®.

Academy Leader A length of black film designated by the Academy of Motion Picture Arts and Sciences (AMPAS) which should be attached to the head of each reel, containing the numbers from ten to two, in descending order, to show where the picture starts. At the number two, a sound cue (beep) is heard, signifying that the picture is about to start. The picture begins where the number one would be. A newer system, designed by the Society of Motion Picture and Television Engineers (SMPTE) and for use in theatrical and television projection of motion pictures, is called Universal Leader.

Academy of Canadian Cinema and Television Organization of film and television industry professionals in Canada. Among its activities, it publishes an annual directory, "Who's

Who in Canadian Film and Television," and presents Canada's key awards shows: English-track Gemini TV Awards, French-track Gemeaux TV Awards, and the feature film Genie Awards. Founded in 1979.

Academy of Motion Picture Arts and Sciences (abbreviated as AMPAS) Honorary organization of filmmakers whose membership is by invitation only. Divided into categorized branches (e.g., directors, actors, cinematographers, art directors, composers), members nominate and vote by secret ballot to determine the annual winners of the Academy Awards®. AMPAS also supports a research and collections library, publishes its *Academy Players Directory* and endorses such issues as film preservation. It is based in Beverly Hills, California. Internet address: http://www.ampas.org. Related term: Academy Award®.

Academy of Science Fiction, Fantasy & Horror Films U.S. organization whose members are professionals in the three named genres, including writers, producers, directors, visual-effects designers and actors. Members vote annually on who shall receive the Saturn Award in various categories. Also presented are a Saturn Service Award, George Pal Memorial Award, President's Award and Life Career Award. Founded in 1972 and based in Los Angeles. Related term: Saturn Award.

Academy of Television Arts and Sciences (abbreviated as ATAS) Los Angeles-based organization of television industry professionals. The Academy of Television Arts and Sciences bestows the Emmy Award for outstanding nighttime programs in the United States (in addition to Emmys for the local Los Angeles market) while the National Academy of Television Arts and Sciences, based in New York City, bestows the Emmy Award for outstanding daytime, news, sports, local (except Los Angeles) and international programs. The organizations are related. Founded in 1948. Internet address: http://www.emmys.org.

Academy Players Directory Multivolume printed or electronic publication listing alphabetically and by casting category (Leading Women/Ingenues; Leading Men/Younger Leading Men; Characters & Comediennes/Characters & Comedians; and Children) a sampling of union actors (also, nonunion actors represented by union-franchised talent agents) who are available to work in film, television, video, stage, etc. Each listing is inserted for a fee and consists of one small full-face photo accompanied by agent, manager and contact information. Additional optional information that may be listed is performing credits, special skills and physical characteristics. Major stars and newcomers list themselves here. Published in January, May and September by the Academy of Motion Picture Arts and Sciences in Beverly Hills, California. First published in 1937. Related term: casting directory.

Academy standard flat Common motion-picture frame-mask size having a widescreen aspect ratio of 1.85:1 (1.85 to 1). "Flat" refers to the photographed image, by means of an anamorphic lens, not being optically squeezed into the 1.85:1 film frame space. Related term: widescreen.

A-camera Film or video camera designated as "A" on a production set, for recordkeeping, blocking and editing purposes. May also be called camera

one. If more than one camera is used, they are designated with consecutive letters, "B," "C," or "2," "3," etc.

accelerated motion Action scene shot with the camera running at a speed of less than 24 frames per second (normal sound speed) so that when it is projected at normal speed, it appears speeded-up. The opposite is slow motion.

accounting department Division or section of a talent or literary agency responsible for managing the agency's financial records, as client billings, commission deductions, and relaying payment to actors or talent. Related term: actor's account.

ace A 1000-watt spotlight equipped with a fresnel lens.

A.C.E. Abbreviation for American Cinema Editors, an honorary professional society of film editors in the United States that promotes the advancement of the art and craft of editing; it also bestows annual editing awards. Membership is by invitation only. Founded in 1950 and based in West Hollywood.

acetate base Slow-burning, chemical film base that has replaced the older, highly-flammable nitrate base. Most older films have been transferred to the more durable acetate base. Related term: safety base

act 1. To portray a character as an actor; to perform a role or play a part. Related term: acting. 2. A short performance by one or a group of entertainers. Related terms: comedy act, dance act, entertainment act, live act, lounge act, music act, nightclub act, opening act, replacement act, singing act, song-and-dance act, variety act, number, performance, routine. 3. The performance and entertainers collectively. 4. One of the divisions that make up a stage play, TV show or opera. 5. To do, operate or function; e.g., "The agent acted as her representative in the process of obtaining film and TV work."

act break 1. Transitional time between the acts of a stage play during which set and costume changes are made; an intermission. 2. In a TV series episode, a transitional pause in the story during which stations identify themselves and run commercials. Related term: station break.

act curtain Stage curtain that opens and closes, representing the beginning or end of an act in a play.

acting coach An individual who works with an actor to develop a valid characterization for an upcoming or current role. An acting coach will rehearse with a performer and provide guidance on proper auditioning techniques and production-set activities. Related term: acting teacher.

acting company Group of actors who perform in productions. Related terms: fringe company, road company, stock company, theater company, touring company, repertory, troupe.

acting credit Acknowledgment of the role an actor has performed in film, television, live theater, radio, a video-game or other performing medium.

acting exercise One or a series of activities that help an actor maintain or improve his performing abilities. Also called an acting practice session. Related terms: exercise, acting scene, improvised play, reading.

acting movement Actor's physical action or manner of moving, e.g., a turn or hand gesture, during his performance. Related terms: false movement, natural movement, unnatural movement, director's directions, eye contact, make an entrance, slapstick, stunt work.

acting name Name by which an actor is hired and known by the entertainment industry and the public. It could be the actor's birth name or a shortened or altered version of it (due to length, similarity, unusualness or difficulty in pronunciation or spelling) or it could be an entirely new name altogether. Talent unions will not allow a new member to use the same name as a current member, so the newly-registered name, or stage name, must be different in some way, even if it is just by the inclusion of a middle initial. For example, Michael Keaton's actual name is Michael Douglas but he had to change it to when he joined SAG. Related terms: name change, stage name.

acting note Comment, suggestion or instruction regarding an actor's performance.

acting stereotype Fixed image of how a particular character in a story should look and behave, e.g., an old and crazy gold prospector, a prim librarian or a high-school nerd. An acting stereotype usually begins when an actor gives a successful portrayal of an original character. Later, productions of the same work will offer close copies of that same character portrayal in an attempt to achieve the same success. The appearance, voice and mannerisms of that type of character soon become fixed and the acting stereotype is born. Related terms: stereotype, typecast, character type.

acting studio 1. Another name for an acting school. 2. Another name for a rehearsal studio.

acting workshop Group of actors who come together to learn and experiment with various acting techniques, usually under the guidance of an acting teacher. An acting workshop may be conducted on a for-profit or non-profit basis. Related terms: acting class, acting school, theater workshop.

action 1. All that takes place in a filmed, videotaped or live shot or scene, according to the script and as per the direction or supervision of the director. Related terms: background action, foreground action, live action, overlap action. 2. Stunts or other forceful physical movement in a script. Examples: running, jumping, falling, fighting, car chases, explosions and weather effects. Related terms: action-packed, nonstop action.

"Action!" Instruction spoken by the director and used as a cue to begin the performance within a shot or scene. Related terms: "And . . . Action!" "Lights! . . . Camera! . . . Action!"

action figure Small, usually plastic, full-color representation of a character from a movie, TV series, comic book, advertising campaign or sports-related field. Often resembles the celebrity who portrays that character. It is purchased as a child's toy or as an investment collectible or is acquired as a promotional giveaway item, as at a fast-food restaurant. *Star Wars* (1977) was the first blockbuster to spawn action figures. Related terms: merchandising tie-in, movie merchandise.

action hero Leading protagonist in an action movie; an action movie's good guy.

action photo Photograph featuring an image of action. Also called an action still. Related term: still photo.

action prop Prop that is used during action in a shot or scene; prop subject to movement. Examples: handgun, sword, knife, baseball bat, golf club, rope and book. Must be handled, or in some way moved, by an actor during the performance. Also called an action property. Related terms: hand prop, prop.

action scene Scene in the script in which any type of swift-paced movement of characters, vehicles, animals, etc., takes place. Related term: action movie.

action still Photograph from an actual frame of a motion picture that has been blown up, as opposed to a photograph taken with a still camera.

action track Film (picture) before music, dialogue or effects tracks are added.

action-adventure Genre of film or television that combines fast-paced action with an exciting journey or unusual risk of some kind. Prototypical examples of the genre include *The Matrix* (1999) and *Star Wars: Phantom Menace* (1999). Related term: adventure.

actioner An action movie. Entertainment trade paper use.

Actor Award Name of the annual award bestowed by the Screen Actors Guild in the United States. The first Actor statuettes were presented during a nationally televised ceremony on February 26, 1995, for work performed during the year of 1994. Related term: Screen Actors Guild Award.

actor development Process of learning how to live and work correctly and successfully as an actor. Also called professional actor development, actor training, or acting instruction. Related terms: acting class, on-the-job experience, on-the-job training.

actor/actress Any person who performs in a play, television show, film, etc. Anyone working on a union film or television project who utters one word has a "speaking part" and must be paid according to the rules and regulations of the Screen Actors Guild (SAG). Productions on tape (audio or video) are under the jurisdiction of the American Federation of Television and Radio Artists (AFTRA). Theatrical productions fall under the jurisdiction of Actors Equity. The gender neutral, all-inclusive term "actor" is more commonly used today to refer to male and female actors.

actor's account The financial record of income received, commission deductions, paycheck statements, and the like that is maintained for each actor in the Accounting Department of a talent agency. Related term: accounting department.

actor's craft Occupational knowledge and skills associated with being an actor.

Actors' Equity Association Union in the United States for performers and stage managers employed in professional theater productions. Also known as (American) Actors' Equity Association, Actors' Equity, or Equity. Founded in 1913 and based in New York City, with offices around the United States. Related terms: AEA (American), British Actors' Equity Association, Canadian Actors' Equity Association, Norwegian Actors' Equity Association, Equity card, non-Equity.

actor's fee Payment to an actor by a production company for the performing of acting services. Related term: scale.

Actors' Fund of America (abbreviated as AFA) U.S. relief and human services organization of the entertainment industry that provides, to qualifying individuals, numerous services, including emergency financial assistance, counseling, nursing home care and retirement housing. It also conducts various programs, e.g., overcoming substance abuse and obtaining employment between engagements. Founded in 1882 and based in New York City.

actor's medium Theatrical stage; acting in plays. The theatrical stage is said to be the actor's medium because it allows the actor the greatest amount of creativity in his performance. The director's medium is said to be film.

actor's production company Production company owned by a successful actor who wants the independence of choosing and developing television, film, or theatrical projects in which he will star. A way for the actor to be in creative and financial control of his own projects. Also called "housekeeping deal" or "vanity deal."

actor's signature Business procedure necessary on work contracts, representation agreements, union forms and paychecks. In the case of a minor, the parent or guardian signs in place of or in addition to the actor. Whether or not a minor-aged actor endorses an acting paycheck depends on the actor's age and the banking program. An actor's signature may also be found or given in the form of an autograph, which can become a collector's item to fans.

actor's time sheet Daily record of an actor's work times, including meal breaks or meal penalties (and their duration) and the time he was released for the day. The actor signs his record each day; a copy is sent to SAG (or AFTRA).

ACTRA Alliance of Canadian Cinema, Television and Radio Artists. In

Canada, a union for performers, scriptwriters, and commentators.

AD Abbreviation for assistant director. Related terms: first assistant director, second assistant director.

ad campaign Short for advertising campaign. Related terms: publicity campaign, television campaign, cross-promotional tie-in.

adaptation Script based on another medium (e.g., a novel, article, play, film, TV series, advertisement, song, news event). The story is adapted (adjusted to suit another medium) for presentation to a different medium. For example, *The Cider House Rules* (1999) was an adaptation of John Irving's novel of the same title. Related terms: faithful adaptation, loose adaptation, TV-movie adaptation, comic-book version, movie version, stage version, TV version.

added scene Scene inserted into a script after said script has been assigned scene numbers. The added scene is noted with a letter beside the number. Related terms: omitted scene, A-page, blue pages.

additional credit Second, onscreen credit, e.g., "The actor got an additional credit as executive producer."

additional dialogue One or more lines of dialogue added to a script before or during production or in the post-production process. (An example of additional dialogue during post-production is the insertion of off-screen dialogue or narration that did not appear in the original script.) Also called added dialogue or extra line(s).

ad-lib To perform without preparation; to improvise dialogue and possibly action that is not in the script (e.g., "I forgot my lines, so I attempted to ad-lib my way through the scene.") Related terms: improvisation, wing it.

ad-lib session Session in which one or more performers originates his or her own dialogue and possibly action. Also called an improv session or creative session.

ADR Abbreviation for automatic dialogue replacement, a system used to dub new or improved dialogue. Instead of the older looping method, the soundtrack and film are played forward during the act of dubbing and then, if needed, rewound quickly back to the beginning for another try. It is still referred to as looping today, though technically, no loop is involved (e.g., "I've got some looping to do this afternoon." Translation: "I've got some ADR work to do this afternoon"). Related term: loop.

ADR editor Individual who edits ADR (automatic dialogue replacement) recordings.

ADR mixer Individual who combines ADR (automatic dialogue replacement) recordings. Related term: dialogue mixer.

ADR recordist Individual in an ADR (automatic dialogue replacement) studio who operates the recording equipment during an ADR session.

ADR session Recording session during which dialogue is replaced using the ADR (automatic dialogue replacement) method.

ADR studio Soundproof studio with a control room, viewing screen, projection and recording equipment necessary to produce ADR recordings during post-production.

adult video Video intended for viewing by adults only. If sexually oriented, it is also called a sex video, porno video, X-rated video or triple-X-rated video. Related terms: blue movie, X-rating.

advance 1. Number of frames by which the sound recording must precede the film image in order to be in sync. For 35mm, the advance is 20 frames; for 16mm, it is 26 frames. 2. Amount of money paid ahead of time to secure talent.

advance teaser campaign Advance publicity campaign consisting of TV or movie theater commercials, print or Internet ads, live publicity events, etc., that occur before a film opens or a TV program is telecast. For a film or TV series, this may include having the entertainment media visit the set during production, a prerelease press tour or junket. It is designed to stir public interest through advance word-of-mouth advertising and name recognition.

advanced television Any television transmission and signal-processing system that is more advanced than the traditional analog systems that have been in worldwide use since the mid 1940s; any current or proposed digital television system. Related terms: ATV, broadcast quality.

advertising 1. Promoting or informing through the use of advertisements. Related terms: product advertising, visual sell. 2. Creation and placement of advertisements. 3. The industry, world, field or profession of advertising.

advertising agency Company representing and servicing the advertising needs of its clients. Also called an "ad agency." Related term: TV commercial producer.

advertising director 1. Individual responsible for the organization and supervision of a product's advertising

campaign. 2. One who directs an electronic advertisement.

advertising rate Fee or charge for placing and running an advertisement.

advertising trailer Commercial shown in theaters. Another name for a movie theater commercial.

AEA 99-seat plan theater Actors' Equity Association (U.S.) designation for a playhouse with fewer than 100 seats and in which its members are allowed to perform for little or no pay (as for showcase purposes and under certain guidelines). Also called an AEA 99-seat theater. Related term: Equity 99-seat theater.

aerial coordinator Stunt pilot who specializes in arranging aircraft stunt sequences for film and TV productions.

aerial shot Scene filmed from a helicopter or plane, etc., using a special camera mount. Related terms: 'copter mount, Tyler mount.

aerial unit Production unit responsible for filming one or more shots from an aerial location.

AFA Abbreviation for Actors' Fund of America.

affil. Short for "affiliate." Entertainment trade paper use.

affiliate Local TV station operating under an agreement with a national or international network to show a certain amount of that network's programming, per their agreed schedule. Related term: network affiliate.

AFI Abbreviation for the American Film Institute.

AFI/Los Angeles International Film Festival An exhibition of independently made films.

AFM 1. Abbreviation for American Film Market. Annual film marketing festival in the United States where national and international producers gather to sell their completed and planned movies, as well as those in production, to distributors from around the world. Many low-budget films (B-pictures) are offered, including independently produced films and those not released theatrically in the U.S. (such films have direct-to-video releases instead). It is organized and presented by the American Film Marketing Association (AFMA), a U.S. trade organization whose members are independent feature film producers and distributors. Founded in 1980 and based in Los Angeles, California. 2. Abbreviation for American Federation of Musicians, the union of professional musicians.

AFTRA Abbreviation for American Federation of Television and Radio Artists. The U.S. union for performers working in live and electronically recorded television and radio commercials, live and recorded television programs (series, talk shows, specials, etc.), and related areas. Founded in 1937 and based in New York City, with offices around the United States.

age range Series of ages, graduating from young to old or vice versa, which an actor can physically portray in a role. Also called "age portrayal range" or "physical age group."

age requirement 1. Qualification or limitation set by an agency as part of its policy for accepting new clients to represent. 2. Minimum age required for purchasing or participating in a production, film or stage play.

agency book 1. Collection of actors' head shots or composites bound in book form. Also called an agency talent book or head book. 2. Such a collection displayed on a computer screen via a specially recorded CD-ROM or by accessing the agency's site on the Internet. Related term: portfolio. 3. An agency's office appointment record book.

agency card 1. Card displaying a represented actor's pictures and personal statistics. Also called a composite card or Zed card. 2. Agency's policy statement card.

agency clearance Approval by an agency of something in question, such as a rate, contract, assignment, working condition, picture or release. Related term: booking clearance.

agency contract 1. Written agreement between an agency and talent detailing the obligations each has and the options by which the agency agrees to act as representation for the talent in obtaining work. Representation usually is for a stated length of time and for a stated percentage of the talent's earnings. Also called an agency representation contract. 2. Any other agreement that may be originated by an agency, as a voucher or release.

agency division Section or department of a talent or advertising agency responsible for the representation of a particular type of client or a department which performs in-house duties for said agency. Examples of agency division types: children's, men's, talent, television, theatrical, voiceover, and women's. Related terms: accounting department, division director.

agency policy statement 1. A list of instructions regarding booking and billing procedures that is given to clients. It is printed on the headsheet, agency book, or separately in some other form. Related term: model booking policy. 2. A statement from an agency regarding its policy on accepting new clients to represent.

agency representative Person employed by and officially authorized to represent its agency in business dealings, public relations, talent hunts or social functions. An example is an agency division director. The terms of an agency representation contract state the conditions under which either side can terminate the agreement. Unions also have rules in this regard, which apply only to union-signatory agencies.

agency switching Change of representation from one agency to another. This may be done for career reasons or it could be due to a change of residence to a new city or because of dissatisfaction with the current agency.

agent 1. Person or company licensed by the state to represent clients and negotiate their contracts for a standard agent's fee (usually ten percent of the client's salary). Representative from the agency who acts as a business representative for his client. An agent obtains interviews, auditions, handles request bookings, negotiates and collects fees, deducts a union-fixed or agreed-upon commission and generally assists in the development of the client's career. Related terms: animal agent, booking agent, children's agent, photographers' agent, talent agent, theatrical agent, rep, representation. 2. Any other type of representational agent. Related terms: advertising agent, press agent, public relations agent. 3. The agency and its operations collectively.

agenting 1. Working as an agent. 2. The field, profession or world in which agents work; e.g., the agenting business or various agenting fields of the entertainment industries.

agent's fee Payment to an agent by a client for services provided. Also called an agent's commission.

AGMA Abbreviation for American Guild of Musical Artists. Union representing opera singers, classical concert singers, classical ballet dancers, modern dancers and the stage directors and stage managers from these fields. Founded in 1936 and based in New York City.

AGVA Abbreviation for American Guild of Variety Artists. Union representing nightclub and variety show performers (singers, dancers, comedians, etc.), circus performers and other types of indoor and outdoor entertainers. Founded in 1939 and based in New York City.

air To show on television or play on radio; to broadcast over the airwaves.

air bag 1. Large, hollow stunt cushion, constructed of nylon sheeting or vinyl-coated polyester fabric, that is inflated with air by one or more electric blower fans connected to wide flexible hoses. It is used to safely stop the descent of a stuntperson performing a stunt fall. 2. In automobiles, a concealed, automatically inflating safety cushion. At the moment of collision, it inflates instantly with nitrogen gas generated from a solid chemical source. The first feature film to use a steering-wheel air bag in a stunt crash scene was *Moving Violation* (1976). In it, American stuntman Vic Rivers drove a deputy sheriff's car head-on into a 16-ton concrete wall at 35 miles per hour (56 km/h). The scene was shot from numerous angles, including an interior shot of the air bag inflating in Rivers's face and chest. Also spelled airbag.

airbrush 1. Small, hand-held spray gun shaped somewhat like a large fountain pen that uses compressed air to blow a fine spray of dye, ink or oil color onto a photographic or artwork surface. It is attached to an air hose and operated by pressing a button that controls the flow of air through the nozzle. Used for retouching or as a special visual effect, an airbrush can be used to eliminate facial imperfections or to add clouds, wisps of steam or smoke or other highlights to an image. Increasingly, it is being replaced by computerized digital retouching and enhancement. Airbrushing is also used to paint latex monster masks, background paintings, T-shirts and other artwork surfaces. 2. To airbrush something. Related term: retouch.

air-to-air Description of a filmed shot of one flying object taken from another flying object, such as filming an airplane from a neaby helicopter.

Alliance of Motion Picture and Television Producers Organization (United States) that represents producers in contract negotiations with labor unions and the like. Founded in 1982 and based in Encino, California. Related term: AMPTP.

alligator clamps Small, pointed spring clips, so-named because they resemble an alligator's jaws; used on a production set to hold objects in place.

allowance Money provided to cover expenses as part of a work contract. Related terms: meal allowance, spousal/companion allowance, travel allowance, travel-companion allowance, wardrobe allowance, per diem.

all-time box-office champ Highest grossing film of all time. (Currently, *Titanic* [1997] is the all-time box-office champ.) Related term: B.O. champ.

alphabetical-order credit listing The positioning of performers' names in alphabetical order on a list of printed or onscreen credits. This may occur when there are many stars of equal rank appearing in a production and a way is needed to avoid credit negotiation problems. Another way to list credits when there is a large, distinguished cast is by order of appearance.

ambience Mood, feeling or presence that pervades a scene.

ambient sound Normal sounds that exist in a particular place (e.g., street noise, chirping birds, wind, room tone).

ambush journalism Practice of a news crew (including reporter, cameraman with camera running and soundperson) confronting an individual without an appointment to conduct an on-camera interview. Such an interview may be called an ambush interview, confrontational interview or cold interview.

American Cinema Editors (abbreviated as ACE) An honorary professional society of film editors in the United States that promotes the advancement of the art and craft of editing; it also bestows annual editing awards. Membership is by invitation only. Founded in 1950 and based in West Hollywood.

American Comedy Award Annual award given to the best film, TV, and stand-up comedy performers in the United States.

American Federation of Musicians of the United States and Canada Union for musicians working in the United States and Canada. Founded in 1896 and based in New York City. Related term: AFM.

American Federation of Television and Radio Artists (abbreviated as AFTRA) The U.S. union for performers working in live and electronically recorded television and radio commercials, live and recorded television programs (series, talk shows, specials, etc.), and related areas. Founded in 1937 and based in New York City, with offices around the United States.

American Film Institute (abbreviated as AFI) Nonprofit U.S. organization dedicated to the preservation and cataloging of feature films made in the U.S. and to the education of filmmakers through its film school, the Center for Advanced Film and Television Studies. Founded in 1967 and based in Washington D.C., with offices in Los Angeles. Internet address: http://www.afionline.org. Related terms: AFT, AFT Life Achievement Award.

American Film Market (abbreviated as AFM) Annual film marketing festival in the United States where national and international producers gather to sell their completed and planned movies, as well as those in production, to distributors from around the world. Many low-budget films (B-pictures) are offered, including independently produced films and those not released theatrically in the U.S. (such films have direct-to-video releases instead). It is organized and presented by the American Film Marketing Association (AFMA), a U.S. trade organization whose members are independent feature film producers and distributors. Founded in 1980 and based in Los Angeles, California.

American Guild of Musical Artists (abbreviated as AGMA) Union representing opera singers, classical concert singers, classical ballet dancers, modern dancers and the stage directors and stage managers from these fields. Founded in 1936 and based in New York City.

American Guild of Variety Artists (abbreviated as AGVA) Union representing nightclub and variety show performers (singers, dancers, comedians, etc.), circus performers and other types of indoor and outdoor entertainers. Founded in 1939 and based in New York City.

American Humane Association Animal protection organization in the United States, providing guidance to filmmakers in the proper treatment of animals used in films, television programs, commercials and stage shows. According to union contracts, the producer must notify the Association prior to using any animal in a production; the Association may opt to have a representative on the set during production.

American Society of Cinematographers (abbreviated as ASC) Honorary organization, comprised of directors of photography and others related to cinematography, that works to advance the art and craft of motion picture and television camera work. Membership is by invitation only. Founded in 1919 and based in Hollywood. The British counterpart is the British Society of Cinematographers (B.S.C.); Canadian counterpart is the Canadian Society of Cinematographers (C.S.C.).

American Society of Composers, Authors, and Publishers (abbreviated as ASCAP) Organization that acts as a clearinghouse for the licensing of musical works and the distribution of royalties to its members. The "authors" and "publishers" in its name refers to lyricists and music companies. Founded in 1914.

amortize, amortization To reduce and settle a debt by regular, periodic payments of principal and interest. In the case of a motion picture, its negative cost is charged against its revenue, thereby lowering the debt.

AMPAS Abbreviation for Academy of Motion Picture Arts and Sciences. Honorary organization of filmmakers whose membership is by invitation only. Divided into categorized branches (e.g., directors, actors, cinematographers, art directors, composers), members nominate and vote by secret ballot to determine the annual winners of the Academy Awards®. AMPAS also supports a research and collections library, publishes its *Academy Players Directory* and endorses such issues as film preservation.

amphitheater Building, room or outdoor site with a tiered seating section arranged around a central performing area. Related term: outdoor theater.

analog 1. Information presented in dial form (with pointer and graduated markings) or in LCD bar-graph form; e.g., a set of circular analog clocks in a newsroom scene showing the current time in different countries of the world. 2. Information recorded and stored in a varying continuous form (with physical variables) in direct correlation to the original information, e.g., the grooves on an old-style phonograph record. (Opposite of analog is the digital method which records and stores information in a discontinuous form—a coded series of ons and offs, represented as "ones [1s]" and "zeroes [0s].")

anamorphic lens Camera lens that squeezes, or compresses, the right and left sides of a widescreen image into the frame space of 35mm motion picture film stock during filming. Another anamorphic lens is used to unsqueeze (expand) the image when it is projected onto a movie screen. Also called a squeeze lens. Related terms: Academy standard flat, widescreen.

anamorphic print Motion picture film print on which a widescreen image is squeezed into each 35mm frame.

ancillary market Additional place or medium where a product, such as a film or rights to manufacture merchandise based on a film, can be sold or licensed. Also called an after-market.

ancillary right That which is supplemental to the main transaction in an agreement, for example, the rights to sell a game, toy, calendar, poster, comic book or literary novel. Related term: merchandising tie-in.

"And. . . Action!" Common variation of the director's, "Action!" The "And . . ." acts as a preliminary cue to alert everyone on the set that the main cue, "Action," will be said momentarily.

angel Financial supporter of a theatrical production. Related term: theater angel.

angle 1. Position of the camera and lens in relation to the subject being photographed. Related terms: camera angle, objective camera angle, subjective camera angle, shot and angle descriptions. 2. Position of an actor onstage or on the set in relation to the audience. 3. To aim or position.

animal actor Animal trained to follow voice or cue signal instructions or to otherwise behave appropriately while performing in a story. Also called an animal performer or non-human actor.

animal handler Individual who transports and controls animals used in a production. Related term: wrangler.

animal trainer Individual who teaches an animal to perform specific movements or sounds (tricks) via sight or sound cues.

animated film Film story told via animation. May also be called a cartoon feature or feature-length cartoon. Related terms: animation, children's movie, featurette.

animatics Technique or process of shooting drawings, still photographs (or elements of either) or stop-motion model miniatures for the purpose of creating sequenced, animated storyboards or finished products. If the animatic is of a storyboard, it is also called an animated storyboard. Related term: photomatics.

animation Specialized branch of fllmmaking in which drawings or three-dimensional objects are photographed frame-by-frame (most commonly, two frames at a time and sometimes, in low-budget production, three frames at a time) so that when they are projected at a normal speed, the illusion of movement is created. Sometimes (particularly in art films) drawing or painting is done directly on the film.

animation bed Specially designed table (with top and bottom lights) used with an animation stand to create animated film; it has pegs that hold the animation cel to be photographed and is turnable, so the artwork, as well as the camera, can move.

animation camera Camera capable of shooting frame-by-frame. Used in animation.

animation cel Piece of transparent acetate, approximately 9" x 12", that contains one in a series of drawings to be photographed for an animated film. Formerly, each cel was drawn by hand; today, the outlines are drawn onto paper, then transferred onto acetate, after which the colors are filled in by hand.

animation stand Elaborately designed and constructed unit that holds the animation camera tightly in place, regulates the movement of the camera by calibration and allows for zooms.

animator 1. Artist who draws animation artwork. Related term: maquette. 2. Individual who prepares and shoots movable (usually miniature) model figures in a step-by-step, stop-motion animation process. 3. Individual who creates animation using a computer. Related term: CGI effects animator.

animator's live-action model Person or creature whose body and movements are the basis or inspiration for animation artwork or computer images. Related terms: live-action reference, figure model, motion capture.

animatronic Of or pertaining to three-dimensional puppet or robotic movements, electronically controlled by the use of servomotors, solenoids or pumps. Related terms: Audio-Animatronic, Videotronic.

animatronic puppeteer Individual who operates the controls of an electromechanical puppet. Depending on its complexity, numerous off-camera (offstage) puppeteers may be required to operate a single puppet. The puppet may also have hand-operated, internal mechanical cables controlling its various body movements; a large puppet may have a human actor inside. Related terms: puppeteer, robot operator.

ankle Term meaning one who voluntarily dissociates from a project or company. e.g., "The exec ankled his studio post to form his own production company." Entertainment trade paper use.

ANN Abbreviation for announcer. Individual who reads the voiceover copy for radio and television spots (e.g., commercials, program introductions and promos, station identifications, equipment-failure interruptions, special report notices, emergency broadcast tests and program and station sign-offs). Also called an off-screen or off-camera announcer. Related terms: commentator, narrator, Voice of God, voiceover artist.

announcer (abbreviated as ANN) Individual who reads the voiceover copy for radio and television spots (e.g., commercials, program introductions and promos, station identifications, equipment-failure interruptions, special report notices, emergency broadcast tests and program and station sign-offs). Also called an off-screen or off-camera announcer. Related terms: commentator, narrator, Voice of God, voiceover artist.

announcing booth Small, soundproof room in which an announcer records the show's announcements. Related term: sound studio.

"Answer back to the camera." Direction to an actor to look into the camera lens.

answer print The lab's first composite print of an edited theatrical film with both sound and images synchronized. Several answer prints may be necessary before all required color corrections are made. Related terms: trial print or approval print.

antagonist Enemy; foe; opponent. The opposite is a protagonist. Related term: villain.

anthology Program (usually for television) featuring a new, unrelated story each week and sporting a different cast and setting in every episode. Examples are the classic science-fiction TV series *The Twilight Zone* (1959-65) and *The Outer Limits* (1963-65).

anticlimax Moment in a story that occurs after the presentation of a highly dramatic sequence of events and the viewer is left feeling disappointed or emotionally cheated because the action or mystery was thoughtlessly or quickly resolved.

anti-halation Transparent coating applied to the cel side of the film negative to reduce halation (unwanted flares or halos on the film). It is removed during processing.

antihero Leading character who lacks traditional heroic qualities. He is often a loner, eccentric or a wrongdoer who is romanticized by the story's action and dialogue. James Dean portrayed a classic antihero in *Rebel Without a Cause* (1955).

A-page Additional page inserted in the script between two already-numbered pages. Subsequent additional pages inserted after the A-page and before the next numbered page are lettered consecutively (e.g., 127, 127A, 127B, 128.) Related terms: added scene, blue pages.

aperture 1. Opening (circular or other-shaped) that allows light (images) to pass from a camera's lens system to the film or CCD chip. The size of the opening is controlled by a mechanical iris diaphragm with a series of calibrated numbers called f-stops. The aperture regulates the amount of light entering the camera while the shutter regulates the length of time the light is allowed to enter (typically a fraction of a second). Related terms: depth of field, exposure, f-stop, iris, lens flare spot, DX-coded film. 2. Academy aperture; the standard aspect ratio of 1:33.1 (4:3) for a 35mm motion picture film-frame dimension, as set in 1932, by the Academy of Motion Picture Arts and Sciences in the United States.

aperture plate Rectangular mask in a camera, in front of the film; it defines the frame by blocking light from the edges of the film.

A-picture Theatrical film that has a high budget or is prestigious because of its cast, director, producer, writer, composer, visual-effects crew or the like. Also called an "A" picture, A-grade film, A-film, A-movie, or A-title. Related terms: B-movie, double feature.

apochromatic lens Lens used in color photography that corrects for chromatic abberation by causing the light rays of different wave lengths to converge at a single point.

applause sign Electrically lighted sign, a type of cue light, positioned above a TV studio audience; the word "APPLAUSE" lights up whenever audience applause is required. (Applause is used to show pleasure or respect for the quality of the production; or as a transitional effect to signify the ending or beginning of a segment or performance.) If there is no applause sign in a studio, or if it is an outdoor production, a crew member stands at the front side of the audience and waves his arms to signal the audience to applaud. He may initiate the applause by being the first one to begin clapping.

applause track Soundtrack made up of audience applause; used mainly in television and radio to take the place of applause from a live studio audience. Related terms: canned applause, sweeten.

apple box Type of sturdy wooden box used to raise the height of an actor or object; derived from the early days of filmmaking, when real fruit crates were used for this purpose. Today, apple boxes are constructed of plywood and are also used as small storage and transport boxes. Also called a riser. There is no standard size for a full apple box, with regard to width and length, but all apple boxes are 8" high (20.3mm). Some typical full apple box sizes are 8" x 12" x 18" or 8" x 12" x 20" or 8" x 14" x 24". Also called a full-apple or full-riser. Related terms: full apple box, half apple box, quarter apple box, pancake apple box.

apprentice editor Member of the editing staff who handles miscellaneous tasks while learning the responsibilities of editor and assistant editor.

approval Permission granted or required. Related terms: cast approval, director approval, picture approval, reporter approval, script approval, writer approval, clearance, right, test deal.

apron Area in front of the proscenium on a theater stage, e.g., the portion of a stage visible to the audience after the curtain is lowered. Related terms: forestage, thrust stage.

Aqua Fire Clear, smokeless, cool-burning fuel used for fire-on-water special effects. It has a low vapor output and is safer to ignite than gasoline or similar fuels. Formulated and sold by Zeller International, Ltd., of Downsville, New York.

Aqua Gel Thick, clear, nontoxic liquid (it can be colored as desired), used to simulate containerized or spilled chemicals, alien body fluids, monster slime or other liquid effects. Formulated and sold by Zeller International, Ltd., of Downsville, New York. Related term: Super Goop.

arbitration Forum for resolving disputes through an informal, non-judicial hearing. Participants in the arbitration agree to be bound by the decision of the hearing for resolution of claims.

arc 1. High-intensity lamp that operates on direct current, either xenon/mercury arc, which requires no adjustment, or carbon arc, which requires frequent adjustment. The carbon arc produces light that approximates daylight (around 4800 Kelvin), so it is often used to simulate sunlight in the studio or as a booster for outdoor color shooting. 2. Progression of various plots woven through the story. In serial television, arcs relate to various storylines for the characters during the season.

arc episode TV series episode that advances a story arc significantly, as opposed to one in which the plot is unrelated or only slightly related to the story arc. Related term: arc.

"Arc out." 1. Direction to an actor who is in front of the camera to walk across a set in a curved path to achieve the appearance of traveling in a straight line; meanwhile, the camera is rotating on a swivel base. 2. Direction to the camera crew to move or swivel the camera in a curved path.

arc shot Camera shot in which the camera moves in a circular path around a subject. Also called a circle-around shot.

arena stage 1. Another name for a theater-in-the-round. 2. Raised stage with the audience located on three sides. Also called an open stage.

armature Internal, solid-wire or ball-and-socket framework of a clay or foam-latex stop-motion animation puppet. Related terms: movable miniature, wireframe.

arrangement 1. Manner in which items, such as props, are placed; the composition of items. 2. Agreement; contract. 3. In music, an adaptation of a musical composition for other types of instruments or voices or for another musical style.

arranger Individual who prepares and adapts previously written music for presentation in a form other than its original form. Often, an arranger will work from a composer's sketch and create parts that will be assigned to voices and/or instruments by the orchestrator. The composer may do his own arranging and orchestrating.

Arriflex (abbreviated as Arri) Trade name for a line of Academy Award®-winning, 35mm motion picture film cameras manufactured by the German company Arnold and Richter Cine Technik. The Arri was the first portable, self-blimped 35mm movie camera. The company, which also manufactures 16mm Arriflex cameras, is represented in the United States by its subsidiary, Arriflex Corporation of Blauvelt, New York and Burbank, California.

art department Crew members who, under the direction of the production designer, are responsible for creating the look of a film in relation to the sets and locations (as opposed to the visual look and costumes). The staff might include the art director, an assistant art director, set designer, draftsman and apprentice.

art director Individual responsible for the design and preparation of the production's visual concepts and set construction (may sometimes be referred to as the production designer or set designer; in theater, may also be called the scenic designer or set designer). For advertising, the art director may be involved with photo layouts, ad layouts, storyboard design and the selection and hiring of talent.

art house Movie theater that principally exhibits foreign and specialty (independent) films. Also called an art theater. Related term: art house film.

art house film Specialized movie whose style or genre falls outside of the more mainstream, studio-made motion pictures. Typically, these are independently made (often, on low budgets) and are shown in smaller, independent movie theaters. Also called an art theater film or limited-market film.

artificial breakeven Mutually agreed-upon amount of revenue generated by a film which, when reached, triggers the payment of profits. Related term: breakeven.

artificial light Opposite of natural light, any man-made light from floodlights, spotlights, etc.

artist 1. Commercial artist, matte artist, scenic artist, special-effects artist or animator. 2. Makeup artist. 3. Another name for a performer or entertainer.

artistic differences Differing of creative opinions. Same as creative differences.

artistic license Freedom granted or conceded to an artist, writer, performer, director, etc., to do things his own way. In film, TV and theater, it is also called dramatic license; in literature, poetic license.

artistic shot Visually appealing and skillfully executed camera shot.

artist's advance Payment to a performer made prior to work actually beginning. Also called an advance payment or advance.

ASA speed rating Internationally accepted system for identifying the emulsion speed (image recording ability) of film. The higher the ASA number, the more sensitive the emulsion. Other rating systems are DIN (the European standard) and ISO (the newest system, also used internationally).

A.S.C. Abbreviation for American Society of Cinematographers. Honorary organization, comprised of directors of photography and others related to cinematography, that works to advance the art and craft of motion picture and television camera work. Membership is by invitation only. Founded in 1919 and based in Hollywood. The British counterpart is the British Society of Cinematographers (B.S.C.); Canadian counterpart is the Canadian Society of Cinematographers (C.S.C.)

ASCAP Abbreviation for American Society of Composers, Authors, and Publishers. Organization that acts as a clearinghouse for the licensing of musical works and the distribution of royalties to its members. The "authors" and "publishers" in its name refers to lyricists and music companies. Founded in 1914. Internet address: http://www.ascap.com

A-scene See added scene.

ASDA Australian Screen Directors Association. Union in Australia for TV and film directors, assistant directors, production managers and television stage managers. Based in Sydney, Australia and established in 1980. Internet address: http://www. asdafilm.org.au.

aside Remark by an actor onscreen or onstage intended to be heard by the audience only and not by other characters in the scene. In an aside, the actor turns for a moment to look directly into the camera or out to a live audience to make the parenthetical comment.

aspect ratio Width-to-height relationship of a projected or printed motion picture frame. There are several different aspect ratios: Academy aperture (1.33:1), Standard (1.85:1) and widescreen (2.35:1). Television is proportionately the same as Academy. (An interesting note: The human eye's range of vision is an ellipse whose proportions are roughly 1.85:1). Related terms: Academy aperture, Academy standard flat, HDTV, matte, SDTV, widescreen process, screen, Cinemascope, cinerama.

aspirin hit Tablet-sized bullet hit (squib) used in gunfight scenes. Small wires are attached, allowing it to be detonated by an off-camera electrical power supply.

assembly First step of editing, during which scenes are put together in script sequence for a rough telling of the story. Related terms: rough cut, fine cut, final cut, editing.

assistant camera One of the possible onscreen credit titles for an assistant camera operator.

assistant camera operator Camera crew member whose responsibilities, depending on the size of the production, may include loading and unloading film or videotape, making lens changes and adjusting the focus,

taking light readings and camera-to-subject measurements, maintaining camera condition and keeping camera reports. On large-budget productions, the responsibility for some of these duties (including clapboard duties) may belong to the second or third assistant camera operator. The assistant camera operator may also be called the first assistant camera operator, assistant cameraperson, assistant cameraman or camera assistant. Related terms: first assistant cameraman, second assistant cameraman, camera-to-subject measurement, clapboard, focus ring, follow focus, loader.

assistant director (abbreviated as AD) Individual who assists a director in administrative and production duties. The responsibilities of an assistant director in film and video may include preparing shooting schedules, filling out production paperwork, summoning and serving as a liaison between the director and actors or other crew members, rehearsing actors, organizing crowd scenes, maintaining order on the set and giving voice commands ("Quiet on the set," etc.). Some of these duties may be performed by a second or third (also called a second second) assistant director. The assistant director may also be called the first assistant director. Related terms: first assistant director, second assistant director, second second assistant director.

assistant editor Member of the editing staff who works with the editor to sync dailies, catalog and keep the dailies organized and accessible, splice film and keeps the editing room in working order. A good filing and coding system helps organize the thousands of feet of film. The assistant editor communicates with the labs and effects companies and, in general, does those jobs that free the editor to edit the film.

assistant photographer An individual who assists a photographer in the studio and on location in administrative duties; setting up camera shots, sets, lighting equipment, fans, etc.; and loading and unloading film. There may be a first, second, etc., assistant photographer. Related term: photographer's assistant.

assistant stage manager Assistant to the stage manager, as on a theater production. Depending on the size of the production, there may be a first, second and third assistant stage manager.

associate director Production crew members for a live or taped television show who assists the director; communicates to the department heads what the director needs before taping begins; ensures that the stage manager and cameras know the director's instructions; makes sure cameras are in position; and keeps a log of the tape during taping.

associate producer Title that varies from one production to another. It can be the title given to the producer's second-in-command who shares business and creative responsibilities, or it can designate an additional credit given to the production manager who also acts as line producer, or it can be an honorary title given to one of the financiers or to the person responsible for bringing the property to the producer.

Associated Actors and Artistes of America Organization whose members are unions in the performing arts fields, including Actors' Equity Association, AFTRA, American Guild of Musical Artists, American Guild of Variety Artists and the Screen Actors Guild. Founded in 1919 and based in New York, New York.

Association of Talent Agents Organization in the United States representing the interests of talent agencies in dealings with entertainment industry unions and the government. Founded in 1937 and based in Los Angeles, California.

Association of Theatrical Press Agents and Managers (abbreviated as ATPAM) Union in the United States representing publicists and stage managers who work in the fields of theater and stage shows. Founded in 1928 and based in New York, New York.

astigmatism Lens imperfection whose effects can sometimes be corrected or lessened by decreasing the size of the aperture (or, "stopping the lens down").

asynchronism Discrepancy between the soundtrack and the image on the screen. Related terms: in sync, out of sync, synchronization.

atmosphere 1. Prevailing mood or sense of environment in a scene, accomplished by visual or audio means; e.g., "Fake cobwebs were strung across the ceilings of the abandoned house to give the scene an eerie atmosphere." 2. Any one or more people, animals, objects, lights, shadows or sounds in a scene that help define an emotional tone or that provide a feeling of authenticity. For people, atmosphere refers to background talent (extras) and their various movements and sounds.

atmosphere vehicle Any form of transportation (car, truck, motorcycle, etc.), used in a scene but not by a principal player or any other actor with a speaking part.

ATPAM Abbreviation for Association of Theatrical Press Agents and Managers.

attitude 1. Emotional or mental state expressed toward a person or activity. 2. Bodily position or bearing; e.g., attitude of the body. Related terms: angle, pose.

attorney Legal advisor and representative for handling contracts, lawsuits, criminal court cases, name changes, emancipation and other business or personal matters. Also called a lawyer. Related terms: entertainment attorney, damage control, name change.

attraction 1. Business, show or exhibit intended to attract admission-paying visitors, e.g., a theme park attraction. Related terms: amusement attraction, main attraction, ride-through attraction, roadside attraction, tourist attraction, amusement park, simulator ride, theme park, throughput, turnaround. 2. Personal magnetism or appeal between two individuals, as between two characters in a script, especially in a romantic sense. Also called physical attraction. Related terms: chemistry, romance movie.

ATV Abbreviation for advanced television. Any of various high-quality methods of digitally transmitting and converting television signals, as opposed to transmission by traditional analog methods. Examples are digital SDTV and digital HDTV. Related term: advanced television.

audience Individuals present to view or to listen to a live or tape-recorded event or program. Also called a crowd. Related terms: computer audience, live audience, paying audience, preview audience, studio audience, theater audience, easy crowd, house, tough crowd, turnaround, TV viewer.

audience movie Theatrical film that paying audiences appreciate more than film critics. The opposite is a critics' movie.

audience plant Individual who is placed (or, planted) in the audience for a specific purpose, e.g., to be part of a comedy sketch or assist a magician; or to prompt or encourage the desired audience reaction, e.g., applause or a specific vocal response, such as laughter, anger or compassion.

audience ringer Another name for an audience plant.

audience walkout A member of the audience who walks out of the theater during the performance, either as a display of protest, displeasure, boredom, etc., or because of a need to be elsewhere. An individual who leaves the theater and returns is not counted as a walkout.

audio Sound portion of the film or tape, as opposed to the video, or visual, portion.

Audio-Animatronic Trade name for the Walt Disney Company's special-effects process of constructing electronically controlled, mechanically animated figures activated by electrical motors/solenoids, hydraulic/air cylinders and/or movable cables; the figures have limbs, a head and lips that can be synchronized by computer to move with the playback of a desired voice or musical soundtrack. An audio-animatronic figure is, essentially, a highly sophisticated, electromechanical puppet. The term was coined and registered as a trademark by the Walt Disney Company (then called Walt Disney Productions) to refer to its realistic theme park robots. The first audio-animatronic figure was built in 1947, and was an 8" electromechanical puppet whose movements were based on a film clip of actor Buddy Ebsen singing and dancing to the song "Swanee River." Related terms: animatronic, puppet.

audiorecord To register sound on audiotape, compact disc, memory chip or other recording medium.

audiotape 1. Flexible plastic tape coated with an iron-oxide composition on which sound can be recorded by magnetically reorganizing its sensitive particles. By electronically reading the analog or digital pattern of the particles formed by this reorganization, sound is played back. Videotape recording and playback work in the same manner except that, on videotape, the audio and visual signals are recorded on separate places on the tape and by separate electromagnetic heads. The audiotape most commonly used to record sound on a production has a width of 1/4" (6.35mm) and is used on a professional reel-to-reel tape recorder. Also called audio magnetic tape or sound tape. Also spelled audio tape. Related term: base side. 2. To record sound on such tape; to audiorecord on magnetic tape. 3. Another name for an audiocassette.

audio-visual Of or pertaining to sound and picture; hearing and sight; recording, playback, projecting and lighting equipment; e.g., an audio-visual presentation.

audit Formal examination, reconciliation and verification of all financial accounts and records. This may apply to production auditing or distribution auditing (revenues generated by the film).

audition 1. To try out for an acting role (in a television show, commercial, motion picture, video, stage production, live promotion activity, etc.), usually in front of a person or group empowered to make casting decisions. Related terms: group audition, live audition, open audition, TV commercial audition, two-person audition, talent test, callback. 2. To conduct or participate in an audition.

audition anxiety Fear, worry, uneasiness, etc., about having to audition for a role. Related term: performance anxiety.

audition piece 1. Another name for an audition scene. 2. Musical composition, dance routine, etc., used by a performer in an audition.

audition report form Sign-in sheet used at auditions; it is a union form.

audition room Location of a casting session. Related terms: casting office, conference room, interview room, rehearsal studio, waiting room.

audition scene Prepared or ad-libbed scene performed by an actor (either solo or with someone else) during an audition. Also called an audition acting scene. Related terms: audition piece, acting scene, monologue, soliloquy.

audition tape Video or audio tape cassette or reel used in an audition. Related terms: audition disc, demo tape.

auditionee Individual being auditioned.

auditioner Individual or group of individuals (casting director, producer, etc.) conducting the audition.

auditor Person responsible for keeping the film's financial records, issuing cost reports, estimating final costs, etc. Related terms: production accountant, location auditor.

Australian Film Institute Organization of movie and television industry professionals in Australia. Among its activities, it presents the Australian Film Institute Awards. Founded in 1958.

Australian Film Institute Award Annual award bestowed by the Australian Film Institute, honoring the best in theatrical and television film work in Australia. The first awards were presented in 1958.

Australian Screen Directors Association (abbreviated as ASDA) Union in Australia for TV and film directors, assistant directors, production managers and television stage managers. Based in Sydney, Australia and established in 1980. Internet address: http://www.asdafilm.org.au.

autofocus Electromechanical system inside a camera that, by a variety of possible sensing methods (optical grids, infrared light or inaudible sound pulses), automatically detects and adjusts the focal length of the lens, thus putting an image into proper focus.

autograph Personal signature of a celebrity. An autograph becomes a collector's item with fans, which in turn, assists a performer's career by creating an ongoing process of publicity and a lasting legacy after the performer has retired or died. Some individuals actively seek autographs from celebrities and sell them to collectors and fans around the world. Some celebrities do not like this commercial aspect of autograph hunting and refuse such requests, while other celebrities, recognizing it as a way to keep their names in the public, will sign autographs willingly.

autograph session Scheduled time during which a celebrity makes himself available to those wishing an autograph. Photographs, books, calendars, etc., are some items requested of celebrities to be autographed.

automatic dialogue replacement (abbreviated as ADR) A system used to dub new or improved dialogue. Instead of the older looping method, the soundtrack and film are played forward during the act of dubbing and then, if needed, rewound quickly back to the beginning for another try. It is still referred to as looping today, though technically, no loop is involved (e.g., "I've got some looping to do this afternoon." Translation: "I've got some ADR work to do this afternoon"). Related terms: loop, ADR.

available light Degree of natural light (sunlight, moonlight, etc.) or nonprofessional artificial light (room lamps, streetlights, etc.) available to illuminate a scene, e.g., "How much available light is there?" If the available light is insufficient, professional-grade artificial lighting is used. Also called existing light.

A-wind Film stock, with the emulsion side down, generally used for projection and printing on positive generations (e.g., interpositive) the original negative and release prints. Related terms: B-wind, wind.

axe To cut or cancel, e.g., "The network decided to axe the low-rated TV series from next season's schedule." Related term: given the axe. Entertainment trade paper use.

ayem Morning, e.g., "New chat show to be scheduled for the ayem." Entertainment trade paper use.

BABA Union in Great Britain for actors, singers, dancers, stunt performers, club and circus entertainers, directors, stage managers, theater designers and choreographers. Founded in 1930 and based in London. Also called British Equity.

baby file A file kept by a children's agent who represents babies for motion picture, television, and modeling work. Each listing includes parental information, statistical data, and one or more current photographs, which are updated regularly.

baby handler Individual experienced in dealing with babies on a production set. Also called (humorously), a "baby wrangler."

baby legs (aka shorty, baby tripod) Short camera stand (tripod) used when shooting from low angles.

baby spot (aka baby, baby keg) Spotlight that is smaller than a junior; usually takes a 500-watt or 750-watt lamp.

back lot Open-air part of a studio where exteriors are shot. Studios save a great deal of money by not having to build new, elaborate sets. Typically, there are different standing sets (e.g., Old New York, Western Town, Modern City). Sometimes written as one word: backlot.

back nine Short for back nine episodes. The last nine episodes of a television series' full season. In the United States, a network may place an initial order for 13 episodes of a new series and then order, or "pick up," the back nine, if the series has done well in the ratings or if it has potential for increased ratings. The maximum number of episodes in a full season in the U.S. is typically 22; however, this can vary, depending on the per-episode production costs and the length of the show (one hour or one-half hour).

back projection Another name for rear-screen projection.

Back Stage New York City-based entertainment industry trade newspaper featuring casting notices, union news, articles on theatrical topics and advertisements for services relating to acting and modeling. Founded in 1960 and published weekly. Internet address: http://www.backstage.com. Related terms: *Back Stage West/ Drama-Logue, Hollywood Reporter, Variety.*

Back Stage West/Drama-Logue Los Angeles-based entertainment industry trade newspaper, published weekly, featuring casting notices, union news, interviews, reviews, how-to articles on theatrical topics and advertisements for acting-related services. It was founded in 1994, as the West Coast sister publication of New York City-based *Back Stage*. In 1998, its parent company, BPI Communications, Inc., acquired the assets of its competitor, the weekly published *Drama-Logue*, and with the June 4, 1998 issue, the paper began calling itself *Back Stage West/Drama-Logue*. Available at newsstands or by subscription. Internet address: http://www.backstage.com.

back story What happened to the characters before the story in progress.

"Back to one." Direction from the director requesting performers go back to their first positions so the action can begin again for another take.

"Back to you." Line used by an on-camera reporter, alerting the director to return the action back to the studio Variations: "Back to you in the studio."

back up schedule (aka cover set) Alternate film location and timetable to be used in the event that shooting cannot proceed as planned, e.g., if exterior shooting is thwarted by weather, it is imperative to have a backup schedule of interior locations which can be substituted.

backdoor pilot Made-for-TV movie (typically, two hours in length) that can readily serve as the pilot for a weekly series. (In the typical method of selling a series to a network, a written series proposal is presented and an order for that series is placed.) Many successful TV series first began as TV movies that achieved high ratings and thus won spots on the regular schedule.

backdrop 1. Sheet or structural material background used in a photographer's studio or on a theatrical stage. Also called a backcloth (if made of fabric). Related terms: backing, background, seamless paper. 2. On-location background selected for a photo, film or video shooting, e.g., "The park makes a nice backdrop for this shot."

back-end deal Type of contract in which payment (or other consideration) is made after a project is produced, released and begins making money. Examples of back-end deals are gross-point deals and net-profit deals. Related term: profit participation.

backer Financier; one who puts up money so that a show or film can be produced. Related term: theater angel.

backer's audition Performance of a show, done in workshop form and presented specifically for an audience of potential backers.

background (abbreviated as b.g., B.G., BG.) 1. Entire area behind an actor, especially as determined by the camera lens or as seen by the audience. Related terms: backdrop, cyclorama, flat, forced perspective. 2. That which is a subordinate accompaniment to the principal dialogue and action of a scene, such as people, voices, movement or lighting. Also called atmosphere.

"Background." Direction from the director to begin background action and noises in a shot or scene

background color Single or prevailing color of a studio backdrop or location background.

background light Any light directed on the background of a shot or scene.

background noise Realistic sounds in a scene other than principal sounds, including indigenous sounds and background voices. Examples are traffic noises, crowd murmur, birds chirping, and leaves rustling. Background noise adds realism to scenes and prevents moments of complete silence on the soundtrack. Related terms: background sound, natural sound, environmental sound, ambient sound, wild sound, presence track.

background prop Any prop located in the background of a set or stage, as opposed to a foreground prop.

background talent Individual or group of individuals hired to perform in the background of a production.

Also known as atmosphere; one such performer is known as an extra.

background voices Conversation(s) between extras in the background of a scene; the voices are mixed together so as to become indistinguishable or unintelligible. Also called walla, indistinct crowd voices, crowd murmur, or talk-talk. Related terms: blah-blah-blah, omnies, walla-walla.

backing 1. Painted or photographic backdrop, as behind a window or door opening on a set. 2. Cloth or other material attached to the inside part of a theatrical costume. 3. Aid or support, e.g., financial backing for a play from a theater angel.

backlight 1. (n.) Light located and directed at a subject or scene from the rear of a set or stage. If it is angled at the back of a person's head and shoulders, it produces a dramatic, halo-like effect when seen from the front. Related term: rim light. 2. (v.) To light a scene from the rear of a set or stage.

backstage Area near and behind the backdrop or scenery of a theatrical stage, including the dressing rooms, wings, etc. Related term: offstage.

backstage entrance Stage door entrance of a theater.

backstage pass Identification granting the holder permission to enter the backstage area or rear staging area of a show.

back-to-back programming Broadcasting, cablecasting or satellite casting of compatible programs, one immediately after the other. For example, a network often airs several sitcoms back-to-back, because their length (half-hour) and genre (comedy) are similar. Also called back-to-back scheduling. Related term: block programming.

back-to-back sequels Two sequels produced and shot in immediate succession or as part of the same overall production. For example, the two sequels to *Back to the Future* (1985): *Back to the Future Part II* and *Part III* were filmed at the same time but released one year apart (1989 and 1990). Related term: shooting the sequel back-to-back.

backup equipment Items, such as cameras, lenses, lights and batteries, that are kept in reserve in case a breakdown occurs with any of the primary pieces of equipment. Also called stand-by equipment.

backup performer Designation of a performer on a backup booking; he would be "on hold." Also called an alternate performer or stand-by performer. Related terms: on hold, understudy.

backup schedule Alternate list of activities prepared in advance in case the primary schedule cannot be used for that day, e.g., a backup shooting schedule.

bad footage Unacceptable film or video footage; damaged footage; out-of-focus footage; poorly framed footage. Related terms: footage, bad take.

bad side Side or angle of a person or object considered less photogenic or visually less appealing than another.

bad take Unacceptable shot or sound recording. Related term: bad footage.

badge Metal identification emblem or symbol of authority worn or carried by a local, state/provincial, military or federal member of law enforcement. There are three leading suppliers in the United States of high-quality prop badges, patches and folding-case credentials for the film, television, and theatrical-stage industries: NIC (National Identification Center), Inc., of Shreveport, Louisiana (current, past and custom made; Internet address: http://www.nic-inc.com/); The Baird Company of Perris, California (current and past); and D.R. Langenbacker & Sons of Riverton, Utah (badges only: U.S. Old West, past law enforcement and custom made).

baffle 1. Sound-absorbing screen inside a loudspeaker which improves fidelity by increasing and decreasing reverberation. 2. Microphone attachment which accentuates high frequencies. 3. Sound-absorbing, movable wall used to prevent reverberation in studio recording (aka baffle blanket). 4. Studio lamp shutter that directs and controls light intensity.

BAFTA Abbreviation for British Academy of Film and Television Arts. In Great Britain, an organization whose members work in film and television. In addition to bestowing the annual BAFTA Awards (also known as the British Academy Awards), BAFTA promotes and advances British theatrical films and television productions. Founded in 1947 and based in London.

BAFTA Award (British Academy of Film and Television Arts Award) Annual award honoring Great Britain's best in films and television, considered the British equivalent of the Oscar® (it is also called the British Academy Award). The BAFTA Award's design is of an ancient Greek mask mounted on a polished marble block pedestal. Presented in separate categories are the Production & Performance Awards and the Craft Awards. Special Awards are also presented to distinguished individuals. Film categories include (subject to change): Film, British Film, Actor, Actress, Supporting Actor, Supporting Actress, Direction, Original Screenplay, Adapted Screenplay, Cinematography, Editing, Production Design, Music, Sound, Makeup/Hair, Costume Design, Special Effects, Film Not in the English Language, Short Film and Short Animated Film. Television categories include (subject to change): Single Drama, Drama Series, Drama Serial, Factual Series, Comedy Programme or Series, Light Entertainment Programme or Series, News Coverage, Sports/Events Coverage in Real Time, Comedy Performance, Light Entertainment Performance, Arts Programme or Series, Children's Programme, Documentary, Foreign Programme, Writing, Original Music, Sound, Editing, Design, Graphic Design, Makeup, Costume Design, Lighting and Photography. Related term: British Academy of Film and Television Arts.

bail out 1. During stunt work, to exit a vehicle or aircraft quickly. 2. To leave or depart, e.g., to "bail out" of a funding deal.

balance 1. As a lighting term, it is the relationship between the key light and fill light. 2. As a sound term, it is the relative volume of the dialogue, music and effects tracks; or, in the music channel, the relative volume of instruments and/or vocals. 3. As a visual term, it is the total composition of a shot so it is eye-pleasing.

balanced print Print that has been color corrected or graded.

balancing stripe magnetic stripe applied to the film edge, opposite the magnetic sound stripe, which keeps the thickness of the film uniform on both sides when it is wound. It protects against damage to the film's surface.

bald cap Rounded, latex, elastic covering that fits tightly over the hair and scalp of a performer; it is used as part of a special makeup process to simulate a bald head or to hold the hair down so that another latex or wig appliance can be fitted on top. A bald cap may also be part of a clown's makeup. Related term: rubber skullcap.

Bambi Award Award presented annually in Germany for achievement in film, television, theater, music and philanthropy.

banana 1. To walk in a curved arc in front of the camera so as to stay in focus. 2. Nickname for a comedian; from the era of burlesque. Related term: top banana.

bank 1. Large number of lamps mounted in a single housing; used for illuminating large areas. Also called coops. 2. Financial institution which may lend money for any phase of filmmaking (e.g., development, production, post-production), based on certain guarentees (e.g., presales, distribution agreements). An investor in a production puts up money and receives a certain percentage of the profits after his investment is recouped; or he may lose his entire investment if the project fails. The bank lends money, making money on the interest charged; it does not take a percentage of the film's profits.

bankable star Actor whose very presence in a film will get it financed; he is acceptable to the project's financial lending or investment sources because his participation is likely to make the project a success. Related term: star.

Banned in Boston Censorship board decision, expression and occasional advertising line derived from news reports regarding the prohibition from general exhibition (outside its X-rated "Combat Zone") of certain controversial theatrical presentations in Boston, Massachusetts. ("Did you hear about that movie? It was banned in Boston.") Films banned in Boston at the time of their release include: *The Birth of a Nation* (1915), *The Lovers* (1958), *I Am Curious Yellow* (1967) and *Caligula* (1980). These films were also banned in other American cities but because of Boston's status as a major northeastern city and the poetic nature of the phrase, "Banned in Boston" became a favorite of newspaper writers and editors when discussing specific or general censorship issues.

"Barefoot on the set." Requirement or caution to crew to remove their shoes before walking onto a set containing a light-colored seamless paper or other fragile floor surface; the order is made to prevent scuff marks or other disturbances that may show up in photographs.

barn doors Metal flaps attached to the front of a theatrical lamp by hinges; used to shape and direct light.

barney Heavily-insulated, yet flexible cover that fits over an unblimped camera to deaden the camera noise during synchronized filming, or one used to protect the camera from the elements (e.g., extreme temperatures, rain).

base Smooth, thin, transparent film onto which light-sensitive emulsion or magnetic recording substance is coated. Since 1952, a slow-burning safety or acetate base has replaced the highly-flammable nitrate base which was used previously. Related term: celluloid.

base location Center of operations and arrival/departure point for on-location productions. Also called the principal location or base camp.

base side 1. Glossy or semi-glossy side of raw (undeveloped) or processed (developed) photographic film. Although the entire material is called the film base, one side is duller in appearance because of various chemicals, dyes and coatings on it. Related terms: base, emulsion side. 2. Glossy, coated side of audiotape or videotape; it is the side that makes contact with the recording and playback heads. (The other side is nonglossy and has an antistatic carbon coating on it.) Recording tape is typically composed of the following layers: polished topcoat/magnetic oxide/polyester base/ antistatic carbon backing.

basher Small, low-powered lamp used as a floodlight or spot; it may be hand-held or fixed.

basic cable Minimum number of cable television channels a subscriber receives as part of a subcription package from the local cable provider. The number and variety of basic cable channels varies between providers and may be subject to government regulations. Channels costing extra to receive are called pay TV (or, premium) channels.

batch number Film manufacturer's code that designates the emulsion's time of preparation. Formerly, it was advisable to use stock from the same batch when shooting a particular sequence so as to assure consistent color and emulsion speed. Today, however, processing has become so sophisticated that differences in emulsion can be corrected in the lab so stock from different batches can be used together. Related terms: emulsion number, emulsion speed.

batten One of numerous long pipes suspended by cables from a grid high in the fly loft above a performing stage. Attached to each batten could be lighting fixtures, scenery or draperies that can be raised (flown) or lowered (set down) as needed by the use of a system of cables, pulleys and counterweights. Related terms: fly loft, flyman, scenery drop.

batteries Portable energy source. There are three basic types of batteries: Wet Cell (rechargeable, but bulky); Dry Cell (non-rechargeable and with a limited lifespan, but portable); and Nickel Cadmium (long life, resistant to high and low temperatures and requires little maintenance, but are more expensive). The camera and the sound equipment run on batteries.

battery belt Compact, portable energy source worn around the waist by the camera operator. When the camera is plugged into the battery belt, the operator has maximum mobility. Used primarily for location newsreel shooting and documentaries.

battle scene Major fight scene involving armed extras or stuntpeople or two or more military fighting machines, such as aircraft, tanks, ships or submarines.

bazooka Studio light support for use on a catwalk.

BBFC Abbreviation for British Board of Film Classification.

B-camera Camera on the set designated as "B," for recordkeeping, blocking and editing purposes. May also be called camera two.

beam light Type of theatrical lamp producing a narrow beam of light; it can be used to simulate a shaft or ray of sunlight or moonlight, e.g., a sun-beam or moonbeam.

beat 1. (n.) Parenthetical direction in a script indicating a required or suggested pause. Related term: dramatic pause. 2. Important event in a story; a story's "pulses." Related term: plot point.

beat sheet Writer's term for a page or two containing one- or two-line summaries of stories. Usually used in episodic or serial television.

beginning credits Another name for opening (or, front) credits.

behind-the-scenes footage Film or video footage taken of a movie's production (or, events behind the camera). Besides cast and key personnel interviews and shooting setups, the footage may include pre-production activities (such as casting and set construction) and post-production activities (such as the creation of special effects and editing). Still photos of such (usually used in press and publicity materials) may be referred to as behind-the-scenes photos, behind-the-scenes shots or production stills. Related terms: production home movie, featurette.

behind-the-scenes photo Another name for a production still.

belly board Small platform used for mounting a camera as close to ground level as possible.

below-the-line Production expenses related to hiring technical and construction crews; renting studio space, cameras and lighting equipment; purchasing and processing film or videotape; and all other costs associated with in-production and post-production activities. Related term: above-the-line.

benefit screening Noncommercial showing of a film at which invitees are requested to make a donation to a named charity in order to gain admission. In some events, celebrities may be invited for free to attract the presence of philanthropic patrons and the media. Also called a charity screening. Related term: premiere benefit.

Berlin International Film Festival Annual film festival held in Berlin, Germany; it screens and honors new German films and other films from around the world. Internet address: http://www.berlinale.de/. Related term: Golden Bear Award.

best boy 1. Second in command to the gaffer. 2. Second in command to the key grip. The best boy/grip is in charge of the rest of the grips and grip equipment; the best boy/electric is in charge of the rest of the electricians and the electrical equipment.

BFI Abbreviation for British Film Institute. Organization in Great Britain promoting film and video production, cataloging and study. It also exhibits noteworthy films in the National Film Theatre and preserves them in the National Film and Television Archive. Founded in 1933.

b.g Abbreviation for background. Also spelled B.G., BG.

bible Television series' master reference source of character information and projected storylines; it may be used initially to help sell the series. A bible for a daytime serial (soap opera) usually projects six months ahead. Also called a series book or long-term projection.

bible run Complete, updated, weekly computerized tally of all accounting activity on a motion picture production.

bicycle Slang term: to work on more than one project at a time.

bicycle the print To screen what is sometimes the only print of a film to more than one audience at the same time (e.g., studio executives in different screening rooms), a messenger on a bicycle waits outside the projection booth as each reel is completed, then he bicycles that reel to the next screening room. This is also the term used when exhibitors rotate prints around the country, from one playdate (theater) to another.

bidding war Auction in which participants compete for a written property (e.g., novel or screenplay); money and other inducements are offered (producing or consulting screen credits, etc.) to obtain a desired property. ("There was a bidding war for the famous writer's spec script.")

Big Apple Nickname for New York City; originated with jazz musicians. New York City is also called the Big Town, Gotham, Metropolitan City, Empire City, Fun City, the City of Towers, the City that Never Sleeps, Madhattan and cement jungle.

big screen 1. Another name for the medium of theatrically exhibited motion pictures, e.g., showing movies to admission-paying audiences in theaters on large screens using projectors. 2. Physically, a large screen in a movie theater.

big-budget film Movie having a high production budget. The actual cost range of a big-budget film is relative to current film industry trends and the international financial marketplace, so the minimum amount needed to be referred to as a "big-budget" film is subject to change from year to year and also to interpretation by labor organizations and national film industries. Film industry trade papers regularly include coverage on what is currently considered a big-budget film, medium budget film and low-budget film. Some actors' unions also provide current definitions, relative to contracts in effect between them and film industry producers. Also called a high-budget film.

billboard 1. An advertisement displayed on a board or metal structure attached to a wall or held in place by ground supports. 2. The structure itself. 3. Sponsor-identification screen title (in the opening or closing credits), logo, picture or message. Related term: sponsor billboard.

billing Placement of names, titles, etc., in the credits. In addition to salary and profit participation in a film, billing is a major issue when negotiating a deal for talent. Other considerations for billing include: size of credit (in relation to the main title and to other performers or crew members); placement on the screen; how many other names are on the same screen, etc. If billing is not found to be satisfactory, it can be considered a "deal breaker." Most guild/union contracts spell out billing clauses.

bin (aka trim bin) Wheeled container, usually made of fire-resistant cloth, that holds film being edited. It has a frame on the top with small hooks, on which film strips are hung.

binaural reproduction Two-channel sound system which closely approximates sound heard by the human ear. If three or more channels are used, it is generally referred to as stereophonic reproduction.

binocular matte Black-colored, light-blocking shield for a camera lens with a centered opening in the shape of two merging circles. Shooting through it produces the effect of a character looking through a pair of handheld binoculars. Director Nicholas Meyer used a binocular matte for a scene in *Volunteers* (1985). Also called a binocular mask.

binocular vision Vision with depth of field, resulting from seeing an object through two separate viewfinders (e.g., human eyes). The resulting, overlapping images allow the viewer to judge distances and sizes. While most film images are planoscopic (flat), 3-D films are stereophonic and try to approximate binocular vision.

bio (short for biography or biographical) Account of a person's life, usually citing only the important or noteworthy aspects; prepared for public relations or news media purposes; e.g., a celebrity bio or performer bio sheet. A self-written biography, in the form of a book, is called an autobiography. The first celebrity autobiography was *Just Me* (1916), written by silent-screen actress Pearl White (1889-1938) who starred in more than 100 films, including the serial *The Perils of Pauline* (1914).

biopic Biographical motion picture, e.g., a movie about a person's life. Entertainment trade paper use.

Bio-Snow 2 Flake Trade name for an Academy Award®-winning, nontoxic, biodegradable fake snow, processed from a white corn-cheese-lactic acid material. It is used to create realistic falling or surface snow. In recognition of Bio-Snow 2 Flake's contribution to filmmaking, its inventor, Dieter Sturm, was honored by the Academy of Motion Picture Arts and Sciences with a 1994 Scientific and Technical Achievement Award. Bio-Snow 2 Flake is manufactured and sold by Sturm's Special Effects International, Inc., of Lake Geneva, Wisconsin, in the United States. Internet address: http://www.wisenet.net/users/Sturm SFX/. Related term: snow effect.

bipack printing Film duplicating process (two pieces of film are printed simultaneously) used in matte shots or for intentional double exposures.

bit 1. Small performing role; also called a bit part, speaking bit part, speaking bit, silent bit part or silent bit. 2. Small amount of action to be performed; also called a bit of business. 3. Routine, act or performance, e.g., "The comedian's Frankenstein bit made the audience laugh." Related terms: comedy bit, shtick. 4. Binary digit; a single unit of computer information meaning on or off and represented numerically as one (1) or zero (0).

bit part Small speaking or nonspeaking role involving some activity. Related term: silent bit part.

bit player Individual who plays a bit part; he has more to do onscreen than a general background extra. Examples of bit-part players are a taxi driver, hotel maid, receptionist, prison guard and store clerk.

black tooth enamel Black-colored liquid, specially formulated for application to one or more of an actor's front teeth to produce a toothless character look that is humorous or grotesque. Related terms: tooth enamel, special teeth effects.

black track print Silent answer print (with picture only, no sound).

black-and-white film 1. Photographic film stock sensitized to shades of black and white only; film without the necessary chemical dyes for processing color. 2. Movie photographed or exhibited without color.

black-and-white shot 1. Photograph produced in black-and-white tones, as opposed to color. 2. Film or video camera shot producing one or more colorless images.

blackout 1. On-screen image fading to black, indicating the end of a scene or the loss of consciousness or death of a character. Related term: fade. 2. Stage lights in a theater turning off, indicating the end of a scene, death of a character or to achieve a special effect. Abbreviated as "B.O." in a script. 3. Blackout skit.

blackout skit Short performance followed by a total darkening of the screen or stage lights. Also called a blackout sketch or blackout.

blacks cloths or drapes used to block daylight from windows or doorways when shooting night interiors; or, used to create the illusion of night when shooting a small, night exterior. (An interesting exception: large portions of the Universal Studios back lot were blacked out during production of *Streets of Fire* (1984) as it was less expensive to use blacks than it would have been to shoot night for night.)

bladder-based makeup Special-effects makeup application containing one or more air-inflatable latex bladders of varying sizes. Attached to each bladder is a tiny air tube running behind or under the actor's clothing or hair to an off camera technician, who inflates the bladder on cue, causing it to expand or pulsate as desired. When used, the actor appears to physically distort in appearance. The same effect can also now be achieved using computer-generated imagery (CGI) and does not require the actor to undergo the lengthy procedures needed to apply and remove bladder-based makeup.

blank 1. Ammunition cartridge used in a weapon firing scene without an attached lead projectile (bullet) at the tip. The blank cartridge, or blank, may contain a full, half or quarter load of gunpowder which is held in place by paper or plastic. When a gun is fired, the blank is expelled from the barrel along with powder residue, flame, smoke and gases. To achieve the visual effect of an imaginary bullet hitting its target, a squib, capsule gun or CGI effect is used. 2. Having no expression or emotion, e.g., a blank stare or blank face.

bleached out (aka burnt up) Film exposed to so much light that all detail is lost.

bleep 1. (n.) Brief, electronic sound that acts as a cue. Also called a blip or bloop. 2. (v.) To edit or censor one or more expletives by replacing them with a brief electronic tone, e.g., "They bleeped out what the comedian said."

blimp Soundproof housing for the camera, usually made of magnesium lined with rubber and plastic foam. The camera is operable with the blimp in place. Related term: barney.

blind bidding Controversial practice, illegal in many states, whereby a distributor requires an exhibitor to bid on, and eventually commit to, exhibit a film before actually seeing it.

blind series commitment Deal made by a television network to purchase a series by a producer that has not yet been developed. Such a series commitment is made usually because the producer has a track record for creating hit shows. Also called a blind network deal or blind commitment.

block booking Controversial practice whereby a distributor requires an exhibitor to buy a group of films (some which the exhibitor may not want to buy), in order to be guaranteed the rights to exhibit a few, high-quality or potentially highly successful films.

block programming Scheduling several similar television shows in a row, a strategy developed by network executives, hoping to keep viewers interested and tuned to the same station, e.g., an evening of half-hour sitcoms. Related term: back-to-back programming.

blockbuster Enormously successful film. Related term: megahit.

blocking a scene Determining where actors, props, cameras (if applicable), etc., will be during the performance of a scene. Related terms: rehearsal, technical rehearsal.

blocking a shot 1. Rehearsing or staging of camera, crew and cast positions and movements before filming the scene. Related terms: lining up a shot, technical rehearsal, "Hit your mark." 2. Obstructing a camera's intended line of sight.

blood capsule Small, thin-walled capsule containing powdered theatrical blood. When an actor bites down on the capsule, the nontoxic powder mixes with the mouth's natural saliva to produce fake liquid blood. Related term: special blood effects.

blood effects Blood-related special effects. Related term: special blood effects.

blood hit Gelatin capsule or plastic ball containing a quantity of fake blood. It is shot from a Sweeney gun or capsule gun at an actor wearing concealed metal body armor.

blood knife Any type of constructed or altered, dull-edged knife that can simulate the cutting of skin and bleeding; used in special makeup effects and stunt work. A blood knife may have a thin tube recessed in a groove on the thick-edged blade of a fake knife or the tube may be glued or taped to the noncamera side of the dulled blade of a real knife. The tube runs to the handle, where it is connected to a squeezable rubber bulb filled with theatrical blood. A less expensive blood knife has a blood-soaked strip of sponge attached to the knife's noncamera side; as the blade and sponge are run across the skin, a trail of fake blood is left behind. Related terms: knife, special blood effects.

bloom Treatment of any glass surface, excluding the camera lens, with a special transparent fluoride coating to reduce glare. Related term: dulling spray.

bloop 1. Clicking noise caused when a faulty soundtrack splice passes through the reproduction equipment. (It happens when the splicer becomes magnetized, putting a magnetic charge on the film.) 2. Opaque, triangular patch applied to the splicing area or painted with blooping ink to silence that noise. The blooping ink can also be used to black out any unwanted areas on the film. (This process is called blooping or deblooping.)

blooper 1. Special effects device, usually a round open tank, used to simulate water explosions. 2. Mistake, blunder or error caught on film, videotape, audiotape. Related terms: acting blooper, flub, outtake, blowing a line, breaking up during a shot, giggles.

blooper reel Short videotape or film reel containing an assortment of individual bloopers that occurred during the production of a theatrical film or television series. Selected segments may be provided to television specials that feature bloopers.

blow up 1. To enlarge one or more photographic images. 2. To create an explosion, e.g., "The pyrotechnic crew will supervise the scene in which the car blows up."

blowing a line Forgetting or misspeaking dialogue. Related terms: blooper, flub, draw a blank.

blowup Enlargement by optical printing. In film, this is typically done from 16mm film stock to 35mm film stock. Individual shots may be blown up and inserted in a film (e.g., stock footage originally shot in 16mm). When this happens, the grain will be slightly different between the two shots. The opposite of a blowup is a reduction print.

blue movie X-rated movie, or one that contains adult content (NC-17). The first theatrically released movie to use the term as its title was Andy Warhol's sexually-explicit *Blue Movie* (1969), which he produced, directed and filmed. *Blue Movie* was banned in New York City after its release and the manager of the theater where it premiered was arrested, tried and convicted for promoting obscene material, a decision later reversed by the U.S. Supreme Court. Related terms: adult video, X-rating, NC-17.

blue pages Added, revised pages inserted into a script that has already been numbered and distributed. The revised pages are printed on colored paper (first blue, then pink, etc.), with the date of the correction on the page. Related term: color coding.

bluescreen process Act of filming of actors or model miniatures against a uniform, nonglossy, bright-blue background and then replacing the blue background with a new background (outdoor scene, starfield, etc.) by means of a special-effects process involving color separation filters, mattes and an optical printer; used to achieve certain visual effects that would be difficult or impossible to create otherwise. For example, the bicycle flying scene *in E.T.: The Extraterrestrial* (1982) was shot in this manner. Parts of an actor's body may also be covered or masked with a blue-colored fabric, for example, covering the head, neck and hands to create the effect of an invisible man. Support structures can also be painted or covered if they are not to be visible in the finished shot, e.g., covering a pole holding up a miniature spaceship. Depending on the type of effects work being done, a bluescreen is either front lit or back lit, the latter consisting of a translucent plastic sheet that is stretched over a frame. If done by electronic means for television, it is also called the chroma-key process. Also called the bluescreen effect. Related terms: underwater bluescreen, chroma key, chroma-key blue, chroma-key board, greenscreen process, orangescreen process, traveling matte.

bluescreen shot Visual-effects shot using the bluescreen process.

blurb Brief publicity statement; can be in the form of a word, phrase, sentence or paragraph, e.g., a blurb on a book jacket; a movie advertisement blurb is often a quote from a reviewer.

BMI Abbreviation for Broadcast Music Incorporated. Music industry company acting as a licensing and royalty clearinghouse for composers, lyricists and other music copyright owners. Founded in 1940, in New York City, with offices now also in other major cities, including Los Angeles, Nashville, and London. Internet address: http://www.bmi.com.

B-movie Low-budget film. In the 1930s, "B" was the designation given to a film shown in a U.S. theater as the second half of a double feature. (An A-picture was a big-budget film and was the main feature.) Typically, production values of a B-movie were not as good as those of an A-movie. Both terms are still in use today, even though the practice of showing two films for a single admission price no longer applies to newly released films. A significant number of B-movies are low-budget horror, science fiction, teen sex comedy and adult sex-drama films and use unknown or marginally well-known actors. A B-movie may have a limited theatrical release, foreign release, video release, direct-to-homevideo release or a combination of any of these. Also called a B-grade movie, B-picture, B-title, low-grade film or low-budget movie.

BN Television rating for "Brief Nudity." Related term: rating.

BNC Abbreviation for Blimped Noiseless Camera, manufactured by the Mitchell Camera Co. Related terms: blimp, barney.

B.O 1. Abbreviation for box office. Entertainment trade paper use. Related term: B.O. champ. 2. Abbreviation for blackout, as in a script.

B.O champ Top-grossing film for any duration (e.g., week, season, year or all-time). Variation: B.O. hero. Entertainment trade paper use. Related terms: B.O., all-time box-office champ, commercial success, hit.

boards 1. Floorboards of a theater stage on which acting or other entertainment is presented. 2. The medium of stage performing, e.g., "The actor is on the boards in New York, appearing in a musical."

body double Individual whose body is similar to that of a principal actor's and is therefore hired to stand in for him during certain camera shots. Related terms: nude body double, double.

body frame/body brace Device that secures a handheld movie camera, such as a Steadicam or Panaglide, to the operator's body during shooting.

body makeup artist According to union rules, a makeup artist may only apply makeup from the top of an actor's head to the breastbone and from the tips of the fingers to the elbow. All other parts of the body fall under the jurisdiction of the body makeup artist.

BodyCam Trade name for a motion-stabilizing, body-mounted camera system that also features a video-assist monitor.

boffo Highly successful, e.g., "The movie is currently enjoying boffo box office." Entertainment trade paper use.

Bollywood Slang for the film industry in Bombay, India, one of the largest film-producing countries in the world. It often surpasses all other countries, with approximately 800 to 900 domestic films produced each year. India's domestically-made films, which typically include song-and-dance numbers, are more popular than the foreign films exhibited there. Nudity is not allowed in Indian films, but violence and sensuality are.

bomb 1. (n.) Unsuccessful; a failure. Related term: flop. 2. (v.) To be unsuccessful, e.g., "The comedian went onstage and bombed." 3. (n.) Explosive device, e.g., "The script requires the hero to disarm the bomb." (Bombs appearing on-camera are actually realistic-looking props. Prop dynamite with fuse attached is available in single sticks or bundles from the special-effects company Tri-Ess Sciences, Inc., of Burbank, California.) Related terms: diaphragm bomb, fire bomb, explosion scene. 4. (v.) To explode by means of a bomb.

boneyard Nickname for an outdoor prop storage yard.

book 1. (v.) To hire or schedule a performer; to schedule a theatrical film for exhibition. 2. (n.) Television series bible. 3. Script for a play, especially a musical; it includes spoken dialogue, action, lyrics for the songs but not the music. The book is written by the lyricist, also called a dramatist. 4. Prompt book for a play.

book flat Another name for a two-fold flat, a type of upright, framed scenery background that opens and closes like a book.

booker Individual who books entertainment acts, guests for news or talk shows or films for exhibition.

booking 1. Job, gig, engagement or contract to work or perform. Examples of booking types: all-day, alternate, backup, canceled, confirmed, convention, cover, day, daytime, final, hour, live-on-tape, live television, major, music video, night, poster, prestige, print, product, request, second tentative, talent, tape, television, tentative, theatrical, trade show, TV commercial, video, videotape, and weather-permitting. 2. Scheduling a movie for theatrical exhibition.

booking agent Another name for a talent agent, especially one whose clients are comedians, singers, magicians and other entertainment acts who perform in nightclubs, performing halls, festivals, fairs and the like.

booking clearance Approval of a proposed booking by an agency or performer.

booking slip Notice of employment.

boom Pole or beam, handheld or on a mobile platform or truck, on which a microphone, camera or other device is attached and controlled. A fishpole boom (or, fishpole) is a long, handheld pole with a microphone attached to its end. Related terms: microphone boom, crane, fishpole.

boom operator Member of the sound crew responsible for the positioning of a microphone boom during a performance. He operates either a handheld boom (fishpole) microphone or an overhead boom swivel microphone attached to and operated from a wheeled platform. Also called a microphone boom operator. Related term: microphone operator.

boom shot (aka crane shot) Continuous shot incorporating a number of different camera angles from different levels, usually accomplished with the use of a crane.

booster Device that increases the voltage of floodlamps to improve their output, and therefore their intensity.

booster light Typically, an arc that illuminates shadowy areas, improving details, especially in exterior day shots.

borderlights Row of overhead lights providing an illuminated border and general lighting on a stage.

bottom line 1. Final or ultimate cost, profit, loss or meaning; the net result, e.g., "What's the bottom line—did we come in under budget?" 2. Place for signing one's name, as on a contract. Also called a signature line or dotted line.

bounce board Another name for a reflector board.

bow 1. To premiere or open, e.g., "The play bowed last week." Entertainment trade paper use. 2. (n.) Forward bend of the body, in acknowledgment of audience applause. A bow may be taken individually or with a group of performers. Related terms: group bow, joint bow, "Take a bow," taking turns bowing, curtain call, curtsy. 3. (v.) To perform a bow. Related term: wow bow.

box office 1. Place at a theater, stadium, concert hall, or the like where admission tickets are sold and information about upcoming events is available. Also called a ticket sales office, ticket sales booth, or ticket booth. Related term: out front. 2. Financial receipts from a film, play or admission-based entertainment event, e.g., "The movie had good box office in its first week." Related terms: domestic box office, foreign box office, worldwide box office, all-time box-office champ, B.O., B.O. champ, gross, house record, opening week, opening weekend, take, ticket sales, long shot, wow bow. 3. Slang term meaning a proposed project which has all the qualities for being a huge success (e.g., "Tom Cruise is considered good box office.")

box rental (aka kit rental) Daily or weekly sum paid to a crew member for the use of his or her personal property (e.g., make-up or hair dressing supplies, special tools) during production.

box rig Safety setup for stunts, consisting of a calculated number of cardboard boxes and mattresses; used by a stuntperson as a landing target for certain types of falls and, in some instances, as a less-expensive alternative to an air bag. Related term: fall.

break 1. (v.) To discontinue or interrupt the action. 2. (n.) Pause or interruption, a break in the action or break in a shooting schedule. Related terms: act break, commercial break, station break. 3. Off-camera hand signal to someone on-camera, e.g., talk-show host or news anchor, indicating it is time to break for a commercial. (The off-camera person repeatedly brings both closed hands together, pretending to break something in half, e.g., an imaginary stick. Related term: cut. 4. Chance or opportunity, e.g., "This acting role is the break I've been waiting for!"

"Break a leg!" Good-luck saying offered to a performer about to go onstage. Derived from the German good-luck phrase "Hals-und-Beinbruch!" meaning "Break your neck and leg!" it originated in the early days of aviation in Germany as a good-luck send-off between pilots. At the time, it was considered unlucky to wish someone good luck because of the superstitious belief that tempting any "evil spirits" would cause them to do the opposite; hence, "Break your neck and leg!" meant "Have a good landing!" The saying is believed to have been transferred to German theater and from there, to more western locales, including the United States. In another story, the saying had its origins in the theater world of the 1800s, as a backstage good-luck saying. In other words, the better the performance, the longer the applause. (The performer, wearing a heavy or hot costume, would have to remain in one spot on stage and keep a steady balance and his knees from buckling and therefore he could fall to the hard stage floor.) In this version, "Break a leg!" translates roughly to mean: "I hope you're so successful on stage that if you fall and break a leg because you've had to stand for a long time and listen to the audience applause, it will have been worth it!"

breakage Additional monies paid to a production company for the services of an actor. Since more money is paid for said actor, it "breaks" the budget.

breakaway costume Theatrical costume or part of a costume designed for quick placement on or removal from the body, by the use of separating segments with snap buttons or Velcro strips. Related term: Velcro shirt.

breakaway glass Fake glass; it is actually a clear or tinted petrochemical-based plastic resin in a hardened state. Breakaway glass is produced by heating the powdered plastic resin until it liquefies; it is then poured into a desired mold and allowed to cool. The finished solid product resembles glass and resists water like glass, yet it is a brittle plastic that varies in strength according to its shape and thickness. For example, the top and bottom edges of a breakaway bottle are stronger than its sides, meaning, if a scene requires an actor to be hit over the head, the bottle should be positioned so that one of its thin-walled sides is the focal point of contact, otherwise the impact could be unnecessarily painful and result in a bruise or cut. A source for powdered breakaway resin and finished breakaway glass products (windows, bottles, drinking glasses, ashtrays, auto windshields, mirrors, etc.; also, breakaway ceramic and furniture items) is the special-effects company Zeller International, Ltd., of Downsville, New York. Related terms: breakaway prop, candy glass, glass prop, glosser, sugar glass.

breakaway line Thin separation line or hairline crack in a large breakaway prop (such as a wooden table or chair). Also called a breaking line or trick line.

breakaway prop Prop designed and constructed, with a thin line or hairline crack, so it will break, collapse, crumble or shatter easily, with little or no danger to the performers who come in contact with it. The most common examples are breakaway sheets of glass and bottles made of a brittle plastic resin or sugar glass (less common today). A spring-loaded or electrically squibbed small device called a glass breaker is used to smash tempered glass a fraction of a second before a performer's body touches it. Breakaway ceramic objects, such as plates, flower vases and planters, are thinly made (or, they are made out of wax or other brittle material) and are not fired in a kiln, which greatly increases their hardness. Breakaway furniture, such as chairs and tables, are constructed of balsa or other soft wood that has been lightly spot-glued together at precut breaking points. Other materials used include rigid polystyrene foam and cardboard. During post-production, a sound effect (foley) of a real item breaking is inserted to give the staged breaking an authentic quality. Related terms: breakaway glass, breakaway line, trick line.

breakdown (aka script breakdown) 1. When prepared by the production manager or assistant director, it is an extremely detailed system of separating each element in the script and rearranging them in the most efficient and least expensive manner for filming. 2. Detailed analysis prepared by the script supervisor for timing the script. 3. Separating individual shots from the dailies during the early stages of editing.

breakdown board See production strip board.

breakeven Term used to identify a specific point at which monies generated by a film equal the monies spent to create, distribute and advertise it. It is that point when profit participation begins. Sometimes, an artificial breakeven point is established at a mutually-agreed income level, one that can be higher or lower than the actual breakeven point. Many times, the definition of "breakeven" varies from profit participant to profit participant within the same film, depending on what kind of deals were made upfront.

breaking news story Important news story that has just occurred or is still developing as it is being reported to viewers or listeners, e.g., "We interrupt our regular newscast for this breaking news story." Related terms: preempt, special report.

breaking up during a shot Laughing suddenly during a film or video shot, usually because of the misspeaking of lines, misperforming of action, misoperation or unintentional breaking of a prop, seeing or hearing something unexpectedly on-camera or off-camera. These occurrences are what constitute "bloopers." Such shots may be assembled into a blooper reel.

breakout role Role that raises a performer to a greater level of success and standing in the industry. (*Pretty Woman* [1990] was Julia Roberts' "breakout role.")

breast tape Any type of adhesive or nonadhesive tape, strap or bandage that is placed on or around the breasts to hold down, lift up or secure them

in place. This is done to alter the actress' appearance or the fit of the costume. Tape may also be used to hold a small microphone in place during production when a clip-on or overhead boom microphone will not work effectively.

breathing Rapid fluctuations in focus, caused by film fluttering in the camera gate.

bright lights Nickname for the stage as a performing medium. Also called the footlights or the boards.

British Academy of Film and Television Arts (abbreviated as BAFTA) In Great Britain, an organization whose members work in film and television. In addition to bestowing the annual BAFTA Awards (also known as the British Academy Awards), BAFTA promotes and advances British theatrical films and television productions. Founded in 1947 and based in London.

British Actors' Equity Association (abbreviated as BABA) Union in Great Britain for actors, singers, dancers, stunt performers, club and circus entertainers, directors, stage managers, theater designers and choreographers. Founded in 1930 and based in London. Also called British Equity.

British Board of Film Classification (abbreviated as BBFC) Limited company (corporation) in Great Britain issuing government-enacted ratings, called Classification Certificates, for theatrical films and videos exhibited in theaters or offered for sale or rental to the public within the country. The Board operates with full-time examiners and is based in London. Related terms: "U"-classification, "UC"-classification, "PG"-classification, "12"-classification, "15"-classification, "18"-classification, "R-8"-classification, motion picture rating board, rating.

British Film Critics Circle Award Award presented yearly by film critics in Great Britain. The first awards were given in 1979.

British Film Institute (abbreviated as BFI) Organization in Great Britain promoting film and video production, cataloging and study. It also exhibits noteworthy films in the National Film Theatre and preserves them in the National Film and Television Archive. Founded in 1933.

broad (aka broadside) Somewhat large floorlight used to increase the illumination of a large area without interfering with the modeling lights. A single broad lamp uses a 500- to 750-watt lamp; a double uses two 1000-watt lamps.

broadcast 1. (v.) To transmit to the public television or radio electromagnetic signals over the airwaves. Receipt of such signals by an electronic receiver is called "reception." Related terms: air, airwaves, telecast, narrowcast. 2. Of or pertaining to broadcasting, e.g., broadcast media (television and radio news companies and departments). 3. (n.) One such transmission. Related terms: delayed broadcast, live broadcast, postponed broadcast, simulcast.

Broadcast Music Incorporated (abbreviated as BMI) Music industry company acting as a licensing and royalty clearinghouse for composers, lyricists and other music copyright owners. Founded in 1940, in New York City, with offices now also in other major cities, including Los Angeles, Nashville, and London.

broadcast quality Of an acceptable condition for transmission by a television station to home television sets. The resolution, or sharpness, of a television picture is determined by the number of picture lines comprising it and by the number of discrete picture elements (pixels) which accurately detail the variations of light, shadow and color information contained in each frame. Most professional-grade video cameras for recording or transmission on TV have three image-sensing CCDS, one for each primary color: red, green and blue. Video images with a resolution that is not of broadcast quality, such as those produced by many single-CCD consumer camcorders in the standard 8mm and VHS formats, are occasionally shown on television but the picture quality is lower; the difference can be subtle or great, depending on the available number of lines of horizontal resolution the camcorder is capable of recording. A professional-grade video camera can produce higher resolution original footage for copying, editing and storage, but is still processed by television broadcast equipment and television sets at the standards determined by the transmission and reception systems in use by a particular country (analog NTSC, PAL, SECAM, etc.).

broadcast schedule List or chart giving the days, times and station channels of television or radio programs. Related terms: airdate log, television schedule.

broadcaster Company or person responsible for the transmission of television or radio signals.

Broadway (New York City) 1. Major thoroughfare in the borough of Manhattan in New York City. Times Square, City Hall, Columbia University and the Theater District are all located along Broadway. Its nickname, the Great White Way, is derived from the thousands of white electrical bulbs that once were used to light the signs along the avenue. Also called the Street of Dreams. "Broadway" is also taken to mean the New York City Theater District itself, especially as the center of commercial theater in the United States. 2. Of or pertaining to a stage play produced in the New York City Theater District, e.g., a Broadway play. Broadway shows typically have higher-paid performers and higher ticket prices and its theaters feature larger seating capacity and better production values. Related terms: Off-Broadway, Off-Off Broadway.

brute Largest lighting unit on a set, using 225 amps, it is a high-intensity carbon arc spotlight with a 48" diameter lens.

buckle Condition occurring when the film accidentally piles up in the camera or projector due to a lost loop. The camera or projector cannot continue operating until buckling has been remedied.

budget The listing of every possible expense in the making of a film before the film begins production. Accurate budgets can only be created after completely breaking down a script and preparing a production strip board, usually prepared by the production manager or, for studio pictures, by the studio's Estimating Department. It is not unusual for many budgets to be prepared during the course of production as more information is supplied, or as unforseen circumstances occur.

budget form Detailed list, separated into categories, of all the elements needed to make a film, how long they will be needed and how much they will cost. Related terms: above-the-line, below-the-line and scheduling.

bug 1. Nickname for the logo of a TV network, station or program, usually found in the lower right-hand corner of the screen. 2. In film, nickname for a corporate, organization or union logo appearing at the end of the closing credits. 3. Slang for an equipment malfunction.

buildup Another name for a publicity or promotional campaign, e.g., to give someone or something a good buildup.

bulldog 1. In stunt work, to jump from a horse, moving vehicle, tree, etc., onto one or more persons, knocking them to the ground. 2. In rodeo, to jump from a horse to the front side of a steer, grab the steer's horns and then twist the animal's neck until it falls to the ground. Bulldogging, or steer wrestling, was introduced to the Wild West show circuit in the 1890s by African-American cowboy Bill Picket.

bullet hit 1. (n.) Small, explosive device used in gunfight scenes. Each electrical detonation of a bullet hit simulates the impact of one lead bullet fired from a gun. Also called a squib. 2. (v.) The effect of a bullet (from a capsule gun or Sweeney gun) striking a surface. Related terms: blood hit, dust hit, glass hit, spark hit. 3. Effect created by CGI, usually a brief flash indicating a ricochet. Also called a CG bullet hit.

bumped 1. To be removed from a scheduled place, e.g., "The network bumped my show to a later time slot." Or, "When Letterman's show ran long, he bumped me." 2. Being moved to a different pay level. Related term: upgrade.

bumper 1. Brief introductory, transitional or exiting logo, image, series of images, animation or voiceover between segments on a television or radio program. Examples of voiceover bumpers are: "We'll be right back," and, "We'll return after these messages." 2. Bumper ads are two short commercials, one appearing before and one appearing after a longer, unrelated commercial.

burlesque Stage entertainment during the era of vaudeville; it featured comedy skits and striptease acts, e.g., a burlesque show. Related term: top banana.

burn gag Fire stunt or effect in which something (clothing, vehicle, side of a building, etc.) is set ablaze. Related terms: fire gag, fire effect.

burn suit Another name for a fire suit.

burn-in 1. To lay white titles, usually captions or subtitles, over the picture in order to identify a person, place or thing. 2. To translate dialogue.

burnt up See bleached out.

bus to Signifying a location day for the crew. Their work (pay) time begins with the bus ride to the location and ends when they are dropped off after competing the day's work.

business 1. Any small movement or action used by an actor in a scene to further the action and/or add depth to the interpretation of his character. 2. Referring to the motion picture industry in general, as in: "He works in the business."

business manager Individual who manages one's financial affairs, including investments and possibly taxes, for an agreed-upon fee or percentage of the earnings (typically, 10 percent). Also called a financial manager or investment manager. Related term: theatrical business manager.

busy 1. Shot or scene with lots of action, e.g., many events occurring at the same time. 2. Full of details, e.g., a busy design.

butt splice In film editing, a type of splice in which two lengths of film, cut straight across in the darkened border area between frames, are joined end to end and fastened by clear tape. Butt splicing is also done on audiotape. Related terms: splice, straight cut, tape splice.

butterfly Device used during filming to diffuse bright sunlight and harsh shadows. Related term: silk

button Television term for a scene's dramatic or comedic punch or for a topper at the end of the scene.

buyer 1. Member of the Prop or Wardrobe Department who finds, buys and/or rents the items necessary for the film. 2. Representative of a theater or theater chain who decides on which films to schedule for exhibition. 3. Syndicated programming buyer.

buyout One-time payment for rights purchased or work done. Related term: flat-rate deal.

buzz Talk on the street or around town about something, e.g., "What's the buzz on the new film?" Related term: word-of-mouth.

buzz track Soundtrack carrying a non-distinct background noise which helps the editor bridge the gaps in dialogue that otherwise might sound unnatural. Related terms: ambiance, walla

buzzer Signal alerting those in or near the production set to remain quiet or proceed with caution because filming is about to begin. Related term: warning bell.

B/W Abbreviation for black and white. Sometimes written as b/w.

B'Way Abbreviation for Broadway. Entertainment trade paper use.

B-wind Film used in the camera and wound so it reads through the base (emulsion side up) and in alternate generations when printing. Related terms: wind, A-wind.

cabaret show Performance taking place at a nightclub or supper club, such as singing.

cable 1. Short for cable television. 2. Insulated transmission wire, e.g., a sound cable. 3. Wire made of twisted strands of metal and used for support and fastening, as in stunt and special-effects work. Related term: wire flying. 4. Metal wire and flexible tubular housing attached to and used to control the movements of a special-effects puppet. Related term: remote control.

cable puller Member of the sound crew who handles the sound hookups and manages the many cables and wires, thus protecting them from damage and the crew from injury. Related term: cableman

cable run Path of cables from the power source (usually a generator) to the equipment being powered. This distance is critical on location shoots, where power sources may be scarce.

cable TV (short for cable television) Closed-circuit system in which television programs are transmitted over coaxial cable or fiber-optic cable to connected subscriber households (as opposed to broadcast TV, in which the television signals are transmitted over the airwaves and received via an antenna attached to the set). Related terms: basic cable, made-for-cable, pay-per-view, pay TV, closed-circuit television.

CableACE Award (Award for Cable Excellence) Award bestowed annually in the United States which honored individuals and programs in the cable television field. Besides U.S. programs, foreign programs shown on U.S. cable networks were also eligible in special categories. Presented by the National Academy of Cable Programming, which was founded in 1985. Formerly called the Ace Award. CableACE Awards were last awarded in 1997. Internet address: http://www.cableace.org.

cablecast 1. (v.) To transmit over a cable system, e.g., to cablecast a program over coaxial cable or fiber-optic cable. Related term: narrowcast. 2. (n.) One such transmission.

cableman 1. Individual responsible for the care, placement and removal of sound equipment cables on a production set. (Electrical cables are handled by the electrical crew.) Also called a cableperson. Related terms: cable puller, sound assistant.

calibration Process of measuring and marking focus settings and f-stops on the lens. While shooting, the first assistant cableman adjusts the lens to pre-set focus stops, allowing the camera operator to concentrate on composition and camera movement.

call 1. Request or notice to one or more actors and/or crew members, etc., to arrive at a specific place and time. Examples of call types: casting, curtain, early, half-hour, 15-minute, 5-minute, one-minute, final, late, makeup, "Places," rehearsal, shooting and wardrobe. 2. Performer wakeup call.

call letters Letters of the alphabet used to identify a television or radio station. In the United States, stations east of the Mississippi River (the eastern half of the U.S.) have call letters preceded by the letter "W." West of the Mississippi (the western half of the U.S.), the letter "K" is used. Also known as a call sign. Related terms: radio station call letters, TV station call letters, station identification, station break.

call sheet List typically posted or distributed at the close of each shooting day. Prepared by the second assistant director under the supervision of the first assistant director and approved by the production manager, the call sheet displays the call time for each cast and crew member (e.g., the time when one must report to the set or to the area for pre-arranged transportation to the location); informs the cast and crew which scenes are to be shot; the order of the scenes to be shot; which sets or locations will be utilized; what the cover sets are; and any unusual equipment needed (crane, Steadicam, etc.).

callback 1. Invitation for an actor to audition again (after the field of competition has been narrowed). For SAG members, there is a limit to the number of callbacks an actor may have before being paid. 2. Actor's automatic invitation to continue working as a day player, unless specifically notified by the end of the shooting day that he has been laid off.

calling the show Announcing the various performer and technical cues for a studio or stage show; e.g., "Who's calling tonight's show?"

cam Abbreviation for camera, e.g., a three-cam show.

camcorder Portable video camera with a built-in video recorder-playback machine and other features, as for editing, picture magnification (zoom), on-screen titling and low-light recording. Also called a video camcorder. Related terms: digital camcorder, disc camcorder, DVD camcorder, flash-memory-based camcorder, video camera, CCD, lux, videocassette.

Camcrane Trade name for a tripod-mounted camera crane capable of raising a camera (weighing up to 20 pounds) over a scene to a height of 10 feet; it also can be rotated 360 degrees. Manufactured and sold by Glidecam Industries of Plymouth, Massachusetts, in the United States. Related term: crane.

cameo lighting Lighting a subject within a neutral or blacked-out limbo setting. Also called vignette lighting.

cameo part Brief role played by a prominent actor or celebrity; it may be a speaking or silent part. Related term: voice cameo.

camera Device with a lens system and, depending on camera type, a film transport system, battery supply and various internal mechanical, electro-mechanical or solid-state electronic image-processing components. It is used by a photographer, cinematographer or videographer to take photographs or to record images for playback or transmission. Examples of camera types: digital still, digital video, film, handheld, hidden, high-speed, MOS production, motion-control, roving, talking, TV studio, and video. Related terms: Arriflex, camcorder, camera mount, Panavision, Polaroid, Showscan, Vista-Vision, 8mm, 16mm, 35mm, 65mm.

camera angle Position and direction of the camera. Related term: angle.

camera assistant Another name for an assistant camera operator.

camera car Vehicle specially outfitted to carry one or more film or video cameras; camera, sound and lighting equipment; and one or more operators, all for the purpose of filming a moving vehicle or person. It is used on traveling shots, either in the studio backlot or on location scenes. Also called an insert car or camera truck.

camera crew Individuals responsible for capturing images onto the film; typical crew consists of the director of photography, camera operator, first and second assistants and a film loader.

camera jam Occurrence when the perforations of the film are not properly engaged in the sprockets; or if the film is damaged and it piles up on itself and jams, causing a buckle. This condition also can occur in a projector.

camera left Camera on the left side of a production set—from the point of view of a camera aimed at the set. Camera left records the area seen in the left side of the screen or photograph. Camera left is the same as house left but is opposite of stage left. Camera left is also called director's left, frame left or left side of frame. Related term: camera right

camera lens Optical portion of the camera attached to the front of its housing; constructed of curved or planed transparent glass, through which the image passes. Related terms: anamorphic lens, fisheye lens, macro lens, night-vision lens, telephoto lens, wide-angle lens, zoom lens, lens, lens flare, lens flare spot, lens hood, single-lens reflex, through-the-lens viewing, camera's eye,

aperture, focal length, f-stop, iris, parallax, shutter, CCD, director's viewfinder.

camera mount Support for a camera that holds it in place during a shot. Related terms: front car mount, rear car mount, side car mount, aerial unit, boom, camera car, camera truss, crane, dolly, monopod, motion-control camera, tripod, BodyCam, Camcrane, Duopod, FlightStick, Flying-Cam, Glidecam, GyroCam, Helmet Cam, MegaCrane, Mini-Crane, motioncam, QuickLift, Panaglide, Skycam, Slingcam, SpaceCam, Steadicam, VISTA Telescoping Tripod, Wescam.

camera movement panning, tilting or tracking of a motion picture camera. Good camera movement, when used with skill and sensitivity, will add depth, drama and rhythm to a scene.

camera one Designation given to a film or video camera on a production set or in a TV studio. Related term: A-camera.

camera operator Member of the camera crew who runs the camera. He takes instruction from the director and director of photography; he is not responsible for creating the lighting or the style of movement, but rather for keeping the action in the frame. Related term: second cameraman

camera report Detailed account, prepared each day by the assistant cameraman, listing scenes shot; number of takes for each shot; amount of film exposed; and instructions as to the disposition of each take ("print," "n.g.", etc.).

camera reverse Camera shot that is intentionally reversed in post-production.

camera right Camera on the right side of a production set—from the point of view of a camera aimed at the set. Camera right records the area seen in the right side of the screen or photograph. Camera right is the same as house right but is opposite of stage right. Camera right is also called director's right, frame right or right side of frame. Related term: camera left

camera shot Particular way of setting up and using a still, motion picture or video camera to photograph or record a subject or scene, e.g., a dramatic camera shot or close-up camera shot. Related terms: angle, shot and angle descriptions.

camera time 1. Electronic digital time displayed on the clock of a video camera. 2. Running camera's duration on a subject, e.g., "The star usually gets more camera time than anyone else." Related term: real time.

camera tracks Metal or wooden rails upon which the camera unit moves during tracking (dolly) shots.

camera trick Special visual effect accomplished with a camera (as opposed to CGI). An example of a camera trick is stopping the camera, removing an item from the set and restarting the camera. When the resultant shot is viewed, the item appears to "vanish" from the set. Actors can be made to disappear and appear this way. Other camera tricks include freeze frame, slow motion, fast motion and reverse motion. Related terms: trick camera shot, "Freeze!"

camera truss Rigid framework (possibly movable) of metal or wood beams on which one or more cameras can be mounted, e.g., an overhead camera truss. Related term: grid.

camera work Physical and mental effort involved in the use of the camera for photographing, filming or video-recording, e.g., "Who did the camera work on that film?" Usually said in reference to the cinematographer, videographer or camera operator. Also refers to the images resulting from this work.

cameraman Individual responsible for lighting the scene and, along with the director, setting up and composing shots. A cameraman is usually chosen because of his lighting style and/or some other particular specialty, such as his ability to shoot action, etc. The DP (known as "DOP" or "Lighting Cameraman" in England and Australia) is sometimes known as the First Cameraman while the camera operator is known as the Second Cameraman. Related terms: cinematographer, director of photography.

camera's eye 1. Round, clear glass lens of a camera. 2. View of what can be photographed or recorded through this lens, e.g., the shot area.

camera-shy Reluctant or uneasy about being photographed, e.g., a camera-shy celebrity. If such a celebrity shuns the camera because of its resultant publicity, the individual may also be called publicity-shy.

camera-to-subject measurement Another name for focal distance; usually taken by one of the assistant camera operators. Related terms: focal distance, follow focus, tape.

camp 1. (n.) Gesture, style or form conspicuously make-believe or pretentious, especially in an amusing way, e.g., "The TV series version of the comic book was pure camp." 2. (v.) To act in an amusingly pretentious or affected way, e.g., "In referring to the character's mannerisms and accent, the director told the actress to camp it up." Related terms: campy, overplay.

can 1. Metal container for storing film. (The term, "in the can," refers to a completed film or scene.) 2. Headphones used by soundmen to monitor a recording. 3. Small, rectangular light that uses a 1000-watt lamp.

Canadian Actors' Equity Association In Canada, a union for stage performers; also called Canadian Equity. Established in 1955 and located in the port city of Toronto, in the province of Ontario.

Canadian Film and Television Production Association (abbreviated as CFTPA) Organization representing the interests of producers in Canada, in labor union contract negotiations and related areas. Based in Toronto.

cancel 1. To discontinue or fail to renew a TV or radio series for another season. 2. To call off, discontinue or make void, as a proposed booking.

candela The internationally recognized unit of measure for gauging the intensity of a light source. Related term: CD.

candid shot Photograph or camera shot that is not planned or staged for the camera.

candy glass 1. Another name for sugar glass, so named because, like candy, it tastes sweet and can be eaten. Breakaway glass used to be made from this material; today, brittle plastic resin is used instead. Related terms: breakaway glass, sugar glass. 2. Carryover nickname for any breakaway glass, including the plastic resin kind.

canned applause Prerecorded applause, stored on an applause track. It can be served up on cue.

canned laughter Prerecorded laughter, as opposed to laughter recorded live from a studio audience. Also

called a laugh track. Related terms: laughs, laugh track.

canned music Prerecorded music.

Cannes International Film Festival & Market World's most famous film industry festival and trade fair. It occurs each May in Cannes, France, a Mediterranean resort city on the southeastern coast of France. Producers, distributors, actors and others (including international media) gather to screen and promote films and make production and distribution deals. Also called the Cannes Film Festival. Internet address: http://www.cannes-festival.fr/. Related term: Golden Palm Award (Palme d'Or).

cannon roll Auto stunt in which a securely attached car roll cannon is used to forcefully push, via a pyrotechnic black powder or nitrogen gas propulsion charge, a vehicle up from the ground into the air.

capsule gun Special-effects rifle using compressed air or nitrogen gas to shoot break-apart capsules (containing powder or other material) or metal balls (to break windows, ceramic lamps, flower pots, etc.). During a gunfight scene, an off-camera capsule-gun operator aims the gun and shoots the capsules or balls at designated targets to simulate bullet hits. It is less time-consuming than having a pyrotechnic crew wire the production set with small explosive charges (squibs). Capsule guns are manufactured in semiautomatic, fully automatic (machine gun) and pump-action single-shot models. Related terms: Sweeney gun, blood hit, bullet hit, dust hit, glass hit.

caption 1. On-screen wording used to introduce or explain a scene, e.g., "The bottom side caption should read: 'FBI Headquarters, Washington

D.C., 3:25 p.m.'" 2. A caption is also called a subtitle when used to translate foreign dialogue. Such captions appear in closed-captioned and open-captioned television programs. Related terms: closed-captioned, open-captioned, subtitle. 3. Printed description or explanation of a photograph or drawing, as in a magazine, e.g., a photo caption. Also called a picture legend.

capture 1. (n.) Motion capture, a process used in computer special-effects work. 2. (v.) To copy or save what is being displayed on a computer screen.

car hit Any stunt in which a stuntperson makes intentional and forceful contact with an automobile. Related terms: hood ride, hood roll, stunt driver, fall.

car roll Any type of stunt requiring an automobile to turn partially or completely over. Related terms: cannon roll, car roll cannon, pipe ramp, stunt driver.

car roll cannon 1. Large, tubular metal device attached securely (or, welded) to the inside bottom frame of a vehicle, open end facing down. The cannon contains a measured black-powder explosive charge, also called a black-powder bomb, that, upon detonation, propels a section of wooden telephone pole downward, striking the ground and causing the vehicle to immediately flip over or upward. The vehicle with cannon in place is called a cannon car/truck. The car roll cannon was developed by stuntman-director Hal Needham, who named his device the Needham Cannon Ram. Related terms: cannon roll, car roll. 2. Similar pneumatic device using nitrogen gas as a propellant instead of black powder, which, in the United States

and most other countries, requires a license at the national (and possibly, local) level to explode.

carbon arc lamps High-intensity lamps and projector bulbs whose light closely resembles sunlight. Related term: arc.

carpenter Production crew member responsible for building the wood-based parts of a set. Related terms: key carpenter, scenery crew.

carry day Day for which the cast and/or crew are paid but are not required to work. Related term: hold.

cartage Term for reimbursement to a musician for the cost of transporting certain musical instruments to the studio for music track recording. If the instruments are brought by public carrier, the courier company is paid directly by the producer.

cartoon 1. Animated film (of any length), made from a series of hand-drawn or computer-generated drawings, e.g., a Saturday-morning cartoon. Also called a 'toon. Related terms: animated film, animated series, animation, toon tune. 2. Short film or video featuring animated characters and settings. 3. Single or series of block-framed, usually humorous, black-and-white or color line drawings featuring characters, backgrounds and dialogue, e.g., a daily newspaper cartoon. (If it's a series of such cartoons, it's also called a cartoon strip or comic strip.) Related terms: comic-book movie, comic-book version.

cassette 1. Lightproof container for film that allows a camera to be loaded in daylight. Related term: magazine. 2. Container that houses audio or videotape, protecting it from damage.

cast 1. Performers appearing in a film. On production forms (e.g., budget and breakdown forms), "cast" refers only to speaking parts and does not include extras. 2. The act of selecting actors for a production. This is typically done by a casting director. Often, casting of a film is done with box office considerations in mind.

cast against type To cast an actor for a role that he normally would not be considered right for, e.g., to cast a comic actor for a starring role in a serious film.

cast approval 1. Approval by an actor of the production company's choices for other principal players; typically, a condition of his agreeing to star in the film. This is a contract right granted only to an actor in a powerful negotiating position. Also called major casting approval. 2. Any approval of a cast by an individual or company as a condition for agreeing to become involved in a production.

cast breakdown Breakdown of a story, storyboard or script into the individual performing parts to be cast. Related term: breakdown.

cast insurance Film production insurance covering principal members of the cast; it financially protects the producers and investors in the event of the injury, illness or death during production of any actor covered. Cast members named in the policy are required to have a medical checkup by a physician approved by the insurance company. The director may also be included in some cast insurance policies. Related terms: insurance, medical checkup.

cast list Listing of the performers (and their character names) appearing in the production. Depending on whether the list is for in-house and union distribution or solely for publicity, the performers' addresses, phone numbers, agents, Social Security numbers (U.S.), salaries/pay rates, etc., may be included. Related term: final cast list.

cast member 1. One of several actors hired to perform in a show, e.g., "The cast members for the new TV series got together for a cast photo." Related term: key cast member.

cast of characters 1. Collectively, the characters in the story, e.g., "That's an interesting cast of characters in your script." 2. Expression referring to any group of real-life individuals, all of whom are distinct in some way. Related term: character.

cast photo Publicity photograph featuring the cast of a show.

cast recording Audio recording of the songs and music from a stage musical or opera. Also called an original cast recording or cast album.

cast-and-crew screening Showing a film to its cast and crew; typically, this is done before the film is released to the public.

casting agency Business hired by a producer to cast performers. Related term: extras agency.

casting agent Individual hired to cast all or specific roles of a production. May also be called a casting director.

casting call Notice, request or invitation from a producer or casting director to actors to submit head shots, composites or demo tapes, or to have them appear in person at an interview or audition. A casting call appearing in print is also called a casting notice. Related terms: commercial casting call, cattle call, character call, model call.

casting data report Statistical sheet submitted on a quarterly basis to the union by the producer; it lists the total number of males and females, age and racial groupings, cast totals, numbers of lead and supporting roles, days worked and forms of hiring (daily and weekly totals) for each film, TV series episode, etc. Used by the union to determine the overall employment status of the industry.

casting director Individual responsible for directing the selection and hiring of actors or other performers for a film, TV program, video, play, or live entertainment event. The casting director screens individuals for the lead roles and presents the best choices to the producer and director for a final decision. Smaller roles, including extras, may be cast entirely by the casting director. A casting director may work on staff at a production company or be hired on a per-project basis (known as an independent casting director or casting agent).

casting directory Any reference source listing performers available for hire. The oldest regularly published casting directory in the United States is the *Academy Players Directory.*

casting notice News or advertising item informing agents, managers and performers of roles being cast for a production. Casting notices appear regularly in entertainment trade newspapers. They may also be delivered directly by hand or electronic means (fax or computer) to agents and managers by companies specializing in such services. Also called an audition notice or tryout notice. Related term: casting call.

casting search Activities conducted to find the best performer(s) for the lead role(s), e.g., a local casting search or regional casting search. Casting searches are also used to help publicize a project. Related terms: national casting search, international casting search, talent search, advance publicity campaign.

casting session Audition or interview held under the direction of one or more production casting personnel. Typically, performers are briefly auditioned or interviewed (or both), one at a time. Related terms: emergency casting session, location casting, audition session.

Casting Society of America (abbreviated as CSA) Organization representing the interests of casting agents and casting directors in the United States.

casting tape 1. Demo, interview or videotape used in the casting of a part. 2. Videorecording of a casting session.

catchlight Tiny reflection of light seen in an actor's or newscaster's eyes.

catchphrase 1. Catchy saying; an interesting and memorable set of words uttered by a character in a movie or TV program. (A movie fan can usually identify a film by its catchphrase.) Examples: "I've a feeling we're not in Kansas anymore." "Rosebud." "Here's looking at you, kid." "May the Force be with you." "Go ahead. Make my day." "I'll be back." "If you build it, he will come." "Bond. James Bond." 2. Advertising slogan used to promote a movie, as in newspaper ads or on posters. Examples: "A cast of thousands." "Garbo talks!" "A long time ago, in a galaxy far, far away . . ." "In space, no one can hear you scream."

cattle call Nickname for an open audition or interview session, usually featuring a large number of auditionees or interviewees trying out for the same part. Related terms: open audition, open interview.

catwalk Suspended overhead structure or walkway on a soundstage that allows lighting and sound equipment to be hung high above the floor. Related terms: rigging, scaffolding, fly gallery.

CC Abbreviation for closed-captioned.

CCD Abbreviation for charged-coupled device. Small, rectangular, solid-state semiconductor; consists of a flat-surface array of thousands (or millions, depending on the type) of light-sensitive photodiodes covered by microlenses and color filters. Found in video cameras and other equipment. Light entering the lens of a video camera strikes the CCD and, through various electronic conversion processes, records images. TV studio and high-grade camcorders have three CCDs, one for each primary color (red, green and blue). Each colored lens and accompanying photodiode underneath it equals one pixel, or picture element. Related terms: digital scanner, pixel.

CCTV Abbreviation for closed-circuit television.

CD 1. (n.) Abbreviation for compact disc, a small, thin, durable, circular plastic disc containing recorded music or other information; the recorded information is decoded optically by laser light as the disc is played in a compact disc player. Related term: Photo CD. 2. (v.) Abbreviation for "curtain down."

CD-E Abbreviation for rewritable compact disc. Blank compact disc, onto which information can be recorded and erased.

CD-R Abbreviation for recordable compact disc. Blank compact disc capable of having information recorded on it, one time only, by means of a compact disc recorder. It is not capable of erasure and re-recording. Related term: RCD.

CD-ROM Abbreviation for compact disc/read-only memory. Compact disc containing digitally encoded visual and audio information, designed to be played on a computer. The "read-only memory" refers to the fact that the disc is for playback use only. Related terms: computer software, agency book, casting directory, portfolio, stock photodisc.

CD-ROM live-action production Video production featuring live actors performing or guiding the events of an entertainment (game) or informational CD-ROM. Related term: CD-ROM production.

CD-ROM production 1. Video production in which a CD-ROM master disc is created; the master is then used to duplicate identical CD-ROMs for promotional distribution or retail sale. Related term: CD-ROM live-action production.

Cecil B. DeMille Award Annual U.S. award, bestowed upon a noted individual in the international film industry by the board of directors of the Hollywood Foreign Press Association and presented during the televised Golden Globe Awards ceremony. The award is named after Cecil B. DeMille (1881-1959), famous director-producer-screenwriter of early Hollywood. Cecil B. DeMille directed and produced many large-scale movie spectacles, including *The Ten Commandments* (1956), his last film, which starred Charlton Heston and featured an all-star cast.

cel Single sheet or frame of clear cellulose acetate; used in the process of cel animation. (Depending on what image is depicted on it and from which film or cartoon, it can be a collector's item.) Individual film frames may also be called cels by collectors, e.g., a film cel. Related term: celluloid.

cel animation Filmmaking process of creating moving characters and objects against changing or stationary backgrounds by placing them on clear cels and shooting them, frame by frame, with an overhead animation camera. As part of the process, original, handmade outline drawings on animation paper with peg holes (24 drawings per second for action characters) are transferred to clear cel sheets (also with peg holes). Colored paint is then applied by hand to the black-outlined areas on each cel. After drying, they are shot in the proper sequence with an overhead animation camera (a special camera that films looking down so each cel remains completely flat). Today, hand-painted cel animation is not the norm; instead, animators do original drawings on white animation paper (with peg holes), which are recorded, one at a time, by a special overhead camera that transfers them to a computer. Once in the computer and displayed on the monitor, each of the drawings are electronically colored and combined with any secondary computer-generated (CG) images. Scenic backgrounds may be hand-painted and combined in the computer with the action images. The result is an animated movie that has both the creative storytelling and artistry of humans and the magic of modern computer technology. Dialogue (recorded earlier), sound effects and music are added at various stages during the production process. Dialogue can also be changed during post-production. The movie's video master is then transferred to 35mm film so release prints can be made for distribution. Related term: animation.

cel side Glossy, uncoated side of film that, depending on the wind, faces outward or inward on the roll. celluloid, A-wind, B-wind.

celebrity 1. Famous or well-publicized individual. Related terms: A-list celebrity, major celebrity, movie celebrity, offbeat celebrity, reluctant celebrity, TV celebrity, child of a celebrity, darling of the media, star. 2. Of or pertaining to a celebrity or having the status of a celebrity. 3. Status or world of a celebrity.

celebrity lookalike Individual who physically resembles a well-known person. Related terms: lookalike talent, double.

celebrity photographer 1. Individual who photographs celebrities as an occupation; a paparazzo. Related term: paparazzi. 2. Famous photographer.

celluloid 1. Originally the trade name for cellulose nitrate, a film base that was used during the early era of filmmaking; it subsequently revealed itself to be dangerously flammable and self-destructing over time to the movies shot on it. Today, cellulose acetate, cellulose triacetate or polyester (Estar) are used; the latter is a heavier base used for visual-effects work, making internegatives and filming and releasing IMAX films (which can also be shot, but not released, on acetate base). 2. Nickname for motion pictures, e.g., "The magazine's cover story was about today's superstars of celluloid."

cement Liquid adhesive used to splice two pieces of film in hot (or chemical) splices.

cement splice Two pieces of film joined together when the scraped ends of film are cemented together. Related terms: splice, hot splice.

censor 1. To delete material on the grounds it is offensive, insulting or supposed to be kept secret. A "bleep" may be used to censor offensive dialogue; or, another word or phrase may be dubbed in its place. If an entire performance or work is censored, it is also the same as being banned. Related terms: "Banned in Boston," bleep, tape delay, television version.

center line Imagined or real line or mark on a stage indicating the division of stage left and stage right. It is bordered downstage (the audience end) by the curtain line.

center stage 1. Middle point or section of a stage; the most prominent performing place on a stage. Also called middle stage or midstage. 2. Expression meaning a place of great prominence, e.g., to take center stage. Same as to be in the spotlight.

Central Casting Corporation Name of a former casting service, established December 4, 1925 by the Motion Picture Producers and Distributors of America (MPPDA), to provide Hollywood productions with extras of particular character types; hence, the saying, "He looks like he's right out of Central Casting." In 1945, the MPPDA changed its name to the Motion Picture Association of America (MPAA), its current moniker. (A behind-the-scenes look at Central Casting Corporation's operations in contemporary 1930s Hollywood can be seen in the Oscar®-winning film, *A Star Is Born* [1937]). The corporation's operations were sold in 1976. Businesses today in various countries, both in and out of the entertainment industry, using the "Central Casting" name are not affiliated with the present-day MPAA in the United States.

Central Park (New York City) Public park of 840 acres, featuring trees, lawns, hills, lakes, ponds, trails, bridges, playgrounds, sports fields, a bandshell, zoo, ice-skating rink, castle (small), open-air theater and restaurant; located in the center of Manhattan Island in New York City. Used for location shootings, outdoor theater and music presentations, and off-hour recreational activities.

century stand Small, three-legged stand with clamps, able to hold, for example, a gobo or small lights. Related term: C-stand

Cèsar Award Award bestowed annually, in a gala celebration, by the French Academy of Motion Picture Arts and Sciences. Categories include (subject to change): Best Film, Foreign Film, Short Film, First Feature, Direction, Actor, Actress, Supporting Actor, Supporting Actress, New Actor, New Actress, Young Actor, Screenplay, Cinematography, Editing, Music, Sound, Art Direction, Costumes and Poster. Established in 1975.

CFTPA Canadian Film and Television Production Association. Organization representing the interests of producers in Canada, in labor union contract negotiations and related areas. Based in Toronto.

CG Abbreviation for computer-generated.

CG actor Character in a film or program that is, in reality, an image created electronically; it is animated, pixel by pixel, on a computer screen. Also called a computer-generated actor, digitally animated actor, digital actor, cyber-actor, virtual actor, or CG performer. Related terms: CG character, synthespian, laser scanner.

CG character Story element (human or otherwise) generated on the computer. The first CG character to appear in a theatrical film was a sword-wielding, stained-glass-window knight in *Young Sherlock Holmes* (1985), executive produced by Steven Spielberg. The CG knight was created by the visual-effects studio Industrial Light & Magic, a company established by George Lucas in 1975, in San Rafael, California. The first theatrical film to use all CG characters and settings was *Toy Story* (1995), featuring the voices of Tom Hanks, Tim Allen, Don Rickles, Annie Potts, John Ratzenberger, Jim Varney and Wallace Shawn. Also called a digital character or cyber-character.

CGI Abbreviated for computer-generated imagery. Related term: 3D CGI.

CGI effects Computer-generated visual effects. Variation: CG effects. Related terms: computer effects, digital visual effects.

CGI effects animator Individual who creates computer-generated, movable images on-screen. Variation: CG effects animator. Related terms: animator, digital effects artist.

CGI effects studio Another name for a digital-effects studio.

CGI effects supervisor Individual responsible for supervising the creation of CG still and animated images. Variation: CG effects supervisor. Also called a digital-effects supervisor. Related term: visual-effects supervisor.

CGI movie Film containing one or more prominent computer-generated visual effects. The first feature-length theatrical movie to use all computer-generated characters and settings was *Toy Story* (1995).

CGI shot Camera shot or still photo featuring computer-generated imagery.

chain movie theater Movie theater owned by a large corporation and is one of a series of similar theaters located in cities around a country. The opposite is an independent movie theater.

"Change!" Instruction from a TV director in the control room to change the onscreen graphic to the next display

change page Script page containing one or more revisions; it replaces another page in the script and is a different color. (When a colored change page itself is replaced, a different color again is used.) In Hollywood, the color order of change pages is typically as follows: white (original), blue, pink, yellow, green, and gold/goldenrod. The word "Revised" (or "Rev.") and the date are printed next to the page number, in addition to a letter of the alphabet next (if the change runs longer than one page, e.g., "152., "152-A.") Added scenes or shots are also accompanied by a letter of the alphabet. A deleted scene or shot is indicated by the word "omitted" or the sentence "Scene [number] omitted" next to the corresponding number in the script. Related terms: revised page, script change.

change-over In film projection, the process of switching between two projectors at the end of each reel so that the film will continue uninterrupted.

changing bag Lightproof bag used by the film loader or second assistant cameraman that allows film to be loaded into the magazine in broad daylight.

channel VHF or UHF frequency pathway assigned to a TV or radio station for its transmissions; represented by a tunable number via a channel selector button or dial. Related term: TV channel.

chaperone Adult who accompanies an unmarried, minor-aged person. Child actors require chaperones to auditions, interviews and bookings.

character 1. The person an actor portrays in a production. 2. Any person, animal or entity portrayed or depicted in a story, e.g., a fictional character or real-life character. Related terms: persona, cast of characters, offbeat celebrity.

character actor 1. Actor (of any age or gender) with the talent and the physical capability to portray a variety of supporting roles. 2. Actor of a certain character type.

character development Process in the script of a character evolving, growing or becoming more interesting or apparent within a story.

character interpretation Another name for characterization.

character makeup Makeup application that changes or distorts an individual's natural features. The opposite is straight makeup. Related terms: highlighting makeup, shadowing makeup.

character number On the production board, the number assigned to the character. Typically, the more scenes an actor has, the lower his number. (The stars in a production usually have numbers one through five.)

character role Acting role other than the lead, e.g., a friend, parent, shopkeeper, hotel clerk, politician, lawyer, nurse, or the like. A character role is usually a supporting role.

character type One of a group or class of individuals having similar personalities or physical features. Examples: airplane-pilot type, army-general type, construction-worker type, cowboy type, grandmother type, school-nerd type, muscle-builder type, rock-musician type and scientist type. Related terms: type classification, acting stereotype, typecast, cast against type, look the part, real-people look, typed out.

characterization Portrayal or interpretation of a character by an actor. Also called character portrayal or character interpretation. Related terms: acting, in character.

Characters & Comediennes/Characters & Comedians Category headings found in and comprising one volume of the *Academy Players Directory*, published by the Academy of Motion Picture Arts and Sciences in the United States. This volume lists male and female character actors and male and female comedy actors. The males and females have their own sections in the volume.

cheat 1. To change the position of a performer, prop, or product to an angle more favorable to a camera or audience, e.g., "Cheat to the camera." Usually, this is done so the performer's face or product's label is seen more fully. 2. To trick the viewer in a clever manner about the contents or action within a shot, scene or edited sequence of shots. Related term: camera trick.

"Cheat the look." Direction to an actor to turn his face more in the direction of the camera, as opposed to the true or natural angle. Also said: "Cheat to/toward the camera," "Cheat the shot." Related term: cheat.

check print Composite print sent by the lab; once the dupe negative is approved, release prints of the film will be struck.

check the gate To look into the gate of the camera and verify there is no buildup of emulsion or other foreign matter that would hinder or prevent proper operation of the camera; it is a function performed by the first assistant cameraman.

checkbook journalism News gathering and reporting based on paying sources for information. Related term: news media.

chemical fade Dipping one end of the negative into a chemical reducer or dipping one end of a positive into a chemical intensifier to make the scene progressively disappear. Chemical fades, which are rarely used, are of poorer quality than optical fades but are quicker to create.

chief lighting technician Another name for a gaffer.

child actor Any actor under age 18; children work under strict rules governing their working hours and conditions. For example, a studio teacher or welfare worker is required on any set using a child actor.

child labor laws Government regulations covering the employment of children, including babies. In the U.S., California is one of many states with specific laws pertaining to children working in the entertainment and advertising industries. Unions also have specific rules covering the hiring and supervision of children. Related terms: chaperone, studio teacher, welfare worker, work permit, emancipation.

Children Category found in and comprising one volume of the *Academy Players Directory,* a directory of union actors published by the Academy of Motion Picture Arts and Sciences in the United States. This volume lists male and female child actors.

china marker Grease pencil used by editors to mark film; it is semiperma-nent but can be rubbed off and does not scratch the film.

Chinese dolly Shot in which the camera is pulled on dolly tracks but is slanted away from the subject; usually combined with a sweeping pan.

choppy-motion video Jerky and disjointed video movement, as opposed to full-motion video.

choreographer Individual who designs and supervises dance or other body movements in a production; e.g., a dance choreographer or fight choreographer. Also called a dance designer (if applicable). Related term: fight director.

choreography 1. Art or process of designing body movements, such as dancing, ice skating, fighting or stunts. 2. Composition of choreographed movements.

chorus Group of singers and dancers in a musical production.

chorus line Row of chorus singers or dancers.

chroma key Electronic process used in television (most predominantly in TV news and weather reports) in which a person or object is placed in front of or within a uniform non-glossy blue or green background; the background is then electronically eliminated and replaced with a selected new still or moving image background. (Blue or green is used because neither color is found in great quantity in human skin tones.) Chroma key is used in television to achieve this visual effect, while in film, the bluescreen, greenscreen or orangescreen process is used. Related terms: matte shot, bluescreen shot.

chroma key blue Bright, nonglossy blue color used in the chroma-key process. Available as paint, blue cloth or plastic sheeting.

chroma key board Large panel in a TV studio, painted with a special, nonglossy blue or green paint or covered with a colored cloth or plastic sheeting designed for this purpose. An example is the one a TV weatherperson stands in front when doing his weather report. The blue or green color is replaced with a geographical map, which is then composited with the weatherperson and a variety of weather symbols, temperature readings or a live radar display. The chroma-key board may also be referred to as a bluescreen or greenscreen. Related term: chroma-key wall.

chroma key green Nonglossy, bright green color used in the chroma key process.

chroma key wall Large-sized chroma key board; a wall in a television studio colored chroma-key blue or green and used for the compositing of onscreen images.

chromatic aberration Distorted image resulting from the fact that light waves do not bend at the same angle when passing through a lens. For example, blue rays bend more than red and would not strike the surface of the film at the correct spot; the resulting image would look soft or out of focus. (This was often used intentionally in silent films for its softening effect.) To correct this problem, at least two lenses must be used: the second compensates for the chromatic aberration of the first. Related term: apochromatic lens.

Chyron Trade name for an electronic device generating on-screen wording and symbols for a television program. Manufactured by the Chyron Corporation of Melville, New York, in the United States.

Chyron operator Off-camera individual operating a Chyron.

cinch marks Scratches on the film's surface caused by pulling the loose end of the film while the reel is stationary. Related term: abrasions.

cinema 1. Motion pictures as a form of art or entertainment. 2. Theater used for showing motion pictures; another name for a movie theater.

cinema verité Candid and real filmmaking; French term meaning "movie truth."

Cinemascope Trade name for 20th Century Fox's widescreen process. It is based on an anamorphic system that uses specially designed lenses during shooting to squeeze the image; the image is un-squeezed during projection. When photographed on 35mm film, the Cinemascope aspect ratio is 1:2.35 (compared with the standard 1:1.85). When filmed on 70mm film, the aspect ratio is 1:2.2. Related term: scope.

cinematic Adaptable to or lendable to film rather than to stage. When used to mean the opposite of theatrical or stagey, it is meant as a compliment to the director that he has used the medium well. Related term: filmic.

cinematize To make into a movie; to adapt to the big screen.

cinematographer 1. Another name for a director of photography; individual who supervises the various usages of a motion picture camera. The cinematographer is in charge of the camera crew and provides expert advice to the director regarding the various shots and angles available and the technical requirements for each. Related terms: director of photography, setup. 2. Individual who is both a director of photography and camera operator, e.g., a documentary cinematographer, underwater cinematographer or wildlife cinematographer.

cinematography Art and science of motion picture photography.

cinemobile Vehicle capable of handling all the required equipment for a film crew of 50, including dressing rooms and bathrooms. Created by Fouad Said, it is principally used for location shooting. The company was bought by Filmtrucks in 1982.

cineplex Movie theater having two or more separate spaces and projectors for exhibiting films. Also called a multiscreen theater, multiscreen complex. Related term: multiplex.

cinerama Widescreen process using three cameras and three projectors to record and project a single image.

cinex strips Test strip provided by the lab which indicates the range of densities possible for that negative, thus enabling the cameraman to see the accuracy of the exposure. Related term: wedges.

circled takes Another name for a good take of a shot; one that the director wants to keep.

clapboard Flat board with a hinged stick on top that produces a clapping noise; its front surface can be marked to display production information. At the beginning of a shot in which sound is also being recorded, an assistant camera operator steps in and holds the board in front of the active camera. Next, depending on the prevailing custom, the scene and take numbers, title, scene location or just the word "Marker" is verbally stated. Immediately after, the clapstick is brought down to create a single clapping sound. This sound and the specific film frame of the clapstick will be the synchronization point when the audio and film portions are ed-

ited together later. The crew member steps out, the director says "And . . . Action!" and the shot begins. The production information may be chalked on, inked on (with removable ink) or written on small pieces of removable tape. Also called a clapstick board, clapper board, marker, slate, take board, number board, production information board or shot information board. Related terms: marker, slate, time-code slate.

clapstick Narrow strip of wood or other material hinged to the top of a clapboard. Its purpose is to create an identifying sound for the audio and visual synchronization of a film during the editing process. Two clapsticks hinged together without a board may be used in some shots. A very large pair of clapsticks may be used to mark a wide or long shot involving a crowd or battle scene. If the clap sticks are used at the end of the shot, they are usually held upside-down and called end slate or end marker. Related terms: clapper stick(s), marker stick(s), or, the sticks.

Class A Program commercial In the U.S., the union designation for a major TV commercial (other than a wild spot) in a union-specified number of market cities during a use cycle. New York City, Los Angeles and Chicago (the three largest cities in the U.S.) count as a certain number of market cities each. The current Commercials Contract between the union and producers (advertisers and advertising agencies) gives detailed information on market city numbers and scale payments to union (SAG and AFTRA) members who perform in them. Also called a Class A spot or network program spot. Related term: network spot.

Class B Program commercial Union designation for a TV commercial (other than a wild spot), shown in the U.S. in a medium number (set by the union) of market cities, excluding New York City, during a use cycle. A related designation is the Special Class B Program commercial, which is one shown in New York City and up to a union-set number of other market cities during a cycle of use. Also called a Class B spot or Special Class B spot.

Class C Program commercial Designation for a TV commercial (other than a wild spot), under the union jurisdiction of SAG or AFTRA in the United States, shown in a small, union-specified number of market cities during one use cycle. Depending on the current union contract, this may be five cities or less. Also called a Class C spot.

classic model Famous or enduring automobile from the past. Classic cars often are used as picture cars in period movies. Also called a collector car. Related term: picture car. For example, classic cars of the '40s and '50s were used in *The Way We Were* (1973).

classical theater 1. Playhouse featuring Shakespearean plays; "classical" in this sense refers to the era of Shakespeare (1564-1616), rather than to the works of the Greek and Roman eras, which are seldom performed. Related term: Shakespearean play. 2. World, field or profession of classical theater. Also called Shakespearean theater.

classically trained actor Actor whose skill in performing comes from the experience of portraying characters in traditional plays, such as those by William Shakespeare, as opposed to experience acquired through portrayals of characters found in modern plays. Related term: Shakespearean actor.

classroom trailer On-set location where the child actor receives mandatory education while working on a production, in lieu of that child attending regular school. A child actor is required to obtain permission from the school district before being allowed to work. Related terms: schooling on a production, studio teacher, welfare worker.

clay animation Animation involving pliable clay figures. Also called "Claymation."

Claymation Trade name for the animation style and technique used by Will Vinton Studios (Portland, Oregon, USA), the industry's preeminent clay animator.

clean entrance Actor's entrance into a scene without first casting a shadow on the set, allowing clothing or a prop to peek around a corner while waiting on a mark, or the like. Also given as a direction by the director, as in, "Make a clean entrance," or "That wasn't a clean entrance. Try it again."

clean exit Actor's exiting from a scene in which he moves far enough out of frame or off-stage so as not to leave a shadow or so a part of the body or a prop does not show. Also given as a direction by the director, e.g., "Make a clean exit."

clean-up Period after an location shooting when the area used is cleaned up or returned to its original state. Related term: wrap time.

"Clear." 1. Spoken notice by a television stage manager or assistant director informing all that the cameras are off, as when a commercial break occurs or the program ends. 2. Spoken notice by one or more stunt or special-effects personnel immediately before and after a hazardous shot, as one involving an explosion.

"Clear frame." Direction by the director requesting one to move out of the shot area

"Clear yourself." Direction by the director to an on-camera actor; the director is asking the actor to move away from a specific object (as a lamp, open door, tree, etc.) blocking the actor's body from the camera.

clearance 1. Permission, paid for or granted free of charge, to use someone else's copyrighted material (a book, song, poem, etc.). 2. Permission, paid for or granted free of charge, to use a location during production of a film, video or television show.

click track Small loop of magnetic film on which the audible clicks of a metronome are placed. Used when recording or scoring a musical number. The clicks are not recorded because the conductor uses headphones to listen to the track; however, when shooting a musical number, the clicks are audible on the playback so the performers can move to the appropriate rhythm.

client list Record of an agency's regular business customers, e.g., a list of its clientele. Related term: stable.

client representative 1. Any client representative, such as an agent, manager, publicist or attorney. 2. Individual responsible for representing the advertising interests of a client at business meetings and on production sets. The client rep may be an employee of the ad agency or client. Related terms: sponsor representative, product representative.

cliffhanger 1. A highly suspenseful, unfinished ending to a film, season-ending episode of a TV series, daytime or nighttime episode of a soap opera or installment of a miniseries or multi-part TV movie. The story is purposely left unresolved so viewers will want to see the conclusion (the next episode). One of the more famous cliffhangers was the "Who Shot J.R.?" season-ending episode of the television series *Dallas* (1978-91). Related terms: season finale, suspense. 2. Film that keeps an audience on the edge of its seat, e.g., "That movie was a real cliffhanger. It had one death-defying scene after another!"

climax Decisive point in a story when a conflict or problem is resolved. For example, the climax of a crime movie is when the criminal is caught or the crime is solved. Related terms: plot resolution, denouement, anticlimax.

clip Small section of film removed from a shot by the editor. Related terms: clip, film clip, trim.

clip clearance Permission to use a portion of someone else's copyrighted audio or visual work. Related terms: film clip clearance, music clip clearance, video clip clearance.

clip episode Another name for a compilation episode; an episode of a television series featuring many flashback clips.

clipping 1. Article from a publication; tearsheet, e.g., a news clipping. 2. Cutoff section of film; a trim, e.g., a film clipping.

clock time Time as measured by a digital or analog clock. Related terms: time, stopwatch, time-code slate.

close 1. Nearby, e.g., a close-up shot. 2. To finish or conclude, e.g., "The host decided to close the show with a few personal comments." 3. The act or instance of closing, e.g., "That was a good close."

closed rehearsal Practice session closed to everyone except the performers, necessary crew and others with special permission, as opposed to an open rehearsal.

closed set Studio set or location set that is closed to anyone not immediately connected with the production. (Sometimes, when an intimate scene is to be shot, only the most necessary crew members are allowed on the set; henceforth, the set will be "closed" to remaining crew members.)

closed-captioned (abbreviated as CC) Dialogue and narration captions appearing at the bottom of the screen, for viewing by hearing-impaired individuals when used with a special decoding device attached to or built into the set, e.g., a closed-captioned TV show. Related terms: caption, OC, subtitle.

closed-circuit television (abbreviated as CCTV) System in which the TV signal is transmitted over metal or fiber-optic cable and received by one or more connected televisions. Subscriber cable TV is an example on a community-wide scale. Or, a closed-circuit television camera and monitor may be used to view an actor's audition. A videocassette recorder-playback machine and its connected television set is another example; these are used by advertising agencies to play audition tapes, new commercials and the like. The "closed circuit" refers to the fact that the TV signal is being transmitted and received directly from the source and is not being broadcast in every direction over the airwaves.

close-up (abbreviated as CU) Shot taken at a short range or through a telephoto lens, or magnified optically or digitally; one that shows details of a subject. Director Ingmar Bergman is noted for using many close-ups in his films.

closing credits Another name for end credits.

closing number Final song and/or dance presented.

closing-night party Party held after the last performance of a theatrical play's run.

cobweb spinner Handheld, special-effects device using a fan to blow a stringy spray of liquid, either a special resin or thinned rubber cement (both flammable), onto portions of a set to create an appearance of spider webs. Large areas are first prepped with one or more thin monofilament (fishing) lines, providing a support base for the cobwebs. To make the webs more visible and nonsticky, they are dusted with fuller's earth or white baby powder. A cobweb spinner typically consists of a handheld drill motor with an attached fan blade protected by a circular wire cage enclosed on the sides and back. Mounted in the center of the fan blade is a cobweb material cup, with removable lid; both spin as a unit with the fan blade. The lid of the cup has a short, extremely thin slot cut into its top. As the blade spins, the liquid cobweb material is forced out by centrifugal force and blown in fine strands onto the targeted area. Also called a cobweb machine, cobweb-maker or cobweb gun (also refers to a compressed-air version). Related terms: web, cobweb maker.

Code and Rating Administration of the Motion Picture Association of America Organization that classifies a film's for audiences. It also rates theatrical trailers. Related terms: ratings, MPAA.

code numbers Numbers placed by an encoding machine on the edge of picture and sound tracks; they keep picture and sound in sync during the editing process.

co-director One of two or more directors on a production. (*The Matrix* (1999) has two co-directors: Andy Wachowski and Larry Wachowski.)

co-feature One of two films exhibited as a single show.

coin Money; funds, e.g., "The film made some additional coin over the weekend." Entertainment trade paper use.

cold interview Interview in which the interviewee is not given advance notice or an opportunity to prepare. Related terms: ambush journalism, interview.

cold lighting Another name for fluorescent lighting; it radiates less heat than incandescent (glowing filament) lighting.

cold reading Reading dialogue from the script without the chance to memorize or prepare an interpretation of it ahead of time, as for an audition. (Typically, an actor is given a few moments to look over the material before the cold reading begins.)

collaboration Act, process or result of working with one or more individuals, as on a film project. Also called a collaborative effort, cooperative effort, shared effort, or teamwork.

color bars Chart containing the color spectrum; the strips of colors are placed side by side and used by the film lab to check the accuracy of colors in processed film.

color coding 1. System used to create a production board during the process of breaking down a script. Items in the screenplay (e.g., cast, props, locations) are assigned different colors and then transferred onto breakdown sheets. A second color-coding system is used on the production board to differentiate interiors from exteriors, day from night, etc. 2. Standard industry system used for designating revisions of a script or revised script pages. (When a revised page is inserted into a script, it is immediately identifiable by its color.) The color sequence is as follows: white, blue, pink, yellow, green and goldenrod.

color correction Changing or altering specific color values; during shooting, it's achieved by means of filters and during processing, it is achieved in the lab.

color film 1. Photographic film stock having color-sensitized elements. 2. Movie photographed using color film.

color reversal internegative (abbreviated as CRI) A negative made directly from the original negative, using reversal film stock; it is used when making release prints. When using a CRI, the progression of generations is as follows: original (negative) to CRI to release print. An alternate method uses an interpositive (aka IP, protection master, master) and the progression is as follows: original to IP to internegative (called IP/IN) to release print. Because an extra step is involved, IP's are more expensive than CRI's, however, most labs prefer IP's because CRI's have a tendency to streak. Also, the overall quality of the IP/IN is superior and the grain is finer. (Usually the more generations involved, the larger the grain. IP/IN, however, is considered to be one generation, not two.) Intermediate stages are used between negative and print to protect the original negative as much as possible. If an IP or CRI gets scratched, a new one can be made so ensuing release prints will be clean.

color timer Individual at the film lab who corrects and/or balances the film to achieve correct color relationships and values. He frequently works with the director of photography to get the desired effects. Related term: timing.

color wheel Circular spotlight attachment; it can be rotated to select one of numerous color filters mounted on it.

colorization Act or process of adding color, manually or via computer, e.g., the colorization of an old black-and-white film.

colorized version Black-and-white film that has been colorized, frame by frame, either manually or via computer, e.g., "Is that the colorized version or the original black-and-white?"

combined print Positive copy of a motion picture containing synchronized pictures and sound. Related terms: married print, composite print.

comeback film Movie featuring an actor who has not been in prominence professionally for a number of years, e.g., "This is his long-awaited comeback film."

comedian 1. Entertainer who tells jokes and performs comedy routines. Related terms: stand-up, warm-up comedian, comic, comic foil, sidekick, straight man, top banana, humorist, impressionist, ventriloquist. 2. Another name for a comedy actor.

comedy 1. One of the two main forms of drama (the other being tragedy). Related term: drama. 2. Movie, TV program, play or the like whose story contains numerous funny verbal or visual elements intended to make the audience laugh or feel cheerful. Comedy can be combined with other forms and story categories, e.g., a comedy-western (*Blazing Saddles* [1974]), horror-comedy (*Young Frankenstein* [1974]) or sci-fi comedy (*Spaceballs* [1987]). Related terms: comedy-drama, comedy of errors, comedy of manners, marital comedy, musical comedy, romantic comedy, screwball comedy, situation comedy, zany comedy, dramedy, sketchcom, slapstick movie, thrillomedy, variety show, vaudeville. 3. Anything funny or humorous. Related terms: comedy material, clean comedy, dark comedy, high comedy, light comedy, low comedy, physical comedy, stand-up comedy, parody, pratfall, satire, sense of humor, slapstick. 4. World, field or profession of comedy. Related terms: American Comedy Award, Montreal International Comedy Festival.

comedy of errors Movie, TV program or play giving prominent attention to the humorous reactions and counterreactions of characters as they respond to one or more central characters' mistakes. The term originated with Shakespeare's play *The Comedy of Errors*, which tells the story of two pairs of twin brothers who are separated at youth and, after many instances of mistaken identity, are reunited as men.

comedy troupe Touring company of comedy performers.

comic 1. Comedian or comedy actor. Also called a funnyman, funnywoman, joker, jokester, comic cut-up or cut-up. 2. Of or pertaining to comedy.

comic foil Member of a comedy team acting as a contrast or opponent to the other(s). Usually refers to a straight man whose on-stage or on-screen character is a strong-minded or intellectual type; thus, by appearing "normal," he highlights the acts of comedy that take place.

comic genius Highly gifted and skilled comedy performer. (Jonathan Winters and Robin Williams are often referred to as comic genuises.)

comic opera Opera or operetta having a humorous storyline, dialogue and usually a happy or sentimental ending. Also called an opera buffa (Italian) or opera comique (French). An example of a comic opera is *The Barber of Seville* (1816) by Gioachino Rossini (1792-1868).

comic relief 1. Another name for a period of comedy relief; one or more funny moments providing a diversion or relaxation from a serious story. 2. Individual, animal or thing providing the humorous relief.

coming attractions Scenes from a film about to be released; or of a television series about to make its premiere. Related terms: coming soon, movie commercial, promo, trailer.

commentator Individual describing the proceedings of a live or recorded event; typically he adds planned or spontaneous comments, e.g., a sports commentator. Related term: narrator.

commercial 1. Filmed, videorecorded or audiorecorded advertisement. Also called a commercial announcement or commercial message. Examples of commercial types: auto, children's, competing product, cosmetics, dealer, demo, endorsement, eye product, fashion, fast-food, food, foot product, hair product, hand product, hidden-camera, holiday, jeans, lingerie, lip product, makeup, movie, movie theater, nail product, national, non-air, non-competing product, piggyback, program, radio, regional, seasonal, skin product, test-market, theme, TV and underwear. Related terms:

documercial, infomercial, spot. 2. Being marketable or directed toward making a profit.

commercial break Pause during which commercials are shown or heard. Related terms: station break, "Welcome back," "We'll be right back," "We're clear."

commercial contract 1. Binding agreement to produce, write, direct, film, tape or perform in a commercial. 2. Contract between a talent union and commercial producers (advertisers and advertising agencies) detailing working conditions and scale payments for union members who perform in commercials. It is called a "[year and union name] Commercials Contract."

commercial head shot Photograph featuring and emphasizing the face of a TV commercial performer; it is used for casting and promotional purposes. Also called a commercial 8" x 10". Related term: head shot.

commercial rate 1. Commercial performing or production work fee. 2. Television, radio or movie-theater advertising time or placement cost, e.g., the fee a station or network charges for running a commercial.

commercial success Money-making hit; a financially positive achievement or attainment. Related terms: B.O. champ, hit.

commercial theater 1. Playhouse offering a variety of staged entertainment to admission-paying theatergoers; this is a for-profit entity. 2. Industry, world, field or profession of commercial theater.

commercial TV For-profit television; it is supported by selling commercial time to various buyers or sponsors.

commissary Cafeteria or dining room located on a film or television studio lot, e.g., a studio commissary.

commission 1. Percentage of earnings paid to an agent or manager for representational services provided. The commission amount varies, usually between 10 percent and 25 percent, and it may be set by a union. In the U.S., an agent is not allowed to deduct a commission from a union actor's scale payment so the hiring producer must pay the commission up to that minimum amount. Agents also receive income from service fees paid by the business clients who hire the talent. Also called an agent's fee or manager's fee. Related term: cut plus ten. 2. Film and television commission.

Comml. No. Abbreviation for "Commercial Number." Identifying number assigned to a commercial; found as an information heading on storyboards, scripts, production records and on-screen displays. Variations: Comm. Title:, Job no.:, Acct. No., or Code:.

"Common marker." Phrase spoken by the clapboard operator when two or more nearby cameras are shooting the same scene at the same time

community theater 1. Small or informal playhouse offering staged entertainment to the residents of its community. 2. World, field or profession of working in community theater productions.

comp 1. Short for "complimentary;" a free admission ticket or pass. 2. Short for "comprehensive drawing," sketch or layout; it includes many details. 3. Short for "composite." 4. Short for "compensation," e.g., payment of some kind.

comp card Short for composite card.

company 1. Acting company. 2. Dance company. 3. Production company;

another name for a production unit. 4. Another name for a business.

completion bond See completion guarentee.

completion guarantee Contractual understanding that a motion picture will be completed and delivered in accordance with certain specifications (e.g., time schedule, cost, conformity to screenplay) and sometimes in accordance with specific creative elements. It usually provides that the guarantor will furnish monies to pay costs over the established budget and contingency; in many instances, the guarantee gives the guarantor the power to take control of the production if it is deemed necessary (e.g., the project is over budget and/or over schedule). Related term: completion guarantor.

composer Individual who writes music. A film composer writes an original score or, with permission, adapts an already existing score, thus producing additional, similar sounding music (as for a sequel). Related terms: songwriter, composition, royalty, score.

composite 1. (abbreviated as "comp") Card, sheet, folder or glossy photo on which two or more pictures of an actor are displayed. Name, personal statistics, garment sizes and contact information are included. Composites are used as promotional pieces and are given to regular and potential clients. Related term: revising composite. 2. Any picture or screen image made by manually, photographically or electronically combining two or more separate images or graphics. Related terms: composite shot, digital composite. 3. Any combination of things, such as visual images synchronized with a soundtrack.

composite card A small-sized composite for models or TV commercial actors, varying in size, with pictures and descriptive wording printed on it. Depending on type, it may have color or black-and-white pictures of the individual on two or more sides that can fold open and close. Also called a comp card, photo card, or model's card. Related terms: agency card, Zed card.

composite dupe negative Piece of duplicate negative with picture and sound in sync. Related term: dupe negative.

composite master positive Fine grain positive print combining picture and sound from which dupe negatives are made.

composite print Positive copy of a motion picture containing synchronized pictures and sound. Also called a married print or combined print.

composite shot Shot in which two or more separate images are combined. Related terms: digital composite, blue-screen shot, matte shot, process shot, visual-effects shot, zone shot, superimpose.

composition 1. Piece of music written by a composer. Related terms: score, song. 2. Arrangement or mixture of elements within a shot. Related term: makeup.

compressed time Reduced time; decreased clock time of a film, video or audio product. (The other two types of time are real time and expanded time.) Compressed time is accomplished a variety of ways, such as editing out brief, irrelevant portions or increasing the speed of the playback. Related terms: time, fast motion, skip frame.

compressed-air catapult General name for a platform that launches a stuntperson; it operates via two attached pneumatic cylinders. This is a device consisting of a metal ram, also called a rod or plunger, that moves in and out of a sealed, tubular metal housing by forcing highly compressed air or nonflammable nitrogen gas into it. Related term: air ram.

computer animation Animated sequences created by a computer; used in television, computer-software products and film. Also called computer-generated animation or computer-generated movement. The general term, computer-generated imagery (CGI), includes both moving and still images created by a computer. Related terms: computer effects, cel animation, screen saver.

computer effects Visual images in television entertainment and news programs, music videos, CD-ROMs, DVDs, theatrical films and the like, created electronically via a computer. Also called computer-generated effects or digital effects. Related terms: CGI effects, digital visual effects, computer animation, Chyron, colorization, laser scanner, morphing, motion capture, paint box, virtual reality, wireframe, wire removal, X.

computer enhancement Another name for digital enhancement.

computer graphics Electronically generated images used in film and tape to create sets, scenes, etc., that are too difficult and/or too costly to build and shoot realistically. *Tron* (1982) was the first feature film to include computer graphics.

concept Idea for a story or image. Related terms: concept sketch, high-concept film.

concept sketch Rough drawing of how an advertisement or production set (or an element of it) will look. From it, a more detailed drawing (comp), such as a blueprint, is created for use as a construction guide.

conductor Individual who leads and directs the performance of an orchestra or band. Often, a film composer will conduct his own score. Related terms: orchestra conductor, bandleader, maestro, baton.

cone light Cone-shaped flood light (in senior, junior and baby sizes) that covers a large area with diffused, soft light.

confab Short for confabulate (to discuss) or confabulation (a discussion). Also denotes a convention or trade show. Entertainment trade paper use.

conflict 1. Incompatibility or interference with another person, product, job or contract. Also called a conflict of interest. Related term: product conflict. 2. Minor or major disagreement or fight between two or more characters or groups in a script.

conflict card Card or sheet on which an actor's competing product advertisements and commercials are recorded. Also called a product exclusivity record.

conforming Matching one piece of film to another (e.g., conforming the original negative to the cut work print). Related term: negative cutting.

console Control panel used in a sound studio for recording, rerecording, mixing, etc.

console dimmer Device used for light changes.

construction coordinator Individual who supervises construction of the set. Also called a construction manager. Related term: scenery crew.

construction crew Individuals who, under the supervision of the construction foreman, perform the tasks necessary to build and complete the sets,

in and out of the studio. The crew is made up of prop makers and laborers.

contact list Compilation of the names, addresses and telephone numbers of the vendors, supply houses, services, etc., that will be used by a motion picture company during production. This list must be constantly updated.

contact print positive or negative made by placing one piece of film in physical contact with another piece of unexposed film; the duplicate is then exposed, frame by frame, on a printer in the lab.

contact printer Device which makes prints (or other generations) from positives or negatives. The two main types of printers are the optical printer, which projects the image onto raw stock for reproduction; and the contact printer, in which the original film is placed in physical contact with the raw stock and exposed to light. There are also two methods of printing: step printing, in which the film is advanced intermittently (with each frame being stationary during exposure); and continuous-motion printing, in which the raw stock and original move continuously during exposure.

contact sheet Large print photograph onto which individual shots from a roll of film are printed, in sequence, in their original negative size; called a contact sheet because the negative strips of film are contacted onto a large sheet of photographic paper. Using an overhead light, the contact sheet is developed into a single, collective, positive print. The numerous rows of pictures can be inspected for quality and detail, usually with the aid of a magnifying lens (or loupe). The selected shots are enlarged, using the negatives, to the desired size. Also called a contact proof. Related term: proof sheet.

contact sheet frame Single, miniature photo on a contact sheet; it is one of many that appear in sequence on the sheet made from the processed roll of film.

contact sheet marks Symbols hand drawn on a contact sheet using a crayon, grease pencil or ink marker, indicating the extent of cropping desired and areas that need lightening or darkening. Examples of marks drawn on a single contact sheet frame (or matching enlarged print): circle around frame (frame to be enlarged); straight line across frame (crop here and do not vary; a definite border); wiggly line across frame (cropping here can vary to match print size; an indefinite border); small circle within frame (make this area lighter to bring out the details); a group of short, straight lines within frame (make this area darker; keep the details in this area from being washed out during processing).

contact-lens special effects Special eye effects used in films and TV involving custom-made, colored contact lenses. Related terms: sclera lenses, special eye effects.

contemporary drama Movie, TV show or play featuring a storyline set in the present day, as opposed to a period drama or futuristic drama.

contingency Certain amount of money, generally ten percent of the total negative cost, included in the budget to cover unexpected costs. Typically, a completion guarantor will not approve a completion guarantee unless a contingency is included in the final budget.

continuing role Performing role continuing regularly from one episode to another or from one performance to another. In a TV series, the actor's character is written into the script of every episode; this is different from a recurring role, in which the character's presence is nonessential or is not expected in every episode. The performer who plays a continuing role is called a regular player. A continuing role is also called a continuing part, continuing character, or running part.

continuing series Television series having the same principal cast and setting in every episode and a story that unfolds with each airing; each new episode begins where the previous one ended. A daytime or nighttime serial (soap opera) is an example of a continuing series. Related terms: daytime serial, nighttime serial, soap opera, arc.

continuity Orderly progression of action from shot to shot to ensure proper development of the story. During production, the script supervisor keeps track of scene details so there are no lapses in the continuity of dialogue, action, set dressing, props or wardrobe.

continuity clerk See script supervisor.

continuity script Script containing precise visual and audio information for each shot; everything in it matches what is seen and heard in the film.

continuity supervisor Individual who maintains continuity records. Another name for a script supervisor

continuous action Action filmed simultaneously from different angles and then edited together as a series of shots. Example: the continuous action of a car chase scene.

contract Legally binding agreement between two or more parties. Related terms: acting contract, agency contract, exclusive contract, TV commercial contract, union contract, credits not contractual, approval, booking, clearance, deal, deal memo, depiction release, location agreement, morals clause, maximum-use period, no-nudity clause, nudity clause, nudity rider, out clause, pact, party, pay or play, perk, right, star commitment, voucher, Producer's Masterguide.

contract negotiation Session or process of discussing, offering, counter-offering, arranging, etc., the specific terms of a contract.

contract player Performer hired to act in one or more unspecified projects during the course of a contract period, as opposed to being hired on a per-project basis.

contrast 1. Degree of difference between the light and dark areas of an image, e.g., high contrast or low contrast. 2. Difference, dissimilarity or unlikeness, e.g., "The contrast between my character, the villainess—and hers, the heroine—is very apparent."

control room Soundproof room in a studio where the director and appropriate technicians are seated at one or more consoles; they control the input, mix and output of video and audio signals. Communication with those on the production set is by wireless headset transceivers, intercom or via loudspeaker.

controlled studio conditions Professional working environment of a studio (for film, video, photography, sound, etc.), as opposed to an outdoor location where conditions such as weather, noise and onlookers are less under the control of the photographer, videographer or director.

cookie See kook.

co-op 1. Short for co-op ad or cooperative advertising; shared cost plan for local advertising between the retailer and the product's manufacturer or regional distributor.

coops Large number of lamps mounted in a single housing; used for illuminating large areas. Related terms: bank, coop.

coordinating producer Television producer responsible for unifying production activities and schedules.

coprod Short for coproducer or coproduction. Also spelled co-prod. Entertainment trade paper use.

co-production 1. Any joint production between two companies. 2. Jointly produced project, as a movie, by a domestic production company and a foreign production company. 3. Film or TV series produced in two countries, e.g., an American TV series filmed entirely in Canada, with post-production and distribution work done in the United States (where the producer's main business offices are located).

'copter mount Camera platform attached to a helicopter, allowing for manned filming (e.g., Tyler mount).

copy 1. Reproduction, duplicate or replica, e.g., a videotape copy. Related terms: first generation, generation loss. 2. To reproduce or duplicate something. Related terms: dub, dubbing. 2. Written material printed, as in a magazine or newspaper; or displayed, as on a TV screen. Related term: hard copy. 3. Wording that comprises the script for a commercial, announcement, news report or live event.

copy sheet 1. Script; short-length script. Related term: sides. 2. Script for an advertisement or press release.

copy space Area where copy is to be printed or displayed.

copycat violence An act of aggression perpetrated as a result of a similar act shown or described on television (news or entertainment) or in a theatrical film, computer game, stage play or printed work (newspaper, magazine or book). If the violence is illegal, it is also called a copycat crime.

copyist Individual who extracts the instrumental parts from the score for use by musicians and the conductor.

copyright Right of legal ownership of a literary, musical, photographic, film, video, computer, artistic, etc., property; it entitles the owner to reproduce and market the work exclusively for a period of time set forth in copyright laws. Related terms: piracy, public domain.

copywriter Individual who writes copy, especially for advertising or public relations purposes.

cordless sync Audio tape recorder that does not need a sync pulse cable to remain in sync with the camera. Instead, it uses a crystal motor whose speed is maintained by an accurate frequency signal from a vibrating crystal; the camera is governed by the same kind of crystal. Sometimes called cableless sync. Related term: Nagra.

core Plastic spool used to store and hold film and raw stock; negatives are usually stored on cores rather than on reels.

corporate television Informational or instructional television programming pertaining to a corporation; such programming is fed via satellite link to its factories, warehouses, dealers or company stores. Private-access corporate websites on the Internet are also used for this purpose.

cost overruns Unbudgeted and unexpected additional expenditures.

cost report Detailed weekly analysis identifying costs to date, costs for the week and estimates of the the costs required to complete the film.

cost to complete Amount of money, as per the budget, required to complete a picture. The financial status of the production is reported weekly on cost reports.

co-star 1. One of two or more lead players who share star billing. 2. One of two or more prominent supporting players who are billed as co-stars. There are also categories such as: special guest star, guest star and featuring. 3. To co-star.

costs to date Current and up-to-date tabulation of money, per budget category, spent on a production. Related terms: cost report, cost to complete.

costume 1. Style of clothing representing a country, sport, celebration, ritual, occupation, period in history or fantasy. 2. Such clothing as worn by an actor, dancer, etc., while performing onstage or in front of a camera. Also called a wardrobe item (single piece). Related terms: breakaway costume, matching costume, outfit, Velcro shirt, wardrobe. 3. Partial- or full-body covering (including head) worn by an actor in a science fiction, fantasy or horror film.

costume department Another name for a wardrobe department.

costume designer Individual who researches, designs and supervises construction or acquisition of costumes worn by performers.

costume fitting Session during which actors try on their theatrical costumes to determine correct size or to make adjustments or improvements. Photographs may be taken for reference purposes. Related term: wardrobe fitting.

costume movie Film taking place in a period of the past; it requires actors to wear historically correct garments. Also called a costume drama. Related term: period movie.

costumer Individual responsible for the care of costumes on the set during production. For productions without a costume designers, the wardrobe supervisor is responsible for acquiring the clothes worn by the cast. (This is a union category separate from costumer.) The antiquated term for costumer is "wardrobe mistress."

countdown Counting down, either verbally or visually, to cue the start of programming or some action, as a special-effects explosion; also may be done as part of an active microphone check. Related terms: In three . . ., "Three . . . two . . . one," "Cue me," "You're on!," leader, mike check, voice cue.

counter programming 1. Scheduling a unique or popular show or special in the same time slot as a competitor's program. 2. The program so scheduled.

cover 1. (v.) To synopsis and critique a script; the result of the Story Analyst's work is called "coverage." 2. (n.) Protective surface, wrapping or lid, e.g., script cover, book cover or video box cover. 3. Photo, artwork or other material used on such a cover. Related terms: cover art, cover material, packaging use.

cover art Visual material appearing on the cover or insert of a music compact disc, CD-ROM, videodisc, magazine, book or other work. It may be hand-drawn artwork, computer-generated artwork, photographs or a combination of these. Related terms: cover, cover material, cover shot.

cover set Alternate set that can be used quickly when circumstances (weather, illness, etc.) prevent originally-scheduled shooting for that day. Related term: back up schedule.

cover shot Additional printed take that can be used in case the preferred take is not usable (e.g., damaged film). Related terms: protection shot, safety shot, insurance shot.

coverage 1. Shooting a scene from various angles and setups to provide options for the editor. Related term: cover shot. 2. Written report about a script, including synopsis and critique; done by a story analyst (also known as a reader). Typically, the coverage includes a recommendation for (or against) further action on the project. Also called a script evaluation or script feasibility report. Related term: synopsis.

co-writer One of two or more writers on a production. Variation: co-scriptor.

crab dolly Small, compact platform with wheels, movable in any direction, on which a camera is mounted. It is typically used in complex shots.

cradle Lens support for extremely heavy and cumbersome lenses.

craft 1. (n.) Occupation or trade requiring specialized knowledge and skills. Related terms: actor's craft, writer's craft. 2. (v.) To make skillfully, e.g., a cleverly crafted script.

craft service Department of a film crew responsible for the coffee, beverages and snacks on a set. Craft service personnel also sweep up and do small chores. (This is a union position on the West Coast.)

craft service table Location where food and drink refreshments for cast and crew are placed. Also called a craft table or food table. Meals also may be served from a trailer or service truck.

crane Large, hydraulic lift, capable of carrying a camera and two people (typically, the camera operator and the director or camera assistant), used on high-angle moving shots. This is one of the most complex pieces of equipment on a set. Smaller cranes are also available for video cameras. Related terms: whirly, Camcrane, MegaCrane, Mini-Crane, boom, camera mount.

crane operator Individual who controls the movements of a crane.

crane shot Camera shot utilizing a crane to pull back and up. For example, a stunning crane shot appears in *Gone with the Wind* (1939), when Scarlett O'Hara (Vivien Leigh) finds herself standing amongst injured Confederate soldiers; as the crane shot pulls back, the screen fills completely with bodies of soldiers.

crash pad Large rectangular block of covered foam rubber or other soft material; used to cushion falls by stunt people, actors doing their own stunts and athletes. Also called a porta-pit.

crawl Rolling titles, typically used for end credits, that begin at the bottom of the screen and roll continuously to the top. (Rolling front credits are rare.) Related terms: crawling title, crawl, roll-up title, roll-across title, rolling title, roller title, creeper title.

created by Onscreen credit designated for the creator of a television series. In the U.S., the creator of a TV series receives an on-screen credit plus a per-episode minimum (or higher) royalty payment. Use of the credit is covered in the Writers Guild of America's contract with producers. Variation: concept by.

creation 1. Originally designed or conceived script, drawing, TV series, song or other artistic work. Related term: original.

creative consultant Screen credit designated for an individual who provides valuable informational assistance to a production or who consults on the project in a creative capacity; without this individual's cooperation, the production possibly could not proceed. For example, a biographical movie about a deceased person's life may have his spouse, parent or adult child listed as a creative consultant in the credits. Also called a creative advisor. Related term: technical advisor.

creative differences Two individuals on a production (e.g., producer and director; director and actor; etc.) who have different approaches to the work and find it impossible to work together. Often, when a key member of the cast or crew is fired or quits, it is due to "creative differences." Related term: artistic differences.

creative director Individual responsible for the creation and development of ideas, as in advertising; such duties may include creating advertising concepts, selecting photographers, models, and locations, attending shooting sessions, coordinating creative activities, reviewing and approving art and copy and developing presentations.

credits 1. List of names and titles of the people who worked on the film. In the front credits, their size and placement are negotiated for above-the-line personnel as well as for some below-the-line personnel (e.g., production designer, costume designer). In the end credits, most union and guild contracts have specific clauses governing the size and placement of their members' names. 2. List of projects an individual has worked on. Related terms: main title and opening credits, end title and closing credits, billing, position number, single card, shared card, uncredited.

credits coordinator Individual who organizes, files and verifies credits for a publication.

credits designer Individual who designs credit sequences for films and TV programs, including the main title, which is part of the opening credits sequence.

credits not contractual Phrase used in early film project announcements meaning credits for actors have not been confirmed; or, credits are tentatively committed until certain conditions are met, such as budgetary financing and scheduling.

credits sequence Segment of a film or TV program during which credits appear on-screen, e.g., an opening credits sequence or closing (end) credits sequence. (The main title is included in the opening sequence.) Related term: pre-credits sequence.

crew Individuals who perform technical and production jobs behind the camera in the creation of a motion picture, video or television show.

crew call List that displays the call time for each cast and crew member (e.g., the time when one must report to the set or to the area for pre-arranged transportation to the location); informs the cast and crew which scenes are to be shot; the order of the scenes to be shot; which sets or locations will be utilized; what the cover sets are; and any unusual equipment needed (crane, Steadicam, etc.). Related terms: call, call sheet.

crew list Sheet containing the names and contact information of those individuals working on a production,

e.g., director, writer, director of photography, all others working in any capacity. The performers' names appear on a cast list.

critical success Favorably reviewed product or production.

critically-acclaimed film Motion picture that has received favorable reviews. Such a film may not necessarily be a box-office success or even have a wide theatrical release. It often does, however, win awards. *Boys Don't Cry* (1999) is such a critically-acclaimed film; it received an Academy Award® nomination for Best Supporting Actress (Chlöe Sevigney) and Hilary Swank won the Oscar® for Best Actress. In addition, it received awards from many critics' associations. Also called a critics' movie. A "critically-acclaimed series" is a television series that receives favorable reviews; it may or may not be a ratings success. A series may improve slowly or dramatically in the ratings after it receives such favorable reviews. *Everybody Loves Raymond* began its network run as a critical darling with low ratings; it has since gained tremendously in popularity, in part helped by its consistently favorable reviews.

crix Short for critics. Entertainment trade paper use.

crop To cut off, eliminate from the frame.

cross cut 1. Alternating shots of action from two independent scenes and locations. For example, to cross-cut shots of a criminal in one part of a city to police detectives tracking down leads in another area of the city. The bank robbery scene in *Heat* (1995) showcases expert cross-cutting. (In an intercut, the action is immediately and closely related; it is considered a single scene, e.g., to intercut shots of the criminal on the phone, talking to a detective, from their different locations in the city.) 2. Alternating shots in such a manner. Related terms: intercut, parallel-action cut.

cross-collateralize Process of combining the profits and losses of the foreign exhibition of a film (or films), so that losses might erase any profits (and successes would, therefore, pay for failures). This controversial practice is employed by the international distribution arms of the major studios and, although the producer may appreciate this simpler accounting report (there is one statement instead of individual ones per country) this practice clearly benefits the distributor. On a smaller scale, a project's individual accounts can be cross-collateralized so that the resulting final figures may appear to be favorable (on or under budget), even though there may have been overages in certain categories.

cross-fade Gradual and simultaneous muting of one sound, while increasing another. Can also be applied to lighting.

cross-light 1. Lighting a subject from one or both sides. 2. Light directed at a subject from a side angle. Also called a sidelight.

cross-over film One that crosses over into a new market audience and therefore has additional box-office appeal. *Waiting to Exhale* (1995) was a successful cross-over film, having found audiences in the African-American as well as the white community.

cross-plot See production strip board.

cross-promotional tie-in Advertising relationship in which two companies promote their products simultaneously as part of a special advertis-

ing campaign. An example is a commercial for a fast-food restaurant that offers toys featuring characters from a current theatrical film. Related term: tie-in.

crowd scene One with a large number of extras. Films by director Cecil B. De Mille are noted for their crowd scenes. Related terms: mob scene, battle scene.

crowd wallas Background voices so numerous they cannot be understood, except possibly for an occasional word. Related terms: walla-walla, crowd noise, talk-talk, omnis.

crowd-pleaser Individual or object found especially entertaining by an audience; typically, he garners applause and/or laughter.

crystal sync Electric device whose speed is adjusted by a vibrating crystal that emits a constant frequency signal. Used in sound recorders and cameras instead of a sync pulse. Related terms: cordless sync, Nagra.

Crystasol Water-soluble, special-effects liquid brushed on glass; it simulates frost (ice particles) when dry. Available from Tri-Ess Sciences, Inc., of Burbank, California. Related terms: Frost Tex, snow effect.

CS Abbreviation for close shot.

CSA Abbreviation for Casting Society of America. Organization representing the interests of casting agents and casting directors in the United States.

CU 1. Abbreviation for a close-up shot. 2. Abbreviation for "curtain up."

cucaloris See kook.

cue 1. Sight or sound signal, used to begin dialogue or action. Related terms: hand cue, light cue, sound cue, visual cue, voice cue, off-cue, on-cue, miscue, cue light, Q, bleep, call the show, countdown. 2. To provide a person or animal with a cue; to signal.

cue cards Large, lightweight cardboard signs on which the actor's lines are written. Mostly used in television, they are held beside the camera so the actor can read them while appearing to speak memorized lines. The TeleprompTer, a newer, more accurate electronic device, is replacing cue cards. Related terms: show cards, idiot cards.

cue light Any type of light used to cue or signal, a performer, newsperson or audience. Related terms: light cue, on-the-air light, applause sign.

cue mark Circle in the upper right hand corner of the film frame, placed several feet before the end of the reel, to alert the projectionist that a reel changeover is approaching. Typically, cue marks come in sets of two, several seconds apart.

cue sheet List of dialogue, music and effects cues, in sequence, as they appear in the sound tracks. Cue sheets are used during the mix. Related term: music cue sheet.

cue track Soundtrack used for cueing purposes. Related term: scratch track.

cult classic Old movie or TV series, it is adored by a devoted segment of the viewing public, e.g., a science-fiction cult classic or Western cult classic. *The Rocky Horror Picture Show* (1975) is a well-known cult classic.

curtain 1. Large, movable drapery that separates the stage from the audience. Related terms: act curtain, final curtain, show curtain, curtain down, curtain up, batten, apron. 2. Short for "curtain time."

"Curtain." Direction to raise or lower, open or close the curtain at the front of a performing stage

curtain call Request to performers on stage to take a bow after the final curtain; in response to continued audience applause, the curtain is reopened and the performers take their bows, individually or as a group. The mark of a successful performance is the number of curtain calls the cast makes.

curtain down 1. Scheduled place in a script when the curtain is lowered. Related terms: "CD," "Bring the curtain down," "Lower the curtain."

curtain line 1. Last line spoken or sung before the curtain closes; there may be additional silent or musical action before the curtain finally closes. 2. Imaginary or real line on a stage where the curtain divides the stage from the audience when it is lowered or closed. Related terms: plaster line, center line.

curtain raiser 1. Short play or skit before the main presentation. 2. First performance in a stage show comprised of numerous separate performances; when the curtain is raised, it is the first to be presented. Related term: opening act.

curtain speech Performer's informal words to the audience; typically, he stands onstage in front of the closed curtains before or at the end of the performance.

curtain time Scheduled time the curtain will be raised, indicating the start of the play. Related terms: show time, curtain up.

curtain up 1. Scheduled place in the script when the curtain will be raised. Related terms: "CU," curtain time, "Bring up the curtain," "Raise the curtain."

cut 1. (v.) To edit or change scenes (shots) without using any optical effects. Also called an editing transition. Related terms: cross-cut, intercut, jump cut, match-action cut, match-image cut, quick cut, straight cut, edit, splice, trim. 4. (n.) Film that has gone through the editing process. Related terms: rough cut, fine cut, final cut, director's cut, uncut. 5. (n.) Share or percentage of something, e.g., an agent's cut. Related term: commission.

"Cut!" Spoken instruction by the director to stop the camera, sound equipment, dialogue and/or action of a shot or scene

"Cut and hold." Direction to the camera crew to stop the camera, to the sound crew to stop recording and to the actors to hold their positions, e.g., stay on their marks. The action may resume shortly after a technical problem is corrected or an on-the-spot script change is made. While in a hold state, the actors are allowed to relax; this is different from the director saying "Freeze!" which indicates the actors must literally become like frozen statues (this is done with the cameras running so visual effects can be achieved, such as characters or objects suddenly popping in or out of the shot).

cut back Editing term used when the film returns to a shot after having cut away from it.

cutaway Editing term used when the film cuts from one shot to another in order to return to the first shot at a later point.

cutter Another term for editor.

cutting Art and science of forming the picture and sound tracks into a logical, rhythmical progression, therefore telling a story. Related terms: editing, editor, montage.

cutting room Room equipped with editing equipment (Kem, Movieola, bins, cores, splicers, etc.); the location where the editor and editor assistants put the film together. Related term: editing room.

cutting script Detailed script used by a film editor; also called a cutting-continuity script.

cutting-room floor Saying referring to a shot or scene being edited out of the film, e.g., "My only scene ended up on the cutting-room floor." During the editing process, unused shots are first placed in a trim bin. Some movies and TV programs are edited on videotape, thus bypassing the traditional cut-and-splice method of film editing.

cyan (bluegreen) One of the three primary colors used in color film; it is sensitive to red light, one of the complementary colors. (Yellow is sensitive to blue light; magenta to green light.)

cyber-character Another name for a CG character, e.g., a computer-generated character.

cyber-double Computer-generated lookalike of a principal actor; typically created as part of a stunt sequence involving CGI effects. *The Matrix* (1999) contains numerous cyber-doubles. Also called a CG double.

cyberspace 1. Computer-generated landscape; the electronically simulated, three-dimensional space within a virtual reality environment. The term was coined by science-fiction author William Gibson in his novel *Neuromancer* (N.Y., Ace Books, 1984). The term was later adopted by computer users to refer to the medium of computer communication, e.g., the electronic space and pathways in which information is digitally transmitted over the Internet and displayed on computer screens. Related terms:

cyberland, information superhighway, electronic frontier.

cyc Short for cyclorama.

cycle Payment cycle; period of time used to calculate payments to union performers working in television. A cycle is thirteen weeks; there are four per year. Related terms: fixed cycle, use cycle, unlimited use cycle.

cyclorama Curved background or backdrop extending to one or both sides of a stage or production set; it is used to give an appearance of infinite space. A soft (fabric) cyc, also called a panorama cloth, typically features a solid color, sky or scene; a hard cyc is made with a hard surface and is set in place permanently; a covered cyc has a curving floor surface eliminating the seam where the back wall meets the floor, thus contributing to the appearance of infinite space (e.g., a limbo setting). Related terms: limbo, limbo set, cyc.

D 1. Abbreviation for day or daytime, as in a script. 2. Television rating meaning dialogue is not suitable for all ages, e.g., sexually suggestive dialogue. Related terms: "AL," "L," rating.

dailies Scenes shot the previous day. At the end of the filming day, the scenes so marked are processed on a rush and delivered by the lab for viewing the next day by the director, producer, cinematographer, editor, etc., hence the term, "dailies" or "rushes." A set should not be struck until the dailies have been approved. Related terms: rushes, video dailies, downprint, video assist, workprint.

Daily Variety **and** *Variety* Los Angeles-based entertainment industry trade newspaper. Founded in 1933; *Daily Variety* is published weekdays while *Variety* is published weekly by Cahners Publishing Company. The first issue was published on September 6, 1933.

damsel-in-distress role Acting part in which a young female character is threatened with great physical harm and is rescued by a male hero, who usually has to battle an evil villain, an alien, paranormal entities or nature's forces to do so. Also called a woman-in-jeopardy role.

dance belt Type of athletic supporter worn by a male dancer to protect and support the genital area while performing a theatrical dance (such as ballet).

dance company Group of dancers performing in dance productions, e.g., a modern dance company or ballet company.

dance director See choreographer.

daredevil Individual performing extremely dangerous stunts as part of a daredevil or thrill show, e.g., a motorcycle daredevil. Evel Knievel may be the world's most famous daredevil. Related term: stunt show.

dark comedy 1. Grim comedy, gruesome comedy; humor involving a serious subject, such as death, illness, violence or crime. *Pulp Fiction* (1994) is considered a good example of this genre. 2. Movie containing dark humor.

darkroom Place used by a photographer or commercial photo lab for handling and processing photographic film. The room is kept completely dark during crucial moments or a safelight color that will not fog the film being developed is used to provide adequate visibility.

darling of the media Celebrity who regularly receives positive publicity from the media, due to the fact that he or she is cooperative about granting interviews, posing for pictures or appearing oncamera, is likable and tends to smile or be funny during interviews. For example, Tom Hanks is a darling of the media. Also called a media darling, media sweetheart or sweetheart of the media.

date movie Theatrical film considered to be a good choice for couples to attend as a social outing. *Notting Hill* (1999) was a successful date movie.

dawn Time of day when light begins to appear in the sky; it can be indicative of a specific look, with pale colors, long shadows, etc. If "dawn" is indicated in a script, it is important that it also be indicated on the breakdown sheet. Related term: magic hour.

day Indication in a script (and, later on the breakdown sheets) that the following scene is to take place during daylight hours. If dawn or dusk is specified, it should be so indicated and noted on the breakdown sheet.

day for night Filming technique that, through the use of special blue filters, allows exterior night shots to be filmed during the day. The technique was devised in Hollywood, and therefore is called, in French, "La Nuite Americaine." François Truffaut's film *Day for Night* (1973) is an excellent example of this practice in filmmaking. Related term: night filter.

day out of days Schedule showing the dates and times an actor is to work.

day player Actor hired by the day who has only a few lines or scenes. Per SAG rules, day players must be individually and personally notified before the end of the day's work if they are laid off, otherwise they automatically will be called back to the set the next day. Related term: guarantee.

day rate Another name for a daily rate.

day shot A shot taking place during daylight hours. As a script term, it is used as a continuity reference to indicate events are occurring during the day, as opposed to the night, dusk or dawn (and it is written in all capital letters). Also called a daylight shot or daytime shot.

day shots scenes to be shot in daylight, in either real or artificial light and on an interior or exterior set.

daylight Amount of measurable light, combining both skylight and sunlight.

day/night 1. Day shot or night shot; time-of-day selection heading found on some clapboards and shot information records. Also written as "D/N." 2. Term found in scripts used to describe a shot or a scene's lighting and uncertain time of day (typically those in outer space, inside spaceships and on alien planet surfaces). It may also be used to specifically refer to a strangely lighted location, as in a dream sequence or on a planet that has no atmosphere and in which the landscape is to appear bright against a nighttime sky. (An example of this effect in real life is what the sunlit surface of the moon looks like against the darkness of space.) On Earth, the clear blue sky over a daytime desert landscape can be replaced by a starry night sky using a visual-effects process to produce an eerie, surrealistic landscape having features of both day and night. For outer-space settings, the term day/night may appear in the script as SPACE DAY/NIGHT.

daytime 1. In the daylight hours; during the day. 2. Short for daytime TV, e.g., "I work in daytime, on one of the soaps."

dead mike Inoperative microphone, either because it has been turned off or has malfunctioned.

deadpan Having an expressionless face.

deal 1. (n.) Hollywood term for an agreement; like a contract, it is legally binding (e.g., "Joe Smith just signed a three-picture deal with Fox."). Related terms: back-end deal, development deal, first-look deal, gross-point deal, movie deal, net-profit deal, package deal, series deal, step deal, test deal, done deal, inked a deal, blind series commitment, contract. 2. (v.) To bargain, negotiate or come to terms. Related terms: negotiation, sweeten.

deal breaker Point of concern in contract negotiations that, if not agreed upon, will terminate the negotiations.

deal memo (abbreviation for deal memorandum) Short, written statement outlining the terms of an agreement. It outlines information regarding services, compensation, etc., and, if not used as a final contract signed by both parties, can serve as the basis for further negotiation or for preparation of a lengthier or union-required contract. Until a formal contract is drawn and signed, the deal memo is fully binding to all parties. Related term: contract.

deal player Union term for an actor hired for one or more movies at a guaranteed minimum salary, as set by a union contract with producers.

debris mortar Any size metal drum or pipe with one end open, used to propel into the air a quantity of debris, such as dirt and fake rocks or building remnants, via an electrically detonated, black-powder explosive charge; used during an explosion scene. Also commonly filled with any combination of fuller's earth, peat moss, cork, vermiculite or other lightweight materials. For some scenes, an air cannon may be used instead; it is easier to test for the desired effect and can be set up more quickly for extra takes. Related term: mortar.

debut 1. (n.) First public performance or appearance. Related terms: acting debut, directorial debut, premiere. 2. (v.) To debut; to show or perform for the first time.

decelerator Device used in stunt work to steadily control the rate of downward movement of a falling stuntperson until stoppage in midair (above the ground) occurs; used in scenes in which an airbag cannot be used, such as an unusual ground location or the director's wish to shoot the scene from an overhead angle. When used, the decelerator's cable is attached to the stuntperson with a special harness. Later, in post-production, the cable is removed digitally by a computer process called wire removal. Related terms: descender, fall.

decibel (abbreviated as DB or db) Unit of measure of sound wave intensity.

deep focus Focus in which every object in a shot, from close-up to infinity, is sharp and clear.

deferred cost/deferment 1. Expense for which payment is postponed. 2. Payment which, by agreement, is contingent upon a film generating a certain negotiated level of income.

definition Sharpness of focus; the clarity of a photographed image.

defocus To take out of focus; to make blurry.

delayed broadcast 1. Television program being broadcast after its scheduled air time, due to the unexpected time overrun of a live program, such as a sports game or government news conference. Also called a delayed telecast. If the program is canceled and rescheduled for a later date, it is called a postponed broadcast. 2. Broadcast seen on a tape-delay basis. Also called a tape-delayed broadcast or tape-delayed telecast. (For example, the Tony Awards are shown on a tape-delayed basis on the West Coast.) Related term: tape delay.

deleted page A page omitted from the script that has been numbered. When this occurs, "page # omitted" is noted on the preceeding or subsequent page, thus eliminating unnecessary and confusing re-numbering. Related terms: added page, blue page.

deleted scene Scene omitted from a script that has already been numbered. When this occurs, it is marked as "scene # omitted" to eliminate unnecessary and confusing re-numbering. Related term: added scene.

delivery 1. Act or manner in which lines of dialogue are spoken, e.g., "She has a good delivery." Or, "Her delivery was not quite right on that take." Related term: rate of delivery.

demo commercial Commercial made for demonstration purposes and not for actual broadcasting or cablecasting to the public. Performers are paid a one-time fee. Also called a demo spot or in-house commercial. Related term: non-air commercial.

demo disc Audio or video disc used for demonstration or audition purposes. Also called an audition disc.

demo reel 1. Spool of audiotape or motion picture film compiled for demonstration or audition purposes; short films are often used as demo reels. 2. Résumé of one's work, in the form of filmed or videotaped samples.

demographics Statistical information about a product's audience, e.g., age, gender, income, education levels, geographic location. Also called audience demographics or audience profile.

denouement Another word for a story's climax.

depiction release Signed statement giving a producer the right to use an individual's picture and voice (in a production, its related advertising and other media, as so stated); often it is a clause that is part of a work contract or voucher. It may also be a separately worded, one-page form. Also called a personal release or group release (for a number individuals). Related terms: extra voucher, feature film rights.

depolarized Device that re-bends polarized light rays so that the object being photographed can be seen clearly through a piece of glass, or without harsh, reflected glare. For example, photographing a piece of art displayed in a glass case or a photograph framed behind glass.

depth of field Distance from the camera at which an object stays in focus no matter where the subject moves within that field. Depth of field depends upon the focal length of the lens and its aperture size and the distance from the camera to the object. The smaller the aperture size, the larger the f-stop, the greater the depth of field and vice versa.

desaturated Having certain colors eliminated from the film, by using filters over the lens or chemicals in the lab. Certain film stocks lend themselves to desaturated color. For example, desaturated color was used to achieve a monochromatic effect in the Dust Bowl sequence from *Bound for Glory* (1976; directed by Hal Ashby).

descender Device, used in stunt work, to steadily control the downward speed of a falling stuntperson; its cable supply is connected to a large, paddle wheel fan producing the necessary slowing effect because of the fan blades' resistance to air while spinning. The stuntperson is connected via a cable and safety harness; the thin cable is later removed by a computer process during post-production. Also called a descending machine. (A decelerator is a device that similarly is used to control the speed of a fall.) Related terms: wire removal, decelerator.

detonation board Flat, wooden board with rows of switches or metal contacts (upright posts) used to detonate, in a desired sequence, explosive charges placed on the production set; the board typically is custom-made by its user, a pyrotechnic operator. On the board, one wire from each charge is connected to its own contact while the other wire is connected to the electrical power supply (e.g., a battery). A metal rod, connected by wire to the other side of the power source, is run across the contacts sequentially; this sends electricity through the wires to detonate each charge. Detonation boards are used to trigger pyrotechnic effects in gunfight scenes or explosion scenes. Also called a nail board or bullet hit board. Commercially-manufactured firing boxes, available in different sizes and designs, are also used. Depending on the task, squibs, fuses, nichrome-wire ignitors, electric matches and household matches are used by licensed pyrotechnic operators on the set to detonate or ignite explosives, flash and sparkle pyrotechnic materials or flammable liquids or gases.

develop Submitting film to a laboratory chemical process that turns the latent image on the exposed film into a visible image.

developer 1. Chemicals used in the lab that turn the latent image on exposed film into a visible image. 2. Individual who oversees the aforementioned process.

development The initial planning stage of a film or television project. A project is said to be "in development" when the rights to the material are being optioned or purchased, a writer is hired, actors are sought to become tentatively and conditionally associated with the project (if applicable) and the script is in one of various writing stages (e.g., it is being written, read, revised, broken down, budgeted). Hopefully, if funding can be arranged, the project in development will receive approval or a "green light." (Some of the work in the development and preproduction stages may overlap.) At this point, the more contractually definite work of preproduction begins, such as casting, crew hiring and set construction. However, it should be noted that most movies in development are never made, usually because investment money cannot be found to meet the costs of production and post-production.

development deal Agreement between a studio and/or production company and a producer or director or writer, to generate one or more film projects for eventual production. Types of development deals vary. Related terms: movie deal, series deal, blind series commitment.

development executive Individual at a production company, studio or network who supervises the development of new projects; these projects may be based on original ideas or stories adapted from a novel, play, comic book, previously-made movie, news events or the like. May also be called director of development, vice president of production, creative affairs executive or some other corporate title.

DGA Abbreviation for Directors Guild of America.

DGA Award Annual award bestowed by the Directors Guild of America honoring film and TV directors in a variety of categories.

DGA trainee Individual accepted into the DGA Training Program; he or she is learning to become a second assistant director. Few applicants are accepted each year; usually, there are more than 1500 candidates for two dozen spots and those accepted must pass rigorous written and oral examinations.

DGC Abbreviation for Directors Guild of Canada.

DGGB Abbreviation for Directors Guild of Great Britain.

diagonal splicing Method of joining magnetic film; the film is cut on an angle to eliminate possible bloops (or pops).

dial Soundman's term for mechanically controlling sound during shooting and mixing. To "dial out" or to "pot it out" is to eliminate unwanted sound. Related term: pot.

dialect coach Individual who is skilled in teaching regional accents. Related terms: accent, drawl.

dialogue Written, printed or spoken conversation between two or more individuals; in a script, dialogue means any one or more spoken lines, even by an actor appearing in a scene alone. Related terms: additional dialogue, off-camera dialogue, overlap dialogue, reprise dialogue, revised dialogue, aside, background voices, copy, line, monologue, narration, pun, recitative.

dialogue coach Individual who rehearses difficult dialogue with an actor prior to a performance; or one who provides instruction in the correct pronunciation of foreign words, accents and dialects. Also called a dialogue director. Related terms: dialect coach, voice coach, voice/speech lessons.

dialogue mixer Individual responsible for combining the production's various dialogue recordings into a single dialogue soundtrack which can then be combined with the sound effects and music soundtracks. Related terms: ADR mixer, sound mixer, soundtrack.

dialogue track Portion of the sound track that carries the dialogue, as opposed to the music track, the effects track, etc.

diaphragm Device that controls the amount of light passing through the lens of a camera, projector or printer, usually made of overlapping metal leaves that form an opening (aperture) in the center. By adjusting the size of the opening (measured in f-stops), more or less light can be let in or out. Related terms: iris, stopping down, depth of field.

diaphragm bomb Drum-shaped explosive device with a thin covering at one end allowing the force of the explosion to be angled in a desired direction; typically used in pyrotechnic special-effects work to explode one or more windows outward. Related terms: mortar, explosion scene.

dichroic filters Gelatin or glass filters used on lamps to omit unwanted red light and to bring out more blue light.

difficult actor Actor reported or rumored to be difficult to work with; uncompromising or hard-to-satisfy actor. Related terms: emergency casting session, hot set, morals clause, out clause.

diffused light Soft, gentle, shadowless light. It is produced when diffusers are placed over lights or as a result of particles in the atmosphere, such as haze, fog. Related terms: silk, silking a set.

diffuser 1. Any translucent material placed in front of a lamp to soften the light shining from it. 2. Any translucent material that softens the focus of the image being shot through it. Related term: silk.

diffusion filter Lens attachment used to put a scene in soft focus (e.g., during a dream sequence). Also called a soft-focus filter.

digital 1. Information presented in number form, e.g., a digital watch or a digital display on a VCR or DVD player. 2. Computer information transmitted and stored in a digital code (the binary system), represented as binary digits called bits (1 or 0; on or off). Each of the numbers represents one bit of information; sequences of these digits represent specific pieces of information, such as sounds or onscreen energizing of pixels. The opposite of digital is analog. Related terms: bit, analog.

digital backlot Computer-generated background or foreground scenes (digital matte paintings); they can be stored in a computer's memory and used in a production, as needed. Movement can be added, such as birds, lights in windows, smoke exiting chimneys and the like.

digital camcorder Compact digital video camera.

digital composite Onscreen picture combining real-life imagery and digital imagery. The process is called digital compositing.

digital department Computer-effects department at a film or television studio.

digital effects See computer graphics.

digital enhancement 1. Process of improving an image via a computer, e.g., digital enhancement of a low-resolution surveillance video picture. Also called computer enhancement. 2. Process of adding to an image via a computer, e.g., digital enhancement of an explosion or fire scene.

digital imaging Process of converting picture information into thousands (or millions) of pixels, each one represented numerically with information describing its position and color. Once digitized, as by the use of a scanner, an image can be copied exactly, without it degrading from one generation to the next.

digital matte painting Scenic picture stored digitally in a computer's memory. Also called a digitized matte painting. Related terms: matte painting, digital backlot.

digital photography Art, science or process of producing still images via a digital still camera, digital scanner or digital/video printer. Also called electronic photography.

digital print Picture produced using digital imaging technology. Also called a digital photo. Related term: photograph.

digital retouching Alteration of a photographic or video image via a computer, e.g., weakening or strengthening the electron beam controlling the colors of individual phosphor-rectangle picture elements (pixels) to produce a desired effect. Facial retouching is done to remove wrinkles, moles, scars, acne and the like; it is also done to repair or restore damaged or old photographs. Related terms: retouch, computer effects, doctored photo, paint box, wire removal.

digital rights Various rights granted in a contract allowing pictures, text or sound to be reproduced in digital form for use in a computer-controlled device or the media. An example is the right to use a digitized photograph of an actor or celebrity on a CD-ROM. Related terms: right, interactive re-use right.

digital scanner 1. Tabletop device that scans a photograph, artwork or text and transfers it to a computer for viewing and manipulation, e.g., a color flatbed scanner, insert scanner or handheld scanner. A digital scanner contains a CCD sensor array; filmstrip, 35mm slide and small-object 3D scanners are also available. Also called an image scanner. 2. Large device used in computer-effects work to scan and digitize a length of 16mm or 35mm motion picture film, e.g., a digital film scanner. 3. Large-object laser 3D scanner used in CGI visual-effects work. Related term: laser scanner.

digital still camera Handheld camera using electronic, digital-imaging technology instead of light-sensitized film to record color still pictures on an internal memory or removable memory disk; these photos can then be downloaded into a computer for viewing and manipulation (enlarging, reducing, etc.). Depending upon the equipment used, the pictures can also be transferred to print photographs or transmitted over phone lines to other computers. Also called a still video camera, video still camera. Related terms: digital print, video still.

digital television Any system of recording, converting or transmitting television picture and sound via digital processing of the information. Related terms: advanced television, broadcast quality, HDTV, SDTV.

digital versatile disc (abbreviated as DVD) Optically encoded plastic disc, the same thickness (1.2mm) and width (120mm) as a compact disc (CD) yet is designed to hold seven times more digital information on a single side or layer. The microscopic pits forming the encoded information on a DVD are about half the size of those on a CD and are read by a narrower laser beam; the data spiral on one side is more tightly packed and can reach up to 11 kilometers in length, which is more than twice as long as a CD's data spiral. For one-sided, dual-layer discs, the laser beam is focused on either the top or bottom layer; the advanced dual-layer design permits both upper and lower data spirals to be read from one side of the disc. However, most DVDs require only one side of recorded information, enough to hold 4.7 gigabytes or over two hours of standard video. The highest capacity DVD, a two-sided, dual-layer disc, has four separate layers and data spirals that can store a total of 17 gigabytes of information, or over eight hours of standard video. The drawback in using a two-sided DVD, besides having to flip it over to access the other side, is that the DVD's title, credits, copyright notice, etc., cannot be printed on either playing surface (such information must be reduced and placed on the circular nonplaying surface area of both sides). Often today, two-sided DVDs have different film formats on each side (e.g., regular format and widescreen format). Most commonly referred to as a digital video disc. The DVD is called "versatile" because it offers a wide range of recording and storage applications, such as movies, music, games, text, etc., and a variety of choices as to how that information is used by the consumer. For a theatrical movie recorded on a DVD, the viewer at home has the option of selecting subtitles in up to 32 languages, eight different language soundtracks, different ratings versions, three aspect ratios (standard 4:3, widescreen letterbox or 16:9 widescreen TV), different camera angles and even different endings or scenes (of course, these options are selected by the company releasing the DVD). Additional DVD player features include instant jumping to any point in the movie, slow motion, fast forward and reverse, freeze frame and single frame advance. DVD images and sound have a higher quality than those produced by a laserdisc or videotape. Credit for the initial development of the DVD goes to Toshiba Corporation and Time Warner, Inc. (they originally named it the Super Density Digital Video Disc); the final format was released in late 1995 and contained the best elements of a competing system developed by Sony Corporation and Philips Electronics (who co-invented the original CD format). When used for video purposes, a DVD is also called a videodisc (the general name). Related terms: DVD, DVD-Audio, DVD camcorder, DVD player, DVD-R, DVD-RAM, DVD-ROM, videodisc.

digital video camera Consumer or professional-grade camcorder or studio camera using digital technology to process still or moving images and sound. Depending on the type, it may use videotape, an optical videodisc or a memory chip as its recording medium. Related terms: digital camcorder, digital videocassette camcorder, disc camcorder, DVD camcorder, flash-memory-based camcorder, CCD.

digital video clip Video clip viewable on a computer, such as through the World Wide Web on the Internet. Major studios and television net-

works produce and maintain advertising websites so the public can access promotional text, video clips and sound clips pertaining to current and upcoming productions. Related term: Internet ad.

digital videocassette camcorder Video camera recording picture and sound digitally on a videocassette. Also called a DVC camcorder.

digital videodisc Digitally encoded, compact optical disc capable of holding more information than a standard CD or CD-ROM. The microscopic pits and spaces on the disc represent offs (0's) and ons (1's) as it is read by a laser beam. Technically, a CD-ROM is a digital videodisc, however, the term is more commonly used to refer to the next generation of higher capacity, digitally encoded discs. Related terms: videodisc, digital versatile disc.

digital videodisc recorder Machine recording picture and sound on an inserted digital videodisc via an internal laser system; depending upon the design, it may also have a playback feature. Related term: DVD recorder.

digital visual effects Another name for computer effects; special effects involving computer-generated imagery (CGI). Related terms: CGI effects, digital backlot, digital composite, digital enhancement, digital retouching, computer effects.

digital zoom Enlarging an image area electronically, rather than optically, by selecting an area of pixel information and converting it to a greater screen size. Optical zooming is done mechanically or electromechanically via a glass lens system.

digital-effects artist Computer artist who creates visual effects for film and TV productions. Related term: CGI effects animator.

digital-effects studio Business or in-house department using computers and skilled artists to create onscreen visual effects. Also called a digital-effects house or CGI studio. Related terms: digital department, visual-effects studio.

dimmer Rheostat that increases or decreases the amount of electricity reaching the object, usually a lamp.

DIN Abbreviation for "Deutsche Industrie Norm," the European system for measuring a film's image gathering ability (or, emulsion speed). Related terms: ASA, ISO.

dinky-inky Small, low wattage incandescent spot, usually 100 to 200 watts.

dinner break Production work stoppage allowing the cast and crew time to eat dinner. Also called a supper break. Related term: meal break.

dinner theater Establishment where dinner is served to patrons simultaneously with a play or similar entertainment. Called a pub theatre in England.

diopter lens Lens with extremely sharp focus placed in front of the normal camera lens for close-up photography.

diorama Miniature version of a set.

direct To work as a director, e.g., to direct a film or an episode from a TV series.

directable Capable of being directed, especially in a theatrical or photographic sense. Refers to a script scene, animal or person.

directed by Production credit designated for a director; its size and positioning is subject to union regulations.

direction Instructions given by the director (on the set), the writer (in the script) or the assistant director (to the background extras), as to the action,

mood, rhythm of a scene, or as to how the scene is to be shot, etc. Related terms: break, clean entrance, clean exit, curtain down, curtain up, hold, lose, overlap dialogue, play it for laughs, play to the camera.

directional mike Microphone with a narrow angle of acceptance; it picks up only selected areas.

director Individual ultimately responsible for all the creative aspects of a motion picture, theatrical or television show. He is hired by the producer, though some directors produce for themselves.

director approval 1. Approval by an actor of a production's choice for a director; often, a condition for the actor agreeing to become involved. This is a contract right granted only to an actor in a powerful negotiating position. 2. Any approval of a director by an individual or company as a condition for agreeing to become involved in a project.

director of photography (abbreviated as DP in the United States and as D.O.P. in Australia) Individual, working in collaboration with the director, who is responsible for lighting, framing and shooting a film. The director of photography doesn't actually operate the camera (that is the job of the camera operator) but makes a major contribution to the overall look of the film and oversees the areas of camera and lighting. Related terms: cameraman, cinematographer.

director's assistant individual who assists a film or TV director; a production assistant who reports to the director.

director's chair Type of folding wooden chair with a canvas seat and back; used on production sets for the director, key cast members, continuity person, etc. Available in standard and tall versions.

director's cut 1. Version of a film approved by the director after the initial assembly of footage by the editor; union contract may allow the director a specified length of time to produce his cut before the producer may suggest changes, if at all. 2. Commercially released version of a film conforming to the director's personal editing choices; typically, this is a version of the theatrically released film that contains unused or deleted footage. For example, there are six different versions of James Cameron's *Terminator 2: Judgment Day* (1991) available on laser disc, many of them featuring special editions, added footage, etc. Also called a director's special edition. Related term: uncut version.

director's finder Short for director's viewfinder.

Directors Guild of America (abbreviated as DGA) Union in the United States for TV and film directors, assistant directors, production managers and television stage managers. Founded in 1959. Based in Hollywood, California. Internet address: http://www.dga.org.

Directors Guild of Canada (abbreviated as DGC) Union in Canada for film and TV directors, assistant directors, production managers and designers, art directors and editors. Based in Toronto, Ontario. Internet address: http://www.dga.ca.

Directors Guild of Great Britain (abbreviated as DGGB) Union in Great Britain for TV and film directors, assistant directors, production managers and television stage managers. Based in London, England. Internet address: http://www.dggb.co.uk.

director's medium Film is said to be the director's medium because it allows the director the greatest amount of creativity in the outcome of the finished product, more so than other types of entertainment directing jobs. The theatrical stage is said to be the actor's medium.

director's viewfinder Portable, calibrated viewfinder, e.g., a see-through, optical viewing device, usually attached to a cord or chain for carrying around the neck; used by a director or cinematographer to frame the desired shot area and to select the proper lens for the camera. Also called a director's finder.

direct-to-video release Release of a feature film directly to the home-video rental and purchase (sell through) market instead of having a theatrical release.

dirty dupe Black-and-white, untimed reproduction of a workprint. Related term: one light print.

disaster movie Movie featuring a storyline showcasing the events before, during and after a disaster (natural or otherwise). If it is a large-scale production, it is also called a disaster epic. *Earthquake* (1974), *The Towering Inferno* (1974) and *Titanic* (1997) are some of the more well-known titles of this genre. Related terms: post-apocalyptic movie, survival movie.

disbursing agent Individual in the accounting department who, with the authorization of the financing entity or studio, is in charge of paying out funds for a film.

disc camcorder Digital video camera using an optical videodisc (e.g., a DVD) as its recording medium. Related terms: camcorder, DVD camcorder, video camera.

disc recording Another name for an optical disc recording, e.g., a CD, CD-ROM, DVD, laserdisc or videodisc.

disclaimer 1. Printed, onscreen or spoken notice informing the audience (reader, viewer or listener) that legal, medical, financial or other-type of material is presented for informational purposes only and that the presenter is not liable for its subsequent use by the audience. Related term: "Don't try this at home." 2. Onscreen statement preceding a presentation, informing the viewer that changes to it have made it different from its original form.

discovery 1. Moment in a film or TV program when the audience learns something new and important; its effect on the story typically is stronger than the normal exposition. Related term: discovery shot. 2. Act or instance of finding that which was previously unknown. Related term: being discovered. 3. Person, thing, method, etc., that was discovered, e.g., "The talent agency was proud of its latest discovery." Also called a find.

discovery shot Shot in which the camera reveals, especially by moving toward, zooming in or angling at someone or something that was previously unknown. Example: a discovery shot of a weapon lying on a floor. Related term: reveal.

dissolve Optical effect that overlays the end of one scene with the beginning of another, so that, simultaneously, the first scene fades out as the second scene fades in. Some cameras are equipped with dissolve controls but most dissolves are done by an optical house or in a lab. Related terms: A and B cutting, wipe.

distressing a set Process of making a production set look old or worn, via painting, staining or abrasive techniques, or a combination of all three.

distrib Short for distributor, distribute or distribution. Entertainment trade paper use.

distribution Process of marketing and delivering products to businesses, which then offer them to consumers, e.g., video movie distribution or feature film distribution to national or world markets.

distribution fees Fee required by distributors for their services.

distributor Company responsible for coordinating all aspects of a motion picture's release. This may include developing and executing the advertising campaign, arranging for exhibitors, striking prints, collecting revenues (and then distributing such revenues to any and all profit participants in accordance with their contracts). Theatrical distribution fees paid to the distributor are based on a negotiated percentage of the revenue generated by the motion picture. Distributors also can be licensed to distribute a film in such nontheatrical markets as television, pay or cable television, home video, in-flight, armed forces, schools, libraries. Most major studios have in-house departments that handle the distribution of their own produced films as well as those acquired through negative pickups. Distribution divisions can contribute to production decisions. For example, the track record of a particular film, or genre of films, will help decide whether or not another film should be produced or acquired. Related terms: film distributor, film producer-distributor, independent distributor, television distributor, video distributor, syndicator.

ditty bag Pouch carried by the assistant cameraman which contains all small items that might be needed during shooting.

doctored photo Picture whose image has been altered in some way, e.g., by compositing, retouching (airbrushing or spotting) or computer methods (digital alteration of onscreen pixels). Related terms: composite, retouch, morphing.

docudrama Theatrical re-creation of actual events, although some points may have been altered for dramatic purposes with the use of actors. An effort is usually made to stay as close as possible to the actual events.

documentary Film of actual events; the events are documented with the real people involved, not with actors.

dog-and-pony show 1. Nickname for a performance or presentation that is routine because it has been done many times. In business, a nickname for a routine promotional speech or sales presentation, as to a potential client. The term originated in the circus world, where it referred to actual trained dog-and-pony acts featured in many small, traveling circuses. The first circus to use the title "Dog-and-Pony Show" in its advertising was the Gentry Bros. Circus, which began operation in 1885, in Bloomington, Indiana, in the United States.

Dolby Sound Trade name for a noise-reducing system in sound recording and reproduction. Since many theaters are now equipped with Dolby systems, the costs of recording in Dolby are often included in the budget under post-production and distribution expenses. Non-Dolby prints should be struck for theaters not equipped with Dolby systems. Owned and licensed to manufacturers by Dolby Laboratories, Inc., of San Francisco, California. Internet address: http://www.dolby.com. A competitive system known as Ultra-Stereo was recently developed and is a less-expensive conversion for theater owners.

dolly Movable, wheeled platform that holds the camera and its operator and is operated by a dolly grip; used in traveling (or dolly) shots. Related terms: crab dolly, Western dolly, Chinese dolly, elemack dolly.

dolly camera Motion picture or television camera mounted on a dolly.

dolly grip An individual responsible for the physical movement of the camera during a shot. Also called a dolly pusher.

dolly shot Shot in which the camera moves while shooting. To "dolly in" means to move in; to "dolly out" means to move away. In the final sequence of *Manhattan* (1979), director Woody Allen uses an extended dolly shot through the streets of the city. Related terms: traveling shot, tracking shot, trucking shot.

dolly tracks Parallel rows of metal rails set down on a ground surface (in connecting sections) on plywood sheets or wooden planks. A dolly camera is smoothly pushed or pulled over the tracks at a desired speed while shooting. Related term: boards.

domestic box office Feature film box-office receipts for a production company's home country, as opposed to the film's gross from foreign distribution.

domestic version Cut of a film released theatrically in the United States; the domestic version possibly may be altered from the film released overseas or from an edited version prepared for television. Related terms: foreign version, director's cut.

done deal One in which the specifics of the contract, arrangement, etc., have been worked out and the legal papers signed, e.g., "My agent phoned to say that it's a done deal."

Don't try this at home. Disclaimer cautioning the audience against attempting a dangerous stunt or scientific demonstration; typically, a warning made to a television audience about to be see a dangerous activity presented as entertainment by one or more qualified individuals. Related term: disclaimer.

doomed time slot Extremely undesirable time slot; one that will likely result in cancellation, usually opposite a very popular show. Also called a terminal time slot.

dope sheet 1. List of all takes of every shot made. 2. List of the contents on a reel of film (including various shots or scenes); usually kept by a film librarian so the viewer doesn't have to run through the whole reel when looking for a specific shot. Related term: camera report.

dot Diffuser consisting of a small, flat, circular plate that reduces the light on the central subject.

double Individual who resembles (or is made to resemble) a particular actor and performs in scenes that do not require acting (e.g., walking through a crowd in a long shot, driving by a location in a car) Related terms: stunt double, photo double, nude body double.

double bill Two films shown consecutively in a movie theater for the price of one admission. Related term: double feature.

double entendre 1. Word or phrase subject to two interpretations. Related term: pun. 2. Word or phrase having a second meaning that is usually sexual in nature.

double exposure Subjecting raw film in a camera or printer to two different images so that one is superimposed over the other; it is one method used to create ghosts, montages and other similar effects. Related terms: exposure, trick camera shot.

double feature Two films exhibited in a theater for the price of one. As with double bill, this term dates back to the early decades of motion picture exhibition; in order to increase attendance at theaters, a high-quality A-picture and lower quality B-picture were offered for the price of a single admission ticket. This is not a common practice today; instead, a featurette, such as a cartoon, may be presented before the main attraction. Related terms: co-feature, B-movie.

double framing Repeating film frames in pairs to slow down the onscreen action. Same as multiple framing, except that only two frames at a time are involved, as opposed to printing three frames, four frames or more.

double hyphenate Individual with three achieved professions or job specialties whose occupational title consists of three words separated by two hyphens, as in "actor-director-producer." The industry's more famous double hyphenates include Charlie Chaplin (for producing, writing, directing and starring in such films as *Modern Times* [1936]); Orson Welles (for producing, directing, writing and starring in such films as *Citizen Kane* [1941]); Mel Gibson (for producing, directing and starring in the award-winning

Braveheart [1995]); and Woody Allen (for writing, producing, directing and starring in *Sweet and Lowdown* [1999]. Related term: triple threat.

double movie During production, to move away from a location and then back to it. Generally, this is an expensive way of shooting and should be avoided.

double scale Twice the union scale payment. Also called twice scale or double time. Related term: golden time.

double system Taping the sound during production on a separate magnetic tape at the same time the action is recorded by the camera—the preferred way to record sound with film. When using a single system, the sound is recorded directly onto the film. Although more portable, the sound quality is poorer and editing options are limited.

double system print work print with separate picture and sound tracks. Related term: interlock.

double time Pay which is twice the basic hourly rate, for work performed on Saturdays, Sundays or union-recognized holidays. Related term: golden time.

doubles shot 1. Another name for a two-shot; a shot in which two people appear. 2. Photograph or camera shot featuring twins or two individuals who resemble each other.

double-take 1. Quick, surprised, second look, e.g., "The scene required her to do a double-take after bumping into an old friend on the street." Also used as a comedy bit and sight gag, e.g., "The teenaged boys did an exaggerated double-take when a girl in a bikini entered the store." 2. Two shots of the same moment of action, from different angles, which are edited to follow each other. Example: a double-take of a car exploding from one angle, followed immediately by the same car exploding from a different angle.

doubling Musician playing more than one instrument during a recording session; musicians receive additional fees for doubling.

down time Period of time lost (before shooting resumes) when the production is required to make necessary equipment repairs, location moves, makeup adjustments, wardrobe changes, etc.

downgrade To lower the status of a performer to a smaller role and lower pay level.

downprint 1. To make a reduction in the size of a photographic print. Example: to downprint 65mm IMAX footage to 35mm so it can be more easily screened as dailies. 2. The reduced print. Also called a printdown.

downstage At or toward the front of a stage. On most stages, walking downstage means walking toward the audience or camera.

downstage foot Foot positioned closest to downstage.

drag rig Protective safety harness and attached rigging worn by a stunt performer who is to be dragged on the ground at the back of a horse or vehicle. Also called a drag harness or drag vest.

drama 1. Story having dialogue and action; it is intended to be acted out by performers on a stage or in front of cameras. The two main forms of drama are comedy and tragedy and, as such, are symbolized by two facial masks: one for comedy (facial expression of laughter) and one for tragedy (facial expression of sorrow). These masks were once worn symbolically by actors in the theaters of ancient Greece. All drama originated as a featured part of religious rituals. Today, the term "drama" is used popularly to connote tragedy when a serious storyline must be differentiated from a humorous one. An example of this is in the labeling of a television program or theatrical film as a comedy, drama or comedy-drama. Related terms: comedy-drama, contemporary drama, crime drama, fantasy drama, futuristic drama, marital drama, musical drama, period drama, docudrama, dramedy, dramatization, melodrama.

drama series Television series that regularly presents episodes with dramatic (serious) storylines. The opposite is a comedy series.

drama teacher Another name for an acting teacher; an individual who teaches the history or performance of drama.

dramatic actor 1. Male or female whose career focuses on primarily serious character roles. The term "dramatic actor" in this sense is used to differentiate between other types of actors, such as the comedic actor. Also called a serious dramatic actor. Related term: serious actor. 2. Any individual who acts in any of the performing arts, as opposed to one who performs only in radio or television commercials.

dramatic irony Story's unexpected contradiction made for dramatic purposes; what one or more characters think will happen is not what the audience knows to be the case because it is aware of contradictory information. Used to build and maintain suspense. Example of a dramatic irony: in a horror film, a group of teenagers arrives at a friend's house and makes plans to party, unaware that a slasher has climbed in an open window and is waiting in a bedroom closet; the teenagers have no reason to believe they are in danger, but the audience knows otherwise.

dramatic license Freedom to be creative with the presentation of the story; a variation of artistic license.

dramatic pause Story's sudden moment of inaction, inserted to heighten suspense. Related terms: beat, shock effects, struggle-then-gunshot scene.

dramatic reading Oral interpretation of a written work, such as a short story, e.g., a dramatic reading of Charles Dickens' "A Christmas Carol." Related term: reading.

dramatic shot 1. Photograph or camera shot featuring the subject in a real or staged dramatic activity. 2. Camera shot set up and performed in a dramatic way, e.g., a dramatic-angle shot or dramatic-lighting shot. (The final shot of the burning sled in *Citizen Kane* [1941] would be considered a dramatic shot.)

dramatist Individual who writes plays or dramatic poetry; another name for a playwright.

dramatization Representation of a real story or situation, in the form of a theatrical film, TV movie, TV series episode or program segment, videogame, stage play, novel or comic book. Related term: docudrama.

dramedy Story containing both serious and comedic elements. Short for dramatic comedy.

drapes Cloths used for decorating the set or for changing the acoustics of the room.

drawl Manner of speaking in which vowels (in English: a, e, i, o, u, and sometimes y) are prolonged, e.g., a U.S. Southern accent with a drawl.

dream factory Nickname for a movie studio, its exact origin uncertain. The most likely first use was in the entertainment news media.

dream role Part coveted by an actor.

dream sequence Transitional scene that begins with a character sleeping, then shifts to a setting within the character's mind where he is shown taking part in an imaginary sequence of events. (The dream sequence of *Oklahoma!* [1955] features a dance ballet.) Related terms: diffusion filter, fade out, montage, psychic-vision sequence, ripple dissolve.

dress To decorate or change the appearance of an item or place so it can be used for shooting. For example, "dressing the set" means putting all furniture, props etc., on the set; to "dress the windows for night" means to change the look of what we see through the windows so it will appear to be nighttime outside.

dress a set To place props on a set. The opposite is to strike a set.

dress rehearsal Practice run-through of a performance with all actors in costume. Related term: rehearsal.

dresser Individual employed to assist in the dressing of one or more performers; he also prepares and cares for clothing articles. Related term: wardrobe assistant.

dressing room Room used by performers for dressing or costuming; it may also be used for applying makeup. Related terms: location dressing room, makeup room, Star Waggons.

drive-in movie theater Outdoor lot with a large movie screen and spaces for automobiles to park; drivers and passengers remain in their cars while viewing the film and sound is heard through an in-car audio speaker provided to each vehicle. There is also a refreshment stand and projection building located centrally on the lot. The first drive-in movie theater was the Camden Automobile Theater in the United States, which opened in on June 6, 1933, in Camden, New Jersey. By 1957, there were approximately 5,000 drive-in theaters across the United States. Their numbers have dwindled since then due to the rise of multi-screen indoor theaters, which are more profitable to operate.

drive-on Permission left at the studio gate, allowing the driver entrance to the studio lot. Related term: gate pass.

drop and pick up Specific union rule for actors stating, there must be at least 10 free days between the last day an actor works and the day he next works on a production, otherwise he must be paid for all non-working days in-between. This rule can be applied once per actor per production.

drop box Overhead rigid container releasing lightweight debris, such as simulated building materials, onto a production set by pulling an attached cord. For some effects, a drop bag is used instead. Related term: snow bag.

dropout 1. Video dropout. 2. In communications systems, a temporary loss of signal.

dry run Another name for a rehearsal.

dry-for-wet Shooting in a dry location and then combining the images with rain or underwater footage in post-production. The opposite is wet-for-wet.

DSS Abbreviation for Digital Satellite System. Trade name for a digital broadcast satellite, direct-to-home television-and-audio system owned and licensed by DirecTV, Inc., a unit of GM Hughes Electronics Corporation, which itself is a subsidiary of

General Motors Corporation (the auto manufacturer). It consists of a satellite signal receiver, remote control, small-sized parabolic antenna dish and necessary connecting hardware. Users pay a monthly fee to a program provider and receive a variety of digitally-encoded channels.

DTS Trade name for sound technology systems licensed for use in movie theaters and home audio equipment by Digital Theater Systems, L.P., of Westlake Village, California. In movie theaters, the system involves the synchronized playback of a digital compact disc containing the entire soundtrack for the movie; the film itself contains a time code along its edge. DTS was first used in 1993 for the film, *Jurassic Park* (1993) and is currently in wide use today. Related terms: soundtrack, time code, time-code track.

dual role Two different parts played by the same performer, e.g., dual role of daughter and mother (the latter with old-age makeup) or dual role of twins. For example, Michael Myers played the roles of Austin Powers and Dr. Evil in the successful *Austin Powers* films. Also called a double role. Related term: multiple roles.

duarc Double ARC used for fill light. Because duarcs cannot be focused, they are not used much anymore.

dub 1. Combining (or, mixing) the different sound tracks to produce a master recording from which the final sound track is made. 2. Replacing the dialogue with another voice or with a different language. 3. Video term meaning to copy or to make a copy. Related terms: mix, loop.

dubbing 1. Process of adding or replacing dialogue, music or sound effects to the soundtrack of a film or videorecording. Related terms: ADR, callback, foley session, loop, sweeten. 2. Transferring some or all of the contents of a video or audio recording onto another tape or disc; copying a recording.

dubbing mixer Another name for a rerecording mixer.

duece Spotlight of 2000 watts, usually equipped with a fresnel lens.

dulling spray Spray, typically aerosol, that leaves a matte finish on objects which otherwise may cause a flare or hot spot on the film. Related term: bloom.

dummy 1. Representation of a human used in film and TV scenes to substitute for a live actor in a dangerous situation (e.g., automobile crash, explosion). Related terms: stunt dummy, character mannequin. 2. Imitation, e.g., a dummy firearm or dummy cartridge.

dummy cartridge Round of ammunition without gunpowder and consisting only of a brass casing and a lead tip; its primer has already been fired or it has no primer at all. Related term: gunfight scene.

dummy firearm Nonworking replica of a real gun. Related terms: dummy prop, gunfight scene.

dummy prop Nonworking prop, such as a plastic, rubber or wooden gun; a rubber or plastic knife; lookalike currency; a breakaway bottle. Also called a fake prop, phony prop or nonworking replica. The opposite is called a practical prop.

dump tank Large-capacity, mechanical water container (some containing a chute in front) used to deliver a gradual or full quantity of water onto a production set. Related term: water tank.

Duopod Trade name for a swivel-head camera mount; it has a telescoping single support pole with an adjustable fold-out second leg and footplate. Manufactured and sold by Band Pro Film/Video, Inc., of Burbank, California, New York City and Ramat Gan, Israel.

dupe 1. (n). Print made from an edited work print; usually made to meet a deadline or to allow the editor to send one print to the negative cutter for conforming and one to the sound mixer. A dupe can also be made from a release print (this is typically the way a film is pirated). More legitimately, however, a dupe can be made from existing film footage, after permission is obtained, which is then used in a new film. This is done for compilation films (e.g., *That's Entertainment* [1974]), when the original negative is not available. 2. (v). To copy a film or tape recording. (For video, the term "dub" can be used.)

dupe negative Negative made from a fine grain master positive or interpositive; used to strike release prints. Related terms: CRI, release negative.

dusk Twilight. When indicated in a script, it must also be so noted on the breakdown sheets. Related term: dawn.

dust effect Appearance of dust; it is a lightweight powdery substance applied by hand, electrical fan or compressed air. Related term: Fuller's earth.

dust hit Gelatin capsule or plastic ball containing fuller's earth; it is shot from a capsule gun or Sweeney gun. A small puff of dust simulating a bullet ricochet is produced upon impact.

duvatyne Black cloth used on flags and gobos to shield light from a particular part of the set.

DVC Abbreviation for digital video-cassette.

DVC camcorder Abbreviation for digital videocassette camcorder.

DVD Abbreviation for digital versatile disc. (The letters originally stood for digital video disc but because of the increased variety of applications since developed, the "V" was changed.) Related terms: digital versatile disc, digital videodisc, master disc.

DVD camcorder Portable digital video camera; it can record images and/or sound on a digital versatile disc (DVD), as opposed to videotape or memory chip. Related term: disc camcorder.

DVD player DVD-Audio or DVD-Video player.

DVD recorder Machine using electro-mechanical and laser technologies to record information digitally on a DVD. Related term: digital videodisc recorder.

DVD-Audio DVD containing only sound, such as instrumental music or singing. The quality is superior to an audio CD.

DVD-Audio player Machine having mechanical, laser and solid-state electronic components capable of playing a DVD-Audio disc; it can also play an audio CD.

DVD-R Abbreviation for digital versatile disc recordable. Blank DVD that is recordable one time and usable for playback.

DVD-RAM Abbreviation for digital versatile disc random-access memory. Type of advanced DVD; it is both recordable and erasable.

DVD-ROM Abbreviation for digital versatile disc read-only memory. Prerecorded DVD for computer playback use; it holds more information than a CD-ROM.

DVD-Video DVD containing images and usually audio, e.g., a prerecorded movie. Related term: digital versatile disc.

DVD-Video player Playback-only machine that reads the information on a DVD videodisc using a fine laser beam; it also plays an ordinary audio CD. Related term: digital versatile disc.

DX-coded film Consumer photographic film with a pattern of coded metallic and nonmetallic squares on its cartridge; these squares are read by sensors inside the camera's film compartment which then automatically sets the film speed f-stop (aperture opening) on the camera. Related term: speed.

dynalens Stabilizer for the camera lens; it has a gyro that helps keep the camera steady in bumpy situations. It is similar to a body frame, but is made for a camera car or helicopter.

early call Scheduled time early in the morning when one is requested to report to the set.

earphone (aka earpiece) Small audio receiver, e.g., a miniature speaker, designed to be worn in or over the ear. An actor or newscaster may be required to wear it while being interviewed remotely by satellite TV. Related terms: earprompter, headset.

earprompter Wired or wireless earpiece communication system consisting of a concealed micro-recorder playback device with a pause switch or a wireless transmitter unit that receives audio transmissions from an offstage or off-camera sender; used to help an actor rehearse or say lines of dialogue during an actual performance. Related terms: earphone, headset, recorded rehearsal.

echo chamber Special room constructed to amplify sound reverberation and repetition.

ECU Abbreviation for extreme close-up.

edge numbers See key numbers.

edit 1. To perform the duties of an editor, e.g., to select, revise, assemble and manage the preparation of visual, audio or written material. In film and television, editing is accomplished according to a script and the directors's instructions. 2. Another name for a splice, cut or other editing transition. Related terms: splice, cut, dissolve, fade in, fade out, wipe.

edit out To eliminate or cut out.

edit point Place where an abrupt or gradual editing transition occurs. Related term: edit.

edited by Production credit designated for a film or video editor.

edited master Originally assembled recording from which copies can be made, e.g., an edited master videotape. Related terms: master tape, master disc.

editing Process of selecting, arranging and assembling a film and its sound track into a logical, rhythmic story progression. The stages of editing are: rough cut (the first logical assembly of the chosen footage), fine cut (a more intricately worked version, final cut (the version to which the negative will be conformed and from which release prints will be struck). However, it should be noted that the editing process evolves rather than being comprised of finite stages. Related terms: cutting, montage.

editing bench Table used during the editing process. It has shelves in the back for storing materials and a light well for viewing film. Related terms: editing table, Kem, Steenbeck, Moviola, flatbed.

editing on tape Process of electronically editing videotaped images that were originally shot on 35mm or 16mm motion picture film or shot on videotape. An example is a television production shot on 35mm film: the footage is transferred directly from the color negative to videotape and then is assembled onto a master tape at a computer-controlled, videotape editing console. Editing on tape bypasses the labor-intensive, traditional process of working to produce a manually spliced, rough-cut to final-cut version of a theatrical movie or filmed television episode. However, if an original, pieced-together negative is needed for creation of a release print, the shots on the videotape can be matched to the unedited negative footage. Related terms: film-to-tape auto conform, film-to-tape transfer, video matchback, assembly, cutting-room floor.

editing room Place where film or video editing is done. For film, also called a cutting room.

editing table A specially-designed workbench for viewing, cutting and splicing film. Related terms: flatbed, editing bench, Steenbeck, Kem, Moviola.

editing video The process of editing using a digital or non-linear editing system. The "film negative" is telecined and assembled onto a master videotape. The master videotape is then edited.

editor Individual responsible for editing the film. Many times, this job can encompass as much creative input as the job of the director. A good editor can take mediocre footage and, by artful cutting, intercutting and with the addition of a moving soundtrack, can turn it into an exciting piece of film. It is not uncommon, these days, for an editor and assistant editor to begin work on a picture during pre-production and to begin assembling dailies during production. If the picture is not complicated, a rough cut can be completed within four to six weeks after principal photography ends. Related term: cutter.

educational theater 1. Theater located in, or associated with, a school's Drama Department, e.g., a university theater.

educational video Video providing instruction or training.

edutainment Short for educational entertainment, as on television or computer CD-ROMs.

effect lighting Stage lighting achieving a particular visual effect. For examples, flickering red lights to indicate fire or flash lighting to represent lightning.

effects Illusory techniques, such as dissolves, wipes, fades, that are typically added to a film during post-production. Related term: F/X.

effects box See matte box.

effects filter Glass or gelatin filter that changes natural light; for example, it would be used to produce the illusion of fog.

effects projector In theater, a lighting device casting a variety of individual visual effects onto a screen or backdrop, such as moving clouds, rain, snow, smoke or fire.

effects track (abbreviated as FX track) The separate channel or mag stripe onto which sound effects are recorded.

EI Abbreviation for Educational/Informational Programming. Symbol used by the weekly publication TV Guide in the United States to identify such programs in its listings. First used on March 1, 1997.

EIA Standard International video industry rating procedure used to determine a video camera's light sensitivity and resulting image quality, as expressed by a number designation called a lux rating; it replaced the variety of older methods used individually by video camera manufacturers. Related term: lux.

8 x 10 résumé Résumé printed and cut to an 8" x l0" size so it can be attached neatly to the back of an 8" x 10" photo. Related term: photo-résumé.

8mm 1. Videotape or film eight millimeters in width. 2. Video format using 8mm videotape cassettes. Hi-8mm (high-band 8mm) has a higher resolution for this size videotape.

18-classification ("'18'—Suitable only for persons of 18 years and over. Not to be supplied to any person below that age."). Rating issued by the British Board of Film Classification for films and videos exhibited or offered for sale or rental in Great Britain. Also called an "18" certificate. Related terms: R18-classification, rating.

eighty-six Turn off; tear down; get rid of, eliminate. Related terms: strike, kill, lose.

electrical truck Specially designed vehicle that holds all the necessary electrical equipment for the production. Oftentimes, these trucks have built-in generators.

electrician Skilled electrical wire and equipment installer-remover. Related terms: stage electrician, best boy, gaffer, grip.

electronic clapboard Another name for a time-code slate.

electronic media Various forms of electronic-based communication, such as television, radio, computers, fax machines and the like.

electronic news gathering (abbreviated as ENG) In journalism, the use of audio and visual recording equipment, computers or telephone-line or microwave (ground or satellite relays) communication systems in the collection of current-event news stories.

electronic photography Another name for digital photography.

electronic press kit (abbreviated as EPK) Another name for a video press kit.

electronic viewfinder Sighting device on a video camera using a miniature vacuum-tube or LCD (liquid-crystal display) video monitor to indicate what is being shot. Related term: viewfinder.

elemack dolly Small, light, maneuverable platform with wheels; it features long, adjustable legs and can fit easily through doorways. It was introduced in the United States from Italy in the 1960s. Related term: spider dolly.

elevator stage Stage or section of a stage that can be raised or lowered mechanically; used to move heavy equipment onstage or to allow a performer to make a dramatic entrance or exit. Also called a rising stage. Related terms: stage, trap door.

eligible performer 1. Nonunion performer who has met the qualifications necessary to join a union and participate in auditions held for that union's members. In May, 1997, the National Labor Relations Board (United States) approved a decision, proposed by Actors Equity Association (U.S.), for a new system of auditioning performers; the "eligible performer" status was phased out over several months and replaced with a system requiring theater producers to hold separate Equity-member (union) auditions and non-Equity-member (nonunion) auditions. Related term: noneligible performer. 2. Actor who is eligible to join the Screen Actors Guild.

ellipsoidal spot Spotlight with a fixed or variable lens providing a sharp beam of light; used to precisely illuminate areas or objects on a stage or set. Related term: lighting.

ELR Abbreviation for Electronic Line Replacement. Related terms: looping, ADR.

ELS Abbreviation for extreme long shot. Also spelled XLS.

emancipation Legal act in which a court frees a minor (e.g., a child performer) from the restrictions of parental control and child labor laws. The minor is required to be of a certain minimum age (14 in California). Minors must appear in court with legal representation before a judge and provide evidence that they can handle personal and business affairs in an adultlike manner; they also must prove that they are able to earn an income and that they will live separately from their parents after emancipation has been granted. Some high-earning teenage child stars, especially in California (United States) which has child labor laws affecting the employment of children in films and television, seek emancipation to have easier access to their income (California law requires a part of this income to be placed in a trust fund until the minor reaches adulthood). Also, emancipation makes it easier for the minor to be hired for child roles that may be offered to youthful-looking actors over the age of 18 (who are legally allowed in the U.S. to work longer hours per day and do not require a studio teacher or welfare worker). There are negative and positive sides to emancipation. Parents can either agree and assist or disagree and fight their child in court. Also, not all child stars want, seek or can handle the responsibilities that come with emancipation. Once a child star petitions the court for a Declaration of Emancipation, it becomes a matter of public record and a permanent part of the child's career biography and public image, even if the emancipation is not approved.

emcee Another name for a "Master of Ceremonies" or, host.

emergency casting session One held on short notice because of a sudden cast addition or the need to replace a performer quickly, as due to no-show status, illness, death or on-the-set/off-the-set trouble.

Emmy Award Award bestowed annually by the Academy of Television Arts and Sciences (United States) upon actors, directors, producers, writers, editors, composers, costume designers, etc., for distinguished merit during the previous television season. The name "Emmy" is a variation of "Immy," which was the nickname for the image orthicon tube used in cameras in the early years of television broadcasting.

emotional recall A technique associated with method acting and other acting systems that is used to help an actor draw upon past experiences involving happiness, sadness, anger, etc., when portraying a role. Example: remembering a childhood pet dog or cat that died when dialogue or action requires sadness or teary eyes.

empathy Identification with or understanding of another individual's feelings or attitudes, e.g., to have empathy with a movie character's plight. The goal of good acting, directing, writing and musical scoring is to achieve empathy from the audience.

emulsion Light-sensitive substance on film; it is dull and faces inward on the roll on B-wind stock.

emulsion number Code number on raw stock indicating the particular batch of emulsion used to create that film stock. Related term: batch number.

emulsion side Dull or semiglossy side of unexposed (raw) or developed film; it contains the various chemicals and dyes that form the photographic image. (The other side is called the base side or glossy side.) In raw film, the emulsion side consists of layers of light-sensitive, silver-halide crystals (which turn dark when exposed to light) and color-dye-forming chemicals, all of which are suspended in gelatin that acts as an adhesive. (Instant Polaroid Spectra film contains 23 micro-thin emulsion layers. More than 5,000 chemical reactions take place as each picture self-develops.) The emulsion side of raw film is positioned inside the camera facing the lens so incoming image-forming light will strike it. Related terms: acetate base, develop.

emulsion speed Light-gathering properties of a film's emulsion, indicated in ASA, ISO or DIN numbers. When shooting in low light, film with a high emulsion speed is required, and conversely, as the light increases, film with a lower emulsion speed is used. The selection of the proper film speed for a given situation is necessary for correct exposure. In controlled lighting situations, emulsion speed is a factor because different emulsions give different visual qualities, e.g., saturated color, desaturated color, rough grain.

encoding machine Device used by the assistant editor to print code numbers at regular intervals on the edge of the work print. Related term: numbering machine.

encore Additional performance brought about by audience demand.

Also called an encore performance, encore presentation or repeat performance (if applicable).

end credits List of individuals (cast and crew) who worked on the motion picture. Size and placement of names on the screen are usually contractual. Any other guaranteed credits, such as acknowledgement of a special location or the IA and MPAA seals, are placed at the end of all credits. Most end credits roll continuously, as opposed to the main credits (aka front credits), which appear one at a time at the beginning of the film. Related terms: closing credits, end title, credit.

end slate Audio-visual mark given by the second assistant cameraman to denote the end of the scene. The clapboard is held upside down so during post-production, the editor will know it is the final shot of the scene.

end title and closing credits End title and list of end credits appearing onscreen at the end of a theatrical film or video. The opposite is the main title and opening credits. Related term: end credits.

ending Finishing or concluding part of a story; a story's final minutes or moments. Related terms: happy ending, predictable ending, surprise ending, weak ending, give away the ending, conclusion, fin.

ENG Abbreviation for electronic news gathering.

engagement Another name for a booking. Related terms: exclusive engagement, holdover engagement, selected engagement.

English-language version Film or video with dialogue spoken or dubbed in the English language.

ensemble cast Cast of performers regarded collectively, each member having a prominent part to play. The television series, *Seinfeld* (1990-98), featured an ensemble cast (Jerry Seinfeld, Jason Alexander, Julia Louis-Dreyfus, Michael Richards).

ensemble movie Film featuring an ensemble cast. Also called an en-semble-cast movie, ensemble film or ensemble piece. *American Graffiti* (1973) featured an ensemble cast, including Ronny Howard, Richard Dreyfuss, Cindy Williams, Paul LeMat, Charlie Martin Smith, Candy Clark, MacKenzie Phillips, Harrison Ford, among others.

entertainment community Occupational group of persons working in or closely associated with the entertainment industry. This is a general term comprising the film, television, radio, live theater, music, nightclub, circus, carnival, fair, festival, ice show, museum show, laser show, air show, roadside attraction, amusement park, and theme park communities. Also called the show-business community, show-biz community, or performing-arts community (theater, singing, dancing, musical-instrument playing, etc.).

entertainment value Worth of a performance, presentation or exhibit, especially in terms of how amusing or interesting it is to audiences or visitors. Related terms: production value, shock value.

entourage Group of personal or professional assistants or associates who are in attendance with someone, as a celebrity, especially when making an appearance at an event. Depending on the circumstances, a celebrity's entourage may include a secretary, driver, bodyguard, hairdresser, makeup artist, nanny, relative, friend, publicist, manager, attorney, or the like.

EP Abbreviation for extra performer; an actor who is an extra. Found on some union forms.

epic Large-scale film production. Director David Lean was famous for his epic films, including *Doctor Zhivago* (1965), *Exodus* (1960), *Lawrence of Arabia* (1962), *The Bridge on the River Kwai* (1957). Related term: spectacle.

epilogue Concluding scene or speech, as opposed to a prologue. Related term: tag.

episode Installment of a TV series, radio serial, website series, miniseries or multi-part telefilm. Related terms: arc episode, bonus classic episode, clip episode, compilation episode, first-run episode, lost episode, two-hour episode, two-part episode, unaired episode, cliffhanger, conclusion, last show of the series, pilot, rerun, season finale, To be continued.

episodic series Television, radio or World Wide Web series featuring the same principal cast and setting and offering a new story (each with a beginning and end) in every episode. Occasionally, there may be two-part episodes. Related terms: two-parter, TV series.

EPK Electronic press kit. Another name for a video press kit.

equalizer Regulating device for shaping the frequency of sound waves in order to produce the desired sound.

Equity Short for Actors' Equity Association.

Equity card Union identification card indicating an individual is a member of the issuing Actors' Equity Association. Related terms: union card, eligible performer.

Equity 99-Seat Plan theater production In the United States, a play presented in a theater with 99 seats or less. Under an agreement with Equity, its members are allowed to perform in such a theater without pay (as for showcase purposes) or for small pay (in accordance with other guidelines).

established 1. Person or object previously seen on camera. 2. Individual well-known in the industry.

establishing shot Wide-angle (long) shot, series of shots, panning shot or a combination, establishing the location, setting and sometimes mood (e.g., showing weather conditions, time of day) of a story's events. A script may contain as many establishing shots as there are new scene locations. A reestablishing shot, also called a reprise establishing shot, reintroduces or reminds the audience of the same location shown earlier.

establishing stock shot Stock footage establishing a story's location, e.g., a stock shot of the New York City skyline or of the Eiffel Tower. Using such preshot footage saves the production from sending a camera crew on location for the same shot. Stock shots are taken from an in-house library of such shots or they are purchased/licensed for use from a stock-footage agency. Related terms: stock shot, stock-footage library.

Estar Trade name for a polyester photographic film base that is stronger that acetate; used for special purposes where durability is required. IMAX movies (shot on either 65mm Estar or acetate base) are released on 70mm Estar base. Related terms: base, celluloid.

ETA Abbreviation for estimated time of arrival. (Spelled E.T.A., especially in script dialogue and location travel paperwork.)

ETOM disc Abbreviation for electron trapping optical memory disc. Type of compact, erasable optical disc

housed in a flat cartridge; it can hold eight times more digital information than a standard CD-ROM. Developed by Optex Communications of Rockville, Maryland, in the United States.

evergreen 1. Old television series that continues to make money for its owners and the stations which rerun it in syndication. Entertainment trade paper use in the United States, where the currency is a shade of green. 2. Article, cartoon or other filler material that can be used at any time because it is not time-sensitive. 3. Type of tree, shrub or plant used on an indoor or outdoor production set that retains its green color year-round. Related term: greenery.

exchange Office responsible for distributing motion pictures to theaters in its region.

exciter lamp Small, bright incandescent lamp that shines light through the printed optical track on the film to activate the optical sound reader, thus converting light waves into sound waves. Used in recording optical sound tracks and when projecting sound films.

exclusive engagement 1. Booking a performer to appear only at the specific, stated location in town. 2. Exclusive scheduling of a theatrical film at one theater for a specified time; if moviegoers want to see the film, they must see it at that particular theater.

exclusive listing Being listed, or signed, with one agency only.

exclusive right Granted contract right granted not shared with others.

exclusivity 1. Limited exclusivity is a contract provision in which talent agrees to refrain from any form of advertising or promotional work for competing products for a specified, possibly renewable, period of time. In complete exclusivity, talent agrees for additional, usually substantial, compensation to refrain from advertising or promotional work for any other company, be it a competitor or non-competitor, for the duration of the contract. Related terms: complete exclusivity, limited exclusivity. 2. Any contract provision in which talent agrees not to work for other employers or clients during the time the contract is in effect. Related terms: exclusive contract, studio system. 3. Any other similar contract provision, such as for talent agency representation, intended to restrict the independent actions of one of the parties.

executive in charge of production Upper-level management employee, usually a vice-president, at a film-TV studio or television network who is responsible for overseeing one or more productions financed all or in part by the company. This is a screen credit most commonly seen at the end of TV programs. Related terms: network executive, studio executive.

executive producer 1. Head of a film or television production company or division who is responsible at the corporate level for the production of one or more theatrical films or television movies, series or specials. Related terms: co-executive producer, producer. 2. Screen credit designated for, or negotiated by, an individual involved in a major or noteworthy way with a production, and who may have a significant personal financial interest in it; without his participation, the project could not go forward as intended or it possibly would not go forward at all.

Executive Speech Prompter Trade name for a popular speaker's podium videoprompter (also called a TelePrompTer) manufactured by QTV of New York City. It is used by business and organization executives and politicians, including the president of the United States, when giving lengthy scripted speeches in public, indoors and outdoors. Related terms: QTV, TelePrompTer, videoprompter.

executive story editor Head story editor on a television series.

exhib Short for exhibitor or exhibition. Entertainment trade paper use.

exhibitor 1. Company that owns or operates a movie theater (or chain of theaters) in which films are shown (exhibited) to admission-paying audiences. Abbreviated as exhib. 2. Company exhibiting products or services at a trade show.

exit poll Moviegoers are survey as they leave a theater and their opinions of the film they just viewed are taken; done for market-research purposes. Depending on the results, changes may be made to the film before it is officially released to the public. One of the companies that does this is CinemaScore. Internet address: http://www.cinemascore.com. Related term: market research.

expanded time Lengthened time; an increased running time of a film, video or audio product while it retains the substance of the work; it is accomplished by a variety of methods, including the addition of duplicate frames (film or video), moments of silence (audio) or by slowing down the speed of the playback. Besides expanded time, there is real time and compressed time. Related terms: time, multiple framing, slow motion.

expendables Items purchased for use on a production that, in all probability, will be used completely (e.g., lightbulbs, tape, gels.)

experimental film Film exploring new ways of dealing with a subject; one offering a new or different style of filmmaking.

experimental theater Theater whose storytelling, acting techniques and production staging (including set and lighting design) are experimental in nature.

experimental video Similar to an experimental film, this emphasizes experimental style of filmmaking rather than usual or familiar methods.

exploitation Advertising, publicity, merchandising, licensing and promotion of a film.

exploitation film Feature film with little redeeming social value and which showcases aspects of the film not necessarily related to the story, e.g., gratuitous sex, violence. Such films usually feature an advertising or publicity campaign that capitalizes on these other elements.

explosion scene Scene in which a real, optically superimposed or computer-generated (CG) explosion occurs. If real, it has elements of fire, compressed water or air (the latter two would be used as a theatrical substitute for a volatile chemical compound or gas). Depending on the size and type of explosion, a stuntperson may be hired to double for an actor involved in the scene. Explosion scenes are carefully planned and the movements of any actors or stuntpeople are thoroughly rehearsed. Related terms: bomb, car roll cannon, "Clear," countdown, detonation board, digital enhancement, double-take, fire effect, "Fire in the hole!" mini-trampoline, mortar, pit, powder, powder person, pyrotechnic effects, pyrotechnic su-

pervisor, safety harness, smoke effect, squib.

expose To subject raw photographic film to visible or invisible radiation (visible light, infrared radiation, X-rays, etc.) to obtain an image through a subsequent developing process. Related terms: exposure, exposure meter, photograph, shoot, aperture, speed.

exposé Media report revealing unfavorable information about a company, organization or individual.

exposed film Film subjected to light but which has not been processed. Related term: latent image.

exposition (abbreviated as expo) 1. Act or process of explaining or disclosing background information to an audience through the use of dialogue or visual images. Related terms: discovery, establishing shot, reveal. 2. Another name for a trade show or convention.

exposure 1. Act or instance of treating raw film to a measured amount of light (by aperture and shutter speed settings) or to other radiation required to produce an image. Related terms: double exposure, expose, overexposure, develop, f-stop, t-stop, emulsion speed. 2. Condition of being seen or made known. Related term: overexposure.

exposure meter Handheld or in-camera electronic photocell device measuring light so the correct aperture size and shutter speed can be selected prior to shooting. Measures the intensity of directed or reflected light. The two basic types of exposure meters are: incident light meter, which measures the amount of light falling on a subject; and reflected light meter, which measures the amount of light bouncing off the subject. For example, a subject dressed in white against a white background would reflect more light than a subject dressed in black against a dark background, even when lit with exactly the same amount of light. Related terms: photometer, light meter.

EXT Abbreviation for exterior.

extension tube Lens attachment permitting the lens to be positioned at a greater distance from the camera housing, to facilitate close-up shots.

exterior Any scene shot out-of-doors, e.g., "According to the shooting schedule, we'll be doing exteriors all day tomorrow."

exterior lighting Another name for outdoor lighting.

exterior shot One that takes place outdoors. Related term: exterior.

extra Actor who speaks no lines (except as part of a group) and who makes no gesture to set him apart from the other extras. Related terms: background, atmosphere, silent bit, Screen Extras Guild.

extra voucher Multicopy form providing an extra performer with a record of employment and payment received, including a depiction release clause, which states that, for payment received, the extra's likeness and voice can be used by the producer in the manner stated; the voucher is signed by the extra and the producer's representative. Related term: depiction release.

extras agency Agency representing or maintaining lists of available film and TV extras. Also called an extras casting agency or extras casting service.

extreme close-up (abbreviated as ECU or XCU) Also called a big close-up or tight close-up (TCU).

extreme long shot Shot taken from some far away, at a high or low angle; such a shot is typically used as an establishing shot. Related term: ELS.

extreme wide-angle lens Another name for a fish-eye lens.

eye effects Special effects related to changing the appearance of the eyes. Related term: special eye effects.

eye light Small light used during a shot to highlight a performer's eyes. Related terms: kicker, catchlight.

eye line Actor's line of vision. It is usually kept clear of people or objects to avoid distraction while working. It is also an important factor in continuity: the director must make sure the actor's eyes are looking in the same direction in the master shot as in the coverage of the scene.

EZ Lite Smoke powder Special-effects powder used to produce smoke when ignited electrically or by a flame. Formulated and sold by Zeller International Ltd., of Downsville, New York.

F Abbreviation for Family rating.

façade False front with nothing behind it. Front part or wall of a building, including doors, windows, ledges, balconies, porches and steps. The buildings on studio backlots typically are façades with accompanying sidewalls. However, a façade may also be constructed on location, as a structure on vacant land or over the front of an existing building.

facial lifts Attachments glued to the upper sides of an actor's face and connected across the top of the head by an elastic fabric strap; they are concealed with hair or makeup and are used to tighten the skin by pulling it upward. They assist in making an older actor look younger.

fact-based movie Film based on events that actually occurred. For example, *Apollo 13* (1995) was a fact-based movie about the traumatic Apollo 13 moon mission. Also called a docudrama.

fade Optical effect causing one scene to emerge or disappear slowly. Movies typically begin with a "fade in" and end with a "fade out." Until the 1960s, it was common practice to begin and end most scenes with fades. However, films today often use straight cuts between scenes unless a specific effect is desired (either for visual reasons, to indicate a passage of time, etc.).

fade in/fade up 1. To go from a black screen to a full picture over a certain time frame, usually a few seconds. (It is the opposite of fade out/fade down.) 2. To gradually increase the level of sound in a scene.

fade out/fade down 1. To go from a picture on the screen to a black screen, over a certain time frame, usually a few seconds. (It is the opposite of a fade in/fade up.) 2. To gradually decrease the level of sound at the closing of a scene.

"Fade to black." Direction from the director in the TV studio control room, meaning the onscreen image should electronically fade to the color black. Variation: "Go to black."

faithful adaptation Script and its resulting production are closely based on their source material; characters, locations and dialogue are exact or very similar. The script to *A River Runs Through It* (1992), written by Richard Friendenberg and directed by Robert Redford, is a faithful adaptation of Norman Maclean's novel. (The opposite is a loose adaptation.)

fall 1. (n.) The fall season. Typically refers to the time of year when some films are distributed (as opposed to summer releases, winter releases and spring releases); also refers to the television season, when new series are introduced. 2. (v.) To drop down, as in stunt work. There are special ways to perform a stunt fall to reduce the risk of injury. Depending upon the type of fall, distance from the camera and willingness of the actor, a stunt double may be used. Special padding typically is worn underneath clothing to absorb the shock of impact. Related terms: high fall, pratfall, stair fall, air bag, box rig, bulldog, car hit, crash pad, dummy, decelerator, descender, hood roll, pit, porta-pit, safety harness, shot, stunt padding, stunt work.

fall premiere Televisions series introduced in the fall.

fall preview Preview of new fall television shows.

fall schedule Networks' planned lineup of shows introduced in the fall. After the season begins and the ratings come in, changes may be made to the schedule; shows may be canceled, put on hiatus or moved. Also called a fall TV lineup.

fall season Same as Fall Schedule. A show that does poorly in the ratings may be taken off the air and replaced at midseason.

false movement Physical move by an actor that is not real or natural to the character being portrayed. Also called an uncharacteristic movement or false gesture.

false start Beginning a movement at the wrong time. Related term: off-cue.

false step Improper step; misstep or stumble.

family hour First hour of prime-time television programming, during which family-oriented shows are aired; these shows are less controversial and appropriate for all ages. Related term: prime time.

family movie Film suitable for viewing by children and parents together. Related terms: children's movie, PG, G.

family rating Abbreviated as "F." Classification issued for theatrical films and videos in Canada, meaning contents of the film or video exhibited, sold or rented are suitable for viewing by all ages. It corresponds to the "G" rating in the United States. Related term: rating.

family show TV program that can be enjoyed by all the members of the family; it does not contain profanity or scenes of nudity or violence.

fan convention Convention organized to attract fans of a particular celebrity, TV series, film genre, comic books, historical period, collecting interest, etc. For example, fans of the *Star Trek* (1966-69) television series and feature films regularly hold fan conventions. Related term: science-fiction convention.

fan magazine Printed periodical devoted to a specific topic, such as science-fiction, teen stars or music performers.

fan mail Correspondence sent to a celebrity (or, a television show or film) from fans. Fan mail is used to gauge an individual's or TV series' popularity; it can also be instrumental in saving a TV series from cancellation or bringing it back after it has been canceled. Related terms: mail pickup, feedback, celebrity stalker.

fantasy movie Film featuring an imaginative, often surrealistic, storyline and equally imaginative characters, sets, props and locations; some also have elements of science-fiction. Related terms: science fiction, surrealistic.

fast film Film with an ASA higher than 100, thereby allowing a scene to be shot in low light.

fast-motion Action faster than normal speed; this is accomplished by editing or shooting at slower-than-normal camera speed or by projecting or playing back the film at faster-than-normal speed (it is a visual effect). Related terms: accelerated motion, speeded-up motion, speeded-up action or time-lapse effect. Related terms: compressed time, skip frame, time-lapse photography.

favored nations Phrase used in negotiations and in informal contracts indicating a party will be afforded treatment by the producer equal to the best treatment to another party. Often used when defining the profits for the participants, the size and placement of billing or even when defining such items as the size of dressing rooms, etc.

favoring Situation in which the camera (or microphone) is placed closer to one actor than the others, resulting in an emphasis on that actor. Related term: cheat.

feature 1. Short for feature film. 2. Prominent role. 3. (v.) To make or hold in prominence. "Feature" in this sense is also a shot angle direction found in scripts, e.g., "Feature Agnes in the shot." 4. Prominent article or story in a magazine, newspaper or TV program.

feature film Motion picture, typically ninety minutes to two hours in length. Also called a feature. Related terms: co-feature, double feature, independent feature, theatrical film.

feature film rights Rights purchased from the owner of a written work (fiction or nonfiction book or article), TV series, life story so that a theatrical film can legally be developed, based on the material, e.g., "There was a bidding war among producers for the feature film rights to the author's latest book." Instead of buying feature film rights outright, a producer may option the right to buy them within a specified time limit (if the other party is agreeable); the owner of the material receives a fee for not selling the feature film rights to anyone else while the option is in effect. An option gives a producer time to raise production money by promoting the project's merits to potential investors. Feature film rights cover such areas as remakes, sequels, TV series, live stage, radio, video, music, books, merchandising, publicity, depiction of names and likenesses and lawsuit protection, among others. Some rights are withheld by the seller; this is a process of negotiation. Also called depiction rights, which is the general term, e.g., a Depiction Rights Purchase (or Option) Agreement. Related terms: contract, option, right.

feature length Film 85 minutes in length (or, longer).

featured player Unofficial term used to designate a principal player who does not have a starring role; typically, a featured player will have higher billing and higher pay than a day player. A featured player is not main character but still is considered a speaking part and is treated as such on the breakdown sheet and budget.

featurette 1. Theatrical film of short length. For example: an animation short (cartoon) shown in a theater before the feature film. Related terms: short film, double feature. 2. Behind-the-scenes film or video showing how a feature film was made; it may also include interviews with key personnel. A featurette is typically half-hour in length and is shown on cable TV (accompanying the feature film's cable run) or as a television special (as part of the film's promotional efforts). Also called a "making of" featurette or behind-the-scenes special. Related terms: behind-the-scenes footage, production home movie.

featuring credit Production credit designated for a featured player.

fee schedule Printed list detailing costs or payments for various services or rights. Also called a rate schedule, fee chart, rate chart, fee scale, payment table or rate table.

feed 1. To give lines or cues to a performer; to prompt. 2. Network feed of programs.

feedback 1. Whistling noise or squeal heard suddenly in an audio system; occurs when an excessive amount of output sound waves from a speaker are picked up by (fed back to) the input end of the microphone. Also called microphone feedback, acoustic feedback or acoustic regeneration. 2. Reaction from the public regarding a performance or other activity. Feedback from a live audience may be in the form of applause and is referred to as instant or immediate feedback; if it is from moviegoers or television viewers, it may be in the form of fan mail or comments from passers-by on the street.

feel-good movie One that leaves audiences with pleasant feelings or a sense of happiness as they exit the theater; most often used by critics, e.g., "It's the feel-good movie of the year." Also called an uplifting movie.

Felliniesque In the manner or style of the films, characters and directing techniques of Italian movie director-screenwriter Federico Fellini (1920-1993). Movies directed by Fellini include: *La Strada* (1954*), The Nights Of Cabiria* (1957), *La Dolce Vita* (1960), *8 1/2* (1963), *Amarcord* (1974).

femme fatale Woman who is irresistibly attractive to men and who leads them into danger; a seductively beautiful woman who deceives men. French for "fatal woman." Also called a siren; used as a casting description. Marlene Dietrich made a career out of portraying femme fatales; Kathleen Turner made her film debut as a femme fatale in *Body Heat* (1981).

Related terms: bad girl, screen siren, TV temptress.

fest Short for festival. Entertainment trade paper use. Also used to form compound words, e.g., filmfest, songfest. Related term: film festival.

F.G Abbreviation for foreground. Also spelled f.g., FG.

FI Rarely used abbreviation for "Fade in."

field of view 1. Area recorded by a camera, as seen through its lens or viewfinder. Another name for shot area. 2. Area visible through an optical instrument, as a director's viewfinder, telescope, microscope or binoculars.

field producer Television producer physically present at a location site to arrange and supervise the filming of a segment for a television news or informational program. A reporter sometimes takes on the additional role of field producer. The opposite is a studio producer. Also called a location producer or on-site producer.

fields Used in videotape. Videotape runs 30 frames per second. Each frame has two fields, one which scans odd lines and one which scans even lines.

15-classification In Great Britain, a rating issued by the British Board of Film Classification for films and videos exhibited or made available for sale or rental to the public. Full wording: "'15'—Suitable only for persons of 15 years and over. Not to be supplied to any person below that age." Also called a "15" certificate. Related term: rating.

15-minute call Announcement made to performers backstage that the show will begin in fifteen minutes. Also called a quarter-hour call. Related term: call.

fight director Stunt coordinator experienced in choreographing one or more fight scenes in a production. Also called a fight coordinator or fight arranger. Related term: choreographer.

fight scene Scene featuring physical violence between characters. Depending upon the complexity of the scene, stunt performers may be called in to double for actors. All such scenes typically are rehearsed carefully. Also called (if applicable) a barroom-brawl scene, hand-to-hand combat scene, martial-arts scene. Related terms: blood capsule, breakaway glass, breakaway prop, fight director, knife, martial-arts film, pulling a punch, special blood effects, stage combat.

fill During the editing process, if a scene is missing, unusable or blank film (fill) is placed in a work print to keep the film in sync. Sound fill is typically footage from a discarded release print.

fill light (aka filler lights) Secondary lamps used to illuminate shadows and soften the harshness that may be caused by the key light. Related term: lighting.

filler Brief report used to fill unused space (in print media) or time (in electronic media). Related terms: padding, stretch.

film 1. Another term for "movie." 2. Acetate-based, emulsion-coated strip with perforations on the edges, used to create photographic images when exposed to light in a camera or when projected through a projector.

film and television commission Government office promoting movie, television and video production in its city, region or country. It also assists producers with permits, facilities, and local suppliers of talent, crews and equipment. Related term: state film and TV commission.

film archive 1. Library of materials that relate to film (e.g., films, posters, aka one-sheets, magazines). 2. Repository for the storage and preservation of films; they may be viewed for research or other purposes.

film budget Descriptive list detailing the planned expenditure of film production funds. Related terms: budget, above-the-line, below-the-line.

film camera Camera using photographic film as its medium for recording images. Related term: camera.

film classic 1. Motion picture produced a considerable time ago (typically, decades) yet is still enjoyed today because of its filmmaking style or techniques, story or value to film history. Also called a classic film. Related terms: cult classic, timeless classic. 2. A recent film regarded as a classic. Also called a modern classic or instant classic.

film clip Portion of a filmed work; often used in electronic film reviews or for promotional purposes. Relatively short section of a film, isolated and used for promotional or other purposes. (A compilation film like *That's Entertainment* (1974) was comprised of film clips.) Also called a film clipping, excerpt, piece, segment, bit, cut, cutting, or snippet. Related term: video clip.

film clip clearance Permission to use a film clip on television or in a motion picture. Related term: clip clearance.

Film Commission In the United States, a bureau or agency at the state government level that assists film or TV production companies in finding locations, obtaining necessary licenses or permits, locating local production services and crew members, providing information on climate conditions, and the like. Most major U.S. cities have their own film and TV promotion bureaus, as do some county and smaller city governments. Also called a Motion Picture and Television Commission (or Bureau or Office. Related terms: film and television commission, Location Expo, location scouting.

film credit 1. Acknowledgment of having performed in or worked on any type of film production. Also called (if applicable) a feature film credit or movie credit. Related term: screen credit. 2. Credit title displayed on a film screen. Related term: on-screen credit.

film direction Instructions, orders or suggestions given by a film director.

film distributor Company distributing theatrical films, for a fee, to various exhibition markets. Also called a film distribution company or film distrib. Related terms: distributor, independent distributor, film producer-distributor.

film editing Process of cataloging, selecting, arranging and splicing motion picture film into a single presentation, synchronized with its various soundtracks (e.g., dialogue, music and sound-effects). Related terms: A and B editing, editing on tape, flatbed editing machine, editing room, cutting room, cutting room floor, cutting script, assembly, cut, trim, trim bin, splice, locked, Kem, Steenbeck, Moviola.

film editor Individual who edits film. Also called a film cutter. Related term: negative cutter.

film extra Individual who performs as an extra in a theatrical film. Also called a movie extra or motion picture extra.

film festival 1. Event in which films are exhibited and premiered, panel discussions or seminars are conducted and, depending on the type of festival, awards or prizes are handed out. A major component of many film festivals is the promotion (and, hopefully the sale) of new and proposed films to distributors. The filmmakers (directors, producers and sometimes the actors) often attend the festival to publicize the work. The following list is a representative sampling of some festivals (there are hundreds of film and television marketing and nonmarketing festivals held worldwide each year): American Film Market, Berlin International Film Festival, Cannes International Film Festival & Market, Los Angeles International Film Festival, MIFED, Montreal World Film Festival, Moscow International Film Festival, New York Film Festival, Sundance Film Festival, Telluride Film Festival, Tokyo International Film Festival, Toronto International Film Festival and Venice Film Festival. Also called a film fest. Related terms: television festival, fest. 2. Scheduled exhibition of old films or the films of a particular genre, actor, director or composer, e.g., an Alfred Hitchcock Film Festival, showcasing all of Hitchcock's films; the festival could be held in a movie theater or his films could be shown on a cable network television station over a series of nights.

film gauge Width of film in millimeters: 8mm, 16mm, 35mm, 65mm or 70mm.

film lab Commercial business offering the services of motion-picture film developing, duplicating, enlarging, visual-effects processing (if equipped), etc. Related term: photo lab.

film leader Length of film, attached to the beginning (head) and end (tail) of the processed film reel; placed onto the reel by the lab to protect the film while it is being threaded onto or winding off of the projector. Related terms: Academy Leader, universal leader.

film loader camera crew member who loads and unloads film magazines; this person also must keep the loading room in an organized, clean condition.

film magazine Lightproof cassette for storing and holding film. For 35 mm film, the standard film loads are 400 feet and 1000 feet. Therefore, the standard film magazines are 400 and 1000 footers. Related term: magazine.

film noir Dark crime movie, most typically made in the 1940s and 1950s. Often shot in black and white, film noir typically used nighttime and shadowy cinematography, sleazy locations and mean, distrustful characters. The term was coined by French film critics to describe such American-made films. Examples of films in this genre include *The Big Sleep* (1946), *D.O.A.* (1950), *The Maltese Falcon* (1941); contemporary film noirs include *Body Heat* (1981), *Chinatown* (1974) and *L.A. Confidential* (1997).

film producer Individual who produces movies shot on film. Also called a movie producer or motion picture producer. The term "movie producer" also applies to a producer of video movies. Related terms: producer, filmmaker.

film production The making of a motion picture, or motion pictures collectively. Related term: production.

film production software Computer programs designed to assist in motion picture production; software is available in such areas as scheduling, accounting and scriptwriting. Related term: computer software.

film rating Rating issued for a theatrical film by a motion picture ratings board. Related term: rating.

film residual Union-determined residual paid to a performer working in a filmed television production. Related term: TV residual.

film series Several related films shown in succession, e.g., a spy film series, space-adventure film series, horror-movie film series. The individual films in such a series following the release of the original are called "sequels" and typically utilize a numeral after the title to identify them from the original. For example, there are several sequels to *Rocky* (1976); *Rocky II* (1979), *Rocky III* (1982), *Rocky IV* (1985), *Rocky V* (1990). Related term: trilogy.

film stock Unprocessed, unexposed film. Related terms: stock, base, film, raw film.

film studio Building or complex where theatrical and television film production takes place. If combined with a television broadcast or video production studio, it is also called a film-TV studio or film-and-television production studio. A film studio is also called a movie studio, movie production facility or movie production complex. Related terms: film-TV studio, studio theme park, studio lot, front lot, back lot, soundstage, dream factory.

film title Name of a short or feature film. The title is found on the script, poster, print and TV advertising, theatrical trailer, clapboard, production documents and forms, copyright certificate and on the film itself. Also called the main title.

film title registration service In the United States, a title listing service offered by the Motion Picture Association of America. Producers who have films in development can have their titles registered to prevent disputes with other producers who may also intend to use the same title.

filmic Trendy Hollywood term meaning cinematic. Entertainment trade paper use.

filming session Period during which filming occurs.

filmmaker Individual who is actively involved in the various stages of making a film. The term "filmmaker" is typically used to refer to a film director or a filmmaking hyphenate, such as director-producer, director-writer-producer, director-writer-editor-producer. Also called a moviemaker. Related terms: independent filmmaker, student filmmaker, young filmmaker.

filmography 1. List of movies with descriptions of their contents. Related term: discography. 2. Individual's résumé of films.

filmspeak Film industry jargon or terminology. Related term: show-biz lingo.

filmstrip Length of processed film containing a series of transparent still photos projected one at a time onto a viewing screen; used for promotional and educational purposes. Also called a slide film.

film-to-tape auto conform Process in which an edited master videotape is produced by skipping the traditional cut-and-splice workprint stage; instead, the images on the film negative are directly transferred to videotape, which then edited electronically. Related term: editing on tape.

film-to-video transfer Process in which filmed images are transferred to a video medium, such as videotape. For older formats, such as 8mm home movies, the transfer uses a film projector, a small screen enclosed in a special housing onto which the images are projected and a video camera which records the images on the screen. For transferring positive-print, 35mm theatrical films to videotape for the home videocassette or television broadcast market, a machine called a telecine is used. Filmstrips and 35mm slides (transparencies) can also be transferred to video. Related terms: film-to-tape auto conform, editing on tape, digital scanner, telecine, letterbox format, pan and scan.

filter Colored or clear plate of glass or gelatin; when placed over the camera or printer lens, it absorbs a particular part of the light spectrum, corrects for color imbalance or diffuses the light. The most basic color filters are: 1) Daylight #85: Produces a crisp, bright, cheerful outdoor image when used with a Neutral Density filter and high-speed film. Related term: fast film. 2) Diffusion: Spreads the light, softens shadows and harsh lines. 3) Fog: Similar to a diffusion filter, except it creates an illusion of fog. Available in varying degrees of greyness. 4) Neutral Density (aka ND): Evenly reduces the amount of light reaching the film; it lowers the contrast and subdues (or desaturates) colors slightly. 5) Polarizing: Controls glare or reflection. (Related term: depolarizer.) 6) UV (ultraviolet, aka sky filter): Reduces the bluish cast caused by ultraviolet light on color film; useful for higher altitudes to reduce distance haze. (Related term: haze filter.) 7) Protection: Optical glass lens used to protect the camera lens from weather, dust, etc.

filter factor Amount by which exposure must be increased to compensate for the light-absorbing qualities of a filter.

fin French for "end." An onscreen end title.

final call Backstage announcement that the upcoming performance will begin in minutes. Depending upon local custom, a final call may be the same as a five-minute call, possibly followed by a "Places" call. The exact practice of how and when such calls are given varies from country to country. All performers should inquire as to the local sequence and definition of the various call times announced at the particular theater. Related term: call.

final cast list Formal list of performers prepared at the completion of casting; it is submitted to the performers' union with jurisdiction over that production.

final curtain Closing curtain at the end of the last act of a stage performance; it indicates the show is over. Also called the final act curtain.

final cut 1. Finished version of the work print from which the negative is conformed and release prints are struck for showing in theaters. 2. Important negotiating point for a director's or producer's contract when determining who has the last word on the form and content of the film that will be released. Related terms: work print, director's cut.

final mix Sound-editing process during post-production in which all the various soundtracks are combined or blended together completely; these include dialogue, music, sound effects, etc. Related term: mix.

finale 1. Closing part of a performance or presentation. 2. Season finale.

financial core status In the United States, a type of dues-paying status of a union; the individual resigns his membership and opts instead to be part of the "financial core" (dues-paying section) only. Individuals who declare financial core status receive a discount on dues and thereafter may work for union and nonunion companies, but they give up the right to run for union office, vote on union issues or receive the union's newsletter. However, they still receive medical and pension benefits and are protected by the terms of union contracts approved by voting members. Readmittance into the rank of membership, which is not guaranteed, depends upon the union's stated policy. In some unions, rejoining requires submission of a special application along with various fees. A 1988 U.S. Supreme Court decision, "Communications Workers of America vs. Beck," resulted in the creation of the financial-core status option by the U.S. National Labor Relations Board. The Supreme Court ruled that a union member, in this case, Harry Beck, could not be forced to pay that percentage of membership dues that goes toward the unions's support of outside activities (political or other causes) with which the member disagrees. Related term: union dues.

financing Monetary support for a film project. Related term: bank.

financing entity Person or company that pays for production of a film. Related terms: backer, theater angel.

financing fees Amount of money paid to the financing entity and/or person who arranged the financing. Related term: executive producer.

fine cut Refined version of the work print (after the rough cut). Related term: editing.

fine grain 1. Film emulsion. 2. Black-and-white positive (like an interpositive) used mainly for producing a dupe negative in which clarity, not speed, is important.

fire bar Metal pipe, with one end sealed, used in special effects; it is of different lengths and has a row of holes or diagonal slots cut into it. Pressurized flammable gas is fed to the bar by an attached hose. When the gas is lit, a directed wall of flames is produced. The height of the flames can be controlled by the level of pressurized gas fed to it. Related term: fire pan.

fire bomb Device specially designed to produce a fiery explosion when detonated. Related terms: bomb, explosion scene, gasoline mortar.

fire effect Use of fire in a scene; the fire, purposely ignited by an off-camera crew of trained fire stunt specialists, is ignited just prior to or during filming. (Actors may sometimes come close to burning props, walls or vehicles which emit toxic fumes.) Fire is also a natural feature of incendiary explosion scenes. In such a scene, flammable paste, gel (jelly) or liquid is applied to or poured onto areas targeted for burning. If a character is to be set on fire, a fire stunt performer is used as a double for the actor. Various layers of fire-resistant clothing, including a full head covering, mask, gloves and a concealed air supply, may be worn; the protective gel or liquid is applied to the stuntperson 's skin and clothing (depending on the type of stunt) to act as additional barriers against heat and flames. Fire scenes are planned and rehearsed carefully and may require the permission and presence of local government fire-fighting personnel and equipment; medical personnel may also be required at the scene. In addition, unions have rules that specifically pertain to fire stunts and smoke in scenes. Fire can also be created or enhanced onscreen by computer digital effects. Related terms: Aqua Fire, fire bar, fire bomb, fire gag, fire gel, fire pan, fireplace rig, Fire Ribbon, fire suit, air cannon, digital enhancement, explosion scene, Flameaway, flash powder, full burn, gasoline mortar, Hydro Fire, partial burn, Pyro Fluid, Pyro Gel, pyrotechnic effects, Road Burn Fluid, smoke effect, stunt gel, stunt mask, torch fluid, Zel-Gel, Zellene Fluid, Zellene Powder, Witch's Fire.

fire gag Any stunt or effect involving fire. Related term: burn gag.

fire gel Thick, flammable liquid spread on objects or clothing in a scene involving fire. Rubber cement or some other flammable liquid is also used for this purpose. Related term: Pyro Gel.

"Fire in the Hole!" Warning voiced by a pyrotechnic operator just prior to detonating an explosive device in a scene. Mining origin.

fire pan Metal pan containing a fire bar, positioned with the bar's slots facing downward. The pan causes the flames to spread, making the fire appear thicker.

Fire Ribbon Flammable paste applied to surfaces from a handheld squeeze tube. It can also be used on water and ice. Available from Tri-Ess Sciences, Inc., of Burbank, California. Related term: Hydro Fire.

fire suit Fire-resistant body garment worn by a stuntperson while performing a fire stunt. Besides the suit, the stuntperson may wear fire-resistant underwear, gloves, hood, goggles, face mask (also called a stunt mask) or stunt gel. The protective garments are the same as those worn by professional race-car drivers. Wearing a fire suit and related garments requires specialized knowledge and trained assistants and safety personnel to help put the suit on; they also should be present while the stunt is being performed. Also called a burn suit.

fireplace rig Realistic simulation of wood logs burning in an indoor fireplace or outdoor campfire; flammable gas is fed to fake logs by a concealed hose and nozzle system.

first assistant cameraman Member of the camera crew who loads and unloads the film magazines (unless there is a second assistant cameraman on the crew); changes lenses; keeps the camera in proper working condition; maintains focus while the camera is in motion; fills out camera reports (if there is no second assistant cameraman); marks the spot where actors will stand; and measures the distance between the object being photographed and the lens.

first assistant director (also called first A.D.) director's on-set aide; the liaison between the director and production manager; he or she sometimes doubles as the production manager on smaller productions; usually a member of the Directors Guild of America (or another guild or union covering production individu-

als outside the United States). During production, the first A.D. is responsible for the extras; keeps the production moving; makes sure that everyone and everything is in the right place at the right time (the call); and maintains order and discipline on the set. He or she orders "Quiet on the set!" before each take and tells the camera operator to roll. Before production begins, the A.D. breaks down the script; determines the number of extras and silent bits needed for each scene; and, with the director's and production manager's approval, hires them. The first A.D. usually has an assistant called a Second. Related terms: second assistant director, second second assistant director, third assistant director.

first camera assistant Onscreen credit variation for "first assistant camera operator." Additional variation: "first assistant camera." Related term: assistant camera operator.

first cut See director's cut, rough cut.

first dollar Term indicating the initial monies generated by a motion picture in release. Gross profit participants and distributors typically take their cuts from the first dollar, while net profit participants must wait until after the picture has broken even. Related term: artificial breakeven.

first draft First complete version of a screenplay, in continuity form, including full dialogue.

first generation 1. Any first printing of film from a negative. Also called the first strike. 2. Original video footage; a copy of the original is called a "second-generation copy." (With digital copying, both the original and copy are identical and the term does not apply.) Related term: generation loss.

first look 1. Initial review privilege; a right of first refusal. 2. Sneak preview.

first position 1. Point or location on a production set or stage where one begins an activity, such as acting or dancing. Also called the number-one position, starting position, starting place or first mark. Related term: "Back to one." 2. Designation given to an onscreen film credit. Related term: position number.

first refusal Right or privilege of being first to have the option to refuse or accept something, usually by a stated time limit. Also called a right of first refusal or first-refusal right. Related terms: first look, tentative booking.

first run First release of a motion picture in a major market area (e.g., in Los Angeles, a first run typically would be in selected theaters in Westwood and Hollywood).

first team Principal actors in a production, e.g., "The first team was called to the set to begin shooting." Also called the first string.

first-choice actor or actress Actor who is the producer's, director's or studio's initial choice to play a role. There also may be a second- (third-, fourth-, etc.) choice actor.

first-draft script First version of a finished script; it is subject to being rewritten, revised and/or polished until a shooting script is approved.

first-look deal Agreement in which one party has the right to look at another party's offering before it is released to other potential buyers; the first party then decides whether to purchase, option, license (for products or technologies) or pass on it. For example, screenwriters often have first-look deals with film studios. In such a deal, the studio has the right to see the writer's spec script before it is offered to any other studios or production companies; the writer receives compensation for being obligated to the terms of a first-look deal. Related terms: first look, first refusal.

first-run episode TV series episode; it is telecast for the first time as opposed to being a rerun.

first-run syndication Shown first in syndication; produced especially for non-network showing. Refers to syndicated TV specials or series that are not network first-run shows or reruns.

fish-eye lens Extremely wide-angle camera or projector lens creating a rounded view on the sides; objects in the center are prominent and appear larger than life when brought closer to the lens. (For example, a fish-eye lens close-up shot of a person's face will give him an oversized nose.) The field of view for a fish-eye lens can vary with the type of lens, e.g., 150 degrees or a full 180 degrees. Such lenses are also used in projectors found in certain specialty amusement theaters. Related terms: IMAX Dome theater, IMAX Ridefilm theater, Iwerks theater, peephole matte.

fishpole Long, hand-held pole with a microphone at the end. Related term: microphone boom.

fitting Session in which garments are tried on to determine their proper fit and look. Related terms: costume fitting, wardrobe fitting.

5-minute call Backstage announcement that a performance will begin in five minutes. Related terms: call, final call.

flack Slang term for a press agent.

flag Sheet of black material (duvatyne), set in a frame and used to shade a particular part of the set, object or camera from the light. Related term: gobo.

Flameaway Liquid flame retardant used to treat production set materials prior to fire stunt scenes. Also manufactured as an additive for water-based paints. Available from Zeller International, Ltd., of Downsville, New York. Related term: fire effect.

flange Found in the cutting room, a metal or plastic disc used to facilitate the uniform rewinding of the film. Related term: core.

flare Bright spot or flash on exposed film, usually from the reflection of a shiny object; can be avoided or eliminated by using dulling spray. Related term: bloom.

flash 1. (n.) short cut or sequence, used for dramatic effect. 2. (v.) Means of increasing overall exposure (especially in shadowy areas) by briefly exposing to the light unexposed and unprocessed film, thus flattening contrast. A tricky procedure, it is typically done in the lab.

flash frames Overexposed film frames at the beginning of a shot; they received too much light because the camera had not yet reached its proper speed. Sometimes, to mark the beginning of a scene for the editor, the cameraman will intentionally flash a few frames.

flash pan Rapid pan (side-to-side movement of the camera rotating on tripod), producing a blur. Related terms: swish pan, whip pan.

flash paper White sheets of pyrotechnic tissue paper; they burn with a quick flash of flame and leave no discernible residue. The paper is shipped wet in a bag and must be air-dried before use. Also available as flash cotton. A source for flash paper is Tri-Ess Sciences, Inc., of Burbank, California.

flash pot Small metal container into which a quantity of flash powder is placed; it is then electrically ignited by an offstage or offcamera special-effects technician. A flash pot is used in scenes requiring a brief flash of bright flame and smoke, such as when a character suddenly appears or disappears in a supernatural or fantasy story.

flash powder Any of various pyrotechnic powders producing brilliant, quick flames when ignited; available in different colors. Related terms: flash pot, powder person, pyrotechnic effects.

flashback 1. (n.) Scene presenting events that occurred in the past; a series of shots or a single, long-playing shot may be used to depict this. An editing transitional effect, such as a ripple dissolve or a soft fade to white, is used at the beginning and ending of a flashback. 2. (v.) To flash back.

flashforward 1. (n.) Scene presenting events that will occur in the future; typically it is part of a dream sequence or psychic-vision sequence. 2. (v.) To flash forward.

flashlight monster Simple, dramatic effect in which the human face is distorted by holding a flashlight (pointing upwards) close to the chin in a darkened room or outside at night. Also called a torch monster (Great Britain, Australia, etc.).

flash-memory-based camcorder Handheld video camera recording images and sound on a special memory chip contained in a removable module. The recorded information can be transferred to a computer or other device.

flat 1. Image with little or no contrast or depth of field. 2. Large, movable section of a set consisting of painted canvas or other material mounted on a wooden or metal frame. Flats can be constructed in different sizes may even contain wooden, glass or screen doors and windows. Related terms: book flat, profile flat, three-fold flat, two-fold flat, background, scenery, wild wall.

flat acting Acting that is not lively or dynamic. Also called one-dimensional acting or dull acting. Related terms: flat, deadpan.

flat print Standard film print, projected normally; as opposed to a squeezed print. Related terms: anamorphic lens, widescreen.

flat rate Set fee paid for services rendered; this differs from a weekly or hourly rate because overtime is not paid. A producer may attempt to negotiate a flat rate for an employee rather than worry about having to pay hourly wages, overtime, golden time, etc.

flat session fee Payment for any type of session calculated at a flat rate.

flatbed editing machine Electrical, motor-driven, playback editing machine having a flat, wide, tabletop surface; 35mm or 16mm films and soundtracks are run horizontally from side to side on circular plates and viewed on an attached screen. Also called a flatbed editor or tabletop editing machine. Related terms: Kem, Moviola, Steenbeck.

flat-rate deal Contract in which a fixed payment is made once; there are no additional payments in the form of residuals or royalties. Also called a flat-rate contract. Related term: buyout.

flicker Shaking of the film when it is erroneously projected at a rate of fewer than 24 frames per second. Related term: persistence of vision.

FlightStick Trade name for a line of handheld, motion-stabilizing camera mounts for video cameras. Manufactured and sold by Classic Video Products of Aliso, California. (The company manufacturers other brands of portable motion-stabilizing camera mounts and video camera cranes.)

flip-card movie Short movie or action sequence consisting of a series of photographic cards, each showing a slight change in the subject's movement; when the cards are rapidly leafed, the appearance of continuous movement is produced. Typically found in old-style penny arcade machines and occasionally in modern printed works as a novelty item.

flipper 1. Nickname for a removable dental prosthesis, e.g., an artificial tooth or extension; for temporary cosmetic use only. It consists of custom-fitted composite plastic and stainless steel wires. The flipper was invented by Dr. Charlie Pincus in the United States. Reportedly, the first child star to wear one was Shirley Temple in the 1930s. The leading industry supplier today is Dr. Robert Smith of West Hollywood, California, whose clients have included child stars Drew Barrymore, Molly Ringwald, Shannen Doherty, Mary-Kate and Ashley Olsen, among others. Also called a plastic partial denture or kiddie partial. 2. Another name for one of the barn doors on a studio light.

floodlight Extremely powerful lighting unit. Standard floods cannot be focused; focusing floods can. Related term: flood.

floor Shooting area of a sound stage.

floor manager Another name for a television stage manager.

floor-level stage Performance area that is no higher than the audience section. However, the audience section may be at the same level as, or higher than, a stage at floor level. Also called a ground-level stage.

flop 1. (n.) Failure, e.g., a flop at the box office or a Broadway flop. 2. (v.) To fail. Related terms: bomb, lay an egg.

Florida look Appearance characteristic or typical of the people, places, scenery or life-styles found in Florida, a peninsular state located at the southeastern corner of the United States. Examples are: stucco-covered buildings painted pink, aqua or other pastel colors; palm trees, swampy grasslands (the Everglades), beaches, mountainless terrains; air boats, speed boats, swamp buggies; and alligators, manatees, flamingos, and pelicans. Related term: Orlando-based (United States).

flub 1. Misspoken dialogue; a botched line; a slip-up or tongue-twisted tangling of words by an actor, TV or radio host, stage speaker, or newsperson. Related term: blooper. 2. To flub one or more lines; e.g., "I flubbed the line. Let's try it again." Related term: blowing a line.

fluid camera Camera in constant movement.

fly Heavy scenery on ropes (cables) above a set.

fly gallery Service walkway high in a theater's fly loft. Related term: catwalk.

fly loft Area above a theater stage where lighting and scenery are located and from where either can be raised (flown) or lowered (set down) before, during or after a performance. A metal framework called a grid, or gridiron, is located at the top of the fly loft and provides structural support for the various pulleys, chains, cables and other fixtures attached to it. Not all theaters have a fly loft; instead, some may have permanent "dead hung" pipes onto which equipment is mounted. Also called a fly space or fly tower. Related terms: fly gallery, batten, grid.

flying scene Scene in which one or more characters defy gravity and are shown levitating or moving above the ground. Related term: wire-flying scene.

Flying-Cam Trade name for an Academy Award®-winning, remote-controlled, small-scale helicopter with a small, motion-picture camera mounted on it; used for aerial shots during which use of a full-scale helicopter with an on-board pilot and camera operator would be too difficult. The Flying-Cam's developer, Emanuel Previnaire, was honored with a 1994 Technical Achievement Award from the Academy of Motion Picture Arts and Sciences. Related term: helicopter shot.

flyman Individual who controls the lines which raise or lower the battens during a stage performance. Scenery, curtains or lighting fixtures are attached to the scenery.

foam latex Type of dense foam rubber made by heating latex with other chemical ingredients; used in the creation of special makeup effects, such as face-altering makeup appliances, stop-motion animation creatures, other types of miniature and life-size puppets and full-body alien and monster costumes. There are alternative materials to foam latex (requiring oven baking), including silicone and urethane foam, the latter of which expands on its own without heating (after combining and mixing its two chemical parts). A leading international supplier of foam latex and all other special-effects related sculpting and casting materials is Burman Industries, Inc., of Van Nuys, California, in the United States. Another Source is Tri-Ess Sciences, Inc., of Burbank, California (also a source for pyrotechnic effects). Both companies have mail-order catalogs (printed in English) and will ship their products to entertainment industry customers throughout the world. Related terms: latex, latex appliance, movable miniature, special makeup effects.

focal distance Measurement from a camera to an area, object or person in focus. Also called focus distance. Related terms: camera-to-subject measurement, depth of field.

focal length Measurement, in millimeters, from the optical center of a camera's lens to the surface of the film or CCD imaging chip inside the camera (when the lens is set at infinity and the image is sharply focused). A wide-angle lens has a short focal length (wide picture area); a telephoto lens has a long one (narrow picture area); a zoom lens has a variable focal length. Related term: depth of field.

focal settings Predetermined positions on the lens focusing ring, allowing the focus puller (aka technician, first assistant cameraman) to correctly maintain focus during shots. Related terms: follow focus, follow shot.

focus 1. (n.) Point of convergence for rays of light refracted by the lens. Related terms: autofocus, deep focus, shallow focus, soft focus, in focus, out of focus, focal length, depth of field.

2. (v.) To adjust the lens of a camera or projector to make a clear, sharply-defined image. Related terms: focus pulling, follow focus, defocus.

focus puller (aka technician, first assistant cameraman) Camera crew member who measures the distance from the lens to the subject and maintains focus while the camera is rolling. The focus puller is also in charge of all cameras and other equipment as well as the other assistants on the camera crew. Related terms: assistant cameraman, first and second assistant cameraman.

focus pulling Shifting focus from one object or person in a shot to another. For example, a camera is focused on a close-up of a flower and then it shifts its focus to a young woman standing some distance away. When this occurs, the flower becomes blurred and the image of the woman becomes sharp. Also called focus shifting or rack focusing.

focus ring Circular part of a lens housing, or barrel, used to adjust the focus by rotating it in either direction. On large motion picture cameras, it may be connected to a dial on the side of the camera for easy use by the assistant camera operator while shooting. Related term: follow focus.

fog effect Appearance of fog (airborne water vapor or a ground-level cloud) in a scene created by a fog-smoke machine, steam, dry ice (solidified carbon dioxide gas) placed in water; a burning solid chemical; computer animation; or a fog filter placed over the lens of the camera. Related terms: fog-smoke machine, rumble pot, smoke effect, steam chips.

fog filter Diffusing filter placed on the camera lens to create the effect of fog.

fog-smoke machine Any of various hand-held or floor-positioned devices containing a supply of water- or synthetic-based fluid used to create the effect of white fog. mist, steam or smoke. In a thermal fog-smoke machine (the most common type), the fluid (also called "fog juice") within the machine is sprayed over a heating element and forced out by a hand pump, pressurized container or blower fan. For a low-lying fog effect, some machines have a front-mounted cooling chamber allowing the vaporized particles to pass over dry ice; as the vapors exit the machine, they fall and stay low to the ground. Different nontoxic fluids are available to produce various fog-smoke effects. Fog-smoke machines can be rented or purchased. A manufacturer of a variety of thermal and nonthermal fog-smoke machines and fluids is Zeller International, Ltd., of Downsville, New York, in the United States. Also called a fog-smoke generator, fog-maker or smoke gun. Related terms: fog effect, smoke effect.

foley Body movement, sound or sound effect recorded in a studio (as the picture runs) and used on the film's completed sound track. For example, for a chase scene on foot, a foley artist would watch the scene and recreate (with believable sounds, e.g., footsteps, panting) the actions of the actor on screen. Or, in a musical, the sound of taps in a dancing number would be recreated by dancers on a foley stage as they watch the dancers move. Related term: streamer.

foley artist Individual who specializes in creating ordinary, synchronized sound effects, such as footsteps, door slamming, keys jingling, glasses clinking, etc., in a soundproofed foley studio. The studio is equipped with various types of sound-effects producing materials and a large screen for watching the necessary film tracks. These types of sound effects, called foleys, are named after Jack Foley (1891-1967), inventor of this process of custom-designing sound effects in a specially equipped sound studio.

foley editor Individual who edits foley sounds.

foley mixer Individual who combines the various foley sounds. Related term: sound-effects mixer.

foley recordist Individual who operates the recording equipment during a foley session.

foley session Session during which foley sound effects are produced and recorded.

foley stage Large room with a variety of floor surfaces and containing objects with which to create sound effects needed for a film or television show.

foley studio Specially designed recording studio capable of projecting picture and sound simultaneously while recording new sounds created by foley artist(s). The sound effects are recorded on full track, usually three- or four-stripe, to give the editor three attempts to get the right sound. The sounds are then cut and sync'ed into the film.

foley tracks Copy (in 35mm) of recorded foley sounds, ready to be cut and sync'ed into the film by the editor. The original foley master is stored for safekeeping until the completion of the film, when it is mixed into the final soundtrack.

folk play Play originating in or featuring the traditions or legends of the common people of a country or region.

follow focus Readjusting the camera's lens during a moving shot so the subject remains in focus. Prior to filming, measurements from camera to subject, at different intervals, are taken; the measurements are used by the assistant camera operator who readjusts the focus of the different camera-subject positions. Related terms: camera-to-subject measurement, focal distance, focus, focus ring.

follow shot Shot in which the camera tracks (or follows) the subject. Related terms: pan, tilt, tracking shot.

follow spot Spotlight that can swivel to follow a performer's movements.

foot End of the film (or tape) reel. Related term: tail.

footage Any length of film, expressed in feet and frames (16 frames = 1 foot of 35mm film); can refer to any part of a film, from one shot to the entire film. Film passes through the camera at 24 frames per second (fps); in 60 seconds, 90 feet of film are exposed.

footage counter Gauge on the camera, projector or printer measuring the amount of film exposed, projected or printed. Film footage is expressed in frames, not inches. Related term: footage.

footcandle Unit of illumination measured at a distance one foot from the light source.

footlights 1. Row of lights positioned on the floor at the front of a stage. Also called a floor light. 2. Expression meaning, "the stage," as a performing medium.

forced call Violation of a union or guild contract caused by bringing a crew and cast member back to work before the minimum amount of required time off.

forced perspective Technique of simulating a three-dimensional depth in a background painting or set, particularly on a set in which space is limited.

foreground Entire area in front of an actor, especially as determined by the camera lens or as seen through the viewfinder. Abbreviation as f.g. or F.G. Related term: downstage.

foreground action Action taking place in front of performers or objects; action nearest the camera or audience. The opposite is background action.

foreground light Any light directed at the foreground of a shot or scene.

foreground prop Any prop located in the foreground.

foreign box office Feature film admissions from outside the country of origin, as opposed to domestic box office. Related term: worldwide box office.

foreign distribution Exploitation and sale of a motion picture in a market outside the United States and Canada (theatrically) and outside the United States (for television/cable and other nontheatrical markets). Related term: cross-collateralization.

foreign sales rep Individual or company authorized to sell rights to and exploit a film in foreign markets. Most foreign sales reps sell country by country, or market by market, and do not cross-collateralize.

foreign version Filmed or printed work that has been changed to accommodate the language or moral standards of one or more foreign audiences. This may include foreign-language dubbing or subtitles or the insertion or deletion of shots involving violence, offensive language, nudity, sex or political references. Related terms: foreign-language version, uncut version.

foreign-language version 1. Filmed work shown or sold outside the country of origin; language translation subtitles or dubbed-over dialogue are added during post-production to match the language of the country where it will be exhibited. Related terms: foreign version, soundtrack. 2. Printed work, such as a movie poster, translated into the language of the country where it will be read.

forestage Front part of a stage. Another name for an apron.

format Width to height ratio of the film as it is projected on the screen (e.g., standard as opposed to widescreen format.) Related term: aspect ratio.

formula movie Movie with a familiar combination of plot elements; it has worked successfully in other, previously-made films.

four-camera Of or pertaining to four film or TV cameras, e.g., a four-camera stunt shot or four-camera TV coverage of a sporting event. Many sitcoms are filmed in the four-camera style.

14-rating Canadian classification issued for films and videos exhibited in theaters or offered for sale or rental to the public. The full wording is: "'14'—Adult Accompaniment Required Under Age 14." Related terms: AA, rating, TV-14, "14" certificate.

four-wall To rent a theater for a flat fee in order to exhibit a motion picture. This practice is usually reserved for low-budget, independent or art house films seeking a distributor or a wider audience. Four-walling can be repeated from town to town, thereby generating good word-of-mouth and revenue.

four-wall set Production set containing four walls, some of which can be moved out of position to allow the camera to shoot from different angles. These movable walls may be called wild walls. Also called a four-walled set.

fps Abbreviation for frames per second (sometimes, feet per second). Related term: persistence of vision.

frame 1. (n.) Film's individual unit of measure. Each frame contains an image and when these images are projected in succession (24 frames per second), an illusion of normal movement is created. Projecting film at more or less frames per second creates the illusion of slow or accelerated motion. 2. (v.) To compose an image through the viewfinder of the camera. 3. To line up the film in the gate of the projector or editing machine so the entire frame (image) is visible.

frame area Another name for shot area.

frame counter Device attached to a camera, projector or printer that keeps track of how many frames have been exposed or projected.

frame down Action taken by the projectionist when the bottom of the picture is cut off the screen; he will move the gate of the projector down to the bottom of the film frame, thus centering the picture properly on the screen.

frame up Action taken by the projectionist to center the picture properly on the screen by moving the gate of the projector up (opposite of frame down).

frames per second (abbreviated as fps) Number of frames of film that pass through a camera, projector or printer in one second.

franchised agency Talent agency that has signed an agreement with a union stating that it will abide by that union's rules with regard to the representation of its members. Related term: union signatory list.

freelance Act of submitting invoices or time cards for services rendered instead of being under long-term contract to the company. Related term: independent contractor.

freeze To stop suddenly during a performance (or just prior to performing) due to nervousness or uncertainty. Also called stage fright.

"Freeze!" Direction from a director or photographer to stop the action and remain still; this is typically done to achieve a special effect, such as making actors or objects appear or disappear. For example, an actor who is supposed to disappear would walk out of the shot while the other actors remain frozen; when the action resumes and the footage is edited, the actor seems to have vanished. Related terms: camera trick, "Cut and Hold."

freeze frame shot in which one frame is printed many times over until it appears as a still image on the screen. Related terms: double printing, skip framing.

Fresnel lens Glass lens for a spotlight; it consists of a series of concentric circular lenses extending from the center to outer margins. They control the light being emitted from the bulb (wide beam to narrow spot) as the lens is moved in or out. Thin, flat versions made of acetate butyrate are used in overhead projectors and other optical equipment. Used on searchlights, spotlights, etc. Invented by French physicist Augustin J. Fresnel (1788-1827).

friction head tripod attachment allowing for smooth camera movement during a pan or tilt.

fringe benefits Additional compensation (typically not paid in cash) over and above salary. Vacation pay and health, welfare and pension benefits are paid to the guild or union of which the individual is a member. Fringe benefits can also include such perks as free screenings, parking, etc. Related term: perk.

fringe company In Great Britain, an acting company performing primarily in fringe theatres.

fringe rates Wages paid on behalf of an employee in addition to that employee's direct wage compensation (e.g., health and welfare, pension, taxes.)

fringe theatre Playhouse located on the edge of the London Theatre District; typically, they are smaller than West End theatres and offer less expensive shows (in the same way that Off-Broadway and Off-Off Broadway theaters do in New York City). Rents and operating costs for fringe theatres are cheaper than playhouses in the main theatre district, hence, their emergence as outlets for new performers, playwrights, producers, etc.

"From the top." Direction from the director (including a casting director) to begin again (such as, the reading of dialogue in a scene). Variation: "Take it from the top."

front car mount Structural support, holding one or more cameras, attached to the front of a vehicle; the camera(s) may be aimed at the driver, passenger or both. In addition to a front car mount, cameras and equipment can be mounted at the rear of the vehicle towing the car being filmed. Or, the vehicle with the actors in it can be mounted on a flatbed trailer and towed during the shot. Related term: camera mount.

front credits Listing, with emphasis on size and position, of the major contributors to the production of the film. Front credits typically appear in the following order: distribution company; producer or production company presenting; (director's) film; stars; film title; actors (in order of importance of the role, alphabetically or otherwise a contractually negotiated order); casting director; costume director; composer; editor; cinematographer; production designer; screenwriter; producer; director. Related terms: opening credits, opening titles.

front light 1. (n.) Lighting unit located and directed at a subject from the front of the set or stage. 2. (v.) To light a subject from the front.

front lot Designated front portion of a film-TV studio complex; typically, where the administrative offices are located. Related term: studio lot.

front projection Projecting moving images or a still image onto the front of a highly reflective screen. Because the special screen is highly reflective, a less-powerful projection light is required to produce a clear, crisp image. (An actor standing in front of the screen does not reflect enough of the image for it to be seen on his body.) Shadows are eliminated because both the projector and camera are aimed straight at the screen by an optically aligned, semireflecting (see-through) mirror system. Also called front-screen projection or front-screen process. Related terms: Zoptic Front Projection System, process shot, projector.

Frost Tex Liquid used in special-effects work to simulate the appearance of winter or freezer frost on glass surfaces; it is applied wet and can be scraped like real frost when dry. Available from Zeller International, Ltd., of Downsville, New York. Related terms: Crystasol, snow effect.

FS Abbreviation for full shot.

f-stop Number on the lens indicating the size of the aperture, thus regulating how much light can enter the lens to expose the film. To find the f-stop, divide the focal length of the lens by the diameter of the aperture. The larger the f-stop number, the smaller the aperture. Related terms: depth of field, t-stop, aperture, iris.

full apple box Box used on a production set to temporarily increase the height of a performer or object. There is no standard size for a full apple box, with regard to width and length, but all apple boxes are 8" high (20.3mm). Some typical full apple box sizes are 8" x 12" x 18" or 8" x 12" x 20" or 8" x 14" x 24." Also called a full-apple or full-riser. Related terms: apple box, half apple box, quarter apple box, pancake apple box.

full body shot Shot of the entire body; head-to-toe shot. Related term: full shot.

full burn Fire stunt in which a stuntperson is set completely on fire. Also called fire gag or full body burn. Related term: fire effect.

full coat Film (35mm) coated with magnetic ferrous-oxide. Typically, production sound (recorded in sync with the picture) is transferred onto full coat so it can be cut in sync with the picture. Sound recorded in a foley or ADR studio may be recorded directly onto full coat. Usually, there are four channels (or stripes) recorded on full coat, although there can be as many as six; this is different from single stripe, which has one channel.

full fee Normal hiring rate or charge for service, as opposed to a half-fee or negotiated fee. Also called a full rate.

full house Movie theater, playhouse or television studio filled to capacity. Also called a packed house or packed audience.

full load Blank ammunition cartridge containing the full quantity of gunpowder normal for that size round, as opposed to a half-load or quarter-load.

full shot (abbreviated as FS) Shot that includes the whole subject, from top to bottom.

Fuller's earth Nontoxic powdered clay used to simulate dust or dirt; available in different grades. When combined with other materials, such as vermiculite, peat moss, sand, methocellulose, etc., a mud or quicksand environment is created. Fuller's earth is more sanitary than ordinary dirt. A source for Fuller's earth is the special-effects company Tri-Ess Sciences, Inc., of Burbank, California. Related terms: cobweb spinner, debris mortar, dust effect, dust hit.

full-face photo Photograph featuring the entire front view of the face. Also called a full-face shot or head shot.

full-length photo Photograph in which the entire length of a subject is shown. Also called a full-length shot, full-body shot or head-to-toe shot.

full-motion video Television or computer images with continuous, real-time movement, as opposed to being choppy or a series of still pictures.

full-scale mock-up Life-size replica, e.g., a full-scale mock-up of an airplane passenger cabin. Related terms: mock-up, process body.

funny man Another name for a comedian.

FV Television rating meaning "Fantasy Violence;" used in reference to children's animated and live-action television programs. Related terms: "V", rating.

FX 1. Abbreviation for "effects." 2. Abbreviation for "special effects."

FXpert An FX expert; a special-effects expert. Also called an FX wizard.

gaffer Chief electrician on the set, responsible for lighting the set per the instructions of the director of photography. The gaffer supervises the crew's placement of lights before and during shooting. Related terms: best boy, electrician, lighting director, lighting technician.

gaffer's tape Strong adhesive tape used to secure objects on the production set; the same as air-conditioning duct tape. Available colors are silver, gray, black, brown, white, and yellow. Also called duct tape, cloth tape, colored cloth tape or grip tape.

gag 1. Joke or comedy trick; a bit of comic business, either audible or visual. Related terms: running gag, sight gag. 2. Another name for a special effect or stunt, e.g., a self-breaking mirror gag or fire gag.

gag writer Another name for a comedy writer.

gangster movie Film featuring a storyline set in the world of organized crime. Related term: crime drama.

gasoline mortar Open-ended metal drum or pipe, varying in size, used to propel ignited gasoline, or petrol, into the air during an explosion scene. The prepared device may consist of the following: a sealed black-powder lifting charge (also called a black-powder bomb) with electrical squib detonator placed at the bottom of the mortar; a gasoline-filled plastic bag on top of the charge; and an electrically squibbed flash-powder charge at the top of the mortar to guarantee ignition of the fuel. If thick black smoke is desired, diesel fuel or liquid tar is mixed with the gasoline; the vaporized, burning gasoline creates a fireball. Other pyrotechnic materials are also used to create an airborne fireball, such as napalm or naphthalene. An air cannon charged with propane gas produces a clean-burning fireball when ignited. To create the effect of a car's hood, trunk, doors or windows being blown into the sky or outward with a fiery explosion, various methods are used, including internally placed shotgun mortars (prepared like a gasoline mortar but filled with gasoline-soaked sand instead). The hood, trunk, etc., of the car is unbolted to allow for easier and more forceful disengagement during the explosion. A gasoline mortar can only be used by a licensed pyrotechnic operator. Related terms: air cannon, mortar, explosion scene, fire bomb, fire effect.

gate Opening over which the film is held in the camera while being exposed, either in the projector or in the printer. It can swing out, like a gate, for cleaning and threading.

gate pass See drive on.

gauge Width of the film.

gauze (aka cheesecloth) Thin, meshed cloth, similar to the type used as a bandage; placed over a camera lens, it achieves a soft effect similar to a diffusion filter.

geared head Complex camera support with gears; it fits onto a tripod or dolly and is wound to allow smooth pans and tilts of the camera. Opposite of friction head.

gel Abbreviation for gelatin. 1. Diffuser that softens the light of a studio lamp. 2. Colored transparency used to change the color of a light source. For example, if a late afternoon look is desired on a location (or on a set in a studio), red-orange gels can be placed on the windows or in front of the lights, thus warming the color of the light. Related term: jelly.

general extra Extra who performs general background or foreground action in a scene.

general release Nationwide distribution to a large number of theaters or marketing outlets (video or music stores), as opposed to a limited release, selected engagements or premiere showing. A wide release is a large-scale general release.

generation Each progressive step from original negative (or tape) to final viewing (or listening) product. For example, to get from original 35mm negative to release print, you can strike a print from the negative (though not advisable); this print would be a second generation print. More commonly, film goes from negative to CRI to release print (third generation); or from negative to interpositive (IP) to dupe negative (this is also considered three generations as IP to dupe neg is considered one generation; the quality is as good as, if not better than, a print from CRI). Generally, the more generations away from the original, the poorer the quality of the final product. A 1/2" video cassette made from a 3/4" cassette will have poorer quality than a 1/2" cassette made from a print. Generation loss does not occur with most digital images.

generation loss Lessening of image or sound quality as a result of duplication. The deterioration may be minuscule or great, depending upon the copying technology used. In an advanced digital system, there is no generation loss. Related term: first generation.

generator Portable power source used on location (or as back-up power at a studio); it runs on gasoline or diesel fuel.

generator operator Individual who turns the generator on at the beginning of the day and off in the evening and ensures it stays in good running condition throughout the production.

genre Category, kind or type of film story, identified by its subject, theme or style. Genres include: action, adventure, comedy, drama, family, fantasy, historical, horror, musical, mystery, romance, science fiction, western. There are also subgenres, such as romantic-comedy, science fiction-fantasy, action-adventure.

gig 1. Slang for a job. 2. Booking involving a music or singing performance.

gimbal stage Platform or enclosure mounted on top of a swivel, fulcrum or other mechanized base allowing it to tilt, twist or shake in any number of controlled directions and speeds so that scripted action or special effects are achievable. On a large, elaborate gimbal stage, numerous hydraulic or pneumatic cylinders are used to precisely control the movements; a small gimbal stage is operated manually by poles or wooden beams projecting out of the sides. The full-scale replica of the submarine's control deck in *Crimson Tide* (1995) was built on a large gimbal stage. The airplane disaster movie *Turbulence* (1997) had most of its action scenes shot on full-scale sets constructed on gimbal stages and a 360-degree revolving stage. *Air Force One* (1997) also used a gimbal stage. Also called a gimbal platform or tilting stage. A revolving stage is different from a gimbal stage in that a revolving stage is mechanically designed to permit a 360-degree rotation of the stage, production set and supporting cylindrical framework exclusively in either a horizontal- or vertical-plane direction; however, some individuals in the industry may refer to a revolving stage as a rotary gimbal stage or rotary gimbal. Related terms: gimbal set, revolving stage.

given the axe To be canceled, cut from the schedule, removed, dismissed or fired, e.g., "The sitcom was given the axe by the network." Related terms: axe, cancel.

glamour shot Photograph or camera shot featuring the glamorous nature or appearance of a person, product, location or activity.

glass breaker Small mechanical device used in a stunt scene to initiate the breakage of tempered glass. Related term: breakaway prop.

glass hit 1. Break-apart gelatin capsule containing a combination of petroleum jelly, metallic glitter flakes and a black felt circle; it is fired from a capsule gun at a window or windshield to simulate a bullet hit without causing damage. 2. Plastic ball containing a clear glass marble; it is shot from a Sweeney gun.

glass painting Another name for a matte painting; it is created on a sheet of glass by a matte artist.

glass prop 1. Drinking glass, used as a prop, made of actual glass or hard

plastic. 2. Breakaway prop made of a brittle plastic resin or from sugar syrup that is boiled, then cooled. Related term: breakaway glass.

glass shot Visual-effects technique used to create the illusion of an expensive and/or difficult set or location, without constructing the set or filming at the actual location. The desired scene is painted on part of a glass plate and the action is shot through it, combining both on the film. Related term: matte shot.

Glidecam Trade name for a line of motion-stabilizing, hand-held camera mounts for video cameras. Manufactured and sold by Glidecam Industries of Plymouth, Massachusetts. Internet address: http://www.glidecam.com.

Glosser Glossy spray coating applied to breakaway glass. Available from Zeller International, Ltd., of Downsville, New York.

glossy 1. (n.) A glossy photograph. 2. (adj.) Having a shiny appearance, as opposed to a dull, or matte, finish. Related term: slick.

go Approval to proceed with the project (e.g., a "go" project.) Related term: greenlight.

go blank To forget lines of dialogue. Related term: draw a blank.

"Go to black." Variation of "fade to black."

gobo 1. Black cloth, sheet, screen or mesh with a particular design or pattern cut from its center, mounted on a stand in front of the camera during filming. It fits in front of a spotlight and is used to cast that image, which could look like scattered sunlight filtering through tree branches, stars, a city skyline or even a television show's name. 2. Shield used to keep unwanted light from entering a camera's lens. 3. Shield to keep unwanted sound from entering a microphone. Related term: windscreen.

gofer Individual who runs errands; nickname for a production assistant or personal assistant. "Gofer" is derived from the phrase "go for." Also called an errand person, errand runner or runner. Related terms: production assistant, personal assistant.

Golden Age of Hollywood Time period in film history that produced many classic films; generally considered to be from the late 1920s to 1949.

Golden Age of Television Time period in television history that produced many classic television shows; generally considered to be from the 1950s through the 1960s.

Golden Bear Award Annual award bestowed in Germany for the best in film at the Berlin International Film Festival; includes the Silver Bear Award.

Golden Globe Award Annual awards presented, in the United States, by the Hollywood Foreign Press Association for noted achievement in motion pictures and television. Members of the organization report on the entertainment world for news media in more than 50 countries around the world.

Golden Palm Award (aka Palme d'Or) Award honoring the best film at the Cannes International Film Festival & Market, held each May in Cannes, France.

golden time Overtime pay. If a union employee is working in a studio or reporting to a location within the studio zone on a straight time day, any time worked over 12 consecutive hours is calculated at double the hourly rate. If the employee does not fall under the on call classification and works on a double time day (Saturday, Sunday or holiday) in a studio or on a location within the studio zone, any time over 12 consecutive hours is calculated at four times the basic hourly rate. Related term: golden hours. If the employee is working on a bus-to location (to which transportation is provided from the studio to the location) or on a distant location, on a straight time day, the hours are calculated at two and one-half times the basic hourly rate after 14 consecutive hours have passed. On a double-time day, the rate is five times the basic hourly rate after 14 consecutive hours.

Go-Motion Trade name for a technique in figure animation utilizing a computerized, motion-control system to operate the precise, choreographed movements of a puppet or model miniature during the exposure of film frames. The incremental stop-action movements normally seen are significantly reduced or eliminated, resulting in more fluid "go" movements, with an appropriate degree of motion blur. In recognition of the technique's contribution to filmmaking, Dennis Muren and Stuart Ziff of Industrial Light and Magic, Inc., were honored by the Academy of Motion Picture Arts and Sciences with a Technical Achievement Award in the Scientific and Technical Awards category for "the development of a Motion Picture Figure Mover for animation photography."

good side Side or angle considered more photogenic or visually appealing than another, e.g., "Make sure you get my good side." Also called a best side. Some actors will insist upon being photgraphed from the side they consider their "good side."

good take Acceptable film or video shot or sound recording. Related term: good footage.

goose 1. (n.) Slang for the camera and sound equipment truck. 2. (v.). To increase or push up (e.g., "goose up" the sound).

Gotham New York City. Entertainment trade paper use.

gothic film Movie about romantic, mysterious or violent events taking place in and around a large, dark mansion, castle, cathedral or other large location. Usually a period, fantasy or horror movie.

Governors Ball 1. In the United States, the formal dinner given by the Academy of Motion Picture Arts and Sciences, following the presentation of the Academy Awards®, for the winners, nominees and presenters; named after the Academy's Board of Governors. A similar event, given by the Academy of Television Arts and Sciences, follows the nighttime Emmy Awards.

grader Lab technician responsible for determining the density of a negative. An experienced grader can do this by eye.

grading Act of determining and balancing the density of each negative frame before printing so the film will be uniform (bright or dark). This is done by a grader.

graduated filter Lens attachment allowing different parts of the same scene to be photographed with different filter densities. For example, a sky filter allows the sky to register more vividly without affecting the rest of the scene.

grand opera Opera on an epic scale, with a serious vocalized storyline and appropriate dramatic music and scenery.

G-rating 1. Rating issued in the United States by the Motion Picture Association of America (MPAA) for a film or video suitable for viewing by all ages. Full wording: "'G'—General Audiences. All Ages Admitted." Related terms: motion picture ratings board, rating. 2. Similar rating for television ("TV-G").

greasepaint Grease-formulated makeup available in a variety of colors; used for theatrical purposes, especially as a base makeup for the face. It is not water soluble and requires a cleansing liquid or cream for removal.

green print New positive print that has never been projected; or, it has not dried sufficiently for projection. Previously unprojected prints may need to be lubricated to prevent them from jamming in the projector.

green room Name for the waiting room of a television studio or stage theater. Also called a guest room or backstage room.

greenery Real and fake plants, trees, shrubs, flowers, leaves, branches and the like. Also called greens. Related terms: greenery department, greensperson, evergreen, set dressing.

greenery department Section of a film-TV studio where greenery is stored and maintained. Also called a greens department.

greenlight When a production is given the go-ahead from a studio.

greenscreen process Similar to the bluescreen process in visual-effects image compositing, except that a bright, nonglossy green color is used as the background or object-masking color; this could be because it is more appropriate or less conflicting than blue to achieve the desired effect. If green or blue cannot be used, orange is the next choice.

greenscreen shot Visual-effects shot using the greenscreen process.

greensman Individual responsible for dressing the set with plants and trees and for maintaining the greenery. For example, if a production is set in the Autumn, a greensman will bring in plants and trees with the appropriate fall colors. Related terms: greensperson, green man or nurseryman.

grey card/grey scale Standardized chart showing tonal gradations from white to grey to black. The card is photographed on the set and when the negative is processed, the resulting image is compared to the lab's grey card to check for the correct tonal values. Related terms: color bars, lily.

grid 1. Framework of metal support beams in the fly loft of a theater stage. Also called a gridiron. 2. Similar framework in the ceiling area of a TV studio where overhead lights are positioned. Related term: camera truss. 3. Pattern of evenly-spaced reference lines.

grip Crew member who provides general labor on the set (in the theater, the term would be stagehand). Grips work in various departments: lighting grips trim, diffuse and mould lights; construction grips build sets, backdrops, etc; dolly grips lay and move dolly tracks and push and pull the dolly, etc. Related terms: key grip, best boy, stagehand, rigger, roadie, scenery crew.

grip package Equipment required to adjust or manipulate lights and camera. The typical grip package consists of: apple boxes, packing quilts, sand bags, gloves, scrims, flags, various light stands, mechanic and carpenter tools, a 12' by 12' frame (with the same size silk and black cloth), a polecat, box of wedges, high rollers and various reflectors.

grip tape Another name for gaffer's, or duet, tape.

Griswold See machine splicer.

gross Total box office receipts a film has generated to date (as reported in the trade papers). In most distribution, financing and participation contracts, the term is defined for purposes of specific agreement and is used to mean film rentals (monies received by the distributor after the exhibitor has retained his percentage) and license fees other than box-office receipts.

gross deal Profit participation in film rentals, as opposed to net profit. These deals are usually reserved for the most powerful above-the-line personnel (e.g., actors, directors and/or producers). Profit participation in the movie industry is a complex area. Accounting methods used are sometimes criticized and the subject of litigation. Because profits, or lack of them, occur after a film is produced and released, a gross-point deal is one type of contract in the general category of back-end deals. Related terms: profit participation, net-profit deal, Hollywood bookkeeping.

gross point One percentage point of the gross income received from the sale or licensing of a product. One gross point is calculated by multiplying the monetary amount by .01. Related term: point.

group audition Audition in which three or more performers are seen at the same time, e.g., a dancer audition. Related terms: three-person audition, two-person audition.

guarantee 1. Negotiated term written into the contracts of, most typically, above-the-line personnel. for example, a director may have a contract stating that, after the first principal player is hired, he is assured of his entire salary whether or not the film is completed or even shot. 2. Written legal agreement between two or more entities, stating that an agreed-upon sum will be paid, either in full or at pre-arranged intervals and after specified conditions in the contract have been met. These guarantees are used in pre-sales, distribution agreements, etc., and can help raise production financing.

guest player Actor performing a prominent role in an episode of a television series, as opposed to being a regular player. Also called a guest actor, guest performer or guest star.

guest star 1. Individual who appears as a guest player on a television program. The term "guest star" or "special guest star" may be a negotiated on-screen credit title offered by the producers as an incentive or show of respect for the performer agreeing to appear on the show. In the case of a TV series, an actor may be a continuing cast member but receive billing as a "Guest Star," "Special Guest Star" or "Special Appearance By" even though the actor appears in every episode and the part lasts for the run of the series. Related terms: special guest star, guest player. 2. Any prominent guest actor or performer on a show.

guest voice Actor or celebrity performing a voice-acting role in an episode of a TV series. The animated television series, *The Simpsons* (1989 -), is known for its use of guest voices. Related term: voice cameo.

guide track Sound track recorded in sync; it is used only as a guide to enable the re-recording of the actual sound track under optimum conditions and is not intended for use in the final film.

guild Another name for a union. The term "guild" is used by labor organizations representing creative individuals in the entertainment and performing arts professions, such as actors, directors, scriptwriters, playwrights and composers.

guild card Another name for a union membership card.

guild member Card-carrying, dues-paying member of an industry union.

gun-catcher Production crew member who catches a firearm thrown off-camera by an on-camera character. In post-production, a foley sound effect is added to the soundtrack to make it seem as though the gun struck the ground.

gunfight scene Scene in which characters engage in a gun battle using conventional firearms or, as in the case of a science-fiction story, imaginary weapons based on technology. Physical, optical or computer-generated effects are used to show guns firing and hitting their targets. A firearm uses a blank cartridge for each shot fired; because staging a gunfight scene has inherent risk, all movements by actors and crew are thoroughly rehearsed ahead of time. Also called a gunfire scene, shooting scene or weapon-firing scene. Related terms: air ratchet, aspirin hit, blank cartridge, blood hit, bullet hit, capsule gun, detonation board, dummy cartridge, dummy firearm, dust hit, fast draw, full load, glass hit, half-load, jerk harness, prop gun, powder, quarter-load, safety harness, shoot, skill test, spark hit, special blood effects, Sweeney gun, weapons master.

GyroCam Camera mount gyroscopically stabilized; used for shooting from an aircraft, such as a helicopter. Manufactured and sold by Aerial Films of Morristown, New Jersey, in the United States.

hair in the gate Cameraman's jargon for any foreign particle or matter in the camera gate.

hairdresser Member of the crew skilled and licensed to cut, color and style the hair of actors on a production; may also be skilled with wigs, if necessary. The hairdresser typically provides all necessary equipment (brushes, hair spray, etc.) and receives a weekly rental (called box or kit rental) for use of this equipment.

hairpiece 1. Small wig used to cover a bald spot or an area of thinning hair. An actor who is losing his hair may opt to wear a hairpiece or he may be required to wear one to match the description of the character he is portraying. Also called a toupee, partial wig, wiglet or rug. Related term: wig. 2. Any supplementary amount of hair. Related term: fall.

hairstylist Individual who designs and consults on hairstyles. Many actors have their own hairstylists, whom they use on all of their films.

halation Any unwanted flare or halo appearing on the film; usually caused by light reflected onto the emulsion from the film base. Today, to counteract this, most film manufacturers put an antihalation coating on the film, which is then removed during processing.

half load Special effects term used to describe one-half of a particular amount of explosive material in a gun or exploding device.

half-apple box Apple box that is one-half the height of the standard version

used. Typical half-apple box sizes are 4" x 12" x 18", 4" x 12" x 20" and 4" x 14" x 24". Also called a half-apple or half-riser. Related terms: apple box, full apple box.

half-hour call Announcement made backstage that the performance will begin in 30 minutes. Related term: call.

half-hour series TV series having episodes that are 30 minutes in length (including commercials, promos, station or network identifications, etc.).

half-rate Half the usual rate for a particular service. Also called a half-fee. Related term: half-hour rate.

ham Actor known for showing off, either with exaggerated gestures or vocalizations; a show-off.

ham it up Expression meaning to overact or to overplay, e.g., to ham up a role.

hamster wheel Nickname for a cylindrical revolving stage. Related terms: squirrel cage, revolving stage.

hand cue Cue given in the form of a hand gesture. Related terms: break, cut, "Pick up the pace," stretch, "You're on."

hand prop Small items used by the actors in a scene (e.g., a book, a gun, a newspaper). These items are bought, made or rented by the property master.

hand puppet Small representation of a real or imaginary person or animal, operated by inserting the hand and fingers into its hollow cloth body and moving its mouth and hands in synchronization with the voice of its operator, another person or an off-stage or off-camera soundtrack. Some hand puppets also have one or both arms controlled outside the puppet's body by attached rods. Related terms: hand-and-rod puppet, puppet.

hand splicer See splicer.

hand-and-rod puppet Puppet controlled by one hand inserted into its back or head section (to operate the mouth and possibly eyes) and by one or more long, thin rods attached to its arms, usually at the wrists. If the puppet is complex, three or more individuals (puppeteers) may be required to operate it offstage or off-camera. The most famous hand-and-rod puppet is Kermit the Frog, star of television series and movies. Jim Henson Productions has since created a host of other Muppets.

hand-cranked Method by which motion picture cameras used to be operated during the silent film era. The cameraman had to approximate the correct speed (24 frames per second) to produce normal motion. With the advent of sound, when camera speed had to be regulated and standardized to keep picture and sound in sync, motor-driven cameras came into common use. However, the concept of cranking left its mark on modern terminology: the terms "overcrank" and "undercrank" are still used and refer to slow motion and accelerated motion cinematography.

handheld camera Camera hand-carried by the operator, as opposed to one mounted on a tripod. Related terms: Steadicam, body frame.

handheld shot Shot made with a camera being held in one or both hands, as opposed to a fixed mount. The end result is an unsteady shot.

handler See trainer, wrangler.

hanging miniature Model of a part of the set; it hangs five to ten feet in front of the camera to give the illusion of something larger in the back of the set.

hard copy Published words or images, printed on paper, as opposed to information stored in a computer or other device using a display screen, e.g., a hard copy of a script.

hard light Bright light producing high contrast and harsh shadows. Used to create certain effects, it is usually less flattering to actors. The opposite of soft or diffused light.

hardware film Movie featuring a lot of high-technology gadgets and machinery. Some or all of the hardware may be make-believe special-effects props. A hardware film is usually a science-fiction film, spy film, military film or computer-world thriller.

have your lines down Saying referring to the memorization of script lines, e.g., "Do you have your lines down yet?" The opposite of having one's lines down (memorized) is to have them "up" (in the air; not memorized). Related term: line.

hazard pay Monetary compensation for participating in dangerous work, such as stunt work or aerial filming (e.g., from an open helicopter doorway while in flight).

haze filter Filter that reduces cloudy or foggy effects by absorbing blue and ultraviolet light. (Haze is caused when light is scattered by dust and other particles.)

HDTV Abbreviation for high-definition television. System in which television images are recorded by a special camera for transmission or playback on home television sets with a wider screen, capable of displaying over 1,000 picture lines of color pixel information (exact number determined by the particular system). The digitally processed images seen are extremely detailed. The aspect ratio for the HDTV screen size is 16:9 (1.777:1). This wide-screen aspect ratio was developed in 1984 by American engineer Kerns H. Powers of Princeton, New Jersey. Also called high-def TV, high-definition video or high-resolution TV. Related terms: aspect ratio, ATV, broadcast quality.

head Beginning of a film or tape reel. Related term: tail.

head frame Individual frame at the opening of a film; it begins the pre-credits sequence or main title and opening credits sequence. Related term: running time.

head shot 1. Close-up or shot featuring the actor's head. 2. Slang for an actor's résumé/photograph.

header Cardboard strip, about 4" wide and either 15" or 18 1/4" long, on which are listed all the key elements making up a script.

headline 1. (v.) To be the star performer; to topline, star or receive top billing. 2. (n.) Title appearing in large, bold print on the page of a newspaper above an accompanying article; the large, front-page headline is also called a banner headline. Related term: "Sticks Nix Hick Pix."

headliner Individual having top billing; the star of the show. Also called a topliner. Related term: top actor.

head-on shot Camera shot in which the subject moves in a direct path toward the lens. Sometimes, an actor may be asked to walk straight to the camera and block the lens so an editing transition effect can be achieved. The opposite is a tail-away shot.

heads out (or heads up) Film wound so it is ready for projection, e.g., the first scenes are on the outside of the roll. Film wound with the end out is called tails up or tails out.

headset Compact microphone-and-earphone two-way communications (transceiver) device designed to be worn over the head or over one ear. It features a thin, swivel-boom microphone and operates as wireless or it plugs into a workstation. Wireless versions are worn by stage performers (with or without an earphone) and film and television production personnel. Production personnel on outdoor location also use hand-held walkie-talkies to communicate with each other. Related terms: control room, earphone, earprompter, walkie-talkie, wireless microphone.

hear When a sound is introduced in a film or television script, the word "hear" is capitalized or the name of the sound itself is capitalized, e.g., "We HEAR a train approaching" or "The doorbell RINGS." This is to clearly identify the sound for production and post-production purposes.

heavy Another name for a villain, e.g., "Remember the actor who played the heavy in that gangster film we saw?"

heckler Audience member who harasses an onstage performer.

helicopter camera operator One who is skilled and/or specially trained to shoot from a helicopter; he works closely with the helicopter pilot.

helicopter mount See 'copter mount, Tyler mount.

helicopter shot Camera shot taken from a helicopter in flight. The first helicopter shot used in a feature film took place on August 21, 1947, for RKO Pictures' *They Live By Night*, helmed by first-time director Nicholas Ray (1911-1979). The achievement was noted in an Associated Press report in the August 23, 1947, issue of the *New York Times*, which stated that (cameraman) Paul Ivano went aloft in a rented helicopter to film two chase sequences of escaped convicts running across a field. Director Ray commented that it saved the production $10,000 (1947 U.S. dollars). Related terms: helicopter unit, aerial shot, Flying-Cam, GyroCam, motioncam, SpaceCam.

helicopter unit Production unit responsible for filming from a helicopter in flight. Related terms: helicopter shot, hazard pay.

helmer Another name for a director. Entertainment trade paper use. Related term: production helmer.

Helmet Cam Type of helmet-mounted camera, as on a skier, skydiver or sports player. A manufacturer of Helmet Cams is Alan Gordon Enterprises, Inc., of Hollywood, California; Headtrip, Inc., also in the U.S., patented a hands-free recording system consisting of a helmet-mounted video camera and a belt-mounted recording unit, microphone and power supply housed in a protective pack. Related term: camera mount.

hero Leading character in a story who is on the side of good and decency; he battles the villain (also called the antagonist). "Hero" can refer to male or female; "heroine" is specifically female. Related terms: action hero, protagonist.

hi hat Small, low tripod or camera mount used to shoot from very low angles. Related terms: high hat, top hat

hiatus Scheduled break or interruption, as in the production of a television series from one season to the next. "Permanent hiatus" means cancellation. Related terms: indefinite hiatus, down time, pulled from the schedule.

hidden camera Camera position and style of shooting in which the camera is hidden from view. First used simultaneously in the United States and Russia in 1924, in two separate silent film projects. Most commonly used today in investigative news reporting, law enforcement and security applications, comedy bits and practical jokes, TV commercials and various types of research. Related term: microvideo camera.

hidden microphone Concealed microphone; it is either used for investigative reporting purposes or so it will not be visible in a camera shot.

hidden parachute In stunt work, a special parachute concealed beneath break-apart clothing; it is packed so that the entire apparatus spreads around the back and sides of the body, giving it a flattened appearance. It is worn by a stunt skydiver (doubling for an actor) who must jump, fall from or be pushed from an aircraft without a parachute; the character appears to fall hopelessly to the earth (and certain death). The stunt concludes when the skydiver removes the outer clothing and pulls the parachute's rip cord, thus activating the parachute. A stunt skydiver is also called a stunt parachutist.

high comedy 1. Comedy based on sophisticated concepts; high-quality humor. 2. Plentiful comedy; joke-filled.

high fall Stunt term indicating a jump or fall from an elevated place.

high key lighting Lighting design used in color photography producing an overall bright tone. High-level illumination emphasizes the lighter tones of the grey scale, resulting in a cheerier or brighter image.

high resolution Extremely detailed; highly defined; having a great number of tightly spaced horizontal lines of picture information, e.g., a high-resolution photograph or TV image. The opposite is low resolution. Related terms: resolution, broadcast quality, HDTV.

high-angle shot Camera shot that looks down on the subject or on the action, from high above it.

high-concept film Movie with a storyline that stands out above the majority of films; movie with an idea that is advanced or greater than usual. For example, *Speed* (1994), described as *"Die Hard* on a bus," was considered a high-concept film.

high-definition television See HDTV.

highlight To brighten or emphasize a specific object or area in a scene.

highlighting makeup Application of light-colored makeup to an actor's face to make specific areas more prominent or others less so. Related terms: makeup, shadowing makeup.

highroller Large, tall century stand.

high-speed camera Camera designed to film at a high rate of speed; when the processed film is projected at normal speed, a slow-motion effect is produced.

historical movie Film about a real-life, noteworthy event. For example, *Elizabeth* (1998) was an historically accurate depiction of Queen Elizabeth's reign. Related term: period film.

historical reenactment Re-creation of an event in history, e.g., a U.S. Civil War battle reenactment. Related terms: reenactment, reenactor.

hit A huge success.

"Hit the lights." A direction to turn on the lights. Also said: "Hit the juice." The opposite is, "Kill the lights" or "Cut the lights."

"Hit your mark." Direction from the director to a performer to step onto a predetermined floor mark during a performance so that camera focus or planned movements (such as dancing or stunt work) will be synchronized correctly. This process of staging a camera shot is called blocking. Also said: "Hit the mark." Related terms: on your mark, off your mark, "Into position."

"Hit your mark and say your lines." 1. Direction to move to the proper spot during a performance and say the proper lines of dialogue. 2. Saying by an actor to describe a performing situation that does not require a lot of creativity, e.g., "All I have to do is show up on time, hit my marks and say my lines."

Hitchcockian In the manner or style of the films, characters or directing techniques associated with director-producer Sir Alfred Hitchcock (1899-1980). Movies directed by Hitchcock include: *Lifeboat* (1943), *Notorious* (1946), *Dial M for Murder* (1954), *Rear Window* (1954), *To Catch a Thief* (1955), *Vertigo* (1958), *North by Northwest* (1959), *Psycho* (1960), *The Birds* (1963) and *Marnie* (1964).

hitcom Very successful sitcom. Entertainment trade paper use.

HMI light Abbreviation for Halogen Medium Iodide, a high-intensity arc lamp that emits a very bright, daylight-balanced light; it uses alternating current and is lightweight and portable.

hold 1. To keep an active camera angled on a subject. 2. To place an actor on hold, e.g., the actor may be used on a particular shooting day but this cannot be determined exactly so the actor's status is placed "on hold."

hold frame Animation term, equivalent to a live-action optical freeze frame.

holding fee Payment to a television commercial actor for exclusivity of his services on a commercial contract for one 13-week cycle; additional holding fees may be paid as each cycle expires and new ones begin. If a holding fee is not renewed, the actor is then free to advertise for a competing product. The holding fee gives the client the right to show the commercial for another 13-week cycle. Related term: on hold.

holdover engagement Extended booking (for a performer or film), usually because of high popularity (as reflected by ticket sales).

Hollywood (United States) 1. Unincorporated section of the City of Los Angeles, California, made famous because of its association with the production of motion pictures, the celebrities who once lived in the area and the "Hollywood" sign positioned on the mountainside overlooking the community. Today, film and television production is spread over the entire city of Los Angeles and its surrounding communities or, the Southern California area in general. Currently, Hollywood is officially called the Hollywood District of Los Angeles; the position of Mayor of Hollywood is an honorary title associated with the Hollywood Chamber of Commerce, which manages the Hollywood Walk of Fame. Related term: Tinseltown. 2. American film and television industry and community as a whole, or that part of it located in Southern California. 3. World of glamour and screen magic associated with making motion pictures anywhere. In this sense, Hollywood is

a nickname for international filmmaking and its celebrities. Related terms: Golden Age of Hollywood, Land of Make-Believe.

Hollywood A-list Literally or figuratively, a list of top film and TV celebrities.

Hollywood bookkeeping Accounting methods and practices used by, or associated with, Hollywood producers and distributors in the calculation of profits and losses for released films and videos. Oftentimes, these methods are called into question by profit participants.

Hollywood Foreign Press Association Organization of foreign entertainment correspondents and photographers based in the United States. Its membership, by invitation only, covers the entertainment world for newspapers, magazines, radio and television in the members' respective countries. Related terms: Cecil B. DeMille Award, Golden Globe Award.

Hollywood Reporter, The Los Angeles-based entertainment industry trade newspaper, published weekdays. Founded in 1930; the first issue was published on September 3, 1930. It is published by BPI Communications, Inc., which also publishes *Amusement Business, Back Stage, Back Stage West, Billboard* and other publications and directories. Internet address: http://www.hollywoodreporter.com.

Hollywood sign Famous landmark and symbol of the entertainment industry. The large metal sign—the most famous popular-culture sign in the world—spells out "Hollywood" in 50-foot-tall, white letters. The 450-foot-long sign is located on Mount Lee in the Hollywood Hills, at the northern boundary of the Hollywood district in Los Angeles. The original Hollywood sign was made of wood and was installed in 1923 as a real estate promotion; it read "Hollywoodland" before it was shortened in 1949, during a restoration project. In 1973, the sign was declared a historic cultural landmark by the City of Los Angeles. Over the years, deterioration and vandalism of the wood continued to take its toll; in 1978, a fund-raising effort by citizens (including many celebrities), brought about the installation of a replacement sign made of metal, which made its debut at night amid searchlights on November 11, 1978, on a nationally televised special. Due to continued vandalism and altering of its letters, it is now illegal to walk straight up to the sign. The Hollywood sign is managed by and is a registered trademark of the Hollywood Chamber of Commerce, which licenses its image to commercial users.

Hollywood Walk of Fame Specially designated sidewalk route on Hollywood Boulevard, Vine Street and the intersection's neighboring streets, where stars and noted individuals of film, television, radio and theater are honored. The celebrity's name appears in brass letters, along with a five-pointed star, embedded in terrazzo inside a brass-bordered square (the terrazzo inside each star is colored with a pink pigment to make it stand out from the surrounding gray); a symbol indicates in which area of the entertainment field the celebrity has made his mark. To be included on the Walk of Fame, a celebrity must be nominated through an application by an individual, group or company; a biography and photograph are required with the application. Awarding of the star is based upon a number of factors: professional achievement,

career longevity (five years or more) and contribution to the community. There is a fee of $7,500 U.S. dollars (subject to change), which covers the cost of the star, administration, installation, unveiling ceremony, crowd and traffic control during the ceremony and a commemorative plaque for the recipient featuring a full-color replica of the star. If the celebrity is living and in good health, he, she or it (the latter in the case of an animal, puppet or cartoon character and its creator) agrees to attend the outdoor ceremony. The Hollywood Walk of Fame was established in 1960 by Hollywood merchant Harry Sugarman and the Hollywood Chamber of Commerce; it was dedicated on November 23, 1960. In 1978, it was designated a historic cultural landmark by the City of Los Angeles. It is managed by the Hollywood Chamber of Commerce, which reviews, through its anonymous Walk of Fame Committee, the yearly list of candidates. Final selections for the 12 new stars dedicated throughout the year are made in June. Recipients of stars are allowed to select their sidewalk locations. The Chamber of Commerce maintains a recorded telephone announcement on upcoming new-star dedication ceremonies.

hologram 1. Three-dimensional picture recorded on a special transparent film by reflected laser light. When it is turned, it shows different angles of what was recorded. 2. Three-dimensional storage of information on holographic film or crystal. Related term: holostor.

holographic model 1. Hologram setup or exhibit. 2. Individual who poses for a hologram. Also called a holography model, hologram model, holographer's subject or 3D model.

holography The art, science or process of making holograms.

holostor (short for holographic data storage) Process of recording digitized text and picture information on a holographic recording medium, such as polymer film or a lithium niobate crystal.

holovideo (short for holographic video) Process of displaying three-dimensional, real-time holographic images on a video screen. Holovideo was first demonstrated on a two-inch square display (a real-time picture showing two holographic dots) in 1989, at the Massachusetts Institute of Technology's Media Laboratory in Cambridge, Massachusetts, in the United States. Also called video holography.

home video 1. Video produced for and sold or rented to consumers for play on their home video machines. For example, how-to videos and exercise videos. Related terms: made-for-homevideo, indie homevid company. 2. Any video sold or rented to consumers for playing on their home machines, including feature films released originally in the theater and later on video, or films made specifically for home video release; may also include DVD and laser disc versions. Also called a consumer video. Related terms: direct-to-video release, sell-through. 3. Home video industry, world, field or profession.

home video rights Various rights purchased or licensed from the copyright owner of a television series or special, feature film, news footage, play, dance performance, beauty contest, lecture, etc., so it can be sold in video format to consumers. Related term: right.

honeywagon Large, mobile location unit, with toilet facilities and dressing rooms; used by cast and crew members.

hood ride Stunt during which a stuntperson holds on to the hood of a moving vehicle while lying on it (typically, he is looking into the windshield). A roof ride involves a similar effect, except the vehicle's roof and windshield chrome or side edges are used as handholds. A lead actor may be required to perform parts of the stunt if close-up shots are needed. Related term: stunt driver.

hood roll Stunt during which a stuntperson jumps on the hood of a vehicle (stationary or moving) and, by means of a performed shoulder roll, exits to the other side.

hoofer Nickname for a dancer, e.g., tap dancer, chorus-line dancer or social dancer (if footwork is involved). Also called a footwork artist or fancy stepper.

hook Idea intended to catch and hold audience interest. Also called a teaser.

horse Editing room stand that holds film reels while the film feeds through the synchronizer or viewer.

horse opera Nickname for a Western movie that uses horses, especially to transport characters from one locale to another.

host 1. (n.) Onscreen, onstage or on-air individual who conducts the activities of a television, stage or radio program. The term "host" can refer to a male or female; a female also can be called a "hostess." Also called an emcee or master of ceremonies. Related terms: chat-show host, guest host, talk-show host, Oscar®-show host, hostess, disc jockey, moderator, ringmaster. 2. (v.) To serve as a host.

hot lights Heat caused by incandescent studio lighting. After a while, hot lights raise the temperature on a set, causing damage to makeup and hairstyling, as well as making a heavy garment or costume uncomfortable to wear. Related term: lighting.

hot prop 1. Prop in its place and ready for use. 2. Prop that has been heated, charged with electricity, loaded or made potentially explosive in any way. Related term: live prop.

hot session 1. Lively or productive photo, film, video, rehearsing, casting, dancing, music or negotiating session. 2. Session in which the working conditions are less favorable due to personal differences between two or more individuals who are present.

hot set 1. Production set that has been prepared for shooting; as such, it should not be entered or changed except by those authorized to do so.

hot splice Method of permanently joining two pieces of film, usually reserved for the original negative or for damaged release prints. The splice is made by overlapping a thin section of two pieces of film from which the emulsion has been scraped; the base of one piece is dissolved into the base of the second, making a chemical weld. The two pieces of film then become one. The alternate method is tape splicing, in which a piece of mylar tape joins the two pieces of film. This is not permanent and allows the film being edited to be spliced and unspliced as often as necessary. Since hot splicing requires the emulsion to be scraped off the areas being joined, at least one frame of film is lost in the process, whereas tape splicing allows frame-for-frame splicing. Related term: cement splice.

hot splicer Machine, used when making a hot splice, that controls the temperature of the cement, enabling it to dry rapidly.

hot spot Portion of the image on the film that is burnt out due to overlighting or insufficient use of gels on an area of the set.

house 1. Movie theater or playhouse. Related terms: opera house, bring down the house. 2. Audience, especially in a movie theater, playhouse, concert or lecture hall or nightclub. Related terms: full house, theater audience.

house left Left side or section of a stage, from the point of view of the audience; same as camera left, but different than stage left, which involves the performer's point of view. House left can also refer to the left side of the audience section.

house light Lighting unit positioned above the audience area in a theater or studio.

"House lights up, please." Direction requesting the overhead lighting in the audience area of a theater or studio be increased

house manager Another name for a theater manager.

house nut Term used in exhibition meaning the theater's expenses, or how much it costs a theater to operate on a weekly basis. (For example, in a 90/10 agreement, the distribution retains 90 percent of the revenues received by the theater after the house nut [expenses] has been paid.)

house record Unbeaten level of admission ticket sales for a day, week, etc., in a playhouse or movie theater. Also called a house box-office record.

house right Right side or section of a stage from the point of view of the audience; same as camera right but not the same as stage right. House right can also refer to the right side of the audience section.

house seat Audience seat in a theater reserved by the management for its own use or for use by the producer.

how-to video Another name for an instructional video.

Hydro Fire Highly flammable liquid used to produce a fire effect on the surface of water. Sold by Tri-Ess Sciences, Inc., of Burbank, California. Related terms: Aqua Fire, Fire Ribbon, fire effect.

hype 1. (n.) Exaggerated publicity or promotion. Also called artificial publicity, manufactured gossip or planned gossip. 2. (v.) To create such publicity or promotion.

hyphenate Individual who has more than one major function on a film. Woody Allen, Orson Welles, Charlie Chaplin, Buster Keaton, Barbra Streisand and Warren Beatty are some of the industry's most famous hyphenates (writer-producer-director-actor).

IATSE Abbreviation for International Alliance of Theatrical and Stage Employees.

idiot cards See cue cards.

illumination Any natural or artificial light source causing an image to be recorded on film.

illusionist Magician whose tricks are visually oriented (sleight of hand or specially designed equipment), as opposed to those of a mathematical nature (coin and card tricks). Some illusionists are part-magician, part-escape artist.

image Photographic reproduction on film. The final decision of what will appear in the frame (hence, the image recorded on film) is made by the director and usually after he consults with the director of photography.

IMAX HD (high definition) IMAX movie footage shot and projected at twice the normal rate (48 frames-per-second, as opposed to 24 fps); this increases picture quality and realism, especially the look of fast-motion images typically found in simulator rides.

IMAX Magic Carpet theater Special IMAX theater constructed with two projection systems and two giant curved screens, one of which is located under the transparent floor of the inclined seating section. Depending upon the film exhibited, the audience can experience such sensations as flying or weightlessness in the air, underwater or outer space.

IMAX Ridefilm theater Eighteen-passenger, compact simulator-ride theater with a projection screen that wraps around 180 degrees. It uses a VistaVision projection system with a fish-eye lens to project a 35mm film at 48 frames per second (eight sprocket holes per frame) as riders sit in an open, motion-base car powered by a patented, three-axis hydraulic system (up-down, side-side, front-back). Ridefilm was invented by special-effects pioneer Douglas Trumbull; he created the first capsule simulator ride in 1974. Trumbull's special-effects work can be seen in the films *2001: A Space Odyssey* (1968), *The Andromeda Strain* (1971), *Silent Running* (1971), which he wrote and directed, among others; "Back to the Future . . . The Ride," designed and directed for Universal Studios theme parks; "Secrets of the Luxor Pyramid," the first Ridefilm theater which opened at the Luxor Hotel and Casino in Las Vegas October 1993; and others. Trumbull is vice-chairman of the Toronto-based IMAX Corporation and also is president and CEO of Ridefilm Corporation, a subsidiary of IMAX, in South Lee, Massachusetts, in the United States. Related term: simulator ride.

IMAX Solido theater IMAX dome theater that exhibits 3D films; audience members wear battery-powered, liquid-crystal shutter glasses (IMAX Electronic 3D Glasses) to view the movie. Solido means "solid" and refers to the solid-like realism of the three-dimensional images.

IMAX theater Specially designed and constructed movie theater that exhibits films shot and projected on the patented, IMAX motion-picture camera and projector system; the curved screen is up to eight stories high. The audience seating section is steeply inclined to allow for a greater viewing experience. Movies shown in IMAX theaters are shot on 65mm, 15-perforation (15 sprocket holes on the sides of each frame) negative film and released to theaters on 70mm, 15-perforation film. The frame area on the film is unusual in that it is positioned lengthwise, resulting in a picture ten times larger than that found on standard 35mm, four-perforation motion-picture film (it is the largest film frame in motion picture history). The 70mm IMAX projection print contains no soundtracks; instead, synchronized sound is provided separately by multiple digital compact discs, 35mm six-track magnetic film or half-inch eight-track magnetic tape. The first IMAX movie premiered at the Fuji Pavilion at EXPO '70 in Osaka, Japan; in March, 1989, astronauts aboard the U.S. space shuttle Discovery used an IMAX camera to film images of the earth from orbit. IMAX theaters are independently owned and are found in museums, theme parks, stand-alone theaters and similar locations. The Oscar®-winning IMAX system was invented and is owned by the IMAX Corporation of Toronto, Ontario, Canada. IMAX is short for Image Max. Related terms: 65mm, 70mm, Estar.

IMAX 3D theater Standard IMAX curved-screen theater, but with a high-efficiency, metallic screen on which 3D or 2D films are exhibited.

For 3D films, audience members wear polarized glasses or electronic shutter glasses.

impersonator 1. Individual who imitates or poses as someone else. 2. Individual hired because of his resemblance to a celebrity or historical figure.

impressionist Stage comedian who does vocal and visual imitations of famous people, cartoon characters, or the like.

improv Short for improvisation.

improvisation Act of performing without preparation; the actors are given a situation and proceed to make up dialogue and action. Also called an improv or ad-libbed routine/sketch. Some comedy troupes, such as The Groundlings (Los Angeles) and Second City (Chicago) specialize in improvisation. Related terms: improvised play, ad-lib, interactive theater, play it by ear.

improvise 1. To create spontaneous action or dialogue, opposed to acting from scripted material. 2. To devise immediate, alternate plans to compensate for an unforeseeable production problem.

improvised play Play in which only the theme is established; the rest is made up by the actors as they go along. Related term: improvisation.

in character 1. In the identity or role of a character. 2. Appropriate for a character, e.g., "That accent is great and totally in character."

in development In the process of being developed; in a stage prior to pre-production. Related term: development.

in every shot Phrase used to describe an actor's large amount of onscreen time in a film.

in focus 1. Of a camera lens: properly focused; sharp. 2. Of the mind: concentrating; directing one's thoughts completely to the task being performed.

in frame In the shot area, e.g., being visible inside the rectangular boundaries of what a camera lens sees and shoots. "Into frame" means moving into this area. Both terms may appear capitalized in a script, e.g., "The snake slithers INTO FRAME."

in shot Same as being "in frame."

in sync 1. Abbreviation for synchronization, which means the sound corresponds to the picture and vice versa. Any other situation is considered out of sync. Related term: lip sync. 2. In a state of moving, operating, talking, etc., at the same time or rate of speed.

in the can 1. Film that has completed principal photography. 2. Scene that has been completed. 3. Exposed film ready to be shipped to the lab for processing.

in the spotlight 1. Illuminated by a spotlight beam. 2. Expression meaning to be in the public eye, e.g., being continuously noticed or brought to the public's attention by the news media. Variation: in the limelight. Related terms: spotlight, limelight.

"In three . . ." Direction, announcement or verbal cue to performers that an activity or performance will begin at the end of the countdown. Variations: "In ten . . ." "In five . . ." Related terms: "Stand by," "You're on!"

in turnaround Term describing a project that has been turned down by a studio or production company and the rights reverted back to the author for a period of time as stipulated in the original option agreement. If the author cannot place the project with another studio or company within that period of time, the rights go back to the studio holding the original option.

in-camera editing Transition effects, such as cuts and fades, which can be done inside a video camera; can also refer to shooting scripted shots in sequence.

incandescent light Warm, glowing light produced by a filament in the lightbulb, as opposed to cold and harsh fluorescent light. Not to be confused with a quartz/halogen light.

incident light Light falling directly onto a subject, as opposed to reflected light; it is measured by an incident light meter. Related term: exposure meter.

indefinite hiatus Shutdown (scheduled or nonscheduled) of production for a TV series; it may be temporary or permanent. Refers to a series with an uncertain future. Related term: hiatus.

independent casting director Casting director who is not a full-time employee of a studio, network or major production company.

independent contractor Individual rendering services but not as an employee on payroll. Related term: freelance.

independent distributor Film, television or video distribution company not associated with one of the major distributors. Related term: indie distrib.

independent feature Film made independently of a major studio; however, a major studio's distribution division may handle its release to theaters. Also called an independent feature film or independent film. Related term: independent production.

independent filmmaker Individual who makes films without a major studio's financial backing.

independent movie theater One not owned by a large movie-theater chain. Also called an owner-operated theater or mom-and-pop theater.

independent producer 1. Producer who raises the funds needed for a production from sources other than a major studio (such as, private or foreign investors, independent distributors or smaller studios). If the film wins an award at a prominent film festival, a major independent distributor or major studio's distribution division may handle the film's release. 2. Any producer who is not a studio employee. Some or all of the money needed to finance the production comes from a distribution agreement with a major independent distributor or major studio-distributor, which in turn receives a sizable share of the film's gross box-office receipts. Such an independent producer is usually well-known in the industry, with a successful track record. Related terms: indie producer, indie prod.

independent production 1. One not financed or controlled by a major studio, though it might be distributed by one. 2. Any film, video, etc., made by an independent producer or production company. Related terms: indie prod, independent feature.

independent production company Production company not associated with a major studio, except possibly as part of a distribution agreement. An independent video production company may use an outside distributor or may sell the finished product itself through an in-house distribution or mail-order division.

independent TV station Television station not affiliated with, or owned by, a network. Also called a nonaffiliated station or non-network station.

indie Short for independent. Entertainment trade paper use.

indie distrib Short for independent distributor. Entertainment trade paper use.

indie homevid company Short for independent home video production company. Entertainment trade paper use.

indie prod Short for independent producer or independent production. Entertainment trade paper use.

indie prod with a (five) pic pack Entertainment trade paper slang meaning an independent producer with, in this case, a deal to produce five films.

indigenous sound Naturally occurring sound; any sound belonging to or matching a location or subject currently being shown onscreen or onstage, e.g., the sound that matches waves crashing on a beach, traffic noises in a city or rain falling outdoors. Also called actual sound, direct sound or real sound. Related terms: background noises, live sound.

indoor location Location for still photo shoot, motion picture or television production situated inside a building or other structure. Also called an interior location.

indoor set Studio or location production set located indoors.

indoor theater 1. Theatrical performing hall located inside a building, as opposed to an outdoor theater. 2. Field or world of working in indoor theaters.

industrial use Exhibiting to management, employees or clients of one or more companies. Also called industrial exhibition.

industrial video Video by and for industry, e.g., the business and manufacturing worlds. Examples are training videos, safety videos, motivational videos and public relations videos.

infomercial Program-length TV commercial. Most infomercials fit into a 30-minute time slot and offer a single product or service for sale directly to viewers. The typical infomercial is shot on videotape and presented in the guise of a talk show or research report.

infotainment Informational entertainment on television, CD-ROMs or the Internet.

infrared Invisible light rays whose wavelengths are longer (and slower) than those of visible light. (If special filters and infrared film stock are used, objects may be photographed in darkness.)

ingenue 1. Innocent, somewhat inexperienced young woman. 2. Acting role of this type. Related terms: good girl, damsel-in-distress role. 3. Any young actress. 4. Member of a category of young actresses capable of playing ingenue and young leading women roles. Related terms: Leading Women/Ingenues, younger leading lady.

in-house Internally generated, distributed or associated, e.g., an in-house designer or in-house video.

inked a deal Signed a contract, e.g., "I just inked a deal for my next film." Entertainment trade paper use.

inkie Slang for incandescent lamp.

in-phase Situation in which two separate motors are running in sync.

insert Quick, close-up shot, cut into a sequence to explain some part of the action or to assist continuity (e.g., a hand circling an item in the want ads, a blood stain on the floor); it is shot separately and inserted into a scene during editing. Also called an insert shot.

insert car Another name for a camera car.

insert stage Sound stage where inserts are shot. There are firms specializing in this work, for feature films and television; their facilities come fully equipped and staffed for this specialized work.

insert title Another name for an intertitle.

instructional video Videorecorded presentation that provides training or how-to knowledge. Also called a how-to video, training video or educational video.

insurance 1. Financial protection against an unexpected problem that may prevent a production from continuing on schedule or at all. Insurance can be obtained to cover a variety of specific production areas, such as cast, equipment, film, video, props, wardrobe and animals. Related terms: cast insurance, medical checkup. 2. Any precautionary step taken.

insurance coverage Contractual guarantee against loss. As it is impossible to predict accurately the cost of insurance on a feature film due to so many variables, an average figure of between two and four percent of the total negative cost is entered in the production budget for insurance. This estimate depends on the shooting schedule, locations, cast members, types of coverage needed (e.g., negative, director, errors and omissions, worker's compensation, etc.).

insurance shot Additional shot of the same action, taken in case the previous one is not usable in the editing process during post-production. Also called an insurance take or cover shot.

Related terms: insurance take, cover shot.

INT Abbreviation for interior.

integral tripack Film with three layers of emulsion, each sensitive to one of the primary colors; used to produce separation negatives in color photography.

intensification Chemical process used to improve the quality of underexposed negatives by increasing the density and the contrast of the image. Related term: thin negative.

intensity Power of a light source, as measured in candelas or footcandles.

interactive movie Feature-length film exhibited in an interactive theater or on interactive television; in such a film, the audience votes on the film's plot points. Also called an intermovie or interfilm.

interactive reuse right Permission to reuse creative material, such as an actor's appearance and voice in a feature film, in an interactive form, e.g., in a videogame or computer CD-ROM game. Also called an interactive right, related terms: digital rights, right.

interactive television Television in which viewers, by using a push-button device or telephone call-in number, can interact with (respond to) what is being presented onscreen. Also called interactive TV.

interactive theater 1. Movie theater specially equipped to show interactive movies. Audience seats feature armrests or boxes with push-button switches so viewers can make choices by majority vote as to the outcome of events and questions displayed onscreen. 2. Play in which the audience is allowed to participate in the performance to some extent. Improvisation is often part of the experi-

ence. 3. World, field or profession of interactive theater.

interactive video User-responsive games, learning aids, etc., viewed on television or computer screens. Related terms: computer game, videogame.

intercut 1. (v.) To alternate shots; cut back and forth briefly between two different individuals in two different locations to give the effect of a single scene. For example: to intercut two people talking on the telephone. Intercutting is different than the effect achieved with cross-cutting. Related term: cross-cut. 2. (n.) An intercut; an alternating of shots in such a manner.

interest Fee charged when money is borrowed; generally based on a percentage of the total sum borrowed at a specific lending rate.

interior (abbreviated as INT) 1. Scenes situated inside a building or other structure and whose light is generally artificial, 2. Short for interior shot, e.g., "The director completed all the interiors for the film." Related term: exterior.

interior lighting Indoor artificial lighting.

interlock System allowing for picture and sound to be projected simultaneously in sync; usually used during editing, to screen a work print.

interlock motor See motor, Selsyn motor.

intermission Period serving as a pause between the acts of a stage show or screening of a lengthy theatrical film. Also called a break or interval.

intermittent movement Start/stop action allowing the film to advance at the speed of 24 frames per second while stopping momentarily so that each frame can be individually exposed or projected.

International Alliance of Theatrical Stage Employees and Moving Picture Machine Operators of the U.S and Canada (abbreviated as IATSE) Organization of local unions in the film, television and theater industries in the United States and Canada. The individual local unions include such professions as art directors, broadcast studio employees, cartoonists, costumers, craft service employees, distribution employees, editors, electrical technicians, first-aid employees, grips, hairstylists, illustrators, lab technicians, makeup artists, matte artists, painters, photographers, prop craftsmen, projectionists, publicists, scenic artists, script supervisors, set designers, sound technicians, story analysts, studio mechanics, studio teacher, welfare workers, ticket sellers and wardrobe attendants. The organization typically is referred to as the International Alliance of Theatrical Stage Employees. Founded in 1893 and based in New York City.

international film industry World business and service activities pertaining to the production and marketing of motion pictures. Also called the worldwide film industry, global film industry or international motion-picture industry.

internegative Negative made from the original negative using reversal film stock. This should not be confused with dupe negative, which is a negative made from an interpositive. Related terms: Interneg, color reversal internegative, CRI).

Internet movie Film presented to viewers on the Internet (they must access a particular site address). The first feature-length movie to be shown on the Internet was the fictional, live-action *Party Girl* (1995), starring Parker

Posey. It was produced by First Look Pictures and transmitted to a worldwide computer audience from Seattle, Washington, in the United States. Due to the limitations of the technology, the moving images were choppy and ostensibly in black and white, even though they were shot in full-motion color. The historic event took place on June 3, 1995 at 6 p.m., Pacific Standard Time (PST). *Party Girl* also had a limited release to theaters in selected major cities during that same summer and a subsequent video release. An Internet movie is also called a cyberspace movie, cybermovie, cyberflick or cyberpic.

interpositive (abbreviated as IP) Positive print made from the original negative; it is identified by its orange base and is typically denser than a positive release print; used to make dupe negatives and not for projection. Related term: CRI.

intertitle Any subtitle or caption appearing onscreen after the beginning titles and before the end titles. Also called an insert title.

"Into positions." Direction to performers to get to their marks because the performance (or filming of it) is about to begin. For some performers, the direction also means to assume a particular body pose while on their marks. Also said: "Get in position," "Get on your marks." Related terms: on your mark, "Hit your mark, "Places."

Introvision Relatively new, patented process for creating visual special effects which allows a matte shot to be seen while filming.

inverse square law Efficiency of illumination (or sound) is inversely proportional to the square of the distance between the subject and its light source (or microphone). For example, if a subject receives ten candelas of illumination when placed five feet away, it will only receive 2.5 candelas when placed ten feet away.

invisible splice Unseen splice between two pieces of film; it is invisible when printed. The occurrence results from use of the A and B rolling (negative cutting) technique.

IP Abbreviation for interpositive.

IPS Abbreviation for Inches Per Second. Unit of measure indicating the speed at which sound is being recorded. Seven and one half IPS (and higher) are used for high-fidelity music recording (30 IPS). Slower speeds are acceptable for recording speech.

iris 1. Set of thin blades in a camera, arranged in an overlapping circular pattern; when moved, they form an opening (aperture) through which light enters from the lens to strike the film or CCD imaging chip. Also called an iris diaphragm. Related terms: f-stop, diaphragm. 2. Similar mechanical device used to control the amount of light exiting a spotlight. Related terms: iris in, iris out.

iris flare spot Another name for a lens flare spot.

iris in 1. Editing transition effect in which a small spot, usually in the center of the screen, opens up steadily into an expanding circle to reveal a new picture. Also called an iris-in wipe or circle-in wipe. 2. In theater, to gradually open the iris on a spotlight to dramatically reveal someone or something onstage.

iris out 1. Opposite of an iris in; the picture area is removed by a contracting circle, leaving a new picture

onscreen. If done at the end of a film, the screen would be left black, followed by the rolling credits. Also called an iris-out wipe or circle-out wipe. 2. In theater, to gradually close the iris of a spotlight so as to end a scene or direct attention to a performer's upper body or face.

issue-oriented Film, TV or stage production featuring a storyline that deals with a particular social, medical, environmental or political issue. Related term: message movie.

Italo helmer Italian film director. Entertainment trade paper use.

IWERKS theater Any of various giant-screen, 3D and simulator-ride attraction theaters designed, constructed, licensed and sold by Iwerks Entertainment, Inc. of Burbank, California, in the United States. Iwerks, a major world supplier of such theaters, was founded in 1986 by two former Disney executives, Don Iwerks and Stan Kinsey. The company's attractions can be found at theme parks, casinos, resorts, fairs, museums, stand-alone theaters and the like. Some of its theater names are: IWERKS 360, IWERKS 870, IWERKS 1570, IWERKS 3D, IWERKS 70mm (five perforation), IWERKSphere, Cinema 180, Cinetropolis, ESI 3D, Freedom Six, Gemini Six, Imagine 360, Magnavision, Motion Master, Omnivision, Transporter Six, Turbo Ride, Video Turbo Ride and Virtual Adventures. Related term: simulator ride.

jelly See gel.

jenny Nickname for the generator used for power on location or for backup power in a studio.

jerk harness Protective, garment-like attachment worn underneath the clothing by a stuntperson in a scene requiring a character to be jerked or pulled off a motorcycle or horse or away from a spot on the ground; the stuntperson is pulled away by a flexible line connected to the harness. Also called a jerk vest or jerk suit. Related terms: air ratchet, pullback, safety harness.

Jetex White foaming agent mixed with water and used to create fake snow. Related term: snow effect.

jingle Musical sales pitch or slogan; a short song used in advertising. Before his pop songs made him famous, Barry Manilow was one of the industry's most successful jingle writers.

jokester Another name for a comedian or comic entertainer.

juice Nickname for electricity. Related term: "Hit the lights."

juicer Slang term for the crew's lamp operator (the individual who installs and activates the lighting units on the sets and "gives them the juice").

jump cut Cut between scenes or within a scene during which the action changes abruptly and unnaturally. A jump cut is achieved by removing a section of film in the middle of a shot or by moving the camera closer or farther away without changing the angle (or POV). Traditionally considered bad filmmaking, many filmmakers insert jump cuts intentionally for effect (e.g., Michaelangelo Antonioni's film *Blowup* [1966].) The technique was brought into vogue by France's Nouvelle Vague (New Wave) directors, most specifically Jean-Luc Godard.

junior spot Lighting unit having a 1,000- to 2,000-watt bulb. Also called a junior spotlight or junior.

keep takes Shots a director wants printed and kept as part of the overall footage selected for film editing. Also called print takes, circled takes, selected takes, hold takes, or OK takes. Related terms: take, "Print it."

keg Spotlight of 750 watts; it resembles a beer keg.

Kem Trade name for a product line of 16mm and 35mm flatbed editing machines.

key carpenter Lead carpenter on a production who is in charge of the construction crew skilled in using wood. Also called a head carpenter or first carpenter.

key cast member Important member of the performing cast; one of the leading principal performers (stars).

key grip Lead grip on a production who works directly with the gaffer and the director of photography and is in charge of the grips. Also called a head grip, first grip or first company grip.

key in To electronically composite one image with another. Related term: chroma key.

key light Greatest source of light on a subject or production set; it is the main light and the one on which all secondary lighting (fill-in, cross and back) is based. It also serves to set the style and mood of a scene.

key number Manufacturer's serial numbers printed on the edge of the film. Used by the negative cutter when conforming negative. They are also used by the editor when ordering effects; for example, he will use the key numbers when telling the optical house where to begin and end the fades and dissolves. (Key numbers should not be confused with code numbers.) Related term: edge number

key second A.D On a production utilizing more than one second assistant director, the key second is in charge of and coordinates the tasks of the other seconds; he or she reports to the first A.D. and to the production manager. Related term: second assistant director.

keyhole matte Light-blocking, black-colored shield for a camera's lens; its centered opening is in the shape of an old-fashioned keyhole. Shooting through it produces the effect of a character peeking into a closed room. Also called a keyhole mask. Related terms: matte, zone shot.

keystone Distorted shape of a projected image usually caused by tilting the projector or the screen. Sometimes, it can be caused by positioning the camera incorrectly.

kick light See kicker.

kicker Small light used for separating an object in the foreground from the background, e.g., outlining an actor's face or hair. Related term: slice light

kidpic Movie designed for children, e.g., an animated feature film or live-action comic-book movie. The plural is kidpix. Entertainment trade paper use.

kidvid Children's home video or television programming. Entertainment trade paper use.

kill To turn off, e.g., "kill the baby" is a request to turn off the small spotlight.

"Kill the lights." Direction to turn off the lights.

Kinescope Copy (in 16mm) of an early black-and-white television program; it was made by filming the live images directly off a TV screen. Before the use of videotape, this was the only way to preserve a copy of what was broadcast on television. Kinescope was the trade name for the cathode-ray (picture) tube on which the images were displayed. Also called a Kinescope recording or Kine.

kit rental See box rental.

Klieg light Type of powerful carbon-arc floodlight or searchlight; open-arc floodlights used in front of theaters for gala openings; also used during production for special lighting effects. Named after its inventors, brothers John Kliegl (1869-1959) and Anton Kliegl (1872-1927).

knife Thin, flat, pointed handheld weapon or instrument with a sharp-edged blade used for cutting or thrusting. In film, television and the theater, prop (rubber or plastic) knives or real knives are used in acting scenes. A real knife has its edge (or both edges for a double-edged blade) and tip dulled, except for close-up shots. Scenes involving one or more knives are carefully choreographed and rehearsed. The property master or weapons master is responsible for providing any knives, swords, spears, etc., used in the production. Related terms: blood knife, rubber knife, retractable, stage combat, sword-fight scene.

kook Metal, wooden or plastic screen with areas cut out in various shapes; when placed in front of a light source, they cast different shadows on an otherwise monotonous surface. Related terms: cookie, cucaloris, kukaloris.

kukaloris See kook.

L Television rating for a program containing language (words or phrases) that may be considered insulting, obscene, profane or vulgar. The rating may be accompanied by a numerical level, such as 1, 2, or 3. Related terms: "AL," rating.

labor of love Work done for reasons of interest and enjoyment and not for financial gain. Many times, independent films or theatrical plays are considered labors of love by their creators.

laboratory (abbreviated as lab) Location where exposed film is developed, processed and printed.

lacquer Protective coating on film that prevents abrasions to the surface.

Land of Make-Believe Nickname for Hollywood or Hollywood-style movie and television production anywhere. A similar nickname, Metropolis of Make-Believe, appears as an opening caption in the Oscar®-winning film *A Star Is Born* (1937).

landing a role Securing a role; getting an acting, dancing, singing, etc., part. Variations: landing a part, landing a guest spot.

lap dissolve See dissolve, a and b cutting.

laser light show Entertainment presentation, indoors in the dark or outdoors at night, featuring a variety of colorful, moving laser beams synchronized to music, action or narration. Pictures, such as animated characters or geometric patterns, formed by the beams (using programmed rotating mirrors) are aimed at a distant wall screen or pressurized water-mist screen. At Walt Disney World in Florida, the nighttime laser-light show in the Epcot theme park is staged by means of a computer-controlled system incorporating a brilliant blue-green argon laser and red krypton laser. Combining the two laser beams produces white light that can be passed through a vibrating crystal filter to selectively create any of up to 16 million colors for use in the show. Related term: screen.

laser scanner Motorized, optical electronic device used to scan a three-dimensional object (such as a model miniature or clay sculpture) or person (actor); this is the first step in the computer-generated (CG) effects process. The information is then converted to digital form in a computer where it is used to map out an onscreen, three-dimensional surface outline (wireframe) replica; this is colored, texturized (or made into a clear "liquid" state) and given movement. The process is harmless (done with eyes closed). It is done to achieve computer-generated character effects seen in science-fiction, fantasy and horror films, music videos, television commercials and computer software products. Related terms: 3D scanner, digital scanner, digital imaging, wireframe, CG actor, motion capture.

laser scanner operator Individual who operates the controls of a 3D laser scanner as it makes a circular scanning pass around an object or person.

laser scanning session Session in which a laser beam scans a three-dimensional surface, such as an actor's head and neck. The session takes place in a dimly lit room so extraneous light will not interfere with the results.

laserdisc Flat, circular plastic plate considerably larger than a videodisc with a durable, clear shiny surface, beneath which, on its laminated recording layer, is digitally encoded visual and audio information. The information is decoded by laser light as the disc spins in a laserdisc player. A laserdisc produces greater picture quality than a standard videotape recorder-playback system. Prerecorded movie laserdiscs are the predecessors of the newer, smaller-sized movie digital videodiscs. Related terms: videodisc, DVD.

last day of shooting Final scheduled day on which filming or video-recording occurs. Also called the wrap day.

last position 1. Point or location on a set or stage where one ends an activity, such as dancing, acting or stunt work. Also called the last mark or final mark. 2. Bodily position assumed last.

last shot Final camera shot of a motion picture or television shooting session.

last show of the series Final episode of a television series scheduled for broadcast. Episodes already shot may exist but they will not be telecast. Related terms: series finale, hiatus.

late call Scheduled time, late in the afternoon or night, that an actor or crew member is requested to report to the set.

late-night TV Any television programming shown between the hours of 11:00 p.m. and 5:00 a.m. (United States), e.g., a late-night talk show. The time period after 1:00 a.m. is also

called late-late night TV or overnight TV.

latensification Process of increasing the density of the latent image by exposing the undeveloped negative to extremely low light for a long period of time. The process increases shadow detail in cases of extreme underexposure.

latent image Image created chemically and present on exposed, unprocessed film.

lateral flicker Effect caused by panning too quickly.

latex Type of rubber used to create special makeup effects, such as aging skin, fake wounds, monster masks and facial-reshaping appliances. In the production process, latex is used in either an air-drying liquid form or mixed with other ingredients and baked in a mold to create a lightweight rubbery foam called foam latex. Foam latex can be used to create latex appliances, such as a nose, forehead or pointy ears; these glued to the actor's skin and blended in with makeup. Foam latex is also used to create model-miniature puppets for stop-motion animation filming. The foam-latex mixture is baked over a metal wire frame or more complex ball-joint frame in the desired shape. This frame, also called an armature, will give the finished stop-motion puppet internal structural support and movability that can be controlled during frame-by-frame shooting. The foam-latex puppet can also be cast hollow and life size so that it can be placed over a shell containing elaborate mechanical and electrical components, such as for eye, mouth and a variety of other muscular movements. The application and removal of latex makeup by a special-effects makeup artist may, depending on the amount and complexity, require the actor to sit for long periods of time in a makeup chair. Related terms: foam latex, latex appliance.

latex appliance Piece or segment of molded latex glued to an actor's skin to achieve a special makeup effect. More than one latex appliance, as is usually the case for advanced old age and monsters, may have to be attached to the skin in adjoining areas to produce the desired visual effect. In some applications, an inflatable rubber bladder is placed underneath the appliance; when filled with air by an offscreen makeup technician, the appliance expands outward or throbs, depending on the particular need. In order to have a latex appliance (especially an elaborate one) fit perfectly on the skin, the actor must visit the makeup artist's studio during preproduction to have a mold made of the area where the appliance(s) will be glued. This mold, which is done in halves or multisections if necessary, may be of a single body part (the face, ears or hands are common), a group of body parts or the entire front and back halves of the body from the neck down and ankles up. A replica of the body part is cast from this mold in a desired material (heated oil clay, plaster, etc.); clay then is used to sculpt the desired visual effect (for example, pointy tips sculpted onto left and right replicas of the actor's ears). A new mold is made from this sculpture, which is prepared for the liquid latex or foam-latex mixture to be poured in or over its inner surface. A shaped, hardened plaster core is suspended inside a foam-latex mold if the finished product is to have a hollow interior. Depending on the type of appliance and mold, the casting is produced through either an air-drying process or baking in a ventilated oven. When the latex appliance is removed from the mold, it is trimmed and painted as needed. The latex may also be colored using a variety of latex pigments before it is cast. Once the appliance (or assemblage of appliances) is attached to the actor using a prosthetic adhesive, colored theatrical makeup is used to blend the edges in with the surrounding skin. Some latex appliances, because of their small size or flat surface area, can be attached to any actor's face or body part. These are called generic or one-size-fits-all appliances and do not require an actor's participation in the mold-making process. Major awards, including the Oscar® and British Academy Award, are given for excellence and achievement in makeup design and application. A latex appliance is also called a makeup appliance, rubber appliance or makeup piece. Check out the award-winning makeup work by Rick Baker and David Leroy Anderson in *The Nutty Professor* (1996) for a superb example of this type of makeup application. Related terms: latex, foam latex, bladder-based makeup, special makeup effects, old-age makeup.

latitude 1. Range in which film can be overexposed or underexposed and still provide a satisfactory image. The faster the speed of the film (the higher the ASA), the greater the flexibility in choosing f-stops. 2. The range which an actor can play and still be credible.

laugh track Tape recording of various kinds of laughter; used on television shows when there is no live audience or when more laughter is needed. The laugh track can be modulated and controlled by a laugh track technician. Related term: canned laughter.

lavender Slang for fine grain master positive; used in making black-and-white prints and so called because of the former color of its base.

lay an egg To perform poorly; to receive mostly negative reviews or little or no applause or laughter (for a comedy) from an audience. Related terms: bomb, flop.

lay in Editing terminology meaning to cut into the film or to place in.

layout Detailed plan of action, movement, special effects, lights, etc., prepared prior to shooting (e.g., to lay out a scene).

LCD TV Abbreviation for liquid-crystal display television. Type of television set or monitor with a flat viewing screen whose individual pixels are electrically activated; appearing in front are liquid-crystal-filled cells with a red, green or blue color filter. Liquid crystal is a material that can both flow and have its molecules realigned when disrupted by electricity or heat; besides its use in television screens, liquid crystal is used in laptop computer screens, hand-held video-game screens and a variety of electronic instrument displays, including calculators. Related term: liquid-crystal display television.

lead 1. One of the principal acting or performing roles in a production. Related terms: romantic lead, starring role. 2. Actor who plays such a role.

lead man Individual in charge of the swing gang in the set dressing department; he is responsible to the set decorator. Related terms: property master, set decorator, set dresser, scenery crew.

leader Clear or black length of film, videotape or audiotape used for edit-ing or machine-feeding purposes; found at the beginning of the reel or used to connect shots in the work print. An Academy leader contains a countdown series of numbers and is used for film cuing purposes by a projectionist. A universal leader, which is more common today, contains words, numbers and symbols; it is used similarly to the Academy leader.

lead-in Anything that comes before something else. The most common use of "lead-in" is in the world of television, when network programming executives schedule shows and must consider the lead-ins to their successful or troubled programs.

Leading Men/Younger Leading Men Two casting category headings found in and comprising one volume of the *Academy Players Directory*. This volume lists adult and young adult male actors who play lead roles.

Leading Women/Ingenues Two casting category headings found in and comprising one volume of the *Academy Players Directory*. This volume lists adult and young adult actresses who play lead roles.

League of American Theatres and Producers (abbreviated as LATP) In the United States, an organization of stage-show producers and theater owners and operators. It represents producers and theaters in contract negotiations with labor unions and co-presents the Tony Awards with the American Theatre Wing. Founded in 1930 and based in New York City.

League of Resident Theatres (abbreviated as LORT) New York City-based organization whose members own and operate professional regional theaters. It works to promote the professional theater industry in the United States and also is involved in labor-management relations. Founded in 1965.

leak light Lighting that is unwanted or eliminated by using a gobo, barn doors or a mask.

leap To jump; go up suddenly, e.g., "The film's box-office revenue leaped in the second week." Entertainment trade paper use.

left by mutual agreement Public relations phrase used to describe an individual's departure from the project, e.g., "A spokesperson said the actor left the show by mutual agreement with the producers." It is a diplomatic response designed to keep the specific circumstances from becoming public knowledge.

legitimate actor/actress 1. Actor who performs on the stage. 2. Actor who works on a professional basis, belongs to one or more actor unions and has acted in at least one production. 3. Any actor who does not work in the adult video industry, also known as the video porn industry. Adult video actors who are hired for traditional acting jobs recognized by the unions are said to have "gone legit" or done a "legit film."

legitimate theater 1. World of commercially produced theatrical stage productions. 2. Any stage production other than vaudeville, burlesque or the like. 3. Originally, a term used to distinguish the professional New York theater world from traveling stage productions and nonprofessional shows. Also used to differentiate stage plays performed in traditional live theater from other types of plays performed in the new media of motion pictures and television (stage plays, as opposed to photoplays and teleplays). The stage was, and still is, referred to as the legitimate home of theater.

legs 1. Slang for tripod. 2. Film in release having enough popularity or drawing power to keep audiences walking into the theaters each week.

lens Optical device that focuses the image onto the film. There are three basic types of lenses (divided according to focal length): Normal, covering a medium field; wide angle, covering an extensive field of view but causing a reduction in the proportional size of images; and telephoto, covering a limited field but having magnifying properties. A zoom lens combines all three capabilities, although with a slight reduction in quality. Prime lenses have single capability but offer the best quality.

lens aberration Imperfection in a lens that causes a distorted image.

lens adapter Device attached to the front of the camera to handle other than normal lenses (e.g., 2X extender).

lens barrel Cylindrical tube that protects the parts of the lens apparatus.

lens coating See antihalation.

lens cover (aka lens cap) Plastic or metal cover that protects the lens when not in use.

lens elements Concave and convex pieces of precision ground glass which comprise a photographic lens.

lens flare Instance of excessive light entering a camera lens; it causes the affected part of the image to be weak or washed out by the light.

lens flare spot Reflection or "ghost image" of the hexagonally shaped diaphragm opening (aperture) appearing in the image area of the picture; it occurs as a result of shooting in the direction of a bright light source, such as the sun. Also called an iris flare spot or iris flare.

lens hood Round, oval, square or rectangular attachment for the front of a camera lens; it shades the lens from unwanted light. Also called a lens shade. Related terms: matte box, gobo.

lens speed Ability of a lens to admit light. The greater aperture size (and, conversely, the smaller f-stop number), the faster the lens. A fast lens can capture images in low light conditions.

lens turret Disc in front of the camera upon which are mounted several (usually four) lenses, any of which can be brought into position and locked into place by rotating the turret. (These are not used much today.)

lenser Nickname for a photographer, cinematographer or videographer. Entertainment trade paper use.

letterbox 1. (adj.) Short for letterbox format. 2. (v.) To place in letterbox format.

letterbox format Manner of displaying widescreen theatrical film images on non-widescreen television sets. To do this, the wide film image is reduced in size, but not in content, so the entire width fills the TV screen; black bars appear at the top and bottom of the image. A widescreen theatrical film that has a subsequent release on videocassette, DVD or laserdisc can retain its widescreen look if it is transferred in the letterbox format. Related terms: letterboxed movie, wide-screen format, pan and scan.

letterboxed movie Theatrical film transferred to home video and presented as it was exhibited in the theater—in the letterbox format so the entire widescreen film image is seen.

level 1. Position of the camera when it is perfectly parallel to the horizontal plane. 2. Decibel range for the best sound reproduction. 3. Sound volume.

level check Another name for a mike check.

library (film/music) 1. Location where films and stock footage are stored. Most film libraries are climate-controlled and have some editing capabilities. 2. Location where pre-recorded music is stored; listening facilities are typically available.

library shot Previously existing scene or shot taken from a film archive and used in the film in place of a scene that would be too expensive, too difficult or impossible to shoot again (e.g., aerial view of New York, sinking ship, battle scene, cars on the highway, street scenes from the 1940's, theater or nightclub marquees). Related terms: stock footage, stock shot.

libretto Script for an opera or operetta.

license 1. (n.) Official government permission to carry on an activity; sometimes, this activity may pose a risk to the public. Related terms: air cannon, car roll cannon, magician, mortar, powder, pyrotechnic operator, pyrotechnic supervisor, squib, weapons master. 2. Conditional right purchased from the owner of a property (movie, TV series, cartoon character, celebrity's likeness, sports team, entertainment event, etc.) allowing the purchaser to use the property in a specified commercial way for a stated length of time. Related terms: right, royalty.

lifecast 1. Three-dimensional casting of an actor's body part, e.g., a lifecast of the face, hand or torso; used in special makeup effects work. 2. Mold containing a real-life impression and into which the casting material is poured to produce a three-dimensional replica.

life-size cut-out Full-scale photographic image of a person, animal, etc., printed on heavy cardboard; it may include a minimal amount of the background image. Used as a point-of-purchase promotional display in a store or theater. Related terms: point-of-purchase display, stand-up, standee.

light box Box with a translucent top and a light inside; used for viewing film, transparencies, animation or film that is being edited.

light comedy Lighthearted, easygoing comedy; humor not based on a serious subject matter. 2. Movie containing light comedy. The opposite is black humor.

light cue Cue given or received in the form of a light switched on or off. Related terms: cue light, visual cue.

light meter Hand-held or in-camera instrument used to measure the available light on or the light reflected off a subject to determine the correct aperture (f-stop) and exposure-time (shutter-speed) settings. An incident light meter measures the light falling on a subject at the location while a reflected light meter, recognizable by the white plastic covering over its sensor cell, measures the light reflected off the subject. The reflected light reading is taken at the camera's location. High-quality, dual-purpose meters can take either reading. Also called an exposure meter. Related terms: exposure meter, reading.

lighting Illumination of a scene to achieve a desired mood or atmosphere in a photographic image. Lighting is the responsiblity of the director of photography, in consort with the director. Because lights are the most cumbersome of film equipment, setting the lighting can be difficult and time-consuming. There are four types of lighting that can be used: key lights, fill lights, backlights and kick lights. Key lights are the main source of lighting on the set, used to provide the principal illumination of the scene. Fill lights are used to complement and supplement the key lights, to lighten shadows or reduce contrast. Backlights are used to illuminate the background and to add depth to the image. Kickers (kick lights) outline hair and face and accent details.

lighting cameraman British term for director of photography.

lighting designer Another name for lighting director.

lighting director Individual responsible for designing the arrangement and type of lighting used on a production. Also called a lighting manager or lighting designer. Related term: gaffer.

lighting technician Individual who sets up, operates, takes down and maintains production lighting equipment. Also called a lighting engineer or lighting crew member. Related terms: best boy, gaffer.

lily Set of color bars and/or grey scale that is shot at the beginning or end of a film roll to assist the lab in checking color accuracy and tonal values.

limbo 1. Background or entire production set with no apparent edges or boundaries; it appears to stretch into infinity without suggesting a specific location. Also called a limbo background, limbo set, or black (white, gray, etc.) limbo. Related terms: cameo lighting, cyclorama, seamless paper. 2. Project with no discernible future, e.g., "The studio put the project in turnaround and it's been in limbo ever since."

limelight 1. Another name for a spotlight. 2. Early type of theatrical lamp that produced light by burning a quantity of lime (calcium oxide). 3. Attention focused on an individual or subject, as by a figurative limelight, e.g., "He loved being in the limelight; that's why he came out of retirement." Related term: in the spotlight.

limited exclusivity Exclusivity applying only to certain areas of marketing or work responsibilities and for a specified length of time. Related term: exclusivity.

limited release Film shown in a small, specific area for the purpose of finding an audience or gauging audience reaction. If a film is known to have limited appeal or a limited audience (e.g., most foreign films, art films) or limited resources, it would be distributed in limited release to lessen the risk of financial loss.

limited run Less than a full run; having a specified number of showings (rather than an open-ended run).

limited-run series TV series that has been scheduled to air for less than a full season. Also called a limited series. Related term: summer series.

line 1. Word, phrase or sentence of speech, as from a script for a commercial, television series, motion picture or stage play. For contract purposes, a script line may be defined as containing ten words or less (a number agreed upon in a labor-management industry contract). Related terms: script line, memorization of script lines, curtain line, have your lines down, "It's your line," "Line," one-liner, punchline, "That's my line," "What's my line?" dialogue, lyrics, tag, under-five. 2. Short, straight mark on

a floor surface indicating a performing location. Related terms: center line, curtain line, plaster line. 3. Electron-beam scanning line inside the vacuum tube of a television set. In the NTSC system used in the United States, Canada, Japan and elsewhere, it takes 525 horizontal scanning lines to form a complete picture every 1/30th of a second. Related term: broadcast quality. 4. Eye line or sight line. 5. Breakaway line or trick line. 6. Log line. 7. Above-the-line or below-the-line. 8. Bottom line.

"Line." Request from an actor onstage during a rehearsal to an individual offstage (a prompter or script person) for the next line of dialogue. During an actual live stage performance, a nonverbal method may be used (it may be as simple as the actor hesitating too long). Related term: "What's my line?"

line producer Supervisor of above-the-line and below-the-line elements during production.; the individual who keeps track of budgetary line expenditures. (The production manager reports to the line producer on below-the-line matters.) Related term: production manager.

line reading Oral interpretation by an actor of one or more lines from a script. Related term: script reading.

linear editing Video editing using standard videotape recording and playback equipment connected to a video mixer and viewing monitor, as opposed to nonlinear (computer) editing. Related term: off-line editing.

liner notes Explanatory text on the cover or insert booklet of a music CD, DVD, audiocassette box, phonograph album or other recording container or sleeve.

lineup 1. Any arrangement of items, e.g., performers, animals, television shows.

lineup sheet Any schedule or chart indicating an arrangement of performers, objects, shows, etc.

lining up a shot Positioning a camera at the proper angle and distance so its line of sight will photograph or record the desired action or subject. Related term: blocking a shot.

lip sync To synchronize one's lip movements with the sound playback of recorded singing or speaking.

liquid gate Procedure, performed by an optical house, for minimizing abrasions and scratches on film while it is being printed. Related terms: wet gate, submerged printing.

liquid-crystal display television Flat-screen television set or monitor (as on a computer or video camera) using liquid-crystal imaging technology. The screen on such a TV set or monitor has hundreds of thousands of tiny liquid-crystal-filled cells or pixels (depending on its size), each with attached positive and negative electrodes and a colored red, green or blue filter. There is no vacuum tube or electron beam scanning to produce a picture. Related terms: LCD TV, television set.

lit Short for literary, e.g., a lit agent or lit property. Entertainment trade paper use.

Little People Individuals of a small size; dwarfs and midgets. Such actors are listed in the *Academy Players Directory* in the United States. One talent agency representing a number of prominent little people actors is the Coralie Jr. Agency of North Hollywood, California. An organization representing the interests of little people is Little People of America,

founded by Billy Barty in 1957, and based in Dallas, Texas. Related terms: dwarf actor, midget actor.

live action Real actors filmed on sets or at actual locations, as opposed to animation or special effects made to look like real action.

live action-animation Combining live actors onscreen with animated characters. *Space Jam* (1996) is an excellent example of a live action-animation film.

live audition In-person tryout for a part in front of individual(s) empowered to make casting decisions, as opposed to being auditioned by submitting a video, audiotape or disc to be viewed or listened to at a later time.

live broadcast Broadcast at or near the moment a performance or event occurs. A slight time delay (a fraction of a second or seconds) may occur before the TV signal reaches home viewing sets because of a national or international satellite relay or other transmission equipment. A live signal may also be tape-delayed slightly for security or censoring purposes. Related terms: live feed, live hookup, live via satellite, live television booking, tape delay.

live cablecast Live program airing on cable television.

live feed Transmission originating from a source live. Related terms: network feed, satellite-fed, telephone-line-fed.

live hookup Connection between two or more locations enabling a live broadcast to occur.

live mike Functioning microphone; one that has been activated and is picking up and transmitting sound, as opposed to a dead mike (or one that has been turned off). Also called a live microphone. Related term: open mike.

live music Music performed at the time of presentation, as opposed to recorded music.

live prop 1. Prop that is real or alive, e.g., a plant or live snake. Also called a living prop. 2. Prop that is electrically charged, loaded or potentially explosive, e.g., "The lamp and the television set are live props but the telephone isn't." Related term: hot prop.

live sound Any type of sound, including background noise, voices and music from instruments, that is recorded live as it is created during shooting. Live sound is indigenous sound, but this may also be any sound effect added during post-production to match what is seen on the screen, e.g., the clopping of a horse's hooves as it walks across the screen; this sound would be too difficult to record live during the actual shooting so it is added to the soundtrack later. Related terms: live recording, wild sound.

live theater Theatrical productions performed live in front of an audience.

live via satellite Broadcast that receives a live feed from a space-based satellite. Related terms: satellite-fed, live broadcast.

live-action model Individual whose scripted movements in a studio serve as the basis for animation artwork or stop-motion model figures. Related terms: animator's live-action model, live-action reference, artists' model.

live-action reference Using frame-by-frame images of an actor, model or animal (videorecorded or filmed) performing scripted movements as the basis and inspiration for making true-to-life, hand-drawn or computer-generated animation drawings.

Related terms: live-action model, motion capture.

live-on-tape Television program, such as a talk show, that is recorded live on videotape from start to finish to fit into a designated time slot of 30, 60, 90 or 120 minutes; the only studio interruptions are for timed commercial breaks and local station messages. Since it is not a live telecast, there is more control over the content of the show which can be aired the same day, the next day, the following week or month or rerun any number of times. Also called a program that is "taped live" or a program that is "recorded live before a studio audience." Related term: tape delay.

living allowance Fixed amount of money paid during overnight location shooting, in lieu of the production company's direct payment for that employee's living expenses. Related term: per diem.

load To put film in the camera (or magazine) before shooting.

loader 1. Individual responsible for loading, unloading and storing film on the production. On most productions, this job belongs to the assistant camera operator. 2. Union worker who loads and unloads production equipment trucks.

loading room Small darkroom on a set or in a vehicle, used for loading and unloading camera magazines.

lobby card Publicity photo still from a movie; it is printed on heavy card stock measuring 11" x 14" and is intended to be framed and put on display in a movie theater's lobby.

local location Any spot within a 30-mile radius of the union agreed-upon center of town where shooting takes place; or, any shooting location where cast and crew do not have to spend the night. In Los Angeles, it is usually 30 miles from the intersection of La Cienega and Beverly Boulevard; in Manhattan, a "local location" is defined as any spot between 125th Street and the Battery (the southern tip of Manhattan). Related term: studio zone.

local media Regional or city newspapers, magazines and television stations. The opposite is mass media.

local spot Television or radio commercial produced for a local advertiser and audience. Also called a local commercial.

local TV Television programming that originates from a nearby region, as opposed to programming that originates on a national level.

location Any place away from the studio that is used for shooting. Location shooting provides special problems for production managers who must arrange for food, shelter, toilet facilities, transportation to and from the location for cast and crew, plus generators and other special equipment. "Local locations" are defined as being within a 30-mile radius of a union-defined center of town; cast and crew will usually have a "Report To Location" call and will return home that night. Distant or overnight locations are defined as those places farther away from the 30-mile radius, where cast and crew are obliged to stay overnight. When a film is shot on location, production usually occurs on a six-day-a-week schedule.

location agreement Contract between the producer and owner of a building or tract of land giving the producer the right to use and depict said location on screen.

location bus Transport vehicle for cast and crew. Also called a location van. Related term: location vehicle.

location casting Selection and booking of performers for a production on location. Also called on-site casting, local casting or remote casting.

location dressing room Room or area used for dressing or costuming while on location. It may be formal or informal, e.g., hotel or motel room, motor home, trailer, tent or back of a van. Related terms: dressing room, honeywagon, star's motor home, star's trailer.

location fee Compensation paid for the use of a site and facilities when shooting a motion picture or television show.

location lighting Portable lighting equipment used on a location, as opposed to studio lighting.

location manager Individual who finds the locations needed in the script; evaluates their suitability; takes photographs of the potential sites for approval by the director and production designer; develops a budget for all locations. Once a location site is approved, the location manager arranges for permission to shoot there and negotiates the terms for using the site. The location manager is then responsible for organizing all details relating to that location, e.g., permits, parking, catering, police, firemen, insurance.

location movie Theatrical film or video shot entirely (or mostly) on location.

location scout Individual, such as a location manager, responsible for finding, traveling to and reviewing locations, local services, etc., for the production; the location scout also seeks and obtains permission for use of the suitable location(s). National, state, provincial, county and local city governments may have agencies, bureaus or commissions that assist in this task. Related terms: film and television commission, state film and TV commission, Location Expo, snow search.

location set Production set not physically located on a studio lot.

location shooting Filming, videorecording or taking still photographs at a non-studio site. Also called a location shoot.

location sound Sound recorded while shooting on location.

location team Group of individuals working on a location production. Also called the location crew, location unit, location family, remote team, remote crew or remote unit.

location vehicle Any of various transport, storage, shelter or service trucks, vans, buses, motor homes, limousines, cars or trailers used during location work. Related terms: camera car, honeywagon, limo, location bus, mobile production unit, picture car, star's motorhome, star's trailer, transportation captain.

location work Production activities that take place at a site other than at a motion picture, television or photographic studio. It may be the actual script location (a New York City side street, as an example) or a similar one (a side street in a different city) with re-created elements. Also called on-location work, on-site work, non-studio work or remote work. Related term: clean-up.

locked Held or secured in place; fixed, e.g., a locked camera.

locked picture Film on which editing is complete; no further changes are planned or desired.

log line One-sentence description or summary of the storyline of a script, film, TV program, play or other production. If story related, it is also called a plot line or plot description.

London Theatre District The West End area of London in which many large and prestigious playhouses are located. Also called the West End Theatre District or Theatreland. Related term: fringe theatre.

long focus lens Lens with a focal length longer than that of a normal lens. Related term: telephoto lens.

long shot (abbreviated as LS) Wide shot of the principal subject. The camera is positioned far enough away to identify the subject in its setting but not to see any great amount of detail. Long shots are used mainly for establishing and master shots.

long-form television Television program over one hour in length, e.g., telefilm or miniseries. One such program may be referred to as a "long-form."

lookalike talent Individual who physically resembles a well-known person and, on that basis, is hired to perform. Related terms: celebrity lookalike, impersonator, double.

loop A length of film or audiotape that is spliced end to end so that it can be machine-played repetitively. In a special sound studio, an actor or voiceover artist would watch a "looped" scene on a screen and, using a microphone and single or dual headphones that are worn on the head or held close to one ear, respeak or resing those words or lyrics that need to be improved or changed. This process is called looping or dubbing. Another way is through the use of an automatic dialogue replacement system (ADR). In this more advanced and popular system, the picture and soundtrack of the scene in question are played forward at normal speed without the use of a physical loop connection. For each new try at recording, the picture and track are rewound at high speed to the beginning of the scene and then played forward again at normal speed. Related terms: ADR, dubbing, scratch track.

loose adaptation Script and its resulting production that are loosely based on another work. Characters, locations and dialogue may have been changed, but the basic story is similar enough to be recognized. The opposite is a faithful adaptation.

Los Angeles International Film Festival Film festival held annually every year in Los Angeles, California, featuring seminars, tributes, award presentations and screenings of films from around the world. Also called the American Film Institute/Los Angeles International Film Festival or AFI/L.A. Film Fest.

lose Slang for get rid of, as in, "Let's lose that extra lamp on the set." Related term: eighty-six.

losing the light Gradually losing the natural sunlight required for outdoor daylight photography or filming; another way of saying that sunset, dusk or twilight is approaching, the sun is going down for the day, or a cloud is moving overhead.

lost episode 1. Unaired episode of a canceled or old TV series. Related terms: last show of the series, bonus classic episode. 2. Script for a TV series episode that was never shot.

lot Area comprising a production studio; it may include office buildings, sound stages, dressing rooms, etc., and is usually protected by guards at

the front gate who regulate entry of non-employees. Related terms: studio, back lot, drive on, gate pass.

loupe Type of pocket-sized magnifying glass used to examine such items as print photographs, photo slides, graphic artwork and precious jewelry. A base magnifier also may be used for these purposes.

low angle shot Shot taken with the camera close to the ground and looking up at the subject.

low comedy Comedy based on unsophisticated concepts; low-brow comedy; low-quality humor.

low key Scene lit at the lower end of the grey scale; it uses dim illumination to produce many shadows.

low resolution Inadequately detailed; poorly defined; lacking a sufficient number of lines of picture element information to offer a sharp image, e.g., a low-resolution photograph or video image.

low-budget film 1. Movie having a low budget. The actual cost of a low-budget film is relative to current movie industry production trends and is subject to change on a yearly basis as the budgets (which include actors' salaries) for medium- and big-budget films set new records. The term "low budget" can refer to any film costing a few hundred to a few million dollars (U.S.). Also called a low-budget movie or low-budget pic. Related term: B-movie. 2. Movie having a budget that falls within a cost range set by a union. In the United States, the Screen Actors Guild determines the amount for low-budget feature status.

LS Abbreviation for long shot.

luminaire Self-contained light; it comes complete with lamp, housing and stand.

lux Unit of illumination on a surface used to indicate a video camera's sensitivity to light. The lower the lux rating, the less light is needed to adequately record a scene. One lux is equivalent to the level of brightness seen on the surface of a white piece of paper held one meter (39.37 inches) from a standard candle flame in a darkened room. In 1996, the BIA Standard (EIA-639) was introduced by the Electronic Industries Association and adopted by international manufacturers as a uniform method for measuring lux ratings for video cameras. The rating procedure involves aiming a newly manufactured video camera at various test charts in a laboratory setting and taking readings according to the protocol established by the Standard. Before 1996, there was no industrywide standard for video camera lux ratings. Related term: EIA Standard.

lyricist Individual who writes the words for a song. Related terms: songwriter, book.

lyrics Words of a song; a single word, phrase or sentence may also be called a lyric; a line from a song is a lyric that has been excerpted for speaking purposes.

M Rating that means viewing is restricted to or intended for mature audiences only (adults). Related terms: TV-MA, rating.

M&E track Abbreviation for music and effects track. Sound track containing everything but the dialogue. It is particularly useful when doing foreign language versions because new dialogue can be recorded without interfering with the music or sound effects.

machine splicer Splicer operated with the hands and feet; used for cutting the negative. Griswold is the brand name machine splicer most commonly used. Related term: splicer.

macro lens Camera lens with the ability to focus on small objects (e.g., coins, stamps, insects, fingerprints) or on the details of larger objects (e.g., engraving on paper currency, brush strokes on a painting).

made-for-cable Program produced originally for airing on a cable network or station.

made-for-home video Video program produced specifically for consumers to purchase or rent, for example, exercise and how-to videos and low-budget video movies. Related term: indie homevid company.

made-for-TV movie Film produced for airing on television. Later, it may have a domestic video or foreign theatrical release. Also called a movie for television, TV movie, telefilm or telepic.

maestro Master; an individual skilled and accomplished in a particular field.

Most often applied to a music conductor or composer.

mag print Release print containing both magnetic and optical sound. Related term: optical print.

magazine 1. Film container or cassette fitting on the camera with two lightproof compartments, one for unexposed film and one for film that has already been exposed. Most magazines can hold up to 2,000 feet of film and are easily loadable into the camera (by changing magazines) in broad daylight. The magazine itself must be loaded in a darkroom or changing bag. 2. Rectangular or circular container holding live or blank ammunition for a gun.

magic hour Time between sundown and darkness, when the light is very warm, the sky is a magical, deep blue and shadows are long; also called twilight. An example of scenes shot at magic hour is Terrence Malick's film, *Days of Heaven* (1978).

magic of television Technological wonder of how television works, e.g., "Through the magic of television, we now take you live to the North Pole for this report."

magnetic film (aka mag film) Perforated film base, the same size as motion picture film, coated with iron oxide instead of light-sensitive emulsion; used for recording sound. Magnetic film is used for editing sound, not production sound, because the perforations allow synchronization with the picture track.

magnetic recording Sound recorded on magnetic tape, synchronized with motion picture film; it later is transferred to mag film for editing, then, after the final mix is complete, is transferred back to film on an optical track.

magnetic soundtrack Magnetic-particle stripe printed next to the image area on motion picture film; it is used to record and play back the film's dialogue, music and sound effects, either on separate soundtrack stripes or mixed together. Related term: soundtrack.

magnetic stripe Coating of ferro-magnetic iron oxide running along the edge of perforated 70mm Dolby film, onto which sound is recorded.

magnetic tape High quality polyester or mylar-based tape coated with a substance containing iron oxide; used for recording sound or for recording sound and picture on videotape. Professional size is 1/4" and generally runs between 7-1/2 and 15 fps for high-quality recording, which is five times faster than magnetic tape used for home recordings.

main title Although specifically referring to the title card containing the name of the film, the main title more generally refers to all credits appearing at the beginning of the film. Under terms of the DGA contract, the director's credit is the last to appear before the beginning of the film.

main title theme Theme music or theme song with the same name as the title of the production.

major sponsor Sponsor who purchases a great deal of advertising time or provides a large amount of funding capital. Also called a major backer or major funding source.

majors Film industry's largest film producer-distributors. Entertainment trade paper use. Related term: mini-majors.

make an entrance To enter a room or stage in such a way that everyone takes notice.

makeup Cream, powder, mascara, eyeliner, etc., applied to the face, and sometimes the body, of an actor or extra. Makeup can enhance the features of the actor; create an effect (e.g., old age) or illusion; cover a blemish or scar (or create a blemish or scar or wound); or transform the actor into a different person altogether (such as the makeup applied to the actors portraying simians in the original *Planet of the Apes* [1968]). Sometimes elaborate makeup will require many hours to apply (e.g., Robin Williams in *Mrs. Doubtfire* [1993]), resulting in an exceptionally early makeup call.

makeup appliance Any type of latex appliance used to change an actor's appearance. Related term: special makeup effects.

makeup artist Member of the production crew skilled (and usually licensed) in applying makeup on the actors; however, the makeup artist may apply makeup only from the top of the head to the breast bone and from the elbow to the fingertips. (A body makeup artist applies makeup to any other parts of the actor's body.) Related term: special effects.

makeup bib Loose, protective covering for the chest and shoulders of an individual about to have makeup applied. Related term: smock.

makeup call Time when the actor must report to the set for his makeup application and still be ready on the set for the first scene. The makeup call is determined by counting backwards from the time the actor will be needed on the set (the call time). The time required for makeup application can be anywhere from 15 minutes to seven hours, as was the case for Eddie Murphy in *The Nutty Professor* (1996). For example, if Murphy had an 8:30 a.m. call, his makeup call would have been 1:30 or 2:30 a.m.

makeup department Section of a production house, studio or theater responsible for the design, construction and application of makeup on actors, dancers, newspeople, show guests and others who appear on camera or onstage.

makeup room Room in a TV or film studio where performers go to have makeup applied. For film productions, it is often a trailer parked outside the sound stage or shooting location. Related term: dressing room.

makeup test 1. Trial effort of a particular style of makeup or makeup effect, done prior to a performance. One or more reference photographs typically are taken of the result.

manager Individual who, depending on the particular field, supervises, directs or guides an administrative department, work activities, one or more careers or money matters. Related terms: business manager, children's manager, location manager, personal manager, production manager, road manager, stage manager, theater manager.

manager's fee Payment to a manager by a client for managerial services provided. Also called a manager's percentage of client's earnings, manager's commission or manager's cut.

Manhattan (New York City) Island and one of the five boroughs of New York City (Manhattan, Bronx, Queens, Brooklyn, and Staten Island), located on the upper west side of the city. Manhattan is also commonly referred to as New York. New York City, with its five boroughs, is also called New York, Greater New York and the City of New York.

man-on-the-street interview News, market research or comedy-sketch interview in which a randomly chosen or targeted pedestrian is interviewed on the sidewalk of a public street.

maquette Three-dimensional, small-scale model of a character or set in an animated film; used as a visual reference by animators during the production process.

marionette Type of puppet manipulated by strings from above to control its body movements.

mark Small pieces of masking tape (or chalk marks) placed on the floor during blocking to identify certain positions, e.g., where the camera should stop dollying, where the actor should stop his movement so the scene will be shot in proper focus. In a scene where many actors are in motion, each actor is assigned a different color tape (chalk) to avoid confusion. Before the scene is shot, the marks are removed so they are not unintentionally filmed.

marker 1. Another name for a clapboard. 2. Anything used to mark something else.

"Marker." Announcement by the clapboard operator as it is activated at the beginning of the shot. Related terms: "Common marker," clapboard.

marquee Large sign above, in front of or near a theater displaying the theater's name and billing information, such as the title of a movie or stage play being exhibited in the theater.

marquee value Name value of a star, e.g., how much minimum box-office income can be expected by having a particular star associated with the film or play. Related term: name value.

married print British term for composite print.

martial-arts film Movie featuring numerous fight scenes involving various Asian forms of fighting using the hands and feet, such as karate and jujitsu.

mask 1. Black frame outlining the screen in a movie theater; it can be altered for different aspect ratio formats. 2. Device in black covering part of the frame, e.g., to create the effect of looking through a telescope or a pair of binoculars. This is done optically, after the film has been shot and processed, rather during filming. 3. Flag or gobo used to keep unwanted light off the camera lens.

masks of comedy and tragedy Two visual symbols of drama: one has a face of laughter and the other of sorrow. Related term: drama.

mass media National or international means of communication to the public, e.g., national or international magazines, newspapers, television, radio, the Internet. The opposite is local media. Also called the national media or international media.

master (aka master positive) Film or tape from which dupe negatives are made for striking release prints. Or, in the case of sound tape or videotape, the material from which subsequent copies (listening or viewing) are made. Related terms: CRI, IP.

master disc Designation given to an optical disc, such as a DVD or CD-R, with original material recorded on

it. The digitally recorded pictures and sound can be copied exactly, with no loss of information from one generation to the next, unlike non-digitally recorded video and audio tape. Related term: edited master.

master scene Scene of primary dialogue or action, in which characters are developed, plot is advanced, etc.

master shot Uninterrupted, complete shot of an entire scene, and to which all other shots in the scene are related. For example, in a scene where two actors are talking, the uninterrupted shooting of the entire scene with all dialogue is the master, which is usually completed to satisfaction before going in for coverage (close-ups, over-the-shoulder shots, etc.) The master shot itself can be used without coverage, if shot with that intent.

master tape Original video or audio recording from which copies can be made. Also called a tape master, video master or audio master. Related terms: edited master, first generation.

master-scene script Early stage in script development in which dialogue and action are included, but specific camera angles are not (some specific camera angles may be included out of storytelling necessity). Since the director typically personalizes the script by selecting the precise shot-by-shot camera angles (e.g., close-up, medium, low-angle), most film scripts are written in the master-scene format.

match 1. To repeat exactly the action and/or dialogue of a scene so that the continuity of subsequent shots is maintained, enabling them to be edited into the master shot. 2. To line up the final cut work print with the negative so they conform, frame by frame. The negative then is cut and release prints are made.

match cut 1. A match-action cut. 2. Match-image cut.

match dissolve Similar to a match cut, except a dissolve is used to change from one image to another.

match-action cut 1. In editing, a change from one image to another having a similar type of visual action, e.g., a cut from a close-up of someone pouring liquid into a drinking glass to a shot of a waterfall. 2. Cut from action in one shot to the same action continuing in another shot as filmed from a different angle, e.g., a cut from a shot of a car approaching a stop sign to a shot of the same car from a different angle, seconds later, as it leaves the stop sign and makes a turn into traffic. Also called a matching-action cut. Related terms: overlap action, match-image cut, pickup shot.

match-image cut Sudden visual change from one onscreen image to a similar one, e.g. a cut from a seagull hovering in the sky to a shot of a kite floating in the wind. Also called a match cut. Related term: match-action cut.

matching costume Garments and accessories worn by a stunt double; they are identical to those worn by the actor who is being doubled in the scene.

matinee 1. (n.) Performing event held in the afternoon. A "bargain matinee" is one in which a reduced admission price is charged. 2. (adj.) Of or pertaining to a matinee, e.g., a matinee performance, matinee show or matinee screening.

matrices Set of three pieces of film used to make color prints via the three-strip Technicolor process. Each strip is sensitive to one of the primary colors (red, green and blue) and contains part of the final image. Each matrix absorbs a dye and transfers the color to the required area of the frame as it comes into contact with the release print stock.

matte 1. (n.) Black-colored shield of any flat shape; it is placed in front of a camera's lens to mask (block out) part of the image being shot. This may be done so a second image can be inserted into the space later in a special composite process; or a desired film-frame aspect ratio or variety of character point-of-view shots can be created. Also called a mask. Related terms: binocular matte, keyhole matte, microscope matte, peephole matte, telescope matte. 2. Glass sheet on which a partial image has been painted to create an unusual scenic or structural background; it is combined with another image in a special composite process. The unpainted area is blacked out or left clear, depending on the composite process used. Also called a matte painting, painted matte or glass painting. Related terms: matte shot, glass shot. 3. Traveling matte. 4. (v.) To block out an image with a matte.

matte artist Individual in the Visual-effects Department who designs and paints mattes; an expert in creating realistic backgrounds and foreground images in the proper perspectives necessary for filming. The matte artist creates the image from information in the script and/or the director and production designer. One of the legendary matte artists is the late Albert Whitlock, whose work appears in such films as *The Birds* (1963), *Marnie* (1964), *The Sting* (1973), *Earthquake* (1974), *Ship of Fools* (1965). He won an Academy Award®

for Best Special Effects for his work on *The Hindenburg* (1975). Also called a matte painter or matte illustrator.

matte box Adjustable filter holder attached to the front of the lens. It shields the lens from unwanted light and holds mattes and filters in place when shooting. Related terms: matte shot, effects box, special effects box.

matte painting Specially prepared, highly realistic painted image of a background, foreground or combination of both; it is used as a matte. Related terms: digital matte painting, glass painting.

matte photo Photograph having a dull finish. Also called a matte-finish photo. The opposite is a glossy photo.

matte screen Specially treated projection screen in which the brightness of the images appears the same from all viewing angles.

matte shot Visual-effects shot in which some type of matte is used. Related terms: traveling matte, composite shot, glass shot, zone shot, rotoscope.

maximum-use period Length of time set forth in a contract, for example, an actor's appearance in a television commercial or print advertisement. Also called the maximum period of use.

MCS Abbreviation for medium close shot.

MCU Abbreviation for medium close-up.

meal allowance Daily (per diem) payment to cover the cost of meals. According to varying union rules, a producer may deduct the cost of each provided meal from this allowance. Also called a meal payment. Related term: allowance.

meal break Pause in a production schedule allowing the cast and crew time to eat. Related terms: dinner break, lunch break, commissary, craft service, craft service table.

meal penalty Payment from the production company to actors or crew members if the company fails to or is late in providing a meal or meal break; the payment is set by union contracts in accordance with the length of time worked.

meat axe Slang for a rod typically used on scaffolding to hold scrims or flags.

media (medium is the singular form) Various forms of communication to large numbers of people. Related terms: electronic media, local media, mass media, multimedia, news media, print media.

media buy Single purchase of advertising time or space.

media buyer Individual at an advertising agency responsible for purchasing advertising space (in magazines and/or newspapers) and time (television and/or radio) on behalf of the agency's clients.

media circus Situation in which there is a large, noisy presence of journalists (reporters, photographers, videographers, sound crews), e.g., "Coverage of Princess Diana's death turned into a media circus, with reporters jockeying for photos and helicopters buzzing overhead to catch a glimpse of the accident scene."

media frenzy Fast-paced, on-scene media efforts to obtain information on a news story, especially in an effort to be among the first to obtain an interview with principals involved, e.g., "There was a media frenzy as the celebrity exited the courthouse." Also referred to as a "crush of reporters."

media interview Interview conducted by a journalist from the news media. Related terms: press interview, interview.

media kit Another name for a press kit. Related term: electronic press kit.

media personality Interesting or influential person frequently seen on the media. The term is typically used in reference to famous authors, lawyers, psychologists, businessmen and experts in such fields as science, medicine, the military and politics. Related term: personality.

media presence News media in attendance, e.g., "There was a large media presence at the awards show."

mediagenic Appealing, at ease and effective as a media subject. Related terms: telegenic, photogenic, presence.

media-shy Another name for publicity-shy.

medical checkup Physical examination required of an actor, director or other production talent for insurance purposes; in the event of injury, sickness or death, the insurance company pays the necessary expenses associated with completing the production. The physical is paid for by the production company. Related term: cast insurance.

medical leave Another name for sick leave.

medium close-up (abbreviated as MCU) Shot in-between a close-up and medium shot.

medium long shot (abbreviated as MLS) Shot in-between a medium and long shot. The subject appears in the middle distance, not in the foreground or background.

medium shot (abbreviated as MS) Camera shot in which the subject appears at a distance midway between a close-up and long shot.

medium-budget film Movie with a medium production budget. The cost range of a medium-budget film is relative to current trends and is subject to change from year to year. Related terms: big-budget film, low-budget film.

medley Musical composition consisting of a series of usually familiar songs or parts of songs.

MegaCrane Trade name for a tripod-mounted, video camera crane available as a stationary unit or with dolly wheels; it can reach heights up to 17 feet and hold cameras weighing up to 25 pounds. Manufactured and sold by Classic Video Products of Aliso Viejo, California. The company also manufactures an Event Crane for cameras weighing up to seven pounds as well as a variety of hand-held, motion-stabilizing camera mounts called FlightSticks. Related term: crane.

megahit Major success. Related terms: smash hit, hit film, blockbuster, top-grossing film.

megaplex Movie-theater complex having a large number of individual theaters. Related terms: cineplex, multiplex.

melodrama Drama, with hero and villain, that emphasizes sensational action and exaggerated emotions rather than in-depth character portrayal; typically, it has a decisive ending with good overcoming evil.

member report In the United States, a multicopy, employment work sheet; it may be required that a principal performer file such a report with his union within 48 hours of certain types of work sessions. It lists various information about the session and is initialed or signed by both parties, as indicated. It may also be called a member-contractor report.

merchandising tie-in Consumer products, such as toy action figures, breakfast cereal prizes, clothing, calendars, etc., associated with an event or entertainment product, such as a popular feature film or television series. Product tie-ins are valued sources of additional income. Related terms: movie tie-in, tie-in, movie merchandise, ancillary market, ancillary right.

mercury vapor lamp Small arc light which emits a bluish light; it is used mainly for close-up work.

method acting Style of acting based on the teachings of Russian actor-director-producer-teacher Konstantin Stanislavsky (1863-1938) and, later in the United States, of director-teacher-actor Lee Strasberg (1901-1982). The technique involves the actor working toward the goal of achieving the same psychological realism as his character, through studying of the character's background, inner feelings and motivations, as if the character was a real person. Emotional recall, also called emotional memory or affective memory, is also used to help assume the identity of the character. A method actor strives to "be" a character, rather than "act" like a character. In the theater world, however, critics of method acting contend that it does not always meet the level of theatricality necessary (facial expressions, body gestures, etc.) to convey particular emotions to the audience, especially for those seated in the back rows who cannot see characters' faces and bodies clearly, as in film and television. Method acting is not universally accepted and is only one of many different acting theories. Parts of it may be incorporated into other systems.

metteur-en-scene French term for "director." It came from the stage and means, literally, the person who places (the action) in the scene. The more modern term is realisateur.

micro-cinematography Photographing an object too small for the ordinary lens. In such a case, one would use a combination of microscope and motion picture camera.

microphone (abbreviated as mike or mic) Device that transforms soundwaves into electrical impulses capable of being transmitted to a receiving device by wire or nonwire; such soundwaves are then processed for recording or amplification and, eventually, are transformed back into the identical soundwaves through a speaker. Examples of microphone types: bi-directional, clip-on/lapel, directional, floor stand, headset, lavalier, omnidirectional, parabolic and ultradirectional/rifle/shotgun. Related terms: hidden microphone, wireless microphone, mike, dead mike, live mike, off-mike, on-mike, open mike, mike check, mike cube, boom, fishpole, headset, Popper-Stopper, windscreen.

microphone boom Handheld, telescopic pole, beam or a more elaborate, multi-jointed movable arm at the end of which a microphone is attached and controlled. In a studio, a microphone may hang from an overhead boom attached to a dolly and be raised, lowered and/or angled in the proper direction by an off-camera operator. Outdoors, it may be attached to the end of a hand-held pole ("fishpole"), which features a changeable length. Related term: boom.

microphone operator Member of the sound crew responsible for the placement, operation and removal of one or more microphones. Related terms: boom operator, sound assistant, soundperson.

microphone shadow Unwanted dark area on a production set caused by an overhead microphone or microphone boom blocking the light. The microphone itself also must be kept from appearing in the shot.

microscope matte Camera lens matte with a single, centered hole; shooting through it gives the impression of a character looking through a microscope. Microscope and telescope mattes may be identical. If a video microscope is used in a scene, no matte is used; in such a case, the magnified image is shown on the entire screen, possibly with part of the television monitor in the shot.

microvideo camera Any solid-state video camera having smaller-than-normal CCD imaging chip, lens and color or monochrome (black-and-white) circuitry; used in investigative news reporting, surveillance, the medicine and special-effects work. Also called a microvideocam. A source for hard-wired (closed-circuit) and wireless microvideo cameras is Supercircuits of Leander, Texas, in the United States. Internet address: http://www.supercircuits.com. Related term: video camera.

midget 1. Small, fill light spot using a 50- to 200-watt lamp. 2. Little person, dwarf. Related term: Little People.

midseason replacement TV series replacing another show that was canceled in the middle of the television season, usually due to poor ratings.

midstage Another name for center stage.

MIFED International film and home-video trade fair held annually in Milan, Italy. Originally, it was an international market for films and documentaries, but was later expanded to include videos. Internet address: http://www.mifed.com.

mike 1. (n.) Another name for microphone. Variation: mic. Related terms: dead mike, live mike, off mike, on mike, open mike, open-mike night, microphone. 2. (v.) To supply with a microphone, e.g., to mike a talk-show guest.

mike check Audio test in which an individual speaks into a live microphone, usually doing a countdown so that the audio level can be adjusted to its proper level. Also called a level check. Related terms: sound check, voice test.

mike cube Station, network or program logo display box that slides onto the shaft of a reporter's handheld microphone. Also called a microphone flag, a term that can apply to any shape, e.g., cube, rectangle, triangle, oval sides, TV screen sides or circular sides. An industry source for mike equipment, as well as other studio and field production equipment, is Markertek Video Supply of Saugerties, New York. Internet address: http://www.markertek.com.

mileage money Amount paid to a cast or crew member during production when he drives his own vehicle to a location. Compensation is a specified amount and is set by union contracts.

mime Character portrayal using body movements and facial expressions only. Related term: pantomime.

miniature Small-scale model of a set used for shooting special effects; often used when a scene is too expensive or difficult to build in life size. Miniature artwork has become a highly specialized branch of the special effects department, due to the special equipment required and the complexity of the work. Related term: model miniature.

minibrute Light of 650 watts used for supplementing sunlight on outdoor sets.

Mini-Crane Trade name for a tripod-mounted crane; a single operator can use this crane to raise a camera up to 12 feet over a scene. It features a remote control for camera panning and tilting. The entire unit can be disassembled to a smaller size for easier transport. Manufactured by Stanton Video Services, Inc., of Phoenix, Arizona, in the United States. Related term: crane.

minilight Compact light with a reflector and barn doors; used mostly for fill light.

mini-majors Small, but still prominent, film producer-distributor. Currently, the most famous and successful mini-major is Artisan Entertainment. Entertainment trade paper use.

minimount Stable camera mount; it can be attached to planes, helicopters, cars or boats.

mini-movie Short film having a story with a beginning, middle and end, e.g., "The movements of the theme-park simulator ride followed the onscreen action of the mini-movie, which was shot by a well-known director." A mini-movie can be as short as a few minutes in length. Related term: short film.

minimum call Fewest number of hours for which an actor or crew member is entitled to be paid, regardless of whether or not the hours are worked.

minimum fee Lowest payment required to hire a person or service. Also

called a minimum rate. Related terms: starting fee, scale.

miniseries Television film in two, three, four, etc., parts; it is in the category of "long-form television." A grand miniseries, or grand series, is a miniseries featuring a distinguished cast, high production budget and a large number of hours or episodes. The industry's first miniseries was ABC's adaptation of Irwin Shaw's novel, *Rich Man, Poor Man* (1976); the industry's most successful miniseries was Alex Haley's *Roots* (1977), also for ABC.

mini-trampoline A small-sized gymnastic or exercise trampoline that is used by a stuntperson to add force to an upward jump in a scene involving an explosion, super muscular strength, or paranormal activity. It is hidden out of sight behind an object or placed below ground level in a pit. A small, compressed-air catapult called an air ram can be used as an alternative (but costlier) method when greater lift is required. A mini-trampoline is also called a trampolette.

MIPCOM Annual festival of film, video, broadcast TV, cable TV and satellite TV (mass communication) program marketing; held each October in Cannes, France. It is attended by international producers, distributors, broadcasters and cablecasters and sponsored by the Reed Midem Organisation of Paris, France, which also organizes MIPAsia and MIPTV. Internet address: http://www.mipcom.com.

mirror shot 1. Shot of an actor's reflection in a mirror; the image in the mirror is called a virtual image. 2. Any other shot using a mirror, as for special-effects purposes.

mirror shutter Camera shutter with reflecting mirrors allowing the camera operator to view the image being shot without having to compensate for a parallax. Related tem: viewfinder.

miscast To cast the wrong performer for a role; cast incorrectly.

miscue 1. To incorrectly give or receive a cue; to mistakenly cue someone. Related term: off-cue. 2. An instance of miscueing.

mise-en-scene French term for direction. The direct translation is "to put into the scene" (stage). Related term: metteur-en-scene.

missing the mark To miss stepping or landing on a predetermined floor mark during a performance. Related term: mark.

Mitchell Motion picture camera; usually, it is used in studios rather than on location, due to its size and lack of portability.

mix 1. (n.) Combination of separate sound tracks into a single sound track on a single piece of magnetic tape with three to four separate channels. The mix is then transferred onto an optical track (or mag/optical track) for use in the composite print. The mix, or re-recording, is done on a mixing console by the mixer (actual film credit is "re-recording mixer"). Related tem: dubbing. 2. (v.) The act of mixing a sound track.

mixed reviews An assortment of separate positive reviews and negative reviews or reviews that contain both positive and negative elements; e.g., "The film is getting mixed reviews."

mixer Related terms: sound recordist, production mixer, re-recording mixer.

MLS Abbreviation for medium long shot.

mobile production unit Van, bus or motor home equipped with various types of film or video production equipment and necessary workspace (depending on the specific purpose). Related term: location vehicle.

mockup Full-scale model simulating an object or place, e.g., a full-scale mockup of the cockpit of a passenger jet. If the mockup is supposed to show movement during a shot, it is constructed on a framework base of hydraulic pistons, metal springs or inflated truck-tire tubes. (For the latter two, arm poles extending from the sides are handled by crew people during the shot.) Also called a "replica" if the mockup is of a real object or place. Related terms: full-scale mockup, gimbal set, process body.

model miniature Small-scale model of something, such as a vehicle, building, city street, cityscape, person or creature. It is constructed to demonstrate how a full-scale version will look or is used in the actual shooting of a scene. A model miniature typically saves the production money; for example, in the case of fantasy, horror and science-fiction projects, one or more model miniatures are often the only way to shoot a scene (e.g., a fairy-tale castle model miniature or futuristic spaceship model miniature). Related terms: movable miniature, scale model, set model, motion control.

modeling light Light emphasizing the contour and texture of a subject. Also called the contour key, it is aimed at the subject in the opposite direction of the key light. Related term: lighting.

modelmaker Artist-craftsman skilled in constructing model miniatures or special props. For props, also called a propmaker.

modern dance Type of dancing originating in the late 1920s; it uses movements different from classical ballet, such as new techniques of stretching, twisting, lifting the body and using the floor to lie and sit on while performing. Martha Graham (1893-1991) was a famous performer and teacher of modern dance. Related term: performance art.

modulation Variations in the amplitude, phase or frequency of continuous sound waves, usually in recorded sound.

mogul Powerful or influential person. Related term: movie mogul.

money shot Highly prominent film or video shot; a shot that is expected to help make a production a commercial success. In *Psycho* (1960), the "money shot" would be the shower scene. Also called a money-making shot.

monitor Screen used with a video camera during filming or taping to check the accuracy of exposure; the quality of an image or sound; or the quality of a performance as seen by the camera.

mono 1. Containing one; single. 2. Short for monophonic; sound recorded, received or transmitted on a single track or channel, as opposed to stereo sound.

monochromatic Term typically applied to black-and-white photography. It can also mean an image composed of a single color or tonal gradations of a single color.

monologue Talk or speech by one person. In a script, it means a lengthy bit of dialogue performed by one character at one time. In an audition, an actor may be asked to perform a monologue in front of casting personnel. On a TV talk show, comedy or variety show, it is typical for the show's host to open the program with a humorous monologue of several minutes. Related terms: opening monologue, prologue, soliloquy, curtain speech, host-chat segment.

monopack Color film in which there are three separate layers of emulsion, each sensitive to one of the primary colors. related term: integral tripack.

monopod Camera mount consisting of a single pole or beam on which a still, motion picture or video camera is attached.

monopole Adjustable device for hanging studio lights.

monotone Speaking or singing in one unvarying tone of voice. Also called a drone. Related term: staccato.

montage Series of brief shots, typically dissolved or superimposed. For example, a passage-of-time montage showing the pages of a wall calendar falling off, dissolved with outdoor shots of the four weather seasons. A montage is sometimes used in a dream sequence and in scenes where a character has to make a moral decision between right and wrong. In the latter, brief shots of the same character (appearing as good and evil), which act as the character's conscience as he makes his decision, are shown onscreen. Related term: double exposure.

Monty Pythonesque In the manner or style of the humor or characters associated with the British comedy troupe Monty Python, which performed during the 1970s and 1980s; its members were Graham Chapman, John Cleese, Terry Gilliam, Eric Idle, Terry Jones and Michael Palin. Monty Python performed in a successful television series, several feature films as well as performing live.

moo print Laboratory term for a perfect print.

morality play 1. Type of stage play in which the characters symbolically portray moral concepts, such as love, hate, friendship, kindness, courage, cowardice, indifference, death or the like. 2. Theatrical film or television program featuring a storyline with characters representing moral concepts. One example is *High Noon* (1952), starring Gary Cooper (1901-1961) and Grace Kelly (1928-1982), and featuring a story pitting lawman against villains; in it, the characters symbolically represent good, evil, cowardice, loyalty and courage. Also called a morality tale.

morals clause Contract provision allowing a performer's employment to be terminated as a result of his immoral or illegal conduct on or off the set. Such a clause is intended to protect the production company's financial investment from the damaging effects of negative publicity and controversy. Related term: contract.

morphing Computer animation effect in which one image is smoothly transformed into another by means of a steady and continuous manipulation of the onscreen pixel information. For example, a human face morphing into a different human face. Derived from the word "metamorphosis," meaning a change of physical appearance or structure. A stunning example of morphing is *Terminator 2* (1991). Related terms: computer effects, doctored photo.

mortar In pyrotechnic-effects work, an open-ended, thick-walled metal tube or drum with a bottom support plate that forcefully angles a desired explosive effect (flames, flash, sparkle, debris, etc.) in a particular direction. Mortars are also used to lift or propel objects into the air with explosive force. Because they involve the use of pyrotechnic materials in significant quantities, they require a government license to operate (in the United States, a federal and possibly a state license is required). Examples of mortar types: angled shotgun (positioned at an angle; diameter of opening less than 4 inches or 100 millimeters), flat/pan (shallow or bowl-like), round V-pan ("V" profile that allows explosion to spread out), square V-pan, straight (positioned upright; large diameter opening) and straight shotgun (positioned upright). Also called a small cannon or short cannon. Related terms: debris mortar, gasoline mortar, pipe mortar, air cannon, car roll cannon, bomb, explosion scene, powder.

mortician's wax General name for a skin-colored, microcrystalline wax-based sculpting material that adheres to the skin and is used by special-effects makeup artists to create cuts, bumps and misshapen appearances. It does not have the resiliency of latex, e.g., it will dent if pressure is applied. Once applied, it can be powdered and painted. Available in different brand names. Related term: special makeup effects.

MOS Abbreviation for "mit out sound" (without sound) or "mit out sprache" (without speech). According to early Hollywood legend, it originated on one of the film sets of German-born director Lothar Mendes (1894-1974), where it was used by the sound crew and clapboard operator as an abbreviation for recording without sound. Its use caught on in the film industry and continues today. Related terms: wild shooting, wild picture.

MOS production camera Any camera that does not have a sound-recording feature built into it. The sound must be recorded separately on another machine, such as a reel-to-reel tape recorder.

mother show Nickname for a television series that is the source for a spinoff series. For example, *All in the Family* (1971-79) would be the mother show to its spinoffs, *Maude* (1972-78) and *The Jeffersons* (1975-85). Related terms: sister show, spin-off.

motion blur Visual fuzziness associated with a quick, natural movement; can be demonstrated by waving one's hand in the air. Depending on the type of animation, motion blur is added as a hand-drawn or computer-generated effect or by a special motion-control technique. Related term: Go-Motion.

motion capture Technical process of recording and transferring three-dimensional movements, such as those of the human body, to a computer to create realistic computer animation. A specially designed and electronically wired exoskeleton body suit, helmet and pair of data gloves may be worn by the individual who is performing the movements; filming or laser scanning the individual's movements in a three-dimensional open space may also be used. Related terms: motion-capture puppet, animator's live-action model, live-action model, live-action reference, capture, computer effects.

motion control Computerized, repeatable movement of a device, such as a camera or puppet. Related terms: motion-control camera, Go-Motion.

motion picture Another name for a movie. Also called a moving picture, talking picture, picture, pic, flick, talkie or film. Abbreviated as MP on union forms. Related terms: locked picture, photoplay.

Motion Picture and Television Fund Relief agency of the film and television industry in the United States funded by employee contributions, bequeathments and memorial donations. The fund conducts alcohol and drug abuse programs, provides qualifying financial assistance and medical care and operates the Motion Picture Country Home/Hospital, which provides a permanent home for elderly performers and others who have had careers in motion pictures and television. It was founded in 1921 and is based in Woodland Hills, California.

Motion Picture Association of America (abbreviated as MPAA) Organization in the United States comprised of major producers and distributors. Among its various activities, it issues ratings (which are trademarked) for theatrical films and direct-to-video movies; promotes foreign distribution of U.S. films; operates a film title registration service; and provides a voice for the U.S. film industry in news media interviews and government hearings on such matters as film and video piracy, censorship standards, the impact of new and future technologies on moviemaking and industry financial trends. Founded in 1922 and based in Washington, D.C. and Encino, California. Related terms: motion picture rating board, Central Casting Corporation.

motion picture rating board 1. Non-government committee of adults comprising the film and video Rating

Board of the Classification and Rating Administration of the Motion Picture Association of America (MPAA) in the United States. The Rating Board consists of a permanent chairperson selected by the MPAA's president and eight to eleven members serving varying terms. The members review submitted films and videos and determine the appropriate rating each should receive. The submitted film is screened with frame numbers; each member makes a note of the frame numbers containing a questionable scene. After members' notes are compared, a discussion is held and a vote taken; the rating is decided by a majority vote. The film's producers, if they disagree with the rating, may appeal the Board's decision or re-edit and resubmit the film for another review and vote. The rating determinations are based on the following criteria (from the MPAA's handbook): "theme, violence, language, nudity, sensuality, drug abuse, and other elements." For theatrical films and videos, the choice of ratings are "G," "PG," "PG-13," "R," and "NC-17." The rating symbols, with additional wording, are registered trademarks of the MPAA. The "NC-17" rating replaced the "X" rating on September 27, 1990 (the "X" rating was never trademarked and has always existed in the public domain). The film and video rating system in the United States is voluntary and began on November 1, 1968. The Rating Board's members are U.S. citizens and have parenting experience. Their identities are kept secret during the course of their terms. As with other rating or classification boards around the world, theatrical trailers and advertisements (including posters) are also reviewed. A fee is charged for rating services performed. Related terms: Motion Picture Association of America, rating, rating appeals board. 2. Any governmental or nongovernmental film and video rating or classification board or commission of a country. Related term: British Board of Film Classification.

Motioncam Trade name for a small-scale, remote-controlled helicopter on which a camera is mounted; used in aerial shots that would be difficult or impossible to capture with a full-scale helicopter. It can stay aloft for approximately 25 minutes per fuel tank. It is operated by and available for rental from Motioncam USA of Castaic, California. Related term: helicopter shot.

motion-capture puppet Three-dimensional puppet with motion-capture data sensors and wires attached to various movable points. As one or more puppeteers move the puppet in open space, per the action in a script, the motion information is fed to a computer where it becomes the basis for a computer-generated (CG) character. Also called a cyber-puppet.

motion-control camera Computerized, camera-mount system used to film model miniatures in visual-effects work (such as in the bluescreen process). The computer controls motors attached to the camera mount, allowing the user to program precise movements in any direction; these movements can be repeated exactly. The first motion-control camera was the Dykstraflex Camera developed by John C. Dykstra at Industrial Light & Magic for shooting some of the model-miniature visual effects seen in *Star Wars* (1977). In recognition of this achievement, the Academy of Motion Picture Arts and Sciences awarded 1977 Scientific and Engineering Awards to John C. Dykstra "for the development of the Dykstraflex Camera" and to Alvah J. Miller and Jerry Jeffress "for the engineering of the Electronic Motion Control System used in concert [with the Dykstraflex Camera] for multiple exposure, visual-effects motion-picture photography."

motivation Relative to acting, "motivation" is the reason a character in a story is prompted to follow his course of action. The motivation for a character's behavior in a scene and throughout the script is something an actor should be aware of in order for a believable portrayal to take place. Often, an actor will research a role for weeks or months in advance of the start of production to learn every relevant piece of background information and nuance of behavior that will lead him to an accurate portrayal of his character onscreen or onstage. Also called the driving force, incentive or *raison d'être* (French for "reason for being"). Related terms: point, researching a role.

motor Mechanized device causing motion. Most professional motion picture cameras are driven by electrical motors which provide a constant speed of operation so that sound can be recorded in sync. Variable speed motors, which can be noisier, are used for shooting slow or accelerated motion (shot MOS) and can be regulated between 45 fps and 50 fps.

movable miniature Small object, usually a small-scale replica, capable of being moved during shooting. Used in visual-effects scenes. For example, a boat, spaceship or creature (puppet) made of foam latex or clay with an internal wire or ball-joint frame (armature). Related terms: model miniature, puppet, scale model, stop-motion animation, foam latex.

movement list Information sheet listing the means by which everyone connected to the production gets to and from a location.

movie commercial Filmed advertisement for a motion picture, typically up to three minutes in length; it is played to audiences in movie theaters. A shortened version, usually 20 or 30 seconds long, is aired on television. A commercial for an upcoming movie on television may be even shorter and referred to as a network movie promo or preview. Also called a movie spot, film commercial, film promo, film preview or theatrical trailer. Related terms: coming attractions, Internet ad, movie ad, trailer.

movie deal Any type of contract regarding the development, production, distribution or marketing of a movie. Related terms: pic pact, deal.

movie house Another name for a movie theater.

movie memorabilia Collectible items associated with a particular film or with films in general, e.g., photos, posters, scripts, autographed documents, props, wardrobe items, commercially produced tie-in products and the like. Major auction houses in New York and Los Angeles regularly present auctions of entertainment industry memorabilia. Some retail stores in the Los Angeles area specialize in selling used costumes and props from movies and television shows. Numerous other companies sell such items through mail-order catalogs (some also hold mail auctions) and advertise in collecting and fan magazines. Related terms: autograph, cel, movie merchandise, movie poster, production jacket, studio auction.

movie merchandise Manufactured consumer products that are associated with a particular movie or with movies in general. They are sold in retail stores or via mail-order/Internet catalogs or they are given away as part of a promotional tie-in campaign. Related terms: action figure, ancillary market, merchandising tie-in, movie memorabilia, studio store.

movie mogul Powerful or influential individual in the film industry. Also called a film industry mogul or movie bigwig. Related term: mogul.

movie poster Large, rectangular, heavy sheet of paper on which is printed a color promotional image (artwork, photograph or photograph montage), title and main credits for a motion picture. Newer posters are often printed on both sides to be brighter and clearer when displayed in lighted cases. Some mail-order and movie-collectible stores specialize in selling posters from recent, past and upcoming theatrical films. Related terms: poster, advance, one-sheet.

movie premiere Theatrical film's first showing, usually held as an event with celebrities attending the screening and fans and media stationed outside the theater to witness the arrival and departure of the celebrities. The first movie premiere in history to be staged as a major event at a single location was the public debut of the Walt Disney animated film *Pocahontas* on Saturday, June 10, 1995; with over 70,000 moviegoers in attendance, the film was projected simultaneously on four giant outdoor screens, each eight stories high, on 13 acres of the Great Lawn in Central Park, in New York City. The event was titled, "The Premiere in the Park" and included pre-show entertainment and an after-show fireworks display. The first feature-length movie to premiere on the Internet was *Party Girl* (1995). Related terms: premiere, Internet movie.

movie preview Advance partial or full showing of a film; screened for promotional or market-research purposes. Related terms: preview, sneak preview, digital video clip.

movie projector Mechanical or all-electronic device that casts moving images from a motion picture film or a video player onto a screen. Related term: projector.

movie screen Flat or curved reflective or translucent surface on which film or video images are projected from a mechanical or all-electronic projector. Related terms: screen, big screen, silver screen, rear-screen projection, front projection.

movie studio Another name for a film studio. Also called a motion picture studio.

movie theater 1. Building or room housing a movie screen, tiered seating audience section, projection room or booth and possibly a refreshment stand and rest rooms. Also called a movie house, picture house, or movie palace (for large, ornate buildings). Related terms: chain movie theater, independent movie theater, art theater, home theater, IMAX theater, interactive theater, IWERKS theater, revival theater, stand-alone theater, cinema, cineplex, megaplex, multiplex, screening room, simulator ride. 2. Drive-in movie theater.

movie theater chain Corporation owning movie theaters in different locations. Related term: chain movie theater.

movie theater commercial 1. Filmed product, service-business or public-service advertisement played to a movie audience just prior to the coming attractions and feature presentation. Also called a trailer. 2. In-house commercial promoting a movie theater or its services.

movie tie-in Connection with a theatrical film. An example is a merchandising tie-in involving products, such as games, dolls, action figures, clothing, etc., that feature the movie's title and pictures or representations of its principal characters. Related term: movie merchandise.

movie tie-in video Music video of a theatrical film's theme song; it incorporates film clips and possibly new footage of the film's stars shot specially for the video. The one or more singers and musicians who perform the theme song also usually appear in the video.

movie version Theatrical or television representation or interpretation of a news event, book, play, etc. Also called a film version or movie adaptation. Related term: adaptation.

movie-of-the-week Term originating in the United States for a film made specifically for television. It began as the title of an ABC-TV network series (1969-1975), which featured two 90-minute, made-for-TV movies each week. Related terms: MOW, telefilm.

Moviola Trade name for machine used for viewing interlocked picture and sound tracks; used extensively in editing for building sound tracks. The Moviola has variable speeds and can be stopped at a single frame so the editor can mark the cuts, optical effects, etc. On a Moviola, the film runs up and down through the viewer instead of side to side, as in a flatbed machine.

MOW Abbreviation for movie-of-the-week. Entertainment trade paper and union-form use.

MP Abbreviation for "motion picture" on union forms.

MPAA Abbreviation for Motion Picture Association of America.

MPAA code seal Certification that a film, its trailers and advertising have been made and rated in conformance with the regulations and standards of the MPAA.

MRAA rating The Motion Picture Association of America's established system of categorizing feature films according to audience suitability. The categories are as follows: "G" (General Audiences); "PG" (Parental Guidance suggested); "PG-13" (Children under 13 not admitted without a parent or guardian); "R" (Restricted—children under 17 not admitted without parent or guardian); "NC-17" (No Children admitted). The MPAA also rates trailers, which receive one of two ratings: "All Audience" and "Restricted." A Restricted trailer may only play with an "R" or "NC-17"-rated film.

MS Abbreviation for medium shot.

MT Abbreviation for main title.

mug 1. To grimace or contort the face voluntarily and usually jokingly, as for the camera, e.g., to mug (make a face) for the camera. Related term: funny face. 2. Nickname for the face, e.g., "Look at the mug on him!" Also called a puss. 3. To threaten or attack with the intent of robbing; e.g., "The script requires the two young male characters to mug the lead character

on the city street at nighttime."
Related term: fight scene.

multiagency representation Being
represented by more than one agency, as in the case of an individual who
is signed with a model agency and
also with a talent agency for television and film work, or the one who
is also represented by an agency in a
foreign country.

multi-beam Small quartz iodine light
used for indoor and outdoor lighting.

multibroad Light that can be focused
by turning a knob.

multicamera Using two or more
cameras to shoot a scene simultaneously from different angles;
recommended for large action shots
or for shots that are difficult or
expensive to create, e.g., a car driving
over a cliff or a bridge exploding.
Multiple cameras are also used in the
medium of live television, especially
sitcoms.

multi-duty motor A special motor
that can drive camera and sound
equipment in sync. Related term:
crystal motor.

multi-head printer Printer capable of
making more than one copy of a film
at a time.

multi-layer film See mono pack,
integral tri-pack.

multimedia Involving or pertaining
to several types of media, such as
television, print, radio and computer,
e.g., a multimedia entertainment
company.

multiple framing Printing or recording duplicates of one or many
frames, either to create a freeze frame
or the effect of slow motion. If done
for film, it is also called multiple-frame
printing or freeze-frame printing.
Related terms: double framing, slow
motion, expanded time.

multiple roles Three or more parts
played by a single performer in the
same production, e.g., multiple roles
of triplets or cloned humans or
multiple roles of grandmother,
mother and daughter in a flashback
sequence. For example, Michael
Keaton portrayed several versions of
his own character in *Multiplicity*
(1996). Related term: dual role.

multiple-image shot Shot in which
the same image appears several times
in a frame. This effect can be achieved
either optically or with a special,
multi-image camera.

multiplex Multi-screen movie theater
complex; a movie theater having
three or more separate screens and
audience sections for viewing different theatrical films at the same
time. Related term: megaplex.

multi-screen Projection system using
several interlocked projectors and
large abutting screens. Related term:
cinerama.

multiyear contract Contract for a
period of more than two years. Also
called a multiyear agreement, multi-
year deal or long-term contract.

mural Large painting or photograph
used as a background.

Murder Your Wife brick Imitation
brick; first used on (and thus, named
for) the film, *How to Murder Your Wife*
(1964), starring Jack Lemmon.

muscle padding Fabric-covered,
simulated foam-rubber muscles.
Related term: muscle suit.

muscle shading Applying dark-
colored makeup to the edges of an
actor's muscle areas to make them
more visible to the camera or an
audience. Related term: shadowing
makeup.

muscle suit Tight-fitting, flexible
costume with exaggerated muscles

made out of shaped foam rubber; intended to dramatically or comically enhance an actor's physique. Related term: muscle padding.

Museum of Television and Radio Formerly called the Museum of Broadcasting. Institution in the United States that collects, preserves and exhibits past television and radio programs and honors individuals associated with them. There are museums in New York, New York, and Beverly Hills, California. Internet address: http://www.mtr.org.

music Harmonious or expressive combination of instrumental, electronic or vocal sounds. Related terms: score, background music, canned music, live music, royalty-free music, segue music, sheet music, taped music, theme music, arrangement, CD, DVD-Audio, soundtrack.

music act 1. Performance of instrumental music. 2. Performance of one or more musicians collectively. A singing act may include the performance of live music or the playing of recorded music.

music bridge Musical segment providing the transition between scenes and/or moods. Related term: segue.

music by Production credit designated for the project's composer. Variation: "music composed and conducted by."

music clip clearance Permission to use copyrighted music, as in a movie, TV program or play.

music contractor Individual responsible for hiring musicians and coordinating all business and financial activities for the film's music (recording) sessions. He must be present at all recording sessions.

music cue sheet List, by reel, of all music cues; used in post-production

and to establish royalties and licensing.

music director Individual responsible for seeing that a film, video or stage show has a music score, either original or from prerecorded sources. May also be called a music coordinator.

music editor Individual who edits music so that it is synchronized with the action and visual elements of the production. May also be called a music mixer.

music library See library.

music mixer Sound person responsible for controlling, balancing and mixing the film's musical score. He is part of a team of re-recording mixers who prepare the final sound track.

music track Channel of the soundtrack onto which the music is recorded; it is separate and distinct from the dialogue and the effects tracks.

music video Song visualized on videotape or film. The first music video was "Elephant Parts," by Michael Nesmith (1981) and since that time, music videos have become part of the culture. MTV, the cable station that broadcasts rock music videos, debuted on cable on August 1, 1981, and helped changed the way we appreciate rock music.

musical Stage play or show or theatrical or television movie having music, solo or group singing and usually dancing. The musical can combine genres, for example, musical-comedy, musical-drama, musical-fantasy, etc. Also called a movie musical, stage musical, screen musical, film musical, musical film, TV musical or musical TV movie.

musical theater 1. Stage plays having songs or song-and-dance routines as part of their productions. 2. World, field or profession of working in musical theater productions.

musical variety Film, television or stage production featuring an assortment of musical performances.

musician Performer of music; a musical instrument player. For example, accordionist, bagpiper, banjoist, bassoonist, bell ringer, castanet player, cellist, clarinetist, cymbalist, drummer, fiddler, flutist, guitarist, harmonica player, harpist, harpsichordist, jug player, kazoo player, keyboardist, maraca player, oboist, organist, pianist, piccoloist, saxaphonist, spoon player, tambourinist, triangle player, trombonist, trumpeteer/trumpet player, violinist, washboard player and xylophonist. Also called an instrumentalist. Related terms: accompanist, band, orchestra, scoring stage.

Musicians Union Any of various unions for musicians around the world bearing this name, including those in the United States, Argentina, Finland, Israel, Norway, Sweden, and Switzerland. The American Musicians Union also has vocalists and band managers in its membership. It was founded in 1947 and is based in Englewood, New Jersey.

mute British term for a print or negative without a sound track.

mylar Extremely strong plastic material onto which the ferromagnetic coating for video and audio tape is applied.

mystery date A person of the opposite sex who accompanies a celebrity on a social or promotional outing and whose name has not been determined by the media by the time the story is reported. Mystery date is a term used in celebrity gossip columns and photo captions to describe an unnamed person who was seen at an event or in public with a celebrity.

N Abbreviation for night or nighttime.

NAB Abbreviation for National Association of Broadcasters.

nabe Local neighborhood. Entertainment trade paper use.

NABET Abbreviation for National Alliance of Broadcast and Electrical Technicians.

Nagra Trade name for self-contained crystal sync sound recorders used for recording sound on the set or on location. Nagra helped free filmmakers from the confines of shooting in the studio by enabling them to produce studio-quality sound with a small, portable machine. Stefan Kudelski received an Academy Award® for developing and perfecting the Nagra.

name actor Actor with a famous or recognizable name. When packaging a project, the addition of name actors help secure financing. Related terms: famous-name actor, name star.

name change A relatively common practice among actors; they will change their name legally or for professional reasons (because of difficulties associated with an unusual birth name, one that is hard to pronounce, hard to spell or identical to someone else's). However, the individual's real name, by itself or in addition to the adopted name, must appear on all documents where legal identification is required by law. Such world-famous performers who have changed their names or used stage names include (birth name in parentheses): Tim Allen (Timothy Allen Dick), Fred Astaire (Frederick Austerlitz), Ginger Rogers (Virginia McMath), Brigitte Bardot (Camille Javal), Tom Cruise (Thomas Cruise Mapother IV), Danny DeVito (Daniel Michaeli), Judy Garland (Frances Gumm), Whoopi Goldberg (Caryn Johnson), Cary Grant (Archibald Leach), Michael Keaton (Michael Douglas), Jane Seymour (Joyce Frankenberg), and John Wayne (Marion Morrison). Related terms: acting name, stage name.

name value Worth or importance associated with a celebrity's name, especially with regard to the ability to attract TV viewers, movie ticket sales or book purchases, etc. Related term: marquee value.

NARAS Abbreviation for National Academy of Recording Arts and Sciences.

narration Guiding account, story or explanation spoken by a narrator. Related terms: narrative, voice over.

narrative Story line.

narrator Individual who provides an oral guide to the story or course of events. A narrator usually follows a planned script and does not offer spontaneous personal comments, as a commentator would. A narrator may be visible to an audience or positioned offstage or off screen.

narrow gauge film Film often used for documentary, industrial and student films and also for commercial and research applications. The most common gauge is 16mm; the quality is poorer than 35 mm, but it is less expensive.

narrowcast 1. (v.) To target or market a program to a specific audience of viewers or listeners, e.g., to narrowcast a Saturday-morning lineup of cartoons and commercials to a target audience of children and their parents. 2. To provide programming to a limited group only, such as a pay-per-view audience. 3. (n.) Program that is narrowcast.

National Academy of Recording Arts and Sciences (abbreviated as NARAS) Organization in the United States comprised of individuals working in the recording industry. It presents the annual Grammy Awards. It was founded in 1957 and is based in Santa Monica, California. Internet address: http://www.grammy. com.

National Academy of Television Arts and Sciences (abbreviated as NATAS) Organization in the United States comprised of television industry professionals; associated with the Academy of Television Arts and Sciences which presents the Emmy Awards. Founded in 1947 and based in Beverly Hills, California. Internet address: http://www.emmys.org.

national ad Advertisement appearing across the country, as one seen by a national magazine's readers in all of its distribution markets.

National Alliance of Broadcast Engineers and Technicians (abbreviated as NABET-CWA) National labor organization affiliated with the AFL-CIO, formed originally for radio technicians and engineers and later expanded to include television technicians and engineers. Recently merged with the Communications Workers of America, now called NABET-CWA. When there was a proliferation of made-for-television movies, an agreement was struck with IATSE (the union for film stagehands and technicians). Now NABET members are typically used for television production while IATSE members are used for film production, though NABET crews are often used on low-budget feature films (especially in New York). Internet address: http://www.union. nabetcwa.org.

National Association of Broadcasters (abbreviated as NAB) Organization whose members are representatives of television and radio stations and networks. Among its activities, it bestows various awards and it sponsors two prominent annual trade conventions in the United States. Founded in 1925 and based in Washington, D.C. Internet address: http:// www.nab.org.

National Association of Television Program Executives (abbreviated as NATPE) Organization of management personnel from television stations, networks and related professions. It was founded in 1963, originally with a U.S. membership and has grown to accommodate the expansion of the global television marketplace; it now has an international membership. After 1987, the organization revised its name to NATPE International. Based in Santa Monica, California. Internet address: http://www.natpe.org. Related terms: NATPE, NATPE convention.

National Association of Theatre Owners (abbreviated as NATO) Organization in the United States representing the interests of movie theater owners. It also bestows annual awards. Founded in 1966 and based in North Hollywood, California. Related terms: NATO

Award, NATO/ShoWest. Internet address: http://www.showest.com.

National Board of Review of Motion Pictures New York City-based organization of individuals actively interested in the art and craft of motion pictures. Founded in 1909, it is considered the United States' oldest film group. In addition to an annual career achievement award, it bestows the D.W. Griffith Award.

national casting search Search conducted across the country, in its largest cities, to find the right actor for a part. It can also refer to an invitation, via national print ad, for performers and agents to mail in photos and résumés. Also called a nationwide casting search. Related term: casting search.

national commercial 1. Commercial airing nationally on all participating stations of a network at the same time. Also called a national spot. Related term: network spot. 2. Any commercial that is aired or distributed nationally, as opposed to regionally or locally.

National Conference of Personal Managers Organization in the United States comprised of personal managers whose clients are performers in the entertainment industry. Founded in 1967 and based in New York City.

national exposure Being seen, examined or exhibited widely across a country, e.g., an acting appearance on a network television program.

National Television Systems Committee (abbreviated as NTSC) An early working group of major broadcasters and television equipment manufacturers in the United States that proposed and created the final standards for the technical aspects of television transmission and reception

systems for submission to the Federal Communications Commission (FCC) for review and approval. 2. Refers to the standard approved by the FCC and other international government agencies for the number and timing of electron-beam scanning lines needed to produce a complete picture on a television set. Related term: broadcast quality.

national TV Television programming available from a national source, as through a network. The opposite is local TV.

NATO Abbreviation for National Organization of Theatre Owners.

NATO/ShoWest Annual convention and trade show in the United States sponsored by the National Association of Theatre Owners. It is held in Las Vegas, Nevada. Its East Coast counterpart, held at a different time of year, is NATO/ShowEast.

NATPE Abbreviation for National Association of Television Program Executives (or, NATPE International).

NATPE convention Annual syndicated programming convention-trade show sponsored by NATPE International. NATPE also sponsors a yearly Animation & Special Effects Expo. Internet address: http://www.natpe.org.

NATPE convention appearance Promotional appearance at the annual convention-trade show of the National Association of Television Program Executives (NATPE International), where network and independently produced syndicated U.S. and international television series are sold to station buyers. Actors, talk-show hosts, game-show hosts, etc., may make scheduled appearances at their show's promotional exhibits to meet and talk with station executives, pose for photographs and sign autographs. First-run syndication shows and reruns of network TV series (off-network syndication) also are sold at this convention. Related terms: convention appearance, exhibit, syndicated programming buyer.

natural light Light from the sun, stars, fire, lightning or chemical reactions (fireflies, glow worms, deep-sea creatures, etc.); light occurring in nature, as opposed to light from human-made sources (electrical filament and arc lamps, fluorescent and neon gas lamps, chemical light sticks, etc.). Related terms: available light, lighting.

natural movement Body movement performed smoothly and unpretentiously; the body moving naturally.

natural reading Script reading that comes across as easy and authentic to the character being portrayed.

nature film Footage of nature, e.g., wildlife, plants, ocean inhabitants, weather activity, volcanic activity, geologic formations, rivers, streams or the like. Also called a nature documentary.

NC-17 Film and video rating issued in the United States by the Motion Picture Association of America (MPAA). Full wording: "'NC-17'— No Children Under Age 17 Admitted." "NC-17" replaced the "X"-rating for theatrical films on September 27, 1990. Related terms: motion picture rating board, rating.

ND 1. Abbreviation for nondescript, e.g., "This scene will require 25 ND office worker extras." 2. Abbreviation for neutral density, e.g., a neutral density filter or gel that evenly reduces the amount of light on the film or on the scene being lit.

ND stunt performer Union designation in the United States for a general (nondescript) stunt performer hired by the day; he is not allowed to stand in for another actor during a stunt without first being upgraded to stunt double status.

negative Exposed and processed film whose image is opposite of the original subject (e.g., the reverse of a positive); the term may refer to unexposed film stock (aka, raw stock) or to stock in the camera before processing.

negative (abbreviated as neg) Film or plate with an exposed and developed photographic image whose light areas appear as dark ones and colors are reversed. Positive prints are made from negatives. Related terms: duplicate negative, original negative, release negative, internegative.

negative cost Total cost incurred in the production of a film; costs necessary to produce the edited original negative. The edited original negative will eventually be duplicated into one or more release negatives and used to make release prints for distribution. The negative cost does not include the additional expenses associated with making release prints, distribution and promotion (trailers, TV commercials, posters and print ads).

negative cutter Individual who conforms the negative to the finished work print and sometimes splices it. (Splicing, however, is often done by an assistant.) The process of matching is made easier by guide numbers printed on the footage of both the negative and work print. The assembled original negative is then used to strike an answer print. Also called a negative matcher or negative conformer. Related terms: rough cut, editing on tape.

negative cutting The process of matching, or conforming, the negative (frame by frame) to the edited work print to produce the different generations of film leading to the answer print and finally, to the release prints. The negative cutter uses the key numbers as a guide.

negative pick-up Term used to describe an agreement between a film's distributor and the producer, whereby the distribution company agrees to pay a fee for the rights to distribute said film. The fee typically is not paid to the producer until delivery of the completed and cut negative. (This is the opposite of pre-production financing.) If the pick-up deal is with a major studio, the producer can usually take the agreement to a bank where it can be discounted (e.g., converted into money for a fee). Many productions are financed, or partially financed, this way.

negotiated rate Rate determined by discussion and bargaining between the two parties involved; specifics of the contract are taken into account. Also called a negotiated fee.

negotiation Act of discussing and bargaining, with the aim of reaching a settlement in the terms of the contract. Related terms: contract negotiation, deal.

net profits See profits.

net-profit deal Contract in which a participant receives a percentage of the net profits. The net profits are arrived at after all expenses, including those to gross-income participants (if any) are paid. Exactly what criteria constitute net profits normally are defined in the contract. Related terms: profit participation, gross-point deal.

network Major television company, responsible for the creation and development of programming; transmission of the programming to the interconnected stations comprising its affiliates (e.g., network owned-and-operated stations plus non-network owned and operated stations); development of technological advancements; sale of air time and programming to advertisers (sponsors). Major networks in the United States are ABC, CBS, NBC, Fox, The WB, UPN and PBS.

network affiliate Television or radio station under contract to air network programming. Also called a network station. Related term: affiliate.

network executive Administrative-level, policy-making or supervisory employee of a broadcast or cable network. Related terms: web exec, development executive, executive in charge of production, network programmer.

network feed 1. Transmission of network programming to individual affiliate stations by means of a satellite link. Related terms: live feed, satellite-feed, 16mm. 2. Programming transmitted to network affiliates from the network's headquarters.

network programmer Executive who schedules the time slots and air times of his network's programs. The actual job title of this individual may be a corporate one, such as "senior vice president of programming and scheduling." Depending on the size of the network, it may be a collective process, with numerous individuals participating. Related term: network shuffling.

network promo In-house advertisement or announcement for the network's upcoming TV-series episode, TV movie, news program, special or the like.

network series Television series that has its initial run on a broadcast or cable network, as opposed to one that is syndicated to individual stations wishing to purchase it.

network shuffling Rescheduling television programs in an attempt to improve ratings or introduce new series to audiences. Related term: time slot.

network spot Commercial airing on network television. Also called a network program commercial. Related terms: Class A Program commercial, national commercial.

neutral density filter Filter for the camera lens; it reduces exposure and contrast without changing the color. Related term: ND.

Never work with animals or children. A saying that may be said jokingly in a situation where an adult actor or entertainer is required to perform in the same scene or stage act with one or more animals or young children. Performing animals and children tend to receive an above-average amount of applause or laughter or are otherwise considered cute and adorable by audiences. This leads to the possibility of the adult performer, who may be billed as the star of the show, being upstaged by the attention given to the one or more animals or children. The saying is likely derived from a quote by actor John Barrymore (1882-1942): "If you ever become an actor, never play a scene with a child or a dog" (Barrymore speaking to author James Bacon, recalled in *Made in Hollywood*, James Bacon. Chicago: Contemporary Books, Inc., 1977). Related terms: upstage, scene-stealer.

New York City Theater District Area between 41st Street and 53rd Street, bordered by 6th Avenue (also known as Avenue of the Americas) and 8th Avenue; many large and prestigious playhouses are located in this area. Related term: Broadway (New York City).

news conference Another name for a press conference.

news media Any area of journalism (e.g., television, radio and Internet news departments; magazines, newspapers, newsletters) reporting on current events. Related terms: ambush journalism, checkbook journalism, confronted by the media, electronic news gathering, interview, media, media circus, media frenzy, media presence, press, press clipping, press conference, press coverage, press kit, press line, press party, press piece, press release, pressroom, press screening, press showing, press tour, puff piece, spinning newspaper, tabloid journalism, tried in the media, unnamed source.

news release Another name for a press release.

news reporter Individual who obtains and reports news. Also called a print journalist, television journalist, radio journalist or photojournalist. Related terms: pool reporter, reporter approval.

news scoop Getting the news story first.

news show Television program consisting of reports on current events, e.g., a morning news show or evening news show. Related term: newsmagazine.

news story Television report, newspaper article, etc., describing or providing information about a newsworthy event. An opening (or, headline) story is called a "lead story" or "top story." Related terms: breaking news story, news scoop, news show.

newscast Telecast presenting current information on one or more topics.

newscaster Individual who presents the news. May also be called an anchorperson.

newsgroup Electronic discussion group on a computer network service. Related terms: computer online fan club, computer online talk show.

newsmagazine Television program reporting on current events, e.g., a network newsmagazine or syndicated entertainment newsmagazine. Related terms: magazine, television magazine, news show.

newsreel Short news film; a short film (generally made before the advent of television) featuring current events of the day, e.g., a 16mm newsreel.

newton rings Colored, odd-shaped circles appearing on film as a result of light bouncing between two smooth surfaces (e.g., filters on a lens) during shooting.

NG Abbreviation for "no good." Typically used to refer to an unusable take of a scene.

Nielsen ratings Television ratings issued at regular intervals by the A.C. Nielsen Company to television networks, stations and other interested subscribers of its various reporting services. The A.C. Nielsen Company is a subsidiary of the Dun & Bradstreet Corporation in the United States.

night effect See day-for-night.

night filter Lens filter used to darken a daylight shot so it appears to be nighttime. Related term: day-for-night.

night premium Adjustment made to the basic rate of pay, per various unions and guilds.

night shot Shot taking place during nighttime hours. As a script term, it is also used to mean that events in a scene are taking place at nighttime, as opposed to the daytime, dawn or dusk.

night-for-day Shooting outdoors at night with enough artificial light to simulate daytime.

night-for-night Night sequences actually shot at night.

nighttime serial Daily or weekly television series shown at night; it may also be called a nighttime soap opera, especially if the stories are primarily relationship oriented.

nighttime TV Television programming shown in the nighttime hours. Nighttime TV includes early evening television and prime-time television. Related terms: prime time, late-night TV.

night-vision lens Special camera lens incorporating electro-optical, low-light amplification technology allowing one to shoot in extremely low-light conditions, as by starlight or moonlight. The images seen are in varying shades of green. In total darkness, an invisible infrared beam can provide the necessary light for amplification.

99-Seat production Play taking place in an Actors' Equity Association (U.S.) 99-Seat Plan theater. Also called a 99-Seat play or (formerly) Equity-Waiver production. Related terms: Equity 99-Seat Plan theater production, showcase production.

99-Seat theater Playhouse having a seating capacity of under 100 seats. Related terms: AEA 99-Seat Plan theater, Off-Off Broadway.

nitery Abbreviation for nightclub. Entertainment trade paper use.

nitrate base Highly flammable film base previouslyused in early days of filmmaking (now obsolete). Related terms: acetate base, safety base.

"No comment." Standard public-relations or legal response, typically given by an individual (or his representative) to a question he doesn't wish to answer. Related term: damage control.

no-holds-barred interview Media interview in which the reporter is free to ask any question of the interview subject; a no-restrictions interview.

noise Any unwanted or distracting sounds picked up during recording.

non-air commercial Advertisement that will not be broadcast or cable-cast; it is produced intentionally for non-airing or it is relegated to this designation due to unforeseen problems. According to U.S. union rules, if the client wishes to redesignate the commercial for airing, then additional compensation must be paid to the one or more performers seen or heard in it. Also called a non-air spot or in-house commercial. Related term: demo commercial.

noncommercial theater Playhouse offering theater entertainment on a not-for-profit basis. An admission price may be charged, which is combined with donations, government and private foundation grants, etc., to help pay expenses. There are no investors, so any extra money that is made is used to expand the quality of future productions. Also called a nonprofit theater or not-for-profit theater. Related term: regional theater.

non-Equity Not associated with or approved by Actors' Equity Association.

nonexclusive Signing or registering with more than one agency or extras service for representation. Related terms: multiagency representation, exclusive listing.

nonexclusive contract Contract in which an individual is not obligated to work solely for the company offering the contract.

nonlinear editing Video editing in which the original videotape footage is transferred to a digital editing system in a computer; then, individual shots can be controlled frame by frame, assembled and transferred back to videotape as a finished master tape. The opposite is linear editing, which is not computer-based. Related term: on-line editing.

nonsignatory Individual or company that is not a signatory to a contract or agreement. Related term: non-union.

nonspeaking part Acting role in which the performer is seen but not heard. Related term: silent part.

nonstop action Continuous action. For example, *The Matrix* (1999) features nonstop action. Related term: action-packed.

non-theatrical Also nontheatrical. Film market designated for limited distribution among specialized audiences, not in theaters. The non-theatrical market includes television, cable, schools, libraries, film clubs, inflight airlines, the Armed Forces, etc. The largest, and newest non-theatrical market today is video-cassettes.

no-nudity clause Stipulation in a performer's contract stipulating that he will not be required to perform any shots or scenes in the nude. This protects the performer from being dismissed from the production for refusing to do a nude scene if there is a change in the script during production. A "no-nudity clause" may specify that additional approval is required or that a body double be used instead. The subject of nudity is also covered in union contracts. Related terms: nudity clause, nudity rider.

nonunion Not associated with a union; performer, crew member, agency, acting role or production that is not a member of, or affiliated in some way, with a union or guild. Related term: nonsignatory.

nonunion film One produced without union performers or crew; film production that is not a signatory to any union contract. Also called a nonunion production.

nose putty Skin-colored makeup applied (after squeezing and shaping) to the nose or another part of the face to change its appearance. It is an alternative to a latex appliance. Spirit gum or other prosthetic adhesive can be used to hold it in place, if necessary; coloring makeup then is applied to match the desired skin appearance. Related term: mortician's wax.

no-show 1. Situation in which an individual fails to appear for a booking, rehearsal, fitting, meeting or other appointment. 2. Individual who fails to show up.

notch Mark on the film's edge showing where an adjustment in printing density is to be made. This is now done by computer.

NR Abbreviation for "Not Rated." Designation given to a film or video by its producer when the work has not yet been given an official rating by a rating board or commission. Variations: "This Film Has Not Been Rated," "This Video Has Not Been Rated." Related term: unrated version.

NTSC Abbreviation for National Television Systems Committee.

nude body double Actor hired to be a body double for one who opts not to do a nude scene. Related term: no-nudity clause.

nude scene Scene in which one or more actors appear nude (partially or fully). The actor may have his private parts covered in various ways, such as with a skin-colored body stocking, skin-colored shorts, G-string, pasties, etc. The actor may elect to do the scene naked. Some actor contracts request nude body doubles to perform their nude scenes; many actors will consider doing a seminude or fully nude scene if there is a justifiable reason for it in the script. A casting decision may be based on an actor's willingness to appear naked in a scene. Casting notices are required to state if nudity is involved in a role. Unions have specific rules pertaining to nudity in acting scenes. (Consult a union office or union-producer labor contract for current regulations, subject to revisions.) Before making a decision as to whether to perform a role in the nude, actors should be aware that the individual film or video frames containing the nude scenes are almost always transferred to the print medium by one or more of the adult magazine publishers for printing in their publications as celebrity nude photographs; this has occurred with and without the permission of the producer and actor. The majority of famous actresses who have done an onscreen nude scene have had at least one shot taken from the scene and published as a celebrity nude photo. Some actresses do not mind the additional publicity received; others do, but decide against taking legal action because of the international publicity that will result and the problematic issues of copyright ownership and freedom of the press. Related terms: sex scene, foreign version, no-nudity clause, nude body double, nudity clause, nudity in an audition, television version.

nudity clause Contract stipulation detailing the conditions under which an actor will agree (if at all) to participate in a nude scene. Related terms: nudity rider, no-nudity clause.

nudity in an audition According to union rules, a performer must be informed of any nudity required before auditioning for the part. Casting notices are also required to state whether a role involves nudity (partial or full). Nudity does not take place in an audition for a theatrical film unless there is a legitimate need for it; for example, to verify a particular type of physical appearance. A photograph or a video demo tape of previous professional nude work may be a sufficient substitute for disrobing in an audition. It is possible that nudity may not be required until the scene is actually performed, which, for a film or video, is done on a closed set, unless the location is in a public setting. Current union rules apply to all auditions involving nudity and may vary from country to country. (In the United States, an actor is allowed to have an individual of his choice present during such an audition.)

nudity rider Separate addition to a contract that contains a nudity clause.

numbering machine Device used by the assistant editor to print code numbers at regular intervals on the edge of the work print. Related term: encoding machine.

numbers Short for rating and share numbers, e.g., "What were the numbers on last week's episode?"

nut Cost of production; expenses, e.g., "The play has a huge nut." Entertainment trade paper use.

oater Nickname for a Western movie. Entertainment trade paper use.

objective camera angle Camera angle when the camera shoots from the point of view of an imaginary spectator (an invisible third person looking on); it is never shot from a clearly defined character's point of view (this is the subjective camera angle). An example of an objective camera angle would be a shot of two people sitting on a couch watching television, taken from behind and above a TV set. An example of the subjective camera angle would be a shot of the TV screen from the point of view of one of the people looking at it.

obligatory scene 1. Scene that is necessary or expected for storytelling, e.g., a gunfight scene in a Western. 2. Scene considered necessary to attract audiences; one expected by those audiences, e.g., a kissing scene in a romance.

obligatory shot Necessary or expected shot within a certain type of scene, e.g., a car crashing into other cars in a car-chase scene.

OC Abbreviation for "off camera."

OC Abbreviation for open-captioned. Symbol used to identify a television program using onscreen subtitles. Related terms: caption, cc, closed-captioned, SL.

off camera (abbreviated as OC) Action or dialogue taking place outside the camera's range; not seen by the camera. Related terms: OC, off-screen.

off mike Also off-mike. Off the line of transmission or outside the range of picking up sound by the microphone; disconnected from a microphone, e.g., "You're off mike."

off screen (abbreviated as O.S.) Of or pertaining to that which is not seen on a movie or TV screen. Related term: off camera.

off your mark An actor not precisely on a predetermined spot on the floor or ground.

Off-Broadway Reference to a stage play in a New York City theater not located in the Broadway theater district; typically, these theaters have an audience seating capacity of between 100 to 300 people and the plays feature performers who are paid at least minimum Equity scale. Related terms: Off-B'Way, Off-Off Broadway, Broadway (New York City), fringe theater.

Off-B'Way Short for Off-Broadway. Entertainment trade paper use.

off-camera dialogue Script lines belonging to characters who are not seen during a shot.

off-cue Not responding correctly to a cue; to begin a cued action at the wrong time. Related terms: false start, miscue.

offline editing 1. Preliminary videotape editing stage; it produces a worktape that can be reviewed for content or shown to a producer or client for approval. If changes need to be made, they can be done at this stage. The offline worktape can be used as a visual reference guide when assembling a master tape in an on-line editing session. 2. Any editing done without the use of a computer system ("offline" refers to the absence of a physical connection to a computer). Also called linear editing, in which, "linear" refers to the linear (straight-line) nature of videotape that is mechanically set up and played, fast-forwarded, rewound, played again, etc., to locate and transfer footage during the editing process. Related terms: linear editing, videotape editing.

off-network No longer on a television network.

off-network syndication Syndication of a TV series originally shown on network television. Half-hour situation comedies are the most common form of off-network syndicated programming. Related term: rerun syndication.

Off-Off Broadway Refers to a play in New York City, performed outside of the Broadway theater district annd produced in a small setting (100 seats or less). Related terms: Off-Off B'Way, 99-Seat theater, fringe theater.

Off-Off B'Way Short for Off-Off Broadway. Entertainment trade paper use.

off-register Accidental or deliberate rocking effect resulting from camera vibration. Explosions are sometimes made to appear more real by intentionally creating camera vibration.

offstage Of or pertaining to a place not visible on the stage. Related terms: O.S., backstage, wings.

old-age makeup Application of theatrical makeup, including latex appliances; it simulates the appearance of old age.

old-timer Slang term for a flexible pole holding flags or scrims.

omitted Taken out, removed or deleted, such as a shot or scene in a script, e.g., "Scene 64 omitted." "Omitted" appears in the script in place of the shot or scene number. Related term: script change.

omnidirectional microphone (abbreviated as omnimike) Microphone receptive to sounds coming from all directions.

omnies 1. Indistinguishable words or sounds uttered by anyone as part of a crowd in the scene. The term is derived from an omnidirectional microphone, which records sound in all directions. Also called atmospheric words/sounds. Related term: background voices. 2. Extras who produce these sounds.

OMNIMAX theater Original name for an IMAX dome theater.

on a bell Every time a production rolls film, a bell is rung by the sound mixer and a red light goes on outside the door of the sound stage as a signal that all activity around the set should stop and no one should come on or off the stage. When shooting on location, there is no red light but the bell is still sounded to warn everyone that a shot is about to begin. When the take is finished, the bell sounds twice to signal an all-clear.

on call Condition when an actor or crew member may or may not be used the next day but must remain available for work.

on camera Any person or object seen by the camera while filming or taping.

On Camera prompter Trade name for a display-screen videoprompter (15" or 17") manufactured by QTV of New York City. The prompter, which consists of a video monitor and slanted glass screen, attaches to the front of a television camera or free-standing pedestal; the script wording is fed to it from a separate delivery system. Related terms: QTV, Tele-PrompTer, videoprompter.

on cue Responding correctly to a cue; taking a cue. The opposite is off cue.

on hiatus On an extended break. For example, the filming of *Raging Bull* (1980) went on hiatus while actor Robert DeNiro gained weight to portray fighter Jake LaMotta in the man's later years. Related term: hiatus.

on hold 1. In a condition of waiting, e.g., "Work on the film was put on hold." 2. In a stand-by position. A payment typically is received for being placed on hold, as per individual union rules. Also referred to as being "on call." 3. In a condition of having a holding fee paid by a client for a talent's exclusive services.

on location On or at a chosen site for filming or performing; understood to mean a place other than inside a film, television or photographic studio. Also called on site, in the field, or remote. Related term: location.

on mike On the line of transmission or inside the range of being heard by a microphone's sensing element. The opposite is off mike.

on spec Abbreviation for "on speculation." Project completed on the creator's own time and money, without guarantee of success, e.g., "The script was written on spec." Related terms: spec, spec script.

on the air In a state of being broadcast, e.g., "We're on the air in ten minutes."

on your mark Standing precisely on a predetermined spot, so indicated by a piece of tape, chalk line, etc., e.g., "Stay on your mark until I cue you."

100th-episode party Cast-and-crew party held to celebrate the completion of a series' 100th episode. The enter-tainment news media is usually invited to cover the event.

one take Of or pertaining to one try at filming or recording, e.g., "This is a one-take stunt." Director W.S. (Woody) Van Dyke (1889-1943), who directed such films as *Tarzan the Ape Man* (1932) and *The Thin Man* (1934), was nicknamed "One-Take Woody" because of his proficiency in completing films on time and on budget.

one-act play Stage play presented in one act with no change of set or background scenery; it has no inter-mission.

one-camera (abbreviated as one-cam) Of or pertaining to one film or TV camera, e.g., a one-camera shoot, one-camera production or one-camera setup.

one-camera shoot Videorecording or filming session in which one camera is used.

one-hour series Another name for an hour-long series.

one-light print An ungraded print made with a single light setting, to be used as a work print only.

one-liner 1. Short, humorous remark; a short joke consisting usually of one sentence and a punchline. (A famous one-liner: "Why did the chicken cross the road?" Punchline: "To get to the other side.") 2. One word, phrase or sentence. Related term: line.

one-man show Play, dramatic reading, concert, etc., in which only one person performs. Hal Holbrook had a successful run of his one-man show, entitled "Mark Twain Tonight." Julie Harris had similar success with her one-woman show entitled, "The Belle of Amherst." Related terms: one-woman show, solo performance.

one-minute call Announcement to one or more performers backstage that their performance will begin in one minute. Related terms: call, "Places."

one-sheet Standard-size movie poster, displayed at theaters or offered for sale to collectors. In the United States and elsewhere, a one-sheet poster measures 27" x 41". Most one-sheets made before 1982 were shipped folded by the studios; after that, they were rolled and shipped in tubes.

one-shot 1. Photograph or camera shot featuring one subject. Also called a single-shot. 2. One-time opportunity, chance or occurrence, e.g., "The special-effects explosion was a one-shot deal."

on-line editing Computer-assisted video editing; it produces a final, high-quality master videotape with precise, clean edit points. "On-line" refers to the physical connection to a computer. Also called nonlinear editing, referring to the lack of machine-played videotape during the actual selection and assemblage of footage during the editing process. Related terms: non-linear editing, off-line editing.

onscreen Of or pertaining to that which is seen on a movie or television screen.

onscreen credit Credit title appearing on the screen at the beginning or ending of a theatrical film or TV show, as opposed to a credit listed on a résumé. The size and placement of the onscreen credit may be covered by the terms of that individual's union contract.

onscreen programming Programming selections, clock time and language settings, etc., made with the assistance of an instructional television screen display.

on-site casting Another name for location casting.

onstage Of or pertaining to a location visible on the stage.

on-the-air light Warning light indicating a radio or television program is being broadcast.

opaque Impenetrable by light, as opposed to transparent or translucent.

open audition Tryout or reading for an acting role; the tryout is open to all who fit the description of the part. Also called an open casting call. Related term: cattle call.

open microphone or mike Microphone that has been switched on and transmits sounds. Related term: live mike.

open rehearsal Stage play, music concert, etc., attended by any interested individuals (typically, those not directly involved with the show), as opposed to a closed rehearsal. There may be an admission fee and limited seating or it may be accessible to news media only.

open up 1. Increasing the size of the lens aperture, and therefore letting in more light and decreasing the depth of field. 2. Broadening the story when translating it from a play to a film. (The story is no longer subjected to the confines of a stage when it is put on film, so the story "opens up" into the larger scope of the real world.)

open-captioned With onscreen subtitles. Related terms: OC, closed-captioned.

open-end run Unlimited run. For example, a play with an open-end run has no scheduled termination date for its performances.

opener Debut episode of a TV series; first performance or showing. Entertainment trade paper use.

opening 1. Beginning or first part of a performance or presentation. Related terms: prologue, teaser. 2. Formal beginning of operations or activities, often held as an event or celebration. Related terms: debut, premiere.

opening act 1. First act of a play. 2. First performance in a stage show featuring two or more performances, e.g., the opening act of a variety show. The opposite is a closing act. Also called a curtain raiser. 3. Collectively, the performance and one or more individuals who are in the opening act.

opening credits List of credit titles appearing onscreen at the beginning of a film or TV show. Also called beginning credits or front credits. Related terms: main title and opening credits, credits sequence.

opening date Calendar date on which a film or play opens to the public. Related terms: playdate, release date.

opening monologue Talk or speech to an audience, offered prior to the regularly scheduled acts.

opening number First dance or song to be presented.

opening star Performer with the starring role in a stage play's premiere run. Later, the opening star may leave the cast, in which case, another performer takes over the role.

opening week First week of a show's run (either film or stage); the term most often is used in reference to box-office ticket sales.

opening-night jitters Feeling of nervousness felt by a performer before the premiere performance of a stage play; not as severe a condition as stage fright. Also called backstage jitters. Related term: performance anxiety.

opening-night party Party held after a premiere. Related terms: premiere party, post-premiere party, party.

opera 1. Play that is entirely or mostly sung; it typically includes elaborate musical accompaniment, costumes and scenery. Also called a lyric drama or lyrical drama. Related terms: comic opera, grand opera, operetta, librettist, libretto, supertitles.

operator See camera operator.

operetta Opera that is less imposing in size and subject matter than a grand opera; opera that includes spoken dialogue (rather than featuring all singing). An operetta may include contemporary songs, dancing and dialogue. Gilbert and Sullivan were famous for their operettas such as *H.M.S. Pinafore, Mikado,* and *Pirates of Penzance.* Also called a light opera.

optical Any effects created with an optical printer. Related terms: optical effects, dissolve, effects, fade, wipe, matte shot.

optical effects Special visual effects, such as fade-ins, fade-outs, dissolves, wipes, rippling, irises, compositing, matting, freeze framing, image reversing, image enlarging, and image reducing; such effects can be achieved on film through the use of an optical printer. Also called opticals.

optical house Laboratory specializing in optical effects and optical printing.

optical print Print of a film made by any means other than contact printing; it is done in an optical house. Related term: wet gate.

optical printer Combination camera and projector capable of reproducing images onto previously processed film; adding images; enlarging or reducing images (e.g., special effects, titles, superimpositions). New images are exposed with existing ones and both are printed onto new stock by the printer light. The newly exposed raw stock then contains both images. Many special effects scenes using matte shots are printed this way.

optical sound track Sound track optically reproduced on photographic film, creating sound when read by an optical sound reader, as opposed to a magnetic sound track which is recorded on magnetic tape or film. The sound is reproduced by light waves and is electronically converted to sound impulses during projection.

optical viewfinder Camera sighting device consisting of a system of lenses and/or one or more prisms. The opposite is an electronic viewfinder. Related term: viewfinder.

option 1. Right to buy or market a property (e.g., a script or a book's movie rights) within a specified time limit (option period); purchased by an individual or company in exchange for a fee. If the option buyer fails to buy the property or its rights in full by the time the option period lapses, the owner can offer the buyer a renewal term, sell the option or the entire property (or the rights) to another party. A producer or studio may purchase an option for a low fee and use the option period to secure funding used to make a film or television series based on the work. If funding cannot be secured, the buyer's loss is limited to the cost of the option fee, which is nonrefundable. An option is a legal contract. Related terms: feature film rights, turnaround. 2. To option an entire property or one or more of its rights. The term "property" also can refer to an indi-

vidual's life story or involvement in a news event.

orangescreen process Visual-effects process similar to the blue and greenscreen processes used in compositing work; orangescreen is used when blue or green already appear prominently in the shot. Support objects, such as poles or wires, may also be painted orange so they will be easier to locate and remove digitally during post-production.

orangescreen shot Visual-effects shot using the orange screen process.

orchestra 1. Large group of musicians and musical instruments, typically including stringed instruments, woodwinds, brass and percussions, e.g., a symphony orchestra. An orchestra is different than a band because it has a larger string section (cellos, violas, violins, etc.) and typically has more musicians; however, some big bands without large string sections call themselves orchestras. An orchestra may be used to perform the score for a theatrical film during a scoring session. Related terms: orchestra conductor, orchestra pit, musician, score, scoring stage. 2. Audience seating section on the main floor of a theater; the section is closest to the stage.

orchestra conductor Individual leading an orchestra in its performance. Also called an orchestra leader. Related terms: conductor, baton.

orchestra pit Area in front of and below a stage; the orchestra conductor and musicians are located here during a performance.

orchestration The art of scoring for different instruments.

orchestrator Individual who takes the composer's or arranger's musical "sketch" and assigns parts to the various voices and/or instruments. Sometimes the composer does his own orchestrations.

order of credits Determined position or sequence (union-dictated or otherwise) of credits onscreen or in print.

order-of-appearance credit listing Positioning of performers' or cast members' names on a list of onscreen or printed credits, according to the order of each person's initial appearance onscreen or onstage.

original Usually refers to original negative.

original negative 1. Processed still camera or movie film containing negative images; it is original and not a copy; the actual exposed film from the camera to be developed. Also called the camera original. 2. Assembled motion picture in the proper sequence consisting of spliced-together shots and scenes of original negative footage. Related terms: negative cost, negative cutter, rough cut, video matchback.

original score New music written by a composer for a production. Related term: score.

original screenplay Script consisting of original material; it is not based on an already created work (this would be an "adaptation"). Also called an original script.

original session First session. The term is found in work contracts.

originator of a roll The first performer to play a newly written, fictional acting part on a formal level, as in a major production for the stage or screen.

orthodontist A dentist specializing in the diagnosis and correction of improperly positioned teeth. Related term: cosmetic dentistry.

O.S. Abbreviation for offscreen or offstage; found in scripts

Oscar® Official alternative name for the Academy Award® statuette bestowed annually in the United States in film production work by the Academy of Motion Picture Arts and Sciences. According to Hollywood legend, the statuette was nicknamed "Oscar" in the early 1930s by Academy librarian (and later executive director) Margaret Herrick, who said it looked like her "Uncle Oscar [Pierce]." "Oscar" made its way around Hollywood as an informal nickname until the night of the 6th Academy Awards® ceremony (March 16, 1934), when Walt Disney, accepting the first Academy Award® of Merit statuette of the evening (Best Cartoon for *The Three Little Pigs*) from host Will Rogers, referred to the gold-plated statuette as "Oscar," thereby giving the name respectability and official recognition in the industry and media. The Oscar® statuette is a man holding a crusader's sword downward, with both hands, in front of the body while standing on top of a reel of motion picture film. The spokes on the film reel symbolize the five original branches of the Academy: Actors, Directors, Writers, Producers and Technicians. The statuette was designed in 1928 by MGM art director Cedric Gibbons and sculpted by artist George Stanley. It is made of solid britannia (a white metal alloy consisting of tin, antimony and copper) and is electroplated with a layer of copper, nickel, silver and, finally, 24-karat gold. The brightly polished statuette stands 13" tall and weighs 8 pounds. The first Oscar® winners were chosen by the Academy on February 15, 1929, announced to the press on February 18, and presented to the winners three months later by Academy president Douglas Fairbanks during a May 16, 1929 ceremony at the Roosevelt Hotel. Since 1949, the Oscars® have been numbered, beginning with No. 501. Since 1950, all winners must, as a condition of acceptance, sign a standard contract giving the Academy the right of first option to buy the Oscar® from the winner for the nominal amount of one dollar ($1 U.S.) should the winner ever decide to sell it. As a result, the only Oscars® to appear at movie memorabilia auctions are those presented prior to 1950, and this is to the great displeasure of the Academy. The 1934 Best Actor Oscar® won by Clark Gable (his only Oscar®) for the romantic screwball comedy *It Happened One Night* sold at auction at Christie's in Los Angeles on December 15, 1996, for a record-setting $607,500 ($550,000 plus auction fees). The anonymous purchaser was film director Steven Spielberg, who, later that same day, donated the Oscar® to the Academy; it was then placed on public display at its Beverly Hills headquarters. Among the winners in the 12 categories at the first ceremony in 1929, which covered the years 1927-1928, were the Paramount film *Wings* (Best Picture), Emil Jannings (Best Actor), Janet Gaynor (Best Actress, Frank Borzage (Best Director) and Lewis Milestone (Best Comedy Direction—the first and last time comedy directors had their own category). Today, the Oscar® is bestowed for Best Achievement in 24 categories in an annually televised ceremony seen (live or prerecorded) by over one billion viewers in approx-

imately 125 countries worldwide (translated into 30 languages). The 24 Best Achievement categories (subject to change—and they have changed over the years) are: Picture, Actor in a Leading Role, Actress in a Leading Role, Actor in a Supporting Role, Actress in a Supporting Role, Director, Original Screenplay, Screenplay Adaptation, Cinematography, Film Editing, Art Direction, Original Dramatic Score, Original Musical or Comedy Score, Original Song, Sound, Sound Effects Editing, Makeup, Costume Design, Visual Effects, Foreign Language Film, Documentary Feature, Documentary Short Subject, Live Action Short Film and Animated Short Film. At the Academy's discretion, special Oscars®, honorary Oscars® and various memorial awards named after prominent past members of the Academy, e.g., the Irving Thalberg Award, Jean Hersholt Humanitarian Award and the Gordon E. Sawyer Award, are bestowed upon distinguished individuals who have contributed greatly to the international film industry. In the three Scientific and Technical Award categories, the Academy bestows to worthy individuals or companies the Academy Award® of Merit (Oscar® statuette), Scientific and Engineering Award (Academy Plaque) or Technical Achievement Award (Academy Certificate). Related terms: Academy Award®, Academy of Motion Picture Arts and Sciences.

Oscar® presenter Film celebrity who comes onstage during the Academy Awards® telecast to read the list of nominees, announce the winner(s) in a particular category and greet the winner(s) as the statuettes are bestowed. Often, a winner from from the previous year's show. He or she may appear as a solo presenter or as one of a pair or group of presenters. Oscar® presenters rehearse their entrances, which microphone they should walk to, their scripted lines, what to say and do if the winner is not present and which wing of the stage to use when escorting the winner(s) offstage. The individual may not be a celebrity and may present one or more special awards or tributes; introduce clips from nominated movies; introduce performances from nominated songs or music; or introduce other presenters.

OSS Abbreviation for "over-the-shoulder shot." Also spelled OTS.

out clause Provision allowing one or both sides to be released from a contract, e.g., an out clause in an agency representation contract. Also called an escape clause.

out of character 1. Out of the identity of a character, e.g., "The mime artist stepped out of character to answer his cellular phone." 2. Not suitable or appropriate to a character, e.g., "That type of clothing is out of character for her."

out of focus Not in focus; blurry, fuzzy. Related terms: defocus, low resolution.

out of frame 1. Anything outside the camera's field of view. 2. Erroneous threading of the film in the projector (or having a poorly positioned projector gate), causing part of two frames (or, the incorrect part of one frame) to be seen on the screen.

out of sequence Not in the proper or scripted order. Related term: shooting out of sequence.

out of sync Picture and sound that do not coincide properly. Related terms: in sync, synchronization.

outdoor location Location situated outside a building or other structure. Also called an exterior location or outside location. Related term: exterior.

outdoor set Studio or location production set located outdoors.

outdoor theater 1. Theatrical performing stage and audience section located outside, as opposed to an indoor theater. Also called an open-air theater. Related term: amphitheater. 2. Field, profession or world of performing in or working on outdoor theater productions.

outgrade Eliminating a performer from a paying production, as opposed to upgrading or downgrading.

outline Narrative screen story written in the present tense; it is shorter than a treatment but longer than a synopsis (a story outline is typically four to ten pages long). Sometimes a story outline is also called a treatment. A scene outline is one in which brief descriptions of individual scenes, preceded by INT. or EXT., the location, and day or night, are numbered and presented in sequence. Because a scene outline contains more information, its length may be longer. A scene outline resembles a screenplay except that it is more compact and the dialogue is described in general terms, rather than being written specifically for each scene. Related terms: scene outline, sketch, treatment.

out-of-town tryout 1. Audition held in another city. 2. Test performance of a stage play or show taking place in another city.

outtake Omitted shot or scene, or photographic print, slide or negative; part of the editing process. For example, a blooper. Some television shows (*The Fresh Prince of Bel Air*

[1990-96]) and theatrical films (*Liar Liar* [1997]) include blooper outtakes as part of their closing credit sequences; some television specials feature blooper outtakes from films and TV series. A filmed outtake that is not a blooper is also called a "trim" because it was trimmed, or cut, from the main footage. Also called an out.

ovation Enthusiastic applause. Related term: standing ovation.

overact To exaggerate the portrayal of a character. Related term: overplay.

overage Production cost exceeding the amount in the prepared budget. Related term: cost overrun.

overcrank To run the camera at a speed faster than normal (24 fps), producing a slow motion effect. The opposite is to undercrank, which produces accelerated motion. The terms come from the days when motion picture cameras were hand-cranked.

overdeveloped Negative film developed for a longer than normal period of time, or in a warmer than normal solution, causing the film to have extreme contrasts.

overexposure 1. When film has been exposed to too much light. 2. When an actor is given too much publicity so the public grows tired of his persona.

overhead Fixed cost of maintaining offices, facilities and personnel for a studio or individual production company. (In the case of a studio, these costs are passed on to the production companies or producers renting facilities on the lot and appear as a percentage of their budgets.)

overhead clusters Groupings of large numbers of suspended lights.

overhead light Light positioned and directed on a subject from overhead. Also called a high-angle light.

overhead shot Shot where the camera captures action from above. Director Busby Berkeley used the overhead shot in nearly all of his musical films.

overhead strips Suspended lighting units used to light a broad area.

overlap action 1. Repeating action at the beginning of a shot from the previous shot so that a smooth transition of the match cut is achieved in the editing process. For example, in one shot, the camera outside captures an actor walking up to and entering a revolving door at the front entrance of a building; in the next shot, shooting from inside the building, the actor is asked to go outside and come in again so there will be an overlap of the same action of him entering the revolving door. The editor cuts the film at the point where the overlapping action seems the most identical. Related terms: match-action cut, pickup shot. 2. In sound, a scene in which one actor speaks over another actor's lines, accidentally or intentionally, or when a sound is carried over between shots.

overlap dialogue 1. To mix lines of dialogue by actors in a scene. For example, two or more actors say all or part of their lines at the same time, as during an argument. In the script, this is indicated by a parenthetical direction: "(overlap dialogue)." The first example of overlapping dialogue occurred in the first talking feature film, *The Jazz Singer* (1927). In it, Al Jolsen portrays the son of a Jewish cantor who decides not to follow in his father's footsteps, becoming a jazz singer instead. He visits his parents' home after a long absence and has a cheerful conversation with his mother (Eugenie Besserer) as he strikes a repetitive background tune on a piano. During their conversation, which lasts less than a minute and a half, Besserer overlaps some of her dialogue with Jolsen's statements, giving their conversation a sense of realism. Audiences found the exchange amazing because, up until that time, all film dialogue between characters, as well as narration, was silent and separate and consisted of white wording on black cards displayed fully onscreen in-between shots. It was technically not possible to overlap dialogue until *The Jazz Singer* demonstrated that it could be done. 2. To carry over dialogue of an actor from one shot to another in which he does not appear; this is done in post-production, during the editing process. Related term: overlap sound.

overlap sound 1. To carry over any sound, as dialogue or sound effects, from one shot into another. For example, in one shot, a telephone is shown ringing inside an empty kitchen of a house; shots that follow show various parts of the empty house with the phone continuing to ring over what is being seen, even though the phone is no longer visible as the source of the sound. Also called overlapping sound. 2. Sound that has been overlapped. Related term: overlap dialogue.

overnight ratings Ratings for network and syndicated television programs, compiled from major market cities and sent to network and other subscriber offices the following morning. Related term: overnights.

overnights Short for overnight ratings; e.g., "The show won its time slot in the overnights."

overplay To perform a role in an exaggerated or overemphasized manner; same as to overact or overdo. Also referred to as "playing it over the top." Related terms: overact, ham, ham it up, camp.

overscale 1. Over the union-set minimum paid for work. Also called above scale. Related terms: golden time, premium pay. 2. Oversize; larger than life.

overshoot Shooting too much footage for a scene. This is a costly practice, although not as potentially costly as undershooting, which may entail going back for reshoots (requiring the rebuilding of sets, etc.).

oversized prop One that is constructed on a scale larger than life, e.g., an oversized shoe or giant telephone. Used in fantasy and science fiction productions, such as those used in *The Incredible Shrinking Man* (1957).

over-the-shoulder shot (abbreviated OTS or OSS) Shot in which the action is seen from a point directly behind (and to the left or right) an actor's head; typically, part of his head and shoulder are also in the frame.

overtime 1. Time spent working outside the designated or regularly scheduled employment time. Related term: golden time. 2. Payment for such work. Short for overtime payment, overtime pay, or overtime wages. Also called time-and-a-half (if applicable). Related terms: overscale, premium pay. 3. Beyond the scheduled time for completion, e.g., to run into overtime.

overture Composition of orchestral music acting as an introduction, as to an opera, play or concert performance.

P Abbreviation for principal performer on union forms.

PA 1. Abbreviation for production assistant. Individual who runs errands for the production; it is now a union (DGA) position. Related terms: gofer, runner. 2. Abbreviation for public address system (an electronic loud speaker system consisting of a microphone, amplifier and one or more speakers).

pacing Rate or rhythm of theme development in a film or of the dialogue or action in an individual scene. Often, timing a script beforehand will help locate pacing problems which can be corrected before shooting begins. Related term: script timing.

package Putting together various elements (script, director, actors, producer, etc.) to make a viable, sellable project. Certain agents/agencies specialize in "packaging" and present their own clients for each element, thus providing the optimum number of agent fees.

package deal Agreement in which a number of assembled factors are brought together, such as the participation of certain individuals, e.g., "It's a package deal."

packaging use Utilization of an actor's picture on a product's package, for the contract terms agreed upon. "Packaging use" may refer to photographic images printed on boxes, cardboard sheets, plastic bags, wrappers, labels, decals, stickers or the like.

packed house Another name for a theater filled to capacity with audience members.

pact Another name for a contract, e.g., "The exec signed a pact to distrib the indie prod's latest pic." Entertainment trade paper use.

padding 1. Adding or placing material into something; e.g., padding a TV program to increase its running time or padding a script with more scenes or dialogue. Related term: filler. 2. Material used to increase comfort or to provide a shock-absorbing layer of protection. Related term: stunt padding. 3. Any soft material used to fill out or make prominent, as in a bra or shoulder areas of a garment. Related terms: muscle padding, padded bra, pregnancy prothesis, stuffing.

page rate 1. Payment by the page. Related term: photographer's fee. 2. Advertising cost for a full-page advertisement.

paint box Electronic image-generating device that allows an operator to "paint" a desired scene or effect on a television screen using a variety of selected colors. Related term: digital retouching.

painter Production crew member responsible for painting sets, as needed. Related terms: scenic artist, scenery crew, matte artist.

PAL Abbreviation for "Phase Alternating Line." Technical standard for television picture formation developed in Germany and used widely in Europe and elsewhere. It is not compatible with other systems used in the world, such as NTSC and SECAM, meaning, a videotape recorded on a European VCR will not play on an American VCR without first being transferred to the technical system used in the United States (NTSC). Related term: broadcast quality.

Palme d'Or "Golden Palm Award," presented at the Cannes International Film Festival & Market in Cannes, France, to the festival's best film, as voted by a panel of judges.

pan 1. (v.) Horizontal (side to side) movement of the camera on the axis of its tripod or mount. The opening credits of director Jack Clayton's *The Great Gatsby* (1974) features a pan shot. Related term: tilt. 2. (n.) Negative review, e.g., "The film got panned in the trades."

pan and scan Process used in the transference of a 35mm widescreen film to a standard-television aspect ratio of 1.33:1. In the process, the lens is moved back and forth in a special scanning machine (telecine) so only the most visually important part of each shot is recorded, e.g., the actors or action, as opposed to scenery. If this is not done, all that appears in the far left and right of the widescreen image is eliminated when telecast. Major theatrical films for the home video market are increasingly being transferred in the letterbox format, a process that retains the widescreen image as it was presented in theaters. Most directors hate pan and scan as it changes their original presentation. Related terms: film-to-video transfer, telecine.

pan and tilt Special fitting on the tripod allowing the camera to pan (move horizontally) or tilt (move vertically).

pan glass Blue-green or brown-yellow filter allowing the viewer to see approximately what the scene will look like when shot; used primarily by the director or director of photography.

Panaclear Two-foot wide rain or spray deflector made by Panavision; mounted in front of the lens, it spins to keep water off the lens.

Panaflex Trade name for an Oscar®-winning, 35mm motion-picture camera system manufactured by Panavision, Inc., in the United States. Related term: Panavision.

Panaglide Trade name for a motion-stabilizing camera mount worn on the upper body of a Panavision camera operator in a vest-like brace; used to control steadiness during handheld shots.

Panavision Trade name for a motion picture camera system featuring a widescreen process using 35mm film and an anamorphic lens. Panavision 70 (Super Panavision) uses 65mm film and an anamorphic lens. (The 65mm film is used when shooting, while release prints are made on 70mm film; the extra 5mm account for the magnetic sound stripe on the edge.) Panavision equipment is manufactured by Panavision, Inc., of Tarzana, California and Panavision International Limited Partnership of New York City. The company has been honored with numerous awards over the years, including two Oscars® in the Scientific and Technical Awards category.

Panavision 70 with Todd A-O Sound Unsqueezed negative (on 65mm film), printed on 70mm film stock. The extra 5mm are for additional stereophonic magnetic sound tracks (in addition to the normal optical sound track) on either side of the perforations. There are five sprocket holes per frame on this film, as opposed to the four in 35mm film.

pancake apple box Apple box that is one-eighth the height of the standard version. Typical pancake apple box sizes are 1" x 12" x 18", 1" x 12" x 20" and 1" x 14" x 24". Also called a pancake, pancake-riser, eighth apple box, or eighth-apple. Related terms: apple box, full apple box.

panchromatic Black-and-white film that is sensitive to all colors visible to the human eye.

panel Also called a patch panel. Electrical board containing necessary connections for the electrical equipment on a production.

pantomime 1. (n.) Performance acted out by physical movements only; speech and other vocal sounds are not used but music or narration by another individual may accompany the performance. 2. In England, a musical play for a young audience during the Christmas season. 3. (v.) Art or technique of performing pantomime. Related term: mime.

paparazzi (singular form is paparazzo) Photographers specializing in candid and semiposed pictures of celebrities for magazines, newspapers and tabloid outfits. Papparazzo is an Italian slang word meaning "buzzing insect;" the term as applied to a celebrity photographer originated in the Federico Fellini's *La Dolce Vita* (1960) with the name of the character Paparazzo, a young newspaper photographer portrayed by actor Walter Santesso. Also called celebrity photographers. Related terms: camera-shy, candid shot, co-op, stalkerazzi.

parallax Difference in perspective of an image framed through a camera's top- or side-mounted viewfinder and that which is actually recorded by the lens. Parallax is avoided in cameras with a single-lens reflex (through-the-lens) viewing system.

parallel Platform used to raise the camera and camera crew above the floor of the set or location in order to take a high-angle shot. Lights are often placed on the parallels.

parallel action cut Also parallel-action cut. Action in two different scenes which, by intercutting (cross-cutting), seems to take place concurrently. Related terms: cross cut, parallel cut.

parenthetical direction One or more instructions for an actor found in a script; such instructions are found in parentheses just before the actor's dialogue. For example: (smiles), (laughs), (embarrassed), (sincerely), (unimpressed), (frightened), (urgently), (motioning toward), (looking at), (into phone), (into camera), (turns), (stepping away), (a moment then . . .), (a beat then . . .), (beat), (overlap dialogue) and (overlap).

pari passu (pro rata and concurrent) Literally, "with equal progress side by side." Used most often to describe the relationship of investors and profit participants in a film, vis-a-vis recoupment of their investment, payment of deferments or profits. Determining the obligation owed to the entire category entitled to pari passu payments requires the identification of the respective rights of each member of the category. The resulting payment is calculated by applying the fraction of obligation to payee, divided by the obligations to entire category to the fund available. For example, assume that two investors are pari passu; each has invested

$100,000 but one has bargained for 10 percent interest while the other for 12 percent. After one year, $100,000 is available to be paid for recoupment. The calculation for the 10 percent investor would be $110,000 (principal and interest)/ $222,000 (total principal and interest) X $100,000 = $49,549.55.

parody Satirical or humorous imitation of a serious subject. Related terms: satire, spoof, takeoff.

part Acting or performing role. Related terms: bit part, cameo part, monster part, nonspeaking part, silent part, speaking part, stock character part, extra, role, under-five, walk-on.

partial burn Fire stunt (also called a fire gag) in which part of a stunt performer's body or clothing is set on fire with a flammable liquid or gel placed over protective stunt gel. Related term: fire effect.

partial nudity Upper-body nudity, backside nudity or sectional side-angle nudity. "Partial nudity" typically is understood to mean any view of the body except the genital area. Related terms: nude scene, nudity in an audition.

pass 1. To decline to purchase, option or become involved, e.g., "The studio decided to pass on the script." 2. Studio pass. 3. Backstage pass.

passing shot Shot in which the camera is stationary and the subject moves, or the subject is stationary and the camera moves. This differs from pan or tilt, as the camera does not follow the action. *Rules of Engagement* (2000), directed by William Friedkin, uses a number of passing shots during the action scenes. Related terms: drive-by, run-by.

pay-or-play Contractual obligation guaranteeing the employer will pay the employee whether or not the services are performed or required. This kind of guarantee is typically given only to high-level people in the industry (stars, directors, writers, etc.). In some cases, acquiring such a guarantee may be a deal breaker during negotiations.

pay-per-view In cable television, the payment of an extra fee by a subscriber to view a one-time special program, such as a sporting event or concert. Related term: narrowcast.

payroll service Another name for a talent payment company.

peephole matte Camera lens matte with a small centered hole; shooting through it gives the impression that a character is looking through a hole in a wall. If the character is looking through a peephole in a door, a fisheye lens is used. Related term: matte.

penalty fee Payment made or forfeited for various punitive reasons. Also called a penalty payment, penalty charge or fine. Related terms: cancellation fee, docking of pay.

pencil test Uninked animation cells (before the picture has been colored in), photographed to see if the animated movement is correct.

per diem Specific amount of money calculated on a daily basis to cover costs incurred by a member of the company while shooting on location. Such costs can include meals, lodging, laundry, etc. Travel costs are usually additional.

perforations (abbreviated as perfs) Regularly and equally spaced holes, four per frame in 35mm, punched on the edges of motion picture film. In most 16mm film, only one side is perforated. positive film (print) perfs are usually stronger than those on negative film because they must withstand the strain of multiple projections. Related term: sprocket holes. 2. One of three registration peg holes punched in animation cels or drawing paper.

performance A show; presentation of skill or talent.

performance anxiety Condition of being apprehensive and physically queasy about performing in public. Related terms: audition anxiety, opening-night jitters, stage fright, shyness.

performance art Presentation intended to be artistic in nature and a reason for contemplation, as opposed to a presentation strictly for entertainment. Related term: tableau.

performer Any actor in a production who has a speaking, dancing or singing part. Extras or walk-ons are not considered "performers." Related terms: featured player, supporting player.

performer's entrance Another name for the theater's stage door.

performing arts Occupations, such as acting, singing, dancing, musical-instrument playing, etc., requiring performing skills.

period drama Movie, television program or stage play featuring a storyline set in the past, as opposed to a contemporary drama or futuristic drama.

period wardrobe One or more historically accurate theatrical costumes.

perk Short for perquisite. Fringe benefit; a privilege or profit over and above a salary; used as hiring incentives. Perks can include cars, expense accounts, wardrobe from films, etc. Often, perks are not left to fate but are written into contracts.

persistence of vision Human eye retaining an image briefly after it disappears. This phenomenon allows the illusion of movement when still images are projected at the rate of 16 or more frames per second.

persona Another name for a character being portrayed.

personal assistant Individual who runs errands and generally assists a producer, director or key actor on a production. He or she may be an employee of the production company or of the talent. Related terms: production assistant, gofer, entourage.

personal manager Individual who guides and develops the career of a professional talent for an agreed-upon percentage of the earnings, usually between 8 percent and 15 percent; he provides advice and assistance in career matters (and also personal matters that may have an affect on the career). He or she is not technically a publicist, nor legally an agent. A personal manager, who may also be a spouse, parent or mate, acts as an additional source of representation for the performer within the entertainment industry and in dealings with agents, publicists, the media and the public. A personal manager typically works for a management firm, which is a commercially run business with clients. However, if the personal manager is a family member, he or she typically has only the one client or counts as clients only the children in the family who perform (e.g., Kit Culkin who managed the careers of his children, including Macauley and Kieran). A family-member personal manager receives a share of the earnings and may act additionally as a traveling companion and live-in advisor (especially for minor-aged children). An actor who has a personal manager is still required to have an agent to obtain union-related work and to negotiate contracts. Also called a career manager, talent manager, celebrity manager, career advisor or talent advisor. Related terms: National Conference of Personal Managers, children's manager, career consultant, business manager.

PG 1. Rating issued in the United States by the Motion Picture Association of America for theatrical films and videos. The full wording is as follows: "'PG'—Parental Guidance Suggested. Some Material May Not Be Suitable for Children." Related terms: MPAA, motion picture rating board, rating. 2. Similar rating or classification issued for films and videos in other countries, such as Australia and Canada. In Canada, the full wording is "Parental Guidance Advised." Related term: rating. 3. Similar rating for television programs. Related terms: "TV-PG," rating.

PG-classification In Great Britain, a rating issued for theatrical films and videos by the British Board of Film Classification. The full wording of the rating is as follows: "'PG'—Parental Guidance. General viewing, but some scenes may be unsuitable for young children." Also called a "PG" certificate. Related term: rating.

PG-13 Rating issued for films and videos in the United States by the Motion Picture Association of America. All ages are permitted to view the film but parents are strongly cautioned because some material may be inappropriate for children younger than 13. The full wording is as follows: "'PG'-13—Parents Strongly Cautioned. Some Material May Be Inappropriate for Children Under 13." The "PG-13" rating was introduced on July 1, 1984 in response to requests from the public for a new rating midway between the "PG" and "R" rating. Related terms: motion picture rating board, rating.

phone numbers used on TV and in films Films and television shows produced in the United States (many of which are seen around the world), are supposed to use telephone numbers beginning with the prefix "555." The Federal Communications Commission (FCC) reserved this prefix for directory assistance, however, most "555" result in the caller hearing a recorded message similar to: "We're sorry. Your call cannot be completed as dialed. Please check the number and dial again." Fake phone numbers are intentionally used in films and TV shows so the public will not be bothered with unwanted phone calls if a viewer tries to call the number given out. Adding an area code ("800" is a toll-free designation) will produce the same result. Writers and producers should first test a phone number before including it in a script; there have been cases of producers being sued because they used a phone number (without the 555 prefix) that belonged to a homeowner or business. Similar care should be taken when mentioning addresses in scripts.

phoned in his performance Phrase used by critics to describe a less-than-enthusiastic performance by an actor. Other descriptions used: wooden, weak, dull, stone-faced, lackluster, looked as though he would rather have been somewhere else/doing somewhere else. Related terms: dull, flat, flat acting.

photo agency Business providing stock or assignment photographs for reproduction use in magazines, books, brochures and the like. Also called a photo rental agency. Related term: stock-photo agency.

photo check 1. Examination of a photograph to determine or verify its quality or content. Also called a photo examination or photo inspection. 2. Instant picture check.

photo credit Acknowledgment of having been the photographer, studio, rental agency, or syndicate that took or provided one or more photos appearing in a printed or computer work or live exhibition. Whether a credit actually appears on the work itself may depend on the contract terms, stated policy or chance; it may instead be a résumé-listed credit. A tearsheet of the printed photo may be used by the photographer for his portfolio. Also called a photo byline.

photo double Extra performer who matches the same physical description of an actor and therefore substitutes for that actor oncamera during a production. Related terms: double, stunt double, body double, nude body double.

photo editor Individual responsible for the selection and preparation of still photographs at a magazine or newspaper.

photo layout Arrangement of photographs found in or laid out for use in a publication or other printed or displayed work.

photo opportunity Chance, favorable time or good moment for taking photographs. If the photo opportunity is a scheduled event, such as for a politician or celebrity, it may also be referred to as a photo call. Also called a photo op.

photoflood High-intensity incandescent tungsten bulb; one side effect of overloading the voltage to produce

such high-intensity light is a shorter bulb life.

photogenic Attractive in a photograph; photographing well or attractively. Related term: camera presence.

photograph 1. (n.) Picture produced by the process of photography and printed on photographic paper, a transparent film base or other medium. Examples of photograph types include: action, advertising, assignment, before and after, cast, celebrity, doctored, editorial, full-face, full-length, glossy, head profile, matte, Polaroid, professional, publicity, still, still-life, stock, and three-quarter face. Related terms: photo, pic, print, shot, snapshot, slide, transparency, negative, hologram, blowup, select, video printer. 2. Digital photograph; an electronically digitized picture that can be transferred to printed form via a computer or digital/video printer. Related term: video printer. 3. (v.) To record an image on a photographic medium; aame as to film, lens, shoot or print. Related term: expose.

photographer Individual who records images using a photographic camera. Also called a photog, lenser, lensperson, shooter, camera bug or shutterbug. Examples of photographer types include: action, amateur, assistant, catalog, celebrity, fashion, free-lance, press, professional, still, still-life. Related term: paparazzi.

photographers' agent Agent or agency specializing in the representation of professional photographers. Also called a photographers' representative or photographer rep.

photographic memory Rare, special mental ability (the scientific name is eidetic memory) of remembering information, such as script lines, in precise detail, as if they had been photographed by the mind. Also called instant recall or total recall. An actor who has good recall may simply be a quick study, not necessarily eidetic.

photography 1. Art, practice or scientific process of producing images on sensitized surfaces by the action of light or other radiations. 2. Digital photography; prints or onscreen pictures produced with the aid of a computer's digital imaging technology.

photomatics Animation processing using still photographs as the medium. The camera may pan various areas of the image to create the effect of movement or portions of photos may be cut out or overlapped and moved around using stop-motion techniques. Often used to create an animated storyboard for a proposed television commercial.

photometer Similar to a light meter, this device accurately measures brightness.

photoplay 1. Script intended to be photographed as a motion picture (theatrical film); it is an anachronistic name for a screenplay. 2. The motion picture itself; a photographed play.

photo-résumé Photograph and résumé; e.g., a head shot with a résumé attached or printed on the back. Related terms: résumé photo, 8x10 résumé.

physical comedy Humor based on or involving movement of the body. Related terms: pie in the face, pratfall, slapstick.

physically demanding role Acting part requiring a lot of physical exertion, such as running, climbing or fighting. For example, Harrison Ford injured his leg in the physically demanding

role of Dr. Richard Kimble during the making of *The Fugitive* (1993).

pic (short for picture) Motion picture or still photograph. The plural is pix. Entertainment trade paper use. Related terms: biopic, kidpic, telepic, vidpic.

pic pact Movie deal, e.g., "The distrib exec signed a pic pact with the indie prod." Entertainment trade paper use.

"Pick up the pace." Direction to increase the rate of speed, e.g., move or talk faster. It may be given verbally or via a visual signal (circling the forefinger of one hand repeatedly in the air). Also said: "Speed it up," "We're running out of time," "We need to move on," "Let's go."

picked up for next season Renewed for the next television season. The opposite is being dropped, canceled or axed.

pick-up 1. (n.) Scenes or shots filmed after the completion of principal photography (usually, to fill any gaps in continuity). 2. (v.) Decision by a studio to take on a project; decision by a network to create a series from a pilot episode or to continue production on a series. 3. (v.) To shoot a portion of a shot that has already been made (without going back to the beginning of the shot) to get a different line reading or to make some other small change in performance. This is called a "print and pick up."

pickup shot One in which the action in a scene resumes at a specific point, usually with the camera shooting from a different angle or distance. This may be done to get additional footage to insert into a master scene, to film action or dialogue a different way or to repair a problem with continuity. Related term: match-action cut.

picture approval Right granted in a contract allowing a performer or other talent to approve which still photographs can be used for a particular purpose.

picture car Automobile appearing onscreen; it may be rented or borrowed and used on a studio backlot or on location. Some businesses specialize in renting picture cars. Also called a film car. Related terms: classic model, transportation captain, vehicle.

picture duplicate negative See duplicate negative.

picture negative Resulting film with image, after the exposed film has been developed in the lab. Related terms: original, negative.

picture print Processed film with a positive image and no sound track. Related term: silent print.

picture quality Level of usefulness or fineness of a photographic or television image. Related terms: broadcast quality, focus, resolution.

picture release negative Negative which has been conformed to the work print; release prints are struck from this negative.

picture-in-picture (abbreviated as PIP) Onscreen video effect in which a small boxed image is electronically composited with a larger one, usually in a corner, so that the two can be viewed simultaneously.

piggyback commercial Advertisement having two or more segments featuring different products manufactured by the same company.

pilot 1. Television program intended to be the introductory episode of a series. It may have a length of 30 or 60 minutes or it could be the length of a telefilm (90 or 120 minutes). More TV pilots are made than actually end up as network or syndicated series. If a network is interested in the produced pilot, it may authorize funding for additional episodes (thus, creating the series), either with the original cast or with cast changes or with revisions to the story (in which case, a new pilot may be requested). Some pilots are purchased and telecast as one-time events. Often, a pilot will be a 90-minute or two-hour Movie-Of-the-Week (MOW). For example, the pilot of the series *Kojak* (1973-78) was "The Marcus-Nelson Murders." Related terms: backdoor pilot, pilot season, series deal, TV series movie. 2. Individual trained and licensed to operate an aircraft. Some plane and helicopter pilots specialize in aerial shots and stunts for films and television. Pilots are considered principal performers for union contract purposes, if their actions meet the current stated requirements. Abbreviated as "P" or "Pil" on union forms. Related term: stunt pilot.

pilot pins Stationary teeth in the gate of a camera (printer or projector), which fit into the sprocket holes (or perforations) of the film as it advances; they keep the film in place. Related term: register pins.

pilot season Time of the year when pilots or backdoor pilots are produced; it occurs when most episodic television series are on hiatus, so the soundstages and crews are available. In the United States, pilot season typically occurs in late winter through early spring. Also called a TV-pilot season.

pin cushion distortion Aberration in a lens; it causes normally square images on the film to curve inward.

pipe mortar In special-effects pyro-technics work, a small-sized mortar used in explosion scenes.

pipe ramp In stunt work, a sloping, metal structure used in shots requiring a moving vehicle to roll over. In such a shot, the vehicle drives up to and over a large inclined pipe connected to a framework. The pipe makes contact with the vehicle's undercarriage, causing it to move upward and eventually turn over. Related term: car roll.

piracy Unauthorized use; copyright, patent or trademark infringement. Related term: video piracy.

pit 1. Hole or cavity in the ground, used for any of a variety of production purposes, e.g., to place a mini-trampoline for a stunt scene or an explosive device for an explosion scene. 2. Specially prepared soft area on the ground for a stuntperson or actor to fall on, as from a horse or other low-level height.

pitch 1. On motion picture film, the distance between two successive sprocket holes (or perforations). 2. A verbal presentation intended to pitch an idea for a TV movie or series to network executives. 3. Of sound: the high or low of a musical tone.

pivot 1. (n.) Body movement in which one or both feet are used to sharply turn the body in a different direction. 2. (v.) To move in such a manner.

pix Another name for pictures. Entertainment trade paper use. Related term: pic.

pixel 1. Picture element; one of the tiny red, green or blue vertical phosphor rectangles on the inner surface of a vacuum picture-tube television screen composing the color image displayed on it when struck by a fast-moving electron scanning beam. The three form a phosphor-rectangle triad. A pixel can be seen with the naked eye or with a magnifying glass. Also called a phosphor dot. Related terms: television, digital, digital imaging. 2. One of the light-sensitive, microscopic photodiodes contained on a CCD image-sensor chip in a video camera or other device. Depending on its size and type, a CCD can contain hundreds of thousands to tens of millions of pixels. Each photodiode, or pixel, on the CCD has a microlens and red, green or blue color filter in front of it. Light rays, which form images, strike the CCD, are converted into electrical signals and then are further processed for recording or transmission. Related term: CCD. 3. Liquid-crystal pixel. Related term: LCD TV.

"Places." Direction to performers to get to their entrance marks offstage or to their performing marks onstage because the action is about to begin. Also called a "Places" call. Also said: "Places, everyone," "Everyone on their marks." Related terms: "Into positions," final call.

plaster line Another name for a curtain line; straight line or series of reference marks on a stage indicating the area behind which it is safe for performers to stand when the curtain is lowered or closed. Related term: curtain line.

plasterer Individual who applies plaster or plasterboard to theatrical sets under construction. Related term: scenery crew.

platform Elevated, flat structure or flooring. Also called a stage, e.g., a speaker's platform.

play 1. (n.) Book, usually divided into acts and scenes, containing dialogue and stage directions, upon which

a theatrical presentation is based.
2. Theatrical presentation, using actors, in front of a live audience.
3. (v.) To work well, e.g., "This scene will play."

play it by ear 1. To play music by memory. 2. To improvise, as in a situation where unrehearsed dialogue or sounds are present.

play it for laughs To perform a scene with the intent of getting an audience to laugh. Related term: laughs.

play to the camera Perform toward the camera without looking into its lens; to move and talk in a direction favoring the camera, e.g., "Outside the awards show, the actress stopped and played to the cameras." Variation: play to the audience.

playback 1. Playing back recorded sound or video images. A scene may be shot with a film and video camera so the director and cinematographer can view the playback of the scene (on video) to check the quality of the shot (or performance) as it appears on-screen without having to wait for the dailies to be processed. Also called an audio playback, video playback or video replay. Related terms: instant replay, video assist. 2. Playing back previously recorded music or singing on a production set during the filming of a musical number. As the audiotape is played and cameras are rolling, performers synchronize their body movements (lip-synching or dancing) to what they are hearing. The scene is shot without microphones, since the sound has already been recorded. The playback soundtrack is then mixed with the final soundtrack during post-production. TV commercials, musicals, dance films and music videos use the play-

back technique; it is also used for rehearsals.

"Playback." Direction to the sound crew to begin the playback tape. Also said: "Begin the track."

playback track Soundtrack containing prerecorded music; it is played back during a live rehearsal or performance. Also called a playback soundtrack or playback tape. Related terms: playback, taped music.

playbill Advertising poster for a stage play.

playdate Scheduled calendar date on which a stage show or concert is performed, a theatrical film or television program is shown or a radio show, song or commercial is run. If broadcast, it is also called an airdate. Related terms: opening date, release date.

player 1. Individual who plays a theatrical part; another name for an actor. Related terms: bit player, contract player, day player, deal player, featured player, guest player, multiple-picture player, regular player, semi-regular player, supporting player, three-day player, weekly player. 2. Individual who plays a musical instrument; a musician.

playhouse Building in which plays are presented; it contains a theatrical stage, backstage area, audience seating section, front lobby, box office and various other storage and service rooms. Related terms: house, theater.

playwright Individual who writes stage plays. Related terms: dramatist, librettist, screenwriter.

plot 1. (n.) Specific sequence of events comprising a story's basic plan, description or idea. Related terms: main plot, subplot, storyline. 2. (v.) To plan or construct the basic events of a story.

plot device Strategy, method or trick used in the telling of a story. Some examples of plot devices include a character's physical handicap or prowess, interracial or age-difference pairing and time travel.

plot hole Story's credibility gap or logic inconsistency, e.g., "That new movie has so many plot holes, if it were a boat, it would sink."

plot line Another name for a log line, e.g., a one-sentence plot description.

plot point Incident occurring in a story; it is important enough to affect the rest of the story. All stories typically have numerous plot points. Related terms: beat, plot point.

plot resolution Moment in a story when the plot is resolved. Also called the climax or denouement.

plot twist Moment in a story when events take a sudden turn and new information is presented; it provides a radically different perspective or point of view to what was previously known. For example, a criminal and the detective pursuing him turn out to be long lost brothers separated at birth. Related terms: plot point, beat.

plug 1. Favorable recommendation or mention, e.g., to plug a new movie. 2. Another name for a television promotional spot.

plus ten Agent's commission, paid on a performer's union-scale contract with a signatory producer. It refers to a scale payment, plus an additional ten percent of the payment's value. According to U.S. union rules, an agent is not allowed to deduct a commission from a scale payment so the agent's ten percent is paid by the producer. Any amount over the scale payment negotiated by the agent is subject to a commission deduction. Related term: scale plus ten.

POC Abbreviation for production office coordinator.

point Percentage (or fraction thereof) of the profits (net or gross) of a motion picture or television project. Points are usually negotiated as part of a director's deal, and sometimes as part of a writer's or actor's deal. If the talent can command it, his points may be based on gross profits rather than on the usual net profits.

point-of-purchase display (abbreviated as P.O.P.) Advertising exhibit located in the same area where a product is positioned; designed to encourage purchasing by consumers. It can also be a display anywhere inside the store selling the product. Also called a P.O.P. display or point-of-sale display. Related terms: counter card, life-size cut-out, stand-up, store display.

point-of-view shot Camera shot from the character's point of view. For example, *E.T. The Extra-Terrestrial* (1982) features many point-of-view shots of the alien. Related term: POV.

Polaroid Trade name of Polaroid Corporation's camera, film and accessories. Instant pictures are often used on film sets for continuity shots. Polaroid Corporation's world headquarters are located in Cambridge, Massachusetts, in the United States.

Polaroid filter Filter that helps eliminate reflections and glare. Related term: pola screen.

polecat Support for lamps.

polish Slight revision of a script; a special classification recognized by the Writers Guild of America, comprising a specific and separate pay scale. If a polish becomes too extensive, it is called a revision.

Poly Vision Forerunner of Cinerama; Abel Gance developed this triple-screen projection system in 1927, for his historic film *Napoleon.*

Pony Express mount In stunt work, a method of mounting a moving horse by briskly running alongside it, grabbing the saddle's horn and then jumping into the saddle while continuing to ride forward. It is named after the Pony Express horseback-relay mail service that operated in the United States between St. Joseph, Missouri and Sacramento, California, during the period from 1860 to 1861. Of the more than 200 riders associated with the Pony Express during its existence, the two most famous were William F. "Buffalo Bill" Cody (1846-1917) and James B. "Wild Bill" Hickok (1837-1876).

pool camera operator News cameraman who records or provides the live feed for other television news stations or networks at an event with restricted attendance. For example, trials featuring celebrity defendents often utilize pool operators because courtrooms have limited space.

pool reporter News reporter selected to represent a number of news-gathering organizations at an event with restricted attendance. See pool camera operator.

P.O.P. See point-of-purchase display.

Popper-Stopper Trade name for a microphone accessory, the main feature of which is a circular nylon screen. It attaches to or is positioned in front of a microphone and helps eliminate unwanted sounds like those caused by uttering the letter "p." Related term: windscreen.

pop-up ad One having three-dimensional features when opened, e.g., a pop-up magazine ad.

portable stage One that can be disassembled and transported to another location, where it is then reassembled and used.

porta-pit In stunt work, a portable foam crash pad used in scenes involving falls.

portray To represent dramatically; to assume the role of or play the part of; to act. Related terms: perform, play, emote.

positive Print made from a negative (or, stock shot in the camera with reversal film) with the proper colors appearing in their proper places.

positive publicity Any report in the media that is beneficial to an individual's reputation or career. It could appear in any media: television news report, magazine article, gossip column, paparazzi photo, etc. Also called good publicity, favorable publicity, the right kind of publicity or good press. Related terms: publicity, "Any publicity is good publicity."

possessory credit Credit title indicating legal or creative ownership or affiliation. For examples, "[name] Presents," "A [name] Film" and "A [name] Production." This auteur credit has been a controversial subject between writers and directors, as the "A [name] Film" has been awarded to the director, even if he or she did not also write the screenplay.

poster Large, printed sheet featuring advertising, promotional, informational, educational or artistic subject matter. Related terms: movie poster, stage-show poster, transit poster.

postponed broadcast Broadcast that did not take place as originally scheduled and is subsequently rescheduled for airing on a different date. Related term: preempted program.

post-production One of the four stages of work of a film, television program, commercial or video production (the other three stages are development, preproduction and production). Post-production includes the steps necessary to complete a project for distribution; it occurs after principal and any second-unit filming has concluded. Examples of post-production work include picture editing, sound editing, dialogue improvement or replacement (ADR), music scoring, the inclusion of optical or computer-generated visual effects, striking of release prints or copies and preparation of promotional materials. Related term: production.

post-synchronization Act of re-recording dialogue or sound in a proper acoustical environment; used when sound has not been recorded satisfactorily at the time of shooting or when it was impossible to record the sounds/dialogue concurrently while shooting. Also used to translate the dialogue from one language to another. Related terms: dubbing, looping, ADR.

POV Abbreviation for "point of view" or "point-of-view shot."

powder 1. Explosive powder (grains) used in special-effects or stunt work involving pyrotechnics. Examples are black powder (a mixture of potassium nitrate, charcoal and sulfur used as an explosive lifting charge, as in a mortar) and smokeless powder (any powder containing mostly cellulose nitrate). Gunpowder is a general term and refers to either black powder (associated with antique firearms) or smokeless powder (used in modern firearms). The special-effects technician who buys, stores, transports, places and detonates explosive pow-

der is required by law to be licensed. Related terms: powder person, explosion scene, gunfight scene, pyrotechnic supervisor. 2. Flash powder.

powder person Supervisor or other member of the special-effects crew responsible for handling pyrotechnic powders. Related terms: pyrotechnic operator, pyrotechnic supervisor.

P.R. Abbreviation for public relations.

P.R. machine. Nickname for a celebrity or company successful in obtaining publicity. (P.R. is an abbreviation for public relations.)

practical 1. Any prop or part of a set that actually works, such as an electrical fan; practical prop. The opposite is a dummy prop. Also called a prac or functioning prop. Related terms: practical set, prop.

practical joke Joke with physical elements; it is played on one or more unsuspecting participants. Also called a prank or trick. Related terms: joke, flashlight monster, rabbit ears.

practical set 1. Production set full of working parts, e.g., lights, appliances, windows, cabinets and the like. 2. Outdoor production set with real buildings and other working parts, as opposed to a set consisting only of facades.

praiser Another name for a publicist, e.g., "The praiser's comments about her client to the press were all favorable." Entertainment trade paper use.

pratfall Intentional fall, executed as part of a comic routine; comic fall backward in which the individual lands on his prat (another name for the buttocks).

pre-credits sequence Opening segment of a film; it appears before the main title and opening credits. In television, it is also called a teaser.

preem 1. (n.) Short for premiere, e.g., "The stars were out at last night's preem." Entertainment trade paper use. 2. (v.) To premiere.

preempt To take over part or all of the time slot of a regularly scheduled television program so that other programming can be shown. A local TV station may preempt network programming to air an emergency news report or a network may preempt one of its own shows to report on a breaking news story of national interest. For example, when President John F. Kennedy was assassinated, all network and local programming was preempted to cover the story of his death.

preempted program Television show that was preempted by a national network or local station; typically, the program is rescheduled for a later date. When the preempted program is finally aired, it is called a postponed broadcast or telecast.

pre-feature short film Short film, such as a cartoon; it is shown in theaters before the main feature. Related term: featurette.

pregnancy prosthesis Rounded, padded attachment worn on the lower front of the body to simulate a pregnancy. Also called pregnancy padding or a pregnancy simulator. For example, Arnold Schwarzenegger wore a pregnancy prosthesis in *Junior* (1994) when he portrayed an impregnated scientist.

premiere 1. (n.) First formal public performance or showing. 2. (v.) To perform or show for the first time.

premiere benefit Opening of a film, play, etc., intended to support a charitable cause through the donation of all or a portion of its admission

ticket sales. Related term: benefit screening.

premium channels Cable television channels requiring an extra payment to receive. Also called pay TV channels.

premium pay Extra pay to a performer; typically given for working on Saturday, Sunday, a sixth consecutive day, holiday or during nighttime hours. The pay is calculated at a rate different than overtime and is specified by the union contract's premium pay rate, which may be anywhere from ten percent to double the regular scale payment. Related term: golden time.

pre-mix Early stage of creating a composite track in which several sound tracks are combined. Related term: pre-dub.

prep To prepare; make ready, e.g., "The director flew to New York to prep his new film." Entertainment trade paper use.

pre-production Time before production when the elements needed for making the film, e.g., preparing the script, script breakdown, budget, location scouting, costume design, set construction, are done.

pre-publicity Activities occurring far in advance; done to promote a product or project long before it is available for purchase or viewing, e.g., "The movie star did a pre-publicity photo shoot for a magazine story that will appear on newsstands later in the year, when the film opens." Related terms: publicity, prerelease.

prequel Film or television episode released (or aired) after the original but which tells a story about events taking place before the original, e.g., *Star Wars: Episode 1 - The Phantom Menace* (1999) was released 22 years after the original *Star Wars* (1977) but the events in the movie take place many years before those of *Star Wars*.

prerecorded Recorded at an earlier time. Related term: playback track.

pre-scoring Preparation of the musical score before a film is shot. Typically, the music is composed, arranged and recorded after shooting is completed.

presence Visible or audible effectiveness. Related terms: camera presence, screen presence, stage presence, photogenic.

press 1. Print and electronic news media. Related term: news media. 2. Print, TV, computer or radio reports or publicity resulting from such reports, e.g., good press or bad press.

press agent Individual providing representational services to clients in media and publicity matters. Also called a publicist or public relations agent.

press book Press kit in the form of a booklet or folder.

press clipping News item cut from a newspaper or magazine and saved for later reference or used for promotional purposes. Related term: tearsheet.

press conference Session, at a set time and place, with members of the media; more formal than encounters with the media at a press party. An actor, singer, etc., may be required to appear at a press conference as part of a promotional campaign, where he may be interviewed by reporters about an entertainment project. The performer may also, through his publicist, call a press conference to answer questions about personal matters (such as, a legal problem or a rumor that has surfaced). There may be a statement read and/or a question-and-answer period, either with the performer or his representative. More often, a printed press release is issued to disseminate news to the media. Also called a news conference. Related terms: interview, "No comment," press party.

press coverage Extent to which information is gathered and reported by the news media. Also called media coverage. Related term: team coverage.

press interview Any interview in which the subject(s) is asked questions by one or more reporters. Related terms: interview, press conference, press party.

press junket Location trip for members of the press, arranged by the film's publicity department so cast, director, producer, etc., may be interviewed during production. Such a junket also may be planned when the film is released. Since this can be expensive, press junkets are usually reserved for big budget productions in need of lots of advance publicity.

press kit Package of materials, e.g., black-and-white stills from the film, color transparencies, production notes, cast biographies, sent to the press to encourage articles/stories about the film. The materials are written and compiled by the film's unit publicist and the studio's public relations department. In the electronic press kits (abbreviated as "EPK"), the same materials appear on videotape and also may include trailers and interviews with key people from the production.

press line One and/or more rows of reporters and camera people stationed outside the location of a newsworthy event, e.g., "The celebrities had to make their way past the press line to get inside."

press party 1. Event to which members of the media are invited to meet some or all of the stars of a production, including key production personnel (e.g., the producer and director), with the goal to obtain positive publicity for the project. Refreshments are served and there may be an announcement by the host, some entertainment, an informal question-and-answer session or arranged interviews with the stars. Press kits may be distributed or they may have been sent with the invitation. The stars are present to make themselves visible in the interest of publicity and to fulfill their contract obligations to publicize the project. They may be photographed, filmed and/or interviewed briefly by any number of reporters for articles and/or TV reports. A press party is more expensive and showy than a press conference (which has a more businesslike atmosphere). Also called a media party, press reception, media reception, press luncheon or media luncheon. Related term: publicity party. 2. Any nonbusiness or social gathering for members of the press, such as a press awards luncheon or dinner.

press release Prepared statement distributed to the media; it provides information about a product, person, place, activity, service or event. Also called a news release, publicity release, media alert or TV alert. Related terms: video press release, damage control, press conference.

press screening Sneak preview screening of a film project for members of the entertainment press; held in the hope of gaining favorable publicity. Related term: sneak preview.

press tour See press junket.

pressroom 1. Location where reporters and camera crews assemble, e.g., "After winning the Oscar®, the actress left the stage and headed for the pressroom to pose for pictures and meet the press." Also called a press conference room or news media room. Related terms: media presence, winner's interview, winner's photo call. 2. Any room where reporters work.

pressure plate Plate behind the aperture of the projector (or camera or printer) holding the film snugly in place.

preview Advance showing of a film before the scheduled release date. A preview can be shown to an invited group, e.g., members of the press, industry executives, friends, to help spread good word-of-mouth, or to the paying public as a test screening to gauge audience reaction. It is not unusual for changes to be made after a preview. Many directors have the contractual right to one or two previews before submitting their final edited version of the film to the studio. Related term: sneak preview.

preview audience Audience that gets an advance look at a film project, play, etc., e.g., "Preview audiences loved the film." Audience reaction to the preview is used to determine if changes should be made. Also called a test audience; preview of a product (not a film) is called test marketing. Related term: test screening.

preview clip Video clip containing preview material, e.g., one or more scenes from an upcoming theatrical film. Related terms: behind-the-scenes preview, promo, video clip.

primary colors In painting, the primary colors (from pigment) are red, yellow and blue. In terms of color photography, there are two ways to create colors: the additive method and the subtractive method; the additive and subtractive primary colors have to do with light. In the additive method, colored lights are combined until the desired color is created. The subtractive method begins with white light; all the colors of the light spectrum are combined in motion until a filtering out (or subtracting) leaves the desired color. The primary additive colors are red-orange, green and blue-violet which, when mixed, produce white light. Varying the proportions of the mixture will produce the other colors. The primary subtractive colors are cyan (blue-green), yellow and magenta (purple-pink), which are the complementary colors to the additive primary colors. The subtractive primary colors absorb the red, green and blue wavelengths, thus subtracting them from the white light. When mixed, they can produce any color in the spectrum, even black (having absorbed all colors of light). Early color cinematography was based on the additive process but today it is based on the subtractive process; even though the subtractive process requires chemical processing, it is the more practical method.

prime lens Individual lens of a specific focal length, as opposed to a zoom lens, which has variable focal lengths.

prime time Period of the evening during which most people watch television; peak viewing hours. In the United States and elsewhere, prime time is typically is during the hours between 7 p.m. and 11 p.m. Network prime time (Monday through Saturday) is 8 p.m. to 11 p.m.; on Sunday, it is 7 p.m. to 11 p.m. Related terms: family hour, late-night TV, nighttime TV.

principal performer Individual who plays an essential or prominent part in a film or stage production. Generally, in union productions, the term "principal performer" is used to designate a performer whose contribution is above that of a background or foreground extra. For contract purposes, a principal performer often is defined as having a minimum number of lines or scenes to perform; union contracts provide a list of minimum qualifications for such status. Also called a principal player or principal actor. Related terms: key cast member, first team.

principal photography Segment of production during which all scripted material covering all speaking parts is filmed. Second unit material (of locations and containing no speaking parts) may be shot at approximately the same time. It is possible for second unit photography to be shot either before or after principal photography. Related terms: principal shooting, second unit shooting.

principal players Members of the cast comprising the main featured actors.

principal shooting Production stage during which the filming of all shots featuring the principal performers (along with any extras) take place. Secondary shooting, also called second-unit photography, involves aerial and underwater shots, visual effects, explosions, certain stunts and other specialized shots. Principal shooting is also called principal photography.

print 1. (n.) Positive, used for projection, made from an original (or dupe) negative. 2. (v.) Lab process in which a positive is created from a negative, or a negative from a positive. By using a special reversal printing process, the lab can also produce a positive from a positive and a negative from a negative. Related term: CRI.

print ad Advertisement appearing in a printed medium, such as a magazine or newspaper.

print advertiser Business or person featured in print advertising and responsible for its cost and content.

print and pick up Filming a portion of a shot without starting at the beginning, either to get a different line reading or to make another small change in a performance.

print interview Interview featured in a magazine or used as the basis for a newspaper story; it may include still photographs, taken at the time of the interview or at a later session. Related terms: magazine interview, newspaper interview, interview.

"Print it." Direction from the director indicating a shot or scene just filmed is acceptable and should be sent to the lab for printing (or, should be marked as a "keep take" and used as a blooper). Also said: "Cut and print," "That's a print," "That's a good one." Related terms: "Save it," keep takes.

print media Various types of printed communication, such as magazines, newspapers, newsletters, books, and the like. Also called the written media. Related terms: news media, press.

printdown Reduction of a film print. The opposite is a blowup. Related term: downprint.

printer Device which makes prints (or other generations) from positives or negatives. The two main types of printers are the optical printer, which projects the image onto raw stock for reproduction; and the contact printer, in which the original film is

placed in physical contact with the raw stock and exposed to light. There are also two methods of printing: step printing, in which the film is advanced intermittently (with each frame being stationary during exposure); and continuous-motion printing, in which the raw stock and original move continuously during exposure.

printer light Control on the printer; when adjusted during processing, it can correct any differences in the density of the negative.

process body Full structure or cutaway section of a vehicle (e.g., automobile, airplane, train) positioned in front of a rear projection screen. Most common is a process shot featuring one or more actors sitting in an automobile while footage of a receding roadway is projected onto the back of the screen. Related term: mock-up.

process shot Shot in which one or more performing actors are physically located in front of an image being projected onto a rear or front projection screen; it is shot in a studio soundstage. During a process shot, the image on the screen becomes the background for the shot. Related terms: process body, front projection, rear-screen projection.

processing Term used for developing and printing film.

prod Short for producer or production, e.g., "The prod is behind schedule." Entertainment trade paper use.

produced by Credit designated for the project's producer; found on the screen, poster, theater program, etc.

producer Ideally, the first person on a project and the last person off. The producer's role is to find and develop a project; hire the writers and develop the script; hire the director, actors, etc.; arrange for financing; oversee the production. (In episodic television, this person is called the executive producer.) Also, the producer may be involved in the release of the film. Some directors and actors who initiate their own projects act as their own producers. Related term: hyphenate.

producer's assistant Individual who provides assistance to a producer on a production.

Producers Guild of America Organization of film and television producers in the United States. Founded in 1950 and based in Beverly Hills, California. Internet address: http://www.producersguild.com.

producer's net profits See profits.

product placement company Business specializing in providing manufacturers' brand-name products for use as onscreen props in theatrical films and television programs. The placement company receives a fee for arranging the deal between the manufacturer and production company. If a brand-name product is not used, the Prop Department will create a fake brand-name product to use instead.

production 1. Act or process of producing or manufacturing. 2. What is produced; a product. 3. One of the four work stages in the creation of a theatrical film, television program, commercial or video (the other three are development, preproduction and post-production). During production, the actual filming of the project takes place. Collectively, it can mean all four stages, e.g., "The latest figures show that movie production is up from last year." Related terms: CD-ROM live-action production, co-production, runaway production, "go" project, principal shooting.

production accountant Accountant who manages the financial records of a film, TV or stage production, which may include (depending upon the size and complexity of the production) the preparation of cast and crew payroll checks. Related terms: accountant, entertainment accountant, talent payment company, Hollywood bookkeeping, production auditor.

production assistant (abbreviated as PA) Entry-level member of the production crew whose job is to perform tasks for the producer, director, production manager, production office coordinator, etc. Related terms: gofer, runner.

production auditor Member of the production staff, working directly with the production manager and the financing entity, whose primary responsibility is to maintain current, accurate financial records of the costs entailed in the production. This position may be covered by a union. Related terms: location auditor, location accountant.

production board See production strip board.

production breakdown See breakdown.

production center Facility, complex, city or region where the production of film, TV, video, music or stage projects takes place.

production company Business that develops (with the goal of producing) one or an ongoing number of film, television, video, music or live entertainment projects. Related term: independent production company.

production coordinator Also called the production office coordinator, which may be abbreviated POC.

Individual on a production staff who prepares, organizes, files, receives and transmits forms, correspondence and other paperwork necessary to produce a project. On large productions, there may be one or more assistant production coordinators. Related term: production secretary.

production credit Acknowledgment of work done on a production. Often the size, position, and/or placement of the credit is subject to union requirements and contractual obligations. Related term: credit.

production designer Individual responsible for designing the overall look of a film project, according to the script and the guidelines established by the director and producer. The production designer may research and supervise set design and construction, location and prop selection, set decoration, costume appearances and credit and title designs. May also be called a senior art director or supervising art director. Related terms: art director, set designer.

production executive Management-level employee of a studio or independent production company.

production helmer Theatrical film or television director, e.g., "The production helmer flew to Sydney to shoot location scenes." Entertainment trade paper use.

production home movie A behind-the-scenes videorecording shot using a small camcorder. Also called a home movie from the set. It is often done for promotional purposes, with the camera being supplied by an entertainment television news program, which then telecasts the footage as part of a report on the project.

production house Business establishment and workplace where production activities occur.

production manager Individual who manages a production's expenditures and schedules on a daily basis. This may involve budgeting; renting locations and equipment; arranging transportation, meals and lodging; and hiring technical production personnel (camera, sound and lighting crews). He or she may also be called a "line producer" on some productions. In the theater world, a production manager has similar responsibilities. Related terms: unit production manager, line producer.

production mixer Chief sound engineer on the set whose primary responsibility is to achieve the best recorded sound possible during production. The production mixer may also be called a sound mixer, floor mixer, recording supervisor, sound recorder, sound recordist or recordist (the latter three may also refer to the individual who actually operates the recording equipment, if it is not done by the production mixer). Related terms: sound mixer, sound recordist.

production number Number in a film or television show featuring music, dancing and/or singing. For example, the Academy Awards® ceremony typically opens with a large production number. Special sets and costumes are created for the musical number.

production report Daily report itemizing all elements used for that particular day of shooting; filled out by the key second assistant director and submitted to the production manager for approval. The completer report is sent to the producer, director, production auditor, studio executive (if applicable) and any other party concerned with the daily costs of the production. The report includes such items as: the scenes shot, the number of pages completed, amount of footage exposed, any abnormalities to explain overage or underuse of material covered, any penalties incurred and their reasons, which crew members and actors were used, etc.

production schedule Another name for a shooting schedule.

production secretary Production office employee who performs secretarial duties for the production company office. Duties may include telephone, mail and computer communications; handling production paperwork; scheduling appointments; arranging for and receiving deliveries; and being the company's initial contact person within the industry, the media and public. Someone, usually with more experience, would be called a production coordinator.

production set Indoor or outdoor studio or location set where actors are filmed according to the script and the director's directions. Also called a shooting set, filming set or taping set. Related term: set.

production set tour A walk-around visit to the various places of a production set; e.g., "The entertainment reporter was given a production set tour by one of the stars of the cast." Also called a set tour. Related term: studio tour.

production staff Group of administrative or technical production employees, including support personnel, such as production manager, production supervisor, production office coordinator, production secretary and production assistants.

production still 1. Still photograph; it is an enlargement of a single frame from a finished production. Also called a production still photo, action still, frame enlargement or frame blowup. Related term: publicity still. 2. Still photograph taken for publicity and/or continuity purposes. It may show the actors performing, director and crew working, a special effect or stunt being performed, set construction, an actor having makeup applied, or the like. Also called a behind-the-scenes photo. Related terms: publicity photo, behind-the-scenes footage.

production strip board Scheduling tool used by production managers and first assistant directors to determine which actors are needed for which scene and exactly how much time it will take to shoot the film. Each scene in the script is marked on a separate strip (Interior or Exterior; Day or Night). These strips are laid on the paneled board and arranged to show the most efficient and least expensive order in which to shoot the project.

production time report Work-time sheet for the performers; it must be completed daily by a designated member of the production team, signed by each actor and submitted to the actor's union, e.g., a Screen Actors Guild Actors Production Time Report. Related term: time report.

production unit 1. Production team assigned or hired to work on a project. Also called a "company." 2. Separate, often specialized, production team performing a specific aspect of the production. Also called a second unit. (The first unit shoots all the major scenes.) Related terms: aerial unit, helicopter unit, special-effects unit, stunt unit, underwater unit. 3. Mobile production unit. 4. Production investment share. Also called an investment unit or partnership interest.

production value Quality of a production, as determined by the amount and effectiveness of money spent on set design and construction, costumes, equipment, special effects, etc. Related term: entertainment value.

professional acting 1. Acting for which payment is received. Also called paid acting, occupational acting or career acting. 2. Acting that adheres to the normal standards of industry professionalism.

professional name Name an individual opts to take when working in his occupation. Actors are particularly known for changing their names. Related terms: stage name, name change.

profile flat On a production set, a structural background flat with irregularly shaped top or sides, e.g., a protruding rock formation, part of a sign, limb of a tree, as opposed to the typical four-cornered, rectangular appearance.

profile shot Photograph of an object's side view, especially the human face. Related terms: head profile photo, semiprofile shot.

profit participation Sharing in the profits from revenues; it is part of an investment agreement or work contract. Related terms: back-end deal, gross-point deal, net-profit deal, film stock, portfolio, production unit.

profits Net and gross profits are redefined on a per-project basis. Although some companies have adopted a standard or have developed a customary definition, the definition is still subject to negotiation. Two issues determine each specific definition: 1) what income is included and accountable; and 2) what deductions may be taken against that income before the participant's percentage is applied to the remainder. Many industryites are cynical about deriving real profits from a picture's earnings, hence, a prospective participant is advised to seek skilled and experienced counsel when negotiating profits.

program 1. (n.) Radio or TV show. Related terms: back-up program, preempted program. 2. List of performers or events to be presented. Related terms: playbill, television schedule. 3. (v.) To schedule or plan, e.g., to program a week's lineup of TV shows.

programmer Individual who sets the schedule of programs. Related term: network programmer.

programming 1. Schedule or plan. Related terms: back-to-back programming, block programming, counter programming. 2. Shows that can be placed on a schedule, e.g., "The station buyers went to the annual NATPE convention to purchase new programming for their fall schedules."

project 1. (n.) Planned undertaking. Related term: "go" project. 2. (v.) To cast one or a series of photographic or graphic images onto a screen. Related terms: projectionist, projection room, projector. 3. To speak, sing or gesture forcefully.

projection 1. Ability to make one's voice carry a great distance. 2. Process of running a film through a projector, during which a beam of light throws the enlarged image onto a screen. Related terms: back screen projection, bluescreen projection. 3. Forecasts about a film's performance at the box office and any revenue-gathering markets.

projection booth Small room in the back of the theater from which the image is projected onto the screen.

projection printer See optical printer.

projection room Room in a theater where the projector and audio equipment are located and operated. Also called a projection booth.

projection sync Spacing between the sounds track and its corresponding picture: 20 frames ahead of the picture for 35mm; 26 frames ahead for 16mm.

projectionist Individual responsible for operating the motion picture or still-image projector; usually a member of IATSE.

projector Light-producing device that throws filmed images onto a screen. When the images are projected at a rate of 24 frames per second, the illusion of motion is created. Related term: persistence of vision.

prologue 1. Introductory scene. Depending on content, it may also be called a teaser. The opposite of a prologue is an epilogue. 2. Introductory or opening speech. Also called an opening monologue, especially on a television talk or variety show.

promo 1. Filmed or recorded promotional advertisement or announcement for an upcoming program on a television or radio station or network. Also called a promotional spot, plug or preview clip. Related term: network promo. 2. Filmed advertisement promoting a theatrical motion picture. It may be shown in the theater or transferred to videotape for airing on television. Related terms: movie commercial, preview clip, trailer.

3. Any promotional short film or videotape. Related term: video promo. 4. Short for "promotional," such as a promo tour or promo work.

promotional appearance Another name for a publicity appearance.

promotional consideration Payment or product of value given in exchange for the advertising (visual or audio) of a product, company or organization; most often occurs on a game show, e.g., "Promotional consideration paid for by the following . . ."

promotional still Another name for a publicity still.

promotional tour Scheduled stops to various locations (inter- or intra-city) where the creator of a new project (film, TV series, music CD, book, or the like) can promote it. Also called a promo tour or publicity tour. Related terms: promo, publicity appearance, talk-show circuit.

prompt 1. To tell a performer his forgotten lines. Related terms: prompter, feed. 2. Quick; fast, e.g., a prompt response from an audience. 3. To urge, e.g., to prompt into action.

prompt box Low, open-sided box or hood built into the floor at the front of a stage; its opening faces the performers and a prompter can be located here during a performance.

prompt card Another name for a cue card.

prompt corner Area offstage, out of view of the audience, where a prompter can be located during a stage performance.

promptbook Script for a stage play containing detailed information regarding blocking, action, cues and various other references pertaining to the production's staging.

prompter 1. Person offstage or in a prompt box who gives lines of forgotten dialogue or cues to onstage performers during a rehearsal or the actual performance. Related terms: script supervisor, "Line," memorization of script lines. 2. Short for videoprompter, e.g., "Look straight into the camera and read your lines off the prompter." Related terms: videoprompter, TelePrompTer.

proof 1. Test, or first, photograph printed from a negative, created to examine its quality. Also called a trial photograph or test print. 2. Proof sheet.

proof sheet 1. Test, or first, printing of a page, poster or the like. Also called a test sheet, trial sheet, trial impression or galley proof. 2. Sheet photograph displaying numerous negative-size print photographs or frames. Also called a contact sheet.

prop See property.

prop gun Real or dummy firearm used in a scene. Related terms: dummy prop, gunfight scene, weapons master.

prop maker Member of the construction department (e.g., carpenter) responsible for making the props for a film. Should not be confused with prop master.

prop master See property master.

prop test kit Any of various fake medical and scientific test kits used onscreen by actors portraying police investigators, laboratory technicians or the like. For example, Simulated Blood Test, Simulated Cocaine Test, Simulated Pregnancy Test and Simulated Latent Serial Number Kit. A source for prop test kits is the special-effects company Tri-Ess Sciences, Inc., of Burbank, California.

property 1. Any movable item seen on a motion picture set and used in a particular scene. For example, the Spalding basketball Sanaa Lathan uses in *Love & Basketball* (2000) and the basketballs in the locker room are considered set dressing. 2. Literary work, such as a book, script, or story, e.g., "The actor's production company purchased the film rights to the writer's latest property." Related terms: hot property, star property, option. 3. Any proprietary idea or concept whose legal rights can be sold as the basis for an entertainment project, e.g., a person's life story.

property master Individual responsible for obtaining, storing and maintaining the props used on a production. He or she may be in charge of a Prop Department and/or supervise the work of prop handlers and propmakers; or the property master may handle all the job duties alone (especially on smaller productions). Someone with a prop-related job may also be called a prop person, prop master or props. Related terms: leadman, modelmaker, set decorator, set dresser, stagehand, stylist, weapons master.

property sheet List and schedule of all props to be used in the film.

proprietary makeup Makeup application or appearance protected by a copyright or other right of ownership. Typically this situation is found in a science-fiction, fantasy, comic or advertising character.

proscenium In a theater, the two side walls and the connecting overhead arch that frames and divides the stage area from the audience section. Related term: apron.

protagonist The leading figure, or hero, of the story; it could be a person, group, animal, alien being, paranormal entity, force of nature or the like. The protagonist opposes the antagonist, or villain. Related terms: hero, heroine.

protection master See interpositive, master positive, CRI.

PSA Abbreviation for public service announcement.

public domain Not protected by a copyright or patent, e.g., many old black-and-white films and classical musical compositions are in the public domain. Noncopyrighted and previously copyrighted works that now exist in the public domain are free to be used and reproduced or sold by industry and the public.

public eye Public watchfulness, attention, scrutiny and examination. Related terms: limelight, spotlight.

public image How one is perceived by the general population.

public opinion Beliefs and judgments of people. Also called public sentiment, the public's attitude or how the public feels about an issue.

public performance Entertainment presented to the public, either for an admission price or for free.

public relations Field of work in which activities are performed to promote or maintain good relations between the public and a company, organization or celebrity. Related terms: P.R., damage control, expose, spin.

public relations agent Individual providing public relations services to clients. Also called a P.R. agent, P.R. person, press agent or publicist.

public service announcement (abbreviated as PSA) Noncommercial advertisement serving the public interest; it is played, without charge, on television, radio or in movie theaters. Also called a public service

spot or public service message. Related term: PSA.

public television Television programming, as in the United States, supported whole or in part by donations from viewers, private foundations and corporations. The opposite is commercial (for profit) television.

publicist Individual responsible for promotion and publicity of a person or film project to the media. The aim of the publicity is to make the client/film more well-known and, hopefully, a more desirable commodity. The individual overseeing all publicity is called publicity director. On a film project, the publicist is called the unit publicist. This is a union position and covered by the Publicists Guild. Related term: press agent.

publicity 1. Public notice or attention acquired through the media. Related terms: "Any publicity is good publicity," negative publicity, positive publicity, pre-publicity, damage control, press, public relations. 2. Act or procedure intended to get the public's attention, e.g., "I'm scheduled to do some publicity for my new film next week." Also called promotion. 3. Of or pertaining to publicity.

publicity appearance To appear before the public to gain publicity for oneself, one's work, a charity or movement. Also called a promotional appearance. Related terms: personal appearance, professional appearance, talk-show appearance, film festival, publicity stunt.

publicity campaign Organized series of activities designed to use the power of the media to inform the public about a person, product, place, event, company or organization. Also called a promotional campaign. Related terms: advance teaser campaign, promotional tour, build-up, hype, puff piece.

publicity date An arranged outing, as to a movie premiere or other celebrity function, with an individual who is likely to provide proper or favorable publicity for one or both of those involved. Also called a promotional date, (event) date, celebrity date, celebrity-escort date, publicity outing, or promotional outing. Related term: mystery date.

publicity gimmick Attention-getting device or scheme, done to gain publicity. Related terms: gimmick, publicity stunt, ratings ploy.

publicity kit See press kit.

publicity party Party held to attract favorable attention from the media.

publicity photo Any photograph distributed to the media for publicity purposes. Related terms: publicity still, cast photo, lobby card.

publicity release Another name for a press release.

publicity still Any still photograph used for promotional purposes; typically, it is an 8" x 10" photo (U.S.). Also called a publicity photo or promotional still. Related terms: production still, still photo.

publicity stunt Something done to attract the media's attention, e.g., "As a publicity stunt, the producers of the new animated children's film hired actors to appear at the premiere in full character costumes." Related terms: publicity gimmick, stage.

publicity tour Another name for a promotional tour.

publicity-seeker Individual who actively seeks the attention of the news media for reasons of self-promotion; individual who wants celebrity status.

publicity-shy Reluctant or uneasy about participating in publicity activities; uncomfortable being in the public eye. An actor's contract may require a certain amount of publicity work to promote the project, such as media interviews and photo sessions. Also referred to as being media-shy (interviews) or paparazzi-shy (photographs and video). Related terms: camera-shy, celebrity, newsworthy, public eye.

puff piece Written article or news segment so flattering to the subject, it appears to resemble a free advertisement.

Puff Powder Special-effects powder; when ignited, it produces an instant puff of smoke. Formulated and sold by Zeller International, Ltd., of Downsville, New York. Related term: smoke effect.

pull focus Somewhat artistic shot: an object in the foreground is out of focus while an object in the background is in focus (or vice versa); then, the focus is slowly switched, so the foreground object is in focus while the background is fuzzy (or vice versa).

pullback Backwards movement of the camera, e.g., from a close shot to a medium or long shot. Director Mike Nichols uses a dramatic pullback shot in *The Graduate* (1967) to establish a change in setting for Elaine (Katharine Ross), from Los Angeles to her college in northern California. 2. In stunt work, pulling or jerking the stunt performer backwards using a thin wire. Related terms: air ratchet, jerk harness, safety harness.

pulled from the schedule Removed from a list of things to occur; e.g., "My TV series was pulled from the schedule and put on indefinite hiatus." Also referred to as being yanked off the schedule or taken off the air. Related terms: cancel, hiatus.

pulling a punch Faking a punch in a fight scene; stopping just short of hitting someone. It may also mean light contact that appears real with the help of post-production sound effects and choreographed movement from the other actor. There are several ways to position actors so the camera does not record actual physical contact; this way, the audience is fooled into believing that punches and physical damage have actually occurred. Physical damage may be simulated with fake blood and other makeup. An actor will receive training on how to pull a punch before a scene is shot, if necessary. All fight scenes are rehearsed, including those involving simulated kicking, head-butting, and actual throwing of objects. Lengthy scenes or those involving many participants or unusual hand weapons may be choreographed by a fight director. The camera and crew filming or videorecording the scene are carefully positioned as well. Related terms: punch, fight scene, stunt, stunt double.

punchline Word, phrase or sentence at the end of a joke giving it humor and meaning. Related terms: joke, setup.

pup Small, focused light source of 500 watts.

puppet Small or life-size three-dimensional representation of a person or animal operated remotely by hand. The type used in film and television typically is a special-effects makeup creation having a metal or plastic internal framework, moving metal or plastic parts, hair and a colored latex exterior skin (or other rubbery material). It is manipulated directly by hand, remote cables or a wireless radio system by one or more off camera puppeteers. Depending on the degree of complexity, it may also be called an animatronic figure. Related terms: hand puppet, hand-and-rod puppet, rod puppet, marionette, animation, animatronic, armature, Audio-Animatronic, cable, movable miniature, remote control, stand-in doll, stunt dummy, wireframe.

puppet stage Any of various staging areas used for a puppet performance. Examples of small-scale puppet stages include proscenium opening, proscenium three-dimensional, curtain wall (the puppeteers hold the puppets from behind a curtain divider or down from above for marionettes) and solid wall (similar to a curtain wall, except that a wooden or cardboard divider is used to shield the puppeteers from the audience).

puppeteer Individual who operates a puppet. The puppet can be made of cloth, wood, foam rubber, latex or other rubbery material and be operated via mechanical, electro-mechanical, string-attached or wire-attached means. In film and television, the puppeteer is a member of the special-effects crew, handling off camera controls to change the puppet's facial, limb and other movements (breathing, pulse, etc.). Related terms: animatronic puppeteer, ventriloquist.

puppetry Production, process or art of operating puppets.

push To process film as if it had a higher (more sensitive) ASA rating (for example, 100 ASA at 200 ASA).

The resulting image will be grainier but, in some instances (e.g., low-light conditions), it may be the only way to get the shot. Related term: force develop.

Pyro Fluid Thin flammable liquid used in fire scenes; it is long burning but leaves no sooty residue. It can also be used to thin Pyro Gel. Sold by Tri-Ess Sciences, Inc., of Burbank, California.

Pyro Gel Thick flammable liquid used in fire scenes as a safer alternative to rubber cement; it does not evaporate quickly and can be applied to vertical and overhead surfaces. Sold by Tri-Ess Sciences, Inc., of Burbank, California. Related terms: Pyro Fluid, fire gel, fire effect.

pyrotechnic effects Explosive or fiery explosive effects; flash, sparkle and smoke effects; fireworks. Also called pyro effects or pyrotechnics. Two leading international suppliers of flash, sparkle, fire and smoke effects and related equipment (as well as other nonpyrotechnic special effects) are Tri-Ess Sciences, Inc., of Burbank, California and Zeller International, Ltd., of Downsville, New York. Related terms: explosion scene, fire effect, flash paper, flash pot, flash powder, smoke effect, sparkle paste, Witch's Fire.

pyrotechnic operator Individual who is licensed to use and be in possession of pyrotechnic materials. Related term: pyrotechnic supervisor.

pyrotechnic supervisor Expert in pyrotechnic effects; he oversees the use of pyrotechnic materials on a production. Depending on the country and local government law, a license is required to purchase, store, transport, and use pyrotechnic materials, especially in significant or dangerous quantities. In the United States, a federal license is required (as well as a state and possibly a city license); there may be several categories of licenses issued to accommodate different pyrotechnic-related occupations. Governments may have different legal definitions for what constitutes "explosives" and "fireworks." Film and television commissions can provide assistance in obtaining current information on laws and licensing/permit requirements for using pyrotechnic materials for theatrical purposes in their geographical area. A pyrotechnic supervisor is also called a pyrotechnic operator (a legal term used in the issuing of licenses in some places), pyrotechnic coordinator, pyrotechnic expert, pyrotechnician, or pyrotechnist. Related terms: pyrotechnic operator, powder person.

Q Abbreviation for "cue." It may be written in a stage script as Q: (or Cue:).

Q score Another name for "TVQ," a rating for television popularity, issued in the United States by Marketing Evaluations of Port Washington, New York. Related Term: TVQ.

QTV New York City-based company; it is a leading world manufacturer of videoprompting equipment. QTV is a division of Q-CO Industries, Inc. Related terms: Executive Speech Prompter, On Camera prompter, TelePrompTer, videoprompter.

quarter apple box Apple box one-quarter the height of the standard version. Typical quarter apple box sizes are 2" x 12" x 18", 2" x 12" x 20" and 2" x 14" x 24". Also called a quarter-apple or quarter-riser. Related terms: apple box, full apple box.

quarter load One-quarter the amount of explosive material used in guns and explosive devices, to create a smaller explosion. Related term: half load.

quarter-hour call Another name for a "15-minute call."

quartz light Light using a quartz bulb around the filament.

quick cut Fast edit; a quick change of onscreen images. Related term: jump cut.

QuickLift Trade name for a telescoping aluminum pole camera mount; available in different heights, it sits vertically on the ground by means of an attached collapsible tripod base and features remote pan, tilt and monitoring capabilities. Manufactured and sold by Treetop Systems of Westport, Connecticut. Internet address: http://www. tretopsys.com. Related term. tripod.

"Quiet on the set!" Instruction voiced by the director or assistant director just prior to the start of filming activities on the set. Said to keep those in the vicinity from making unwanted sounds that would interfere with the recording. On a large or outdoor set, it may be spoken through a voice amplification device (an electronic bullhorn/loudspeaker or old-fashioned megaphone) and accompanied by a warning light, warning bell or buzzer. When filming ends, and depending on the local custom, a bell or buzzer may be sounded twice to indicate that the shot has been completed. Related terms, director's directors, warning bell, warning alight.

rack 1. Archaic term for threading film in a Moviola, Kem or other viewing device or projector. 2. To line up a frame in the gate on a camera, projector or editing machine. 3. Shorthand command given by the DP to the operator to adjust the focus to a predetermined position. Related term: rack focus.

rack focus Changing focus from an object in the foreground to an object in the background (or vice versa). Related term: focus pulling.

rackover Feature of early motion picture cameras that allowed the entire film mechanism to shift to one side so the operator could see through the lens during rehearsal; the lens had to be re-racked into position before shooting. Cameras today have through-the-lens viewing systems.

radio drama Dramatic performance on the radio. When recording such a drama, actors stand in front of microphones and perform dialogue from scripts; sound effects and music are added as needed. Often, radio plays are performed before an audience. Related terms: radio play, radio show, episode.

radio microphone Microphone that operates by sending audio signals over a radio frequency. Another name for a wireless microphone.

radio play Dramatic work presented on, and produced especially for, the medium of radio. Performers read their parts into microphones and are accompanied by live or recorded music and sound effects. Related term: radio drama.

radio station call letters Combination of letters which officially identify a radio station. Related term: call letters.

rails 1. Scaffolds high above the set where lamps are mounted for overhead lighting. 2. Dolly tracks.

rain effect Simulating rain on a set (indoors or out) with hoses, perforated pipes and/or sprinkler systems. Several systems are used: the most common is the Rain Standard, which features a sprinkler head mounted on a movable stanchion about 25 feet above the set or actors. Rain Clusters are sprinkler systems used to cover large areas. For a more realistic look (with puddles), the area can be drenched beforehand and glossy material can be applied to the ground and walls. It is also possible to add rain (or snow) to a dry scene after it has been shot by optically superimposing stock footage of rain (or snow) over the scene. In this case, the actors' clothing should be presoaked. Gene Kelly's famous dance number in *Singin' in the Rain* (1952) was filmed on a set utilizing rain effects.

ramp 1. Slanted platform used to move a dolly alongside actors as they travel across an uneven surface or up and down levels. 2. Equipment used by a stuntperson that allows a moving object (a person, vehicle, etc.) to pass above another object.

Rank Cintel Trade name for a large, professional-grade telecine used to transfer filmed images to digital electronic signals which are then recorded on a video medium, such as videotape. Manufactured by Rank Cintel, Ltd., of England.

rate 1. (n.) Cost, charge or payment for a service. Related terms: advertising rate, commercial rate, flat rate, full day rate, half-day rate, half-hour rate, half rate, hourly rate, page rate, TV commercial rate, fee.

rate of delivery Pace or speed at which script lines are read, e.g., "The acting coach told the actress to slow down her rate of delivery."

rating appeals board Special committee of individuals that considers an appeal by a producer who is dissatisfied with a rating given to his film or video. In the United States, the Motion Picture Association of America's Rating Appeals Board is separate from the Rating Board and has 14 to 18 members who meet, as needed, to view the film or video in question. Afterward, a hearing is held, during which the producer and chairman of the Rating Board state their positions and are questioned by members of the Appeals Board. A secret ballot then is conducted. The original rating issued by the Rating Board can be overturned only by a two-thirds majority vote and their decision is final. The only options left to the producer are to reedit and resubmit the work or to release it with the given rating or unrated. Related term: motion picture rating board.

ratings period 1. Designated length of time, such as one month, during which program ratings are gathered and used to determine commercial advertising time rates. In the United States, the ratings period occurs four times per year (February, May, August, November). Also called a sweeps period, sweeps month, sweeps week or the sweeps. Related term: sex and violence. 2. Any period of time during which ratings are or were gathered for review.

ratings ploy Something done or added, usually temporarily, to a TV series or news show to attract public attention so the show's ratings will increase; typically done during a ratings period. For example, news shows may broadcast more sex-related stories or a series may feature a wedding or birth. Also called a ratings gimmick.

ratio See aspect ratio, shooting ratio.

raw film Unexposed, unprocessed photographic film. Related term: stock.

RCD Abbreviation for Recordable Compact Disc. Blank compact disc (CD) capable of having information digitally recorded on it. Related term: CD-R.

reaction shot Shot, usually a close-up, of a person reacting to something said or done in a previous shot or to something off-camera.

read 1. To register on a light meter (e.g., "will the image read?"). 2. To register to the eye; to detect whether an object will be noticeable on screen (e.g., "is that sign too small to read on film?") 3. In the case of a scene in a script, to play smoothly and coherently. 4. To audition an actor for a part.

reader Another term for story analyst. Individual who reads, synopsizes and critiques written material (e.g., screenplays, novels, plays), submitted to the studio or production company for consideration as a film. The resulting analysis is called "coverage."

reading 1. Oral interpretation of written material, such as an actor in an audition or as part of a dramatic performance. Related terms: dramatic reading, script reading, staged reading, acting exercise. 2. Measuring available light on a light meter.

read-through Another name for a script session.

real time 1. Actual time it takes to perform a scene. Related terms: camera time, clock time, time. 2. Filming, recording or playing back at the actual speed at which the event naturally occurs, as opposed to compressed time, expanded time, fast motion or slow motion. Related terms: full-motion video, time.

realisateur French term for director. Related term: metteur-en-scene.

reality-based series Any television series featuring real-life events, as opposed to a fictionalized drama or comedy. This includes news programs, talk shows, courtroom and crime reenactment series, health and science programs, fashion and how-to shows, cooking and gardening programs, talent shows and the like. For example, *Rescue 911* is a reality-based series while *E.R.* is a dramatic series. Also called reality programming.

rear car mount Structural support for one or more cameras attached to the rear of an automobile. Cameras also can be mounted on a wheeled platform towed by the vehicle or mounted on the front of another vehicle attached by a trailer hitch or it can be attached to a car driving on its own. Related terms: camera car, camera mount.

rear screen projection System of projecting film onto the back of a translucent screen (as opposed to the front of the screen, as in standard projection). It is sometimes used in theaters but its main use is in production, usually as an exterior background more easily shot in a studio. For example, in a shot in which two characters are driving in a car, you would see scenery in the background (streets, buildings, trees, mountains, etc.). In a rear screen projection shot, the live action is shot in the studio against the projected background (it could be stock footage or footage shot by a second unit); the filmmakers must make sure the camera and projector are carefully synched to prevent flickering. This is referred to as a process shot. For extremely large scenes, the more complex matte shot (or travelling matte) is used.

recast To cast over again; to select a different performer to play a role. For example, Harrison Ford stepped into the Jack Ryan role in the Tom Clancy series (*Patriot Games* [1992]) replacing Alec Baldwin (*The Hunt for Red October* [1990]).

recitative Style of singing dialogue, as by an opera singer, without following a regular rhythm so it mimics the sounds of speech.

record 1. To audiorecord or videorecord. 2. Any electronic, photographic or mechanical recording of music, singing, dialogue, sound effects or visual events, including CDs, DVDs, audiotapes, films, videos and the like.

recorded music Music fixed in place as magnetically or optically encoded information on an audiotape, CD, DVD, memory chip or phonograph record. The opposite is live music.

Related terms: canned music, taped music.

recorded rehearsal Rehearsal that is recorded (audio or video) so it can be played back and used to help performers memorize, understand or improve their parts. Related term: earprompter.

recording Technique of putting a live or previously recorded sound or image on magnetic tape. Related term: mix.

recording industry Branch of business and service activities pertaining to the production and marketing of recorded sounds, such as singing, instrumental music and speaking; such recordings are done on audiotape, compact disc (CD), digital versatile disc (DVD), memory chip or phonograph record. Related terms: music industry, National Academy of Recording Arts and Sciences.

recording session Session during which any type of recording takes place: sound, video or both. Related terms: ADR session, foley session, videorecording session, session.

recording studio Another name for a sound studio.

recordist Crew member responsible for recording sound during production. During post-production, the mixer is responsible for mixing sound tracks into the final composite track, which is then placed onto the film, either on an optical track or a magnetic stripe. Related terms: production mixer, sound recordist.

recoupment Recovery of one's investment.

recurring role Acting part played by the same performer from time to time in an episodic television show or film with a continuing storyline. Also called a recurring character. The performer who plays such a role is called a semiregular player. For example, on the television series *Seinfeld* (1990-98), Jerry Stiller had a recurring role as George Costanza's father, Frank.

red warning light Red lamp used to signify active filming or recording. Related term: warning light.

re-dress To change the look of a set. Related terms: dress, set designer, art director.

reduction print Print made from a wider-gauged original, for example, a 16mm print made from a 35mm original. The opposite is a blow-up.

reel 1. Metal or plastic wheels holding film; for projection or storage purposes. The standard size reel (35mm) typically holds up to 900 feet of film, although it is capable of holding 1000 feet (10 minutes). Today, double reels are commonly used; they hold 2000 feet of film. The 10-minute reel was a standard for so long that people still refer to a film length in terms of the number of (1000 foot) reels. (A reel of processed film is stored inside of a can.) Related terms: core, spool. 2. Referring to the film on a particular reel, e.g., "That scene is located in the first reel of the picture."

reenactment Theatrical, documentary, historical or news production that matches, as closely as possible, the original event. Related terms: historical reenactment, reality-based series.

reflected light Illumination bounced off the subject being photographed. Related term: exposure meter.

reflector Reflective panel, usually made of silver or gold flake material, used to direct light. Sometimes, white cards, called bounce boards, made of cardboard or foam core, are used as reflectors.

reflector board Rectangular or square panel made of or covered with a light-reflecting material; used to bounce natural or artificial light onto a subject or set to fill in shadows or highlight certain areas. Also called a reflector card, reflector flat, bounce board, white card or gray card. Related term: silver card.

reflex camera Camera that, through a system of mirrors, permits through-the-lens viewing while shooting. This systems eliminates the parallax problem.

regional commercial Advertisement (television, radio or movie theater) playing in a specific geographical region of a country. Also called a regional spot or regional ad.

regional theater 1. Playhouse offering professional, noncommercial (not-for-profit) stage entertainment to playgoers in a large community. Performers and crew are paid and admission is charged, but the theater's operating expenses may also be subsidized by donations. Regional theaters may feature classics, revivals and premieres of new works. Related term: resident theater. 2. Such a theater in the United States affiliated with the League of Resident Theatres (LORT). 3. Industry, world, field or profession of working in regional theater productions.

registration Correct alignment with another object; refers to film, an animation cel, photograph, drawing, etc.

registration pins Stationary teeth in the film gate of a camera or projector; they fit into the sprocket holes and pull the film down to advance it. Related term: pilot pins.

registration shot Visual-effects shot in which the image of an onscreen still photograph or drawing transforms to its matching live action shot, usually after the camera moves in for a close-up. For example, a registration shot appears at the very end of the front screen credits in *The Happiest Millionaire* (1967), signaling the end of the animated titles and the beginning of the film.

regular player Permanent cast member who performs a continuing role, as opposed to being a semiregular player (with a recurring role) or a guest player. Also called a regular cast member, regular or series regular. Related terms: series regular, continuing role.

rehearsal Practice session before a formal or official performance, presentation, reading or showing. Also called a run-through, walk-through, read-through, dance-through, sing-through or dry run. Related terms: closed rehearsal, dress rehearsal, open rehearsal, recorded rehearsal, technical rehearsal, blocking a scene, blocking a shot, prepping, prompter, script reading, script session, stage ready, trial run, warm-up.

rehearsal call Request or notice to performers to appear at a scheduled rehearsal.

rehearsal fee Money paid for attending and participating in a rehearsal session.

rehearsal studio Large room at which a rehearsal is conducted. Sometimes auditions are held in such a location. Also called a rehearsal space. Related terms: acting studio, dance studio, studio.

R18-classification Rating issued in Great Britain, by the British Board of Film Classification, for adult videos.

The full wording is: "'R18'—Restricted. To be supplied only in licensed sex shops to persons of not less than 18 years." Also called an "R18" certificate. Related terms: 18-classification, X-rating, rating.

reissue 1. To release or distribute again, such as a film or CD. Related term: rerelease.

release 1. To put a motion picture into general or limited distribution. 2. To dismiss (e.g., "release" an actor after his workday has been completed). 3. To free from contractual obligation. 4. Notice to the press, sent out by the publicity department. 5. Legal document giving the production company permission to include the likeness of a person who has been photographed in a film or video to be exhibited.

release date Day, month and year a theatrical film, video, compact disc, etc., is released to the consumer marketplace. Related terms: opening date, playdate.

release negative Complete master negative of a theatrical film, from which release prints are made; it is copied from the original negative in a series of processing steps. Numerous release negatives may be made to facilitate the printing of a large number of release prints, as in the case of a film with a wide national or international release. By using release negatives to make prints, the one-of-a-kind original negative is protected from possible damage by overhandling. Also called a duplicate negative or dupe negative. Related terms: duplicate negative, internegative, interpositive.

release print Final composite print of a theatrical film distributed to the theaters for exhibition. Also called a distribution print or show print.

Related terms: release negative, rough cut.

remake New version of a previously-made film. For example, the original version of *A Star Is Born* was made in 1937, starring Janet Gaynor and Frederic March; it had two remakes (one starring Judy Garland and James Mason [1954] and another starring Barbra Streisand and Kris Kristofferson [1976]).

remote 1. Distant; located far away, e.g., a remote camera crew, remote camera or remote microphone. 2. Instance of video or audio live transmission from a distant location, e.g., "We're going to do a remote from the site of the news story."

remote control 1. Battery-powered, wireless handheld device using invisible infrared radiation to turn switches on and off at a distance. Examples are a TV remote control and VCR remote control. Also called a remote or channel changer. 2. Similar device that operates over longer distances via radio waves. 3. Mechanically-operated device (located off camera or offstage) using one or more push/pull cables to control the actions of a machine, such as a special-effects puppet, or elements of a special-effects costume. Related term: cable.

remote crew Another name for a location team.

rendition 1. Artistic interpretation, such as a drawing, sketch, painting, sculpture, etc., based on a fixed subject. 2. Interpretative performance, as of a musical or dramatic literary work, e.g., "I like Los Lobos' rendition of 'La Bamba.'"

renew 1. To restore a television or radio series for another season. Same as to pick up, bring back, keep on the schedule, give another chance to or survive the programmer's ax. Related term: picked up for next season. 2. To restore a contract's provisions for an additional period of time.

renewed series Television series that has been given the go-ahead, or green light, for the production of another season's worth of episodes. Related term: renew.

rep 1. (n.) Short for representative or representation, e.g., an actor's rep (agent). 2. (v.) To represent.

repeat See rerun.

repeating take In post-production editing, replaying the same shot (an exact copy) to achieve a desired dramatic, comedic or fantasy effect.

repertoire List of dramas, comedies, musicals, operas, songs, routines, etc., that an actor, singer, dancer, etc., is prepared to perform.

repertory Acting company that regularly performs a varied selection of stage works. Also called a repertory company.

repertory theater Playhouse having a permanent acting company presenting a varied repertoire during a performing season. Also called a resident theater.

replay 1. To rewind and rerun a scene; to rewind or rerun only the audio or visual portion of the scene to see if it has been recorded properly. Related term: playback. 2. To rerun a musical piece during filming so the actors can dance, or react to, music which will be added later in the mix.

report sheet Log or data sheet filled out daily by the Camera and Sound Departments; it lists each take and notes which ones are to be printed and which ones are NG (no good).

report to Instruction written on the call sheet, indicating where the crew

member is working that day (studio or local location) and that his work begins upon his arrival at the set.

reporter approval Approval by a celebrity of a particular reporter as a condition for being interviewed. Related terms: approval, writer approval.

representation 1. Act of representing; state of being represented. 2. Person, agency or organization acting as a spokesperson, go-between or negotiator for another in business, legal, career or personal matters. Related terms: rep, agency, agent, attorney, personal manager, public relations agent, union. 3. Portrayal or performance, as on a stage, e.g., a musical representation of a children's fairy tale. 4. Depiction or likeness, such as a drawing or portrait. Related term: rendition.

representative 1. Person or business representing others, such as a talent agency, attorney, manager or publicist. Also called representation. Related terms: agency representative, client representative, product representative, sponsor representative, rep. 2. Typical example, e.g., "This photo is representative of her work."

reprise shot Shot, such as an action shot or one of a character speaking dialogue, that is repeated at a later point, usually to indicate a character remembering.

reprising a role Performer who plays the same character more than once. For example, Jack Lemmon and Walter Matthau reprised their roles of Felix and Oscar® in *The Odd Couple II* (1998), 30 years after originating the roles in the 1968 film. Also referred to as returning to a role. Related term: originator of a role.

re-record Transfer of an audio or video track from one medium (film, tape, disk) to another. Also describes the act of combining the many sound tracks in the final mix of the film.

re-recording mixer Chief sound engineer responsible for the final mix, when all sound tracks, including dialogue, music and effects, are mixed together and balanced to create the picture's final sound track. Also called a dubbing mixer. Related term: sound mixer.

rerelease 1. (v.) To release again. 2. Act or an instance of releasing a film, video, music recording, etc., typically long after its initial release. A rerelease is due to renewed interest in the item or to the potential for renewed interest once it is rereleased. For example, *Star Wars* was rereleased in 1997, 20 years after its initial theatrical release. Also called a second (third, etc.) release. Related terms: reissue, repremiere. 3. (n.) Project rereleased.

rerun 1. (v.) To reshow (reair, retelecast, rebroadcast or recablecast) a TV series episode, TV special, news segment, etc., e.g., "The network plans to rerun the episodes that had the highest ratings." Related term: repeat. 2. (n.) Show, episode, segment, etc., that is rerun. Also called a repeat, encore presentation. 3. (v.) To run anything over again, e.g., to rerun an ad in a magazine.

rerun syndication Reshowing in syndication; refers to television series, made-for-TV movies, specials, etc., originally shown on a network, cable or in first-run syndication and is now being offered for sale (the licensing rights to telecast) to individual, independent and network-affiliated stations for showing in their own markets. The stations recoup the cost of syndicated rerun programming and make a profit by selling commercial advertising time. Related term: syndication.

reshoot 1. To photograph, film or record over again. 2. Session in which this takes place. Also called a reshooting.

resident theater Playhouse with a permanent acting company for its performing season. In the United States, most resident theaters located in large cities around the country are also referred to as regional theaters. Related terms: repertory theater, League of Resident Theatres.

residuals Additional compensation (equivalent to an author's royalty) paid to actors, directors, etc., according to their union contracts. Not all union members receive residuals.

resolution 1. Level of detail, as on a photograph or video image. Related terms: high resolution, low resolution, broadcast quality. 2. Act of solving, e.g., "The storyline in that crime movie has no resolution."

résumé One-page summary of a performer's personal information (name, agent/contact information, union memberships, height, weight, eye color, hair color, age range), training, special skills and performing credits/experience. Only brief, important information is given. Related terms: 8x10 résumé, photo résumé, credit, skill, skill test, training.

résumé photo Photograph intended to accompany a résumé. Related terms: 8x10 résumé, photo-résumé.

résumé-listed credit A credit that appears on a performer's résumé or other type of job applicant's (director's, writer's, makeup artist's, etc.) résumé.

re-take To re-shoot a scene that was previously filmed, to unsatisfactory results.

retouch To add details or conceal imperfections on a photographic or video image. Photographs are re-touched manually or electronically, the latter by means of a computer. Related terms: digital retouching, airbrush, spot, doctored photo.

retoucher Photographic or computer specialist who retouches images.

retractable Knife, bayonet, sword, etc., having a lightly spring-loaded blade that retracts when pressed against the body of an actor; used in a fight scene. When the weapon is withdrawn, the blade, which has a blunted tip and edge, resumes its extended shape. Related terms: knife, sword-fight scene.

retrospective Film, television, museum, etc., showing of past works of an individual, group, organization, company, industry or the like; it may include whole works or samplings, e.g., a retrospective of film clips from an actor's career or a retrospective featuring film screening of a director's body of work. Related terms: compilation episode, compilation film.

re-use payment Money paid for the re-use of something, such as an actor's photo in a new advertising campaign by the same client. Related terms: print residual, use payment.

revamp To rearrange a set for use in another sequence or in another production.

revamp a show Revise a show; make changes in its content. Related term: makeover.

reveal Shot that opens up or pulls back to show something that wasn't previously visible.

reversal dupe Duplicate positive made from a positive.

reversal film Special type of raw film stock used to produce a positive image from a positive or a negative image from a negative. The "reversal" refers to the chemical processes involved and not to a reversal of the image. Related term: internegative.

reverse action Technique of showing filmed action going backwards. Mainly used as a special effect. Related term: reverse motion.

reverse angle shot Also known as a reverse. Shot taken from an angle almost directly opposite the preceding shot; typically used when two actors are facing each other in a scene or when one actor is shown going through a doorway or entering a room. *The Godfather* (1972) ends on a reverse shot of actress Diane Keaton.

reverse motion Action played backward to achieve a desired visual effect. Also called a reverse shot. Related term: camera reverse.

reverse scene Scene flipped during printing so the image looks reversed, as if it is reflected in a mirror.

revised dialogue Script lines that have been altered slightly or changed altogether. Also called revised lines, revised copy or changed dialogue.

revised page Script page with one more more changes (of dialogue, location, camera angle, character, etc.) handwritten or printed on it. Revised pages inserted into a script are marked as such and dated; typically, they are different in color. Related terms: change page, script change, blue pages.

revised scene Script scene that has been altered slightly or changed completely. A revised scene is different from an added scene. Related terms:

change page, script change, blue pages.

revised shot Shot in a script that is changed in some way. Since a scene may be comprised of numerous shots, it is possible that one particular shot may be revised slightly or completely from the way it was written in the script; it is the director's creative prerogative to do so. A revised shot is not the same as an added shot. Related terms: change page, script change, blue pages.

revision Step of script rewriting; it is greater than a polish but less than another full draft. This is a special classification recognized by the Writers Guild of America and has a specific and separate pay scale. Revisions to a screenplay made after it has been distributed are printed on different color paper with the date of the revision noted on the page. The color sequence of revised pages is: blue, pink, yellow, green, goldenrod and, if necessary, white again. Related terms: script change, blue pages.

revival New production of an old stage show.

revival theater Movie theater exhibiting old films.

revolving set Production set constructed on the horizontal top or cylindrical sides of a revolving stage. Also called a revolving-room set.

revolving stage 1. Horizontal-plane revolving stage. Motorized theatrical or exhibition stage, usually circular; it rotates slowly in a directional plane parallel to the ground. Found in some playhouses as a built-in feature allowing for quick set changes. Portable types are used for exhibits, as at automobile shows. Also called a revolving platform/base or rotating platform/base. Related term: tableau.

2. Vertical-plane revolving stage. Motorized or manually turned film or video production stage consisting of an outer metal cylindrical framework held in place by a curved roller support base or a center-mounted axle attached to two separate support towers. Bolted to a wooden base on the inner side of the framework is a production set with an open end that faces the camera. During operation, the framework, with its attached interior production set, is rotated (by hand or by electric motor) in a directional plane perpendicular to the ground, e.g., up and around in a circle. Reference marks on the framework's outer edge provide a visual guide so that a uniform speed can be maintained. Depending on the scene being shot, the interior elements of the production set are fixed in place or allowed to tumble over as the stage revolves. The camera also can be fixed in place and turned with the stage or it can shoot the revolving stage as it is mounted offstage. The performer is not fixed in place and must change locations to maintain a normal upright position as the various elements of the production set come around. In a scene in which the camera is mounted to turn with the stage, the resulting perspective is that the performer inside appears to be magically walking or dancing on the walls and ceiling. Films in which a vertical-plane revolving stage was used include *Upside Down* (1898), *The Human Fly* (1902), *At the Circus* (1939), *Royal Wedding* (1951), *2001: A Space Odyssey* (1968) and *Turbulence* (1997). Also called a cylindrical revolving stage, revolving drum stage, rotating stage, giant squirrel cage or oversized hamster wheel (the

latter two are nicknames). Related terms: revolving set, squirrel cage, gimbal stage.

revue 1. Stage show featuring dancers and/or singers in a series of skits, songs and/or dance numbers. 2. French for "review."

rewind 1. (n.) Geared device used to rewind film; it consists of two cranks with shafts, one for the feed reel and one for the take-up reel. Electric rewinds are used in projection booths. 2. (v.) To return film to its original reel or onto a core using a rewind.

rewrite 1. (v.) To write again; to make changes to a written project, e.g., to rewrite a script, script page, scene or dialogue exchange. 2. (n.) Script or other work containing rewritten elements. Also called a revision. Related terms: script change, blue pages.

ride-through attraction film/video Any short film or video produced specifically for a ride-through attraction. Related terms: theme-park attraction film/video, mini-movie.

rifle mike See shotgun mike.

rifle spot Spotlight producing a long, slim beam of light.

riggers Crew members responsible for the construction of the scaffolding (aka rigging) on a set and the placement of the lights that go on the rigging.

rigging 1. (n.) Scaffolding. 2. (v.) Placement of studio lights before shooting.

right 1. Privilege, just claim, authority or power, e.g., a right granted in a contract. Related terms: ancillary right, copyright, digital rights, exclusive right, feature film rights, home video rights, interactive re-use right, ancillary market, approval, clearance, entertainment attorney, fee schedule, first refusal, license, perk, property, proprietary makeup. 2. Direction corresponding to the right side. Related terms: camera right, stage right.

right-to-work state One of the 50 United States with a state-level constitutional or statutory provision specifically prohibiting anyone from requiring an individual to join a union in order to be employed. Unions are still allowed and may be joined voluntarily. In a non right-to-work state, the state government remains uninvolved and the matter is decided by the unions, workers and various industries through negotiated contracts and the requirements of the Federal Taft-Hartley Act (also called the Labor Management Relations Act of 1947). The 21 right-to-work states are: Alabama, Arizona, Arkansas, Florida, Georgia, Idaho, Iowa, Kansas, Louisiana, Mississippi, Nebraska, Nevada, North Carolina, North Dakota, South Carolina, South Dakota, Tennessee, Texas, Utah, Virginia and Wyoming. Related term: union member.

rim light Light used to produce a halo effect when it is placed behind the subject. Related term: backlight.

ringer Impostor. Related term: audience plant.

ripple dissolve Dissolve using a wavering effect; it resembles ripples on the surface of water as the scene changes from one to the next. Commonly used at the beginning and ending of dream sequences and flashbacks.

riser Stepped platform used to elevate actors, props, etc.

rising stage Another name for an elevator stage.

Ritter See wind machine.

Road Burn Fluid Rapidly burning liquid used to create flaming tire tracks on a roadway. First used in the science-fiction film *Back to the Future* (1985). Sold by Tri-Ess Sciences, Inc., of Burbank, California.

road company Group of performers that travels to various scheduled locations to perform. The production equipment and sets are transported with the company. Related term: touring company.

road manager Individual who travels with and is responsible for making the arrangements (e.g., transportation, lodging, meals) related to scheduling and setting up a traveling entertainment show.

road show Stage production, such as a play or music concert, that moves between cities. Also called a road production or bus and truck show.

roadie Another name for a stagehand or grip who travels with a road show.

robot operator Individual who controls the movements and functions of a robot. Theme park robots are usually preprogrammed to perform a series of scripted movements as part of a ride, show or exhibit. Related term: animatronic puppeteer.

rod puppet Puppet attached to one or more long rods (thin wooden sticks or metal poles); the rods are held and manipulated by a visible or concealed puppeteer. Related term: puppet.

Rodeo Drive (Beverly Hills) A famous street in the city of Beverly Hills, California, along which are many expensive, fashionable stores. Often used as a location in films and TV programs to symbolize a rich and glamorous lifestyle in the Los Angeles area. Pronounced "Roh-DAY-oh."

role Character identity assumed and played by a performer.

roll Film of any length on a core. Related terms: spool, reel.

"Roll it!" or "Roll camera!" or "Roll, please!" or "Rolling!" Statement made by the first assistant director to the production company, alerting all that a take is about to commence. This is the cue for the camera and sound to start. When the camera is running, the camera operator says, "Rolling!" and when the sound is running at the proper speed, the sound man says, "Speed." After this, the director calls, "Action!" and the take begins.

roll number One or more numbers assigned to a roll of motion picture film for recordkeeping and editing purposes. Letters of the alphabet may also be used. Related terms: A and B editing, A-camera, B-camera, C-camera.

"Roll sound." Direction from the director or assistant director; it is said to the sound recordist to start the tape recorder that will be recording sound. Related term: "Roll 'em."

rolling title Film credits, typically the end credits, rolling from the bottom to the top of the screen. Related terms: crawl, creeping title, running title.

romantic comedy Film, TV program or play featuring a storyline with elements of comedy and romance. *Keeping the Faith* (2000) is an example of a romantic comedy. Related term: romance movie.

romantic lead One of two leading characters in a romance movie. Related term: love interest.

roof ride Stunt in which a performer lies flat on the roof of a moving vehicle while holding onto the windshield chrome, side roof or door edges. Related terms: hood ride, stunt driver.

room tone Existing presence or ambience in a room, recorded onto a buzz track, to be mixed in later with the dialogue track. Room tone makes a scene sound more realistic and hides cuts in the dialogue track.

roster List of members available for work; kept by various unions and guilds.

rostrum Small base on folding legs, upon which a camera or lighting unit may be mounted.

rotary gimbal Another name for a revolving stage.

rotating stage See revolving stage.

rotoscope 1. (n.) Device used to project single frames of positive-image film onto the undersurface of a hard, flat viewing screen so that a rotoscope artist can hand-draw certain matte and animated effects (e.g., laser beams from weapons). The first rotoscope was invented and patented by animator Max Fleischer (1889-1972) in October, 1917. Rotoscoping is still used in filmmaking, but is increasingly being replaced by more advanced computer methods. 2. (v.) To rotoscope.

rough cut Initial version of a film in which scenes and shots have been spliced together by an editor in the approximate finished order, according to the script and creative input from the director. The process of putting together a rough cut is called "assembly." The assembled film is called the "work print." After the rough cut is screened by the director, scenes may be shortened, shots changed, etc., until a fine cut of the film is produced. After this cut is screened by the director, producers, studio executives, etc., and if any further changes are needed, a final cut is created. Using the final cut and its reference numbers along the edges of the film as a guide, the individual strips of negative corresponding to each selected shot are carefully spliced by a negative cutter to exactly match the final cut of the film. This spliced-together, original negative is then used to make an answer print (also called a trial print or approval print). If no additional changes are made (e.g., to meet the requirements of a particular film rating), release prints are manufactured from the release negative (a copy of the one-of-a-kind original, or master, negative). Before the processing laboratory begins manufacturing a large number of release prints, it will require that a sample print, which may be the answer print, be approved by the producer (who is paying the laboratory fees). The rough cut is also called the first cut. Related term: editing on tape.

roving camera Moving camera.

royalty Calculated payment to the creator (author, composer, lyricist, inventor, etc.) or owner of a property each time his creation (book, musical composition, invention, etc.) is sold or licensed. Related terms: residuals, American Society of Composers, Authors, and Publishers (ASCAP), Broadcast Music Incorporated (BMI).

royalty-free music Music that can be performed or included on a soundtrack without having to pay royalties to the owner (who may be the composer) or to the company that owns the rights to the music. Royalty-free music is typically music existing in the public domain or music composed by a company specializing in producing and selling such music to filmmakers, videomakers and others.

R-rating (abbreviated as R) 1. Film and video rating in the United States issued by the Motion Picture Association of America's Classification and Rating Administration. The full wording is as follows: "'R'—Restricted. Under 17 Requires Accompanying Parent or Adult Guardian." The age restriction may be raised to 18 in some areas. Related terms: motion picture rating board, rating. 2. Similar film and video classification issued in Australia, Canada and elsewhere. In Canada, the full wording is: "Restricted—Admittance Restricted to Persons 16 Years of Age and Older." Related term: rating. 3. Abbreviation for "Rehearsal" on union forms.

rubber knife Fake knife made of painted flexible rubber; it is used as a prop in an acting fight scene. (A real knife would be used for close-ups and for cutting/puncture demonstration shots.) Related term: knife.

rubber skull cap Another name for a bald cap; plain, latex-rubber covering stretched over an actor's hair and scalp in a special makeup process to simulate baldness. Sections of hair and makeup appliances may be glued to it to create a variety of looks on the actor's head.

rumble pot Open metal receptacle containing water into which a quantity of dry ice is placed and allowed to melt; this causes a rumbling sound, along with visible, white foglike vapors. Heating the water increases the output of rumbling and vapor. Related term: fog effect.

run lines To rehearse dialogue, something actors typically do before shooting a scene, so as to be well-prepared.

runaway production 1. Film or television project whose principal activities take place in an area (another country, state/province, or city) where the low number or lack of union or government regulations benefit the producers and therefore equal lower production costs. 2. Collectively, all such productions.

run-by Shot in which a moving car (or other vehicle) travels past a stationary camera.

runners 1. Scaffolding on which lights, backdrops and other equipment can be hung. 2. The production assistant (aka gofer) who runs errands for the producer, director, production manager, etc.

running gag A joke, bit of visual humor, etc., that is repeated at various times throughout a theatrical film, TV program, TV series, play, computer game, etc., either in its original form or slightly altered or adapted each time. Also called a running joke. Related term: gag.

running shot Shot in which a moving camera keeps pace with a moving object or person. Related terms: tracking shot, dolly shot, traveling shot.

running speed Rate at which film runs through a camera or projector, or at which tape runs through a recorder or playback machine. The running speed for film is measured in frames per second; for tape, it is in inches per second. Related terms: fps, ips.

running time Length of time a movie, TV program, video, commercial or stage presentation runs, from start to finish. A theatrical film's running time is clocked from the head frame to the last frame of the end credits sequence. Most feature films are between 85 and

120 minutes long, though in recent years running time has increased.

run-of-show Contractual term meaning an individual (usually a principal cast member) has been hired at a specific salary for a specific number of weeks (the entire show), no matter how many days the actor works during that time, as opposed to being hired on a daily or weekly basis.

run-through Complete rehearsal of actors without film running in the camera. Related term: walk-through.

rushes Another name for dailies, e.g., film shot that day and rushed to and from the processing laboratory to be viewed by the director the next day.

S American television rating for a program containing sexual-related visual images or language. The rating may be accompanied by a numerical level, such as 1, 2 or 3. Related terms: rating, sex and violence.

safe action area Shot area within a film frame corresponding to the aspect ratio of standard television. The action performed in the area, which may be indicated by a graphically framed area in the viewfinder, will safely make it to television screens during playback. Related terms: aspect ratio, Academy aperture, safe title area, shot area.

safe title area Slightly smaller area within the safe action area; main and credit titles can be safely positioned within this area so they will be seen on television screens.

safelight Photography studio darkroom lamp; it is safe to use for a recommended period of time because of its minimal effects on photographic materials during processing. It consists of a housing, electrical connections, bulb and colored filter suitable to the particular type of film or paper being used.

safety base Slow-burning film base (usually cellulose with acetate) which is noncombustive. Most films shot before 1950 used highly-flammable nitrate base stock; now, many old films have been transferred to safety base. Related term: safety film.

safety harness Protective attachment for the body; typically consists of a combination of nylon webbing, buckles, loops and possibly one or more sewn-in supporting plates or ribs. It is worn by a stunt performer or actor in a stunt scene (e.g., hanging onto a tall or moving object, an explosion pullback, gunshot pullback or execution of certain types of high-risk jumps and falls (between two rooftops, over a waterfall, etc.). Related terms: decelerator, descender, drag rig, jerk harness, play, ride up, wire flying, wire-flying scene, wire removal.

SAG Abbreviation for Screen Actors Guild.

SAG card Union identification card providing evidence of membership in the Screen Actors Guild. Related term: union card.

SAG eligible Meeting the requirements to join SAG; the next acting job allows the actor to join SAG.

saga Detailed history of a family, people, country, city, etc., history.

sagebrush saga Nickname for a Western movie. Also called a sagebrusher. Entertainment trade paper use.

sample print Composite print of a motion picture; typically, it is submitted by the processing laboratory to the producer, who inspects and approves it before release prints are made. Related term: rough cut.

sandbag Small, divided burlap or plastic bag, filled with sand and used to temporarily steady or hold down certain pieces of equipment; standard equipment found in all grip packages.

satellite dish Ground-based antenna designed to receive television microwave signals relayed from a space-based satellite.

satellite television Using ground- and space-based satellite microwave-transmission technology to provide programming quickly and efficiently over long distances. Related terms: satellite dish, satellite-fed, DSS.

satellite-fed Sent from a satellite, e.g., an electronic telecommunications device capable of receiving and transmitting signals from its position in orbit high above the Earth. Television-signal satellites remain in fixed geosynchronous orbits above the equator. The world television industry relies on satellites to deliver live and prerecorded programming (including news reports) to local and non-network stations, local cable TV providers and individual consumers. Related terms: live feed, network feed, corporate television, teleconference, TV interview.

satire 1. Screen or literary work in which the idiocies, vices or abuses of government, business or private citizens are ridiculed, either unkindly or with good humor. Related term: parody. 2. Such works collectively.

saturation Measure of color intensity in a photographed image. A higher saturation gives richer, more vivid colors (see, for example, *The Patriot* [2000], *Anna and the King* [1999], *Fly Away Home* [1996] and *The Right Stuff* [1983]), all shot by Caleb Deschanel); a lower saturation (or, "desaturated") results in subdued and more subtle colors. Colors desaturated many times are used to create certain effects (see the look of the dustbowl sequence shot by Haskell Wexler in *Bound for Glory* [1976]).

"Save it." Direction from the director to save the footage just shot. Related term: "Print it."

scale 1. Minimum payment for a particular type of work done, as opposed to below-scale or overscale; the amount is fixed in an industry contract approved by a union and employers. Related terms: double scale, overscale, minimum fee, overtime, starting fee, straight time. 2. Union payment table listing graduated minimum payments for various types of work, e.g., performing, technical, service. Related terms: union fee scale, fee schedule. 3. Series of relative measurements for determining or comparing sizes, e.g., small scale, full scale or overscale/large scale. Related term: scale model.

scale model Object constructed in proportion to the original. Related terms: model miniature, puppet.

scale plus ten Common practice, especially regarding an actor's salary, in which the person is paid scale plus and extra ten percent to cover the agent's fee.

scenario Old term for screenplay; most commonly used today to refer to plot or storyline.

scenarist Another name for a screenwriter. Entertainment trade paper use.

scene 1. A single shot or a series of shots taking place in a location or which present a main action or activity. 2. When breaking down a script, a scene (each numbered individually) can mean a unit of action or dialogue occurring in the same location at the same time. Generally, a scene number will not change if an actor enters or leaves the scene, but this rule is not absolute.

scene dock Offstage storage area where scenery pieces, such as backdrops and flats, are stored until they are needed.

scene name Identification of a location where the action of the scene will take place (e.g., "Amy's Room"); identification of the action itself (e.g., "The Knife-Throwing Scene").

scene number Reference number assigned to each scene (or shot, depending on script format) in a script. Numbers begin at one and graduate upward (1, 2, 3, etc.); revised or added scenes or shots may be accompanied by an alphabetical letter (1A, 23B, etc.). The scene number also appears on the information clapboard displayed in front of the running camera prior to filming that scene. Related term: shot number.

scene outline Type of specially formatted theatrical story for a film or video project. Related term: outline.

scene stealer Individual (or, animal) who unintentionally or purposely draws attention away from the principal performer or action in a scene. Related terms: show-stealer, "Never work with animals or children," upstage.

scenery Elements of a production set which give the scene its particular look. Related terms: scene dock, scenery drop, background, backing, cyclorama, effects projector, facade, flat, forced perspective, gobo, greenery, prop, scrim, set, set piece, wild wall.

scenery crew Individuals responsible for building, plastering, painting, dressing, striking, and storing theatrical sets; may also be called the set construction crew. Related terms: carpenter, construction coordinator, electrician, greensperson, grip, lead-man, painter, plasterer, property master, roadie, scenic artist, set designer, set dresser, stagehand, swing gang.

scenery drop Painted, cloth scenery piece; it is unframed and hangs from above. Related term: batten.

scenic artist Individual from the art or scenery department responsible for painting window and door backings, large background murals, signs, props and the like. Depending on the size of the production, the scenic artist may also do any needed wallpapering and hanging of drapes. For prepping purposes, they usually precede the crew onto a location. Also called a set painter or stage painter. Related terms: painter, scenery crew.

scenic designer Theatrical set designer; he prepares plans of proposed theater sets for approval by the director and producer and then oversees their construction. Related terms: set designer, art director.

schedule 1. Broadcast schedule, cable schedule or television schedule. 2. Shooting schedule. 3. Fee schedule. 4. Ahead of schedule. 5. Behind schedule. 6. Pulled from the schedule. 7. "sked."

schooling on a production Tutoring (elementary or secondary school) provided to one or more minor-aged performers working on a film, television or stage project; tutoring is provided according to state law and the terms of the union contract. Related terms: classroom trailer, studio teacher, welfare worker.

science fiction (abbreviated as sci-fi) Genre of fictitious stories in literature, film, television, theater, computer games, simulation rides, art, etc., dealing with real or imaginary scientific possibilities. "Fantasy" is a related genre dealing more with myths, legends and strange biology (giants, talking animals, etc.). Some fantasy movies, as well as some horror movies, have elements of science fiction in them.

sci-fi Abbreviation for science fiction.

sclera lenses Special, oversized contact lenses covering the entire area of the exposed eyes ("sclera" refers to the white part of the eye). Such lenses are often used by actors in horror, fantasy, and science-fiction movies and TV shows. Also called a scleral lens. Related terms: contact-lens special effects, special eye effects.

scoop Wide-angle floodlight.

score 1. (n.) All the music heard in a film, TV show or stage play. Related terms: original score, underscore, soundtrack, theme music. 2. (v.) To compose or provide a score. Related terms: composer, music clip clearance, songwriter. 3. Printed copy of a musical composition showing the various instrumental and vocal (if any) parts. Related term: music.

scoring stage Sound stage where a production's music score is performed and recorded. A conductor and musicians perform the music in front of a large viewing screen while sound personnel monitor recording equipment in a visible adjoining room. Only the conductor sees the screen; the musicians are seated with their backs to the screen so they are not distracted by the onscreen action.

scout An individual who searches or maintains an observance for something. Also called a scouter. Related terms: location scout, model scout, talent scout.

scraper Device, used with a hot splicer, for removal of emulsion from the film before the splice is cemented.

scratch print 1. Duplicate of a finished motion picture workprint used for dubbing, sound mixing or as an editing guide. It's not necessary for the scratch print to have a high picture quality, since it will not be released to theaters. Related term: slop print. 2. Sample footage from a stock-footage library sent to an editor with scratches on it to prevent unauthorized duplication. The footage is examined by the editor and director for possible inclusion in the final cut of the film. If the footage is used, a clean copy is sent and used according to the terms of the agreement. 3. Any motion picture or video footage that has been deliberately scratched to prevent unauthorized duplication.

scratch track Synchronized audio recording made during filming; it later will be used as a guide for respeaking lines or for creating better sound effects during an ADR or other sound-editing session. Its quality does not have to be perfect, since it will not be used for duplication; if it accidentally is damaged during editing, the original soundtrack is still protected. Also called a cue track, guide track or reference track.

scratches Deep grooves on the surface of film caused by poor or overly frequent projection, improper handling or camera friction. Scratches are more serious than abrasions because they are deeper and often damage the emulsion.

scream queen 1. Actress who has had prominent roles in numerous horror movies. For example, Neve Campbell is a scream queen in *Scream* (1996), *Scream 2* (1997) and *Scream 3* (2000). 2. Female voice actor who expertly provides different types of screams for live or recorded theatrical uses.

screamfest 1. Another name for a horror movie, especially one containing lots of screams by frightened characters. 2. Showing on television of numerous horror movies in succession, e.g., a "Halloween TV screamfest."

screen Surface onto which films are projected; usually made of opaque reflective material (although, rear projection screens are translucent). The screen is perforated to allow sound to pass through.

Screen Actors Guild (abbreviated as SAG) In the United States, the union for actors working in motion pictures, television and commercial productions shot on film and released on film, videotape or videodisc. Founded in 1933 and based in Hollywood, California, with offices around the United States. Internet address: http://www.sag.org. Related terms: Screen Actors Guild, Screen Actors Guild Award, Actor, SAG card, SAG eligible, Station 12, AFTRA, Screen Extras Guild, union initiation fee.

screen credit Another name for a film credit. Also called a big-screen credit or silver screen credit.

Screen Extras Guild In the United States, the name of a now-defunct union for extras performers; when it ceased operations in 1992, its jurisdictions were assumed by the Screen Actors Guild.

screen parent Mother, father or legal guardian of a child actor. Unlike the term "stage parent," it does not have a negative connotation.

screen presence Individual's exhibited use of body movements, facial expressions and voice in presenting an onscreen appearance and personality. Related terms: camera presence, presence.

screen test Audition recorded on film or tape to see if an actor is right for a part, to see how an actor looks on film or to test the chemistry between two actors. There were a multitude of screen tests done on actresses who auditioned for the role of Scarlett O'Hara in *Gone with the Wind* (1939); the part went to Vivien Leigh.

screen title Name, word or series of words appearing onscreen. Related term: title.

Screen Writers Guild See WGA.

screening Private showing of a film, or portions thereof, for a selected audience (e.g., friends of the filmmakers, members of an industry guild, distributors). No admission is charged.

screening room Mini-theater or conference room equipped with a projection booth for showing films or films in progress. Major studios, film labs, optical houses, etc., typically have several screening rooms at their facilities. Dailies are usually screened in such a room, unless circumstance (or preference) calls for them to be screened on an editing machine.

screening-in-progress light Illuminated sign outside a screening room; it flashes "Screening In Progress" as a film is being viewed inside.

screenplay Completed manuscript upon which a film is based. It contains dialogue; it is divided into scenes; it often includes some camera directions; it is written in the generally accepted screenplay format. Changes to the screenplay, even during production, are not uncommon. Related terms: teleplay, script, scenario.

screenplay by Credit awarded the writer(s) of a screenplay. This credit differs from "written by" in that it implies the original story was not conceived by the writer. "Written by" implies story and screenplay are created by the writer(s). If the movie is produced under the jurisdiction of a writers' union or guild, the ownership and placement of the credit is subject to the union's regulations.

screenwriter Individual who writes screenplays, treatments, stories and outlines for theatrical or television motion pictures. Also called a scriptwriter, film writer, film author or scenarist. Related terms: produced screenwriter, scriptwriter, first-look deal, Writers Guild of America, Writers Guild of Canada, Writers Guild of Great Britain, co-writer.

screenwriting 1. Working as a screenwriter. 2. Field, profession or world in which screenwriters work. Related term: scriptwriting.

screwball comedy Movie in the style of 1940s-era film comedies featuring eccentric or whimsical characters and situations. Preston Sturges, who wrote such films as *The Lady Eve* (1941), *The Great McGinty* (1940), *Christmas in July* (1940), *Sullivan's Travels* (1941), *Unfaithfully Yours* (1948), among others, was the father of the screwball comedy.

scrim 1. In production lighting, a mesh material used to diffuse light coming from a natural or artificial source. 2. In theater, a sheer cloth material used to achieve certain visual effects. For example, when a scene is lighted onstage in front of a scrim, it appears solid; when the lighting in front is shut off and a scene in back of it is lit, the scrim appears transparent. A scrim is also used to make backgrounds appear less defined, e.g., a hazy appearance associated with a scenic distance over land.

script 1. Written text in a special format serving as a guide for the course of action, dialogue and setting. Related term: screenplay.

script approval 1. Authorization of the script's final contents. Script approval is sometimes granted to high-powered stars who want to read the finished product before agreeing to portray a character in it; this is a contract right granted only to an actor in a powerful negotiating position. 2. Any other approval of a script by an individual or company before agreeing to become involved in a project. Related term: approval.

script breakdown See breakdown.

script change Alteration or modification of the script's text. Related terms: added scene, additional dialogue, omitted, polish, revised dialogue, revised page, revised scene, revised shot, revision, rewrite, scene number, strike, stet.

script girl Archaic term for "script supervisor."

script note Comment, suggestion or instruction regarding something that appears in a script.

script reading Reciting script lines from memory or reading them from the script or videoprompter screen, as for rehearsing or auditioning purposes. An actor is expected to dramatically interpret lines of dialogue as his character would say them. Related terms: cold reading, line reading, natural reading, reading, blowing a line, delivery, quick study, straight copy.

script session Meeting attended by members of the cast and creative staff (e.g., director and writer) to rehearse and gauge the script's dialogue effectiveness and sometimes its action. It may take place sitting around a large table or on the set. Also called a script read-through, script run-through or script rehearsal (also applies to the blocking of camera movements, lighting, etc.). Related term: rehearsal.

script supervisor Individual who records detailed notes on every take, including dialogue, gestures, action, lens used, costumes, makeup, etc., to ensure continuity of all elements from shot to shot and scene to scene. Since films are typically shot out of sequence, the script supervisor's notes, filed at the end of each shooting day, are critical to the continuity of the finished product. They also are an essential tool for the editor and director when putting the film together. Some feel the script supervisor is the second most important job on the set after the director. Without the aide of this person, the director's job would be infinitely more difficult, as there are so many details to keep track of while shooting. This is often a union job. Related term: continuity.

scripter Another name for a scriptwriter. Entertainment trade paper term.

scriptwriter Individual who writes scripts for films, TV or radio shows, videos, CD-ROM or DVD productions, play-format publications (comic books, photo soap-opera magazines, etc.), or the like. Also called a scriptwriter, scripter or dialogue writer. Related terms: comedy writer, co-writer, screenwriter, Writers Guild of America, Writers Guild of Canada, Writers Guild of Great Britain, written by, librettist, playwright.

scriptwriting 1. Working as a scriptwriter. 2. Field, profession or world in which scriptwriters work, including screenwriting.

SDTV Abbreviation for standard-definition television. System in which television images with less than 1,000 lines of picture information are processed digitally for transmission to home television sets with the traditional screen aspect ratio of 1.33:1 (4:3). SDTV and HDTV are two types of digital television, also referred to as advanced television (ATV). Related term: standard-definition television.

SE Abbreviation for "sound effect" or "sound effects". May appear on some union forms and production worksheets. Related term: SFX.

seamless paper A wide sheet of disposable background paper hung from the ceiling in a roll in a photographer's studio. To use it, a long section is pulled down and out across the floor where it is fastened, usually by adhesive tape. This creates a set without visible seams, a limbo set, for subjects to stand and move around on while being photographed, filmed, or videorecorded. Seamless paper is available in different widths, lengths, and colors. Also called no-seam paper, backdrop paper, or background paper. Related terms: backdrop, barefoot on the set, footprint watch.

season finale Season-ending episode or performance. Also called the last show of the season, season-ending episode or season-ending cliffhanger.

SECAM Abbreviation for Sequential Couleur à Memoire. Technical standard for television picture formation developed and used in France and other countries. Related term: broadcast quality.

second assistant cameraman Member of the Camera Department; the second assistant cameraman reports to the first assistant cameraman and prepares the camera equipment for the first A.C. In addition, he or she loads and unloads magazines from the camera, fills out the camera reports, slaps the clapsticks at the beginning and end of each take.

second assistant director (abbreviated as second AD) Production position who reports to the first assistant director and the production manager; generally the second AD is responsible for all cast and crew. Duties include preparation and distribution of daily paperwork (call sheets, production reports, actor's time sheets, extra's vouchers, etc.); acting as liaison between the production manager and/or the production office and the first assistant director; assisting the first AD in the placement of extras and in the maintenance of crowd control; supervising and directing the work of any DGA trainee. On union productions, the second AD is a member of the DGA or some equivalent union covering production personnel (e.g., Directors Guild of Canada, Directors Guild of Great Britain). This position can be upgraded on the second unit to first AD. Related terms: key second, second second, first assistant director, third assistant director.

second camera Additional camera used to shoot a sequence at the same time as the principal camera. A second camera is typically used in a scene that is difficult to restage, such as an explosion. Also called B-camera. Related term: multiple cameras

second camera assistant Assistant camera operator; third in rank on the director of photography's crew, after the director of photography and first camera assistant. Onscreen credit variations: second assistant camera, second assistant camera operator.

second cameraman See camera operator.

second second assistant director (abbreviated as 2nd 2nd AD) Additional second assistant directors, hired by and reporting to the key second assistant director. They are typically used on large productions. Second seconds are hired on a day-to-day basis and are called upon to help with a large cast or extra call or in large crowd scenes. An exception was *Taxi Driver* (1976), which had a complex schedule (a great deal of the shooting was done at night on the streets in New York); an additional second assistant director (Bill Eustace) was hired for the entire schedule.

second team Stand-ins for the principal performers, typically used when lighting the set. Also called the second string.

second unit Additional production crew, handled by the second unit director, used for shooting sequences that do not involve principal players, such as background shots at remote locations, backgrounds for process shots, large-scale sequences shot with multiple cameras and inserts. Often, the second AD becomes the first AD of the second unit and, on nonunion productions, the camera operator may become the second unit director of photography.

second unit director Individual in charge of directing sequences not involving principal players. Related terms: second unit, insert.

second unit director of photography (abbreviated as 2nd unit DP) Cameraman hired to shoot second unit scenes—shots the principal unit does not have time to shoot, shots that are complicated or require special skill or equipment (e.g., underwater scenes), shots that are at a distant location or inserts. The first unit camera operator and assistant cameraman can be upgraded for second unit work.

secondary location Similar to principal players and supporting players, there are locations that are deemed important (primary locations) and those which are less important (secondary locations). When scouting locations, it is advisable to find the primary locations before finding the secondary locations.

SEG Abbreviation for Screen Extras Guild.

segment producer Television producer responsible for the production of one or more segments on a news or informational program.

segue To move from one scene to the next, usually accompanied by a short piece of music (bridge); the term is derived from the early days of radio and television.

segue music Brief musical piece providing a segue point between two performances or segments, as on a radio show or live stage show.

select cast Cast of top-choice performers.

selected engagement 1. Booking to perform at a specific location as part of a planned tour. 2. Booking to exhibit a theatrical film in a particular city as part of a limited release.

selective focus Another name for a shallow focus.

sell-through Retail store sales as opposed to the rental market. Related term: direct-to-video release.

Selsyn motor Trade name for a device that runs two pieces of equipment in synchronization (e.g., camera and sound recorder).

semidocumentary A partial documentary. It contains both facts and fiction, the latter usually because all of the facts are not known. Related term: docudrama.

semiprofile shot Photograph or camera shot featuring a partial profile of a person or object. Also called a three-quarter face shot.

semiregular player Performer on a television series whose character is not in every episode; rather, he plays a recurring character who appears at the option of the show's creators. Also called a semiregular cast member.

senior producer Supervising producer on a television news or information series or special who oversees the work of segment producers.

senior spot High-intensity, 5,000-watt spotlight. Also called a senior spotlight or senior.

Sensurround Trade name for a sound system developed by Universal Studios; it adds low-frequency vibrations to the sound track, thereby increasing the believability of the action. Sensurround first appeared in *Earthquake* (1974).

separate card Refers to screen credit positioning; another name for a single card.

separation negatives Three individual negatives, each sensitive to one of the primary colors of light; used in three-stripe Technicolor. The three negatives are bonded together to produce an integral tripack.

sequel Film, TV program, video, book or the like that continues the story of its source material. It sometimes picks up where the previous story ended, either immediately or at a later point in time. A sequel typically features all or some of the same characters featured in the original work. For example, *The Godfather* (1972), directed by Francis Ford Coppola, spawned two sequels, *The Godfather Part II* (1974) and *Part III* (1990). *The Godfather* won Academy Awards® for Best Picture, Actor and Screenplay, while *The Godfather Part II* was the first sequal to be equally successful to its original work, winning Oscars® for Best Picture, Director, Screenplay, Supporting Actor, Score and Art Direction/Set Direction. Related terms: back-to-back sequels, shooting the sequel back-to-back, prequel, film series.

sequence Series of shots with a continuity of location, action, time or story; usually contains a beginning, middle and end.

serial Another name for a soap opera. Related terms: daytime serial, night-time serial.

series Weekly or daily program on television or radio, usually one half-hour or one hour in length. Related term: pilot.

series book Another name for a TV series bible. Related term: bible.

series deal Contract with a television network to create a series pilot and a certain number of episodes. Related terms: blind series commitment, development deal.

series finale Final episode in a TV series. Related term: last show of the series.

series of shots Number of related shots shown in succession, e.g., a series of shots of a fast-moving train. Related terms: continuous action, montage.

series regular Actor who appears on every episode of a television series.

serious actor 1. An actor who accepts mainly dramatic roles to perform. Another name for a dramatic actor. 2. An individual who is pursuing acting in a professional manner and as a career occupation.

sesh Short for session. Entertainment trade paper use.

session Period of time at one location during which an activity occurs. Related terms: ADR session, audition session, casting session, filming session, foley session, laser scanning session, original session, photo session, recording session, script session, shooting session, still session, TV commercial session, video session, rehearsal, set, shoot, shooting.

session fee Payment for or cost of participating in a session.

set Exterior or interior location where a film or television show is shot. Also called a designated shooting/performing area. Examples of set types: cover, four-wall, gimbal, hot, indoor, location, outdoor, practical, production, revolving, studio, three-wall, two-wall and standing. Related terms: distressing a set, silking a set, backlot, concept sketch, facade, scenery, scenery crew, stage, strike.

set construction area Place where a production set is built.

set decorator Individual responsible for dressing the set with furnishings relevant to the scene according to the production designer's or set designer's decoration plans for the production set. On some smaller (or, low-budget) productions, the jobs of set designer, set decorator, set dresser, property master, leadman, etc., may be done by the same person.

set design Plan for a production set. Related terms: virtual-reality set design, concept sketch.

set designer Individual responsible for preparing detailed architectural drawings (and, sometimes, three-dimensional models) of production sets; they are made from concept sketches created by the production designer. The actual duties and title of "set designer" may vary from production to production. On some smaller productions, the jobs of production designer and set designer are combined, with the individual doing both the initial concept sketches and finished blueprint drawings. Related terms: art director, set decorator.

set dresser Individual responsible for placing and removing various objects (e.g., furniture, paintings, lamps) on the production set prior to shooting. The set dresser works under the supervision of the property master or leadman. On smaller productions, the three jobs may be combined. A set dresser is also called a prop handler or prop person. Related terms: property master, leadman, grip, stagehand.

set dressing Furnishings, etc., used to decorate the set. Related term: props.

set estimator Member of the art department responsible for preparing cost estimates for the construction of the sets, based upon detailed drawings or verbal descriptions.

set list List containing information on the various production sets and locations.

set model Small-scale, three-dimensional replica of the production set. Also called a production set model or production set miniature. Related term: virtual reality set model.

set piece Prop or item of scenery standing upright, on its own, on a production set, e.g., a piece of furniture or fake tree. Related terms: flat, greenery, prop, set dressing.

set to roll Expression for a production with a scheduled start date, e.g., "The film is set to roll in Vancouver next week." Related term: "Roll 'em."

set tour Short for production set tour.

setting Time and place of events portrayed in a photograph, TV commercial or program, movie, play or other work of fiction or nonfiction.

setup Arrangement or positioning of equipment, materials, performers, action or dialogue, e.g., "The director and cinematographer are discussing the setup of the next shot."

seventy millimeter (70mm) Projection print film 70 millimeters (two and three-quarter inches) wide, with perforations (sprocket holes) on both sides and space for numerous soundtracks. A widescreen movie shot on 35mm film may be enlarged to 70mm as part of a special theatrical release. A movie shot on 65mm film may be transferred, without enlarging, to 70mm film (the extra 5mm of space on the edges allows for easier handling and provides room for numerous optional soundtracks). IMAX 70mm movies, which are shot on 65mm film stock with each frame positioned lengthwise, have no soundtracks directly on the finished projection print. Instead, the sound is played separately by one of three methods: multiple digital CDs, 35mm film with magnetic-tape soundtracks printed on it or half-inch eight-track magnetic tape. A leading 70mm film consultant is 70MM, Inc., of Culver City, California, in the United States. Related terms: 65mm, IMAX theater, Panavision, perforation.

sexploitation movie Film using sex scenes in its storyline to attract a larger audience. Related term: exploitation film. *Porky's* (1981) and *American Pie* (1999) are examples of classic sexploitation films.

SF Abbreviation for science fiction. Also FX.

SFX Common abbreviation for sound effects.

shadowing makeup Application of dark-colored makeup giving an actor's face the appearance of prominent wrinkles or underlying bones. Also done on other body areas (e.g., muscles or cleavage) to give them increased prominence. Such an application may also include highlighting makeup between the shadowed areas. Related term: character makeup.

Shakespearean actor Actor trained to perform the rich dialogue and artistic style of characters featured in plays written by William Shakespeare (1564-1616). Related term: classically trained actor.

shallow focus Camera shot in which one person or object is in focus but everything else is out of focus (blurry). Also called selective focus.

share That portion of television sets in use which are tuned to a particular program during a ratings measurement period. Related term: rating.

shared card Onscreen credit billing consisting of two or more names appearing at the same time, as opposed to a single card, on which a single name only appears onscreen.

sharp Crisp image in proper focus.

shock effect Visual, audio and editing element and/or technique designed to induce surprise and fear in an audience; commonly found in horror films. A classic example of a shock effect is the near-final shot in *Carrie* (1976), when the hand pops out of the ground. Related term: shock value.

shock value Worth of a shock effect; the degree to which an audience will be surprised at what they are seeing or hearing. Related term: entertainment value.

shoot 1. (n.) Slang for a motion picture or television show, etc., in production (e.g., "How did the shoot go today?" or "This shoot is driving me nuts!"). 2. (v.) To film any part, or all, of a motion picture or television show, etc. (e.g., "Get ready to shoot this before we lose the light.")

shoot around To reschedule camera shots when production problems occur, such as the illness of an actor, an unexpected delay with special effects or inclement weather.

shoot day Day on which shooting takes place.

shoot-'em-up Nickname for a Western or other movie featuring gunfights. Entertainment trade paper use.

shooting 1. Recording one or more pictures using a camera. Related terms: first day of shooting, last day of shooting. 2. Session in which this takes place. Short for shooting session. Also called a shoot. 3. The pictures themselves. For film and video, also called footage. 4. Discharging a firearm, e.g., shooting a gun.

shooting call Request or notice to be at a certain place, at a certain time, where moving or still pictures will be shot.

shooting company Crew of a film in production.

shooting location Place where film, video or still photography images are shot. Related term: location.

shooting out of sequence Shooting a film out of its sequential order (scenes 1, 2, 3, 4, etc.), as listed in the script. Almost all productions are shot this way for reasons of practicality and budget. Once all the footage is shot (or even as soon as the dailies are ready), the editor will take it and, using the script as a guideline, combine the footage into a story that has continuity from beginning to end. Related terms: out of sequence, continuity.

shooting ratio Amount of film exposed while shooting relative to the amount of film in the final release print. A lower ratio is better for a film's budget. For example, a 4:1 ratio is considered economical while a 20:1 ratio is considered wasteful. Luis Buñuel was known for shooting on a ratio of 1:1.

shooting schedule Listing of the numbered shots, actors, director, producer(s), crews, times, locations, props and equipment for one or more days of production. Also called a production schedule. A Production Report details the activities actually accomplished each day. Related term: shooting script.

shooting script Approved final version of the screenplay, complete with dialogue, detailed camera setups and other instructions used by the director.

shooting session Period during which images are recorded on still photographs, motion picture film, video-tape or any other photographic or electronic medium. Related terms: shooting, shoot, filming session, photo session, still session, video session.

shooting stage Another name for a production sound stage.

shooting the sequel back-to-back Filming the sequel to a film project immediately following the completion of the original production; or, shooting the sequels at the same time. For example, *Back to the Future, Part II* (1989) and *Back to the Future, Part 3* (1990) were shot back-to-back even though they were released in different years; the two sequels to *The Matrix* (1999) are scheduled to be shot back-to-back. Related term: back-to-back sequels.

short end Length of unexposed film left over after the exposed part is cut off. Many student and experimental films are made from short ends.

short film Also called a short subject. Any film of short length (it can be a theatrical or television film). Typically, this means 30 minutes or less in length. The exact length range (sometimes defined in linear length, as opposed to time) varies among unions and contest entry rules. Short films often are used by filmmakers as demo reels; they are also produced as school projects. Live-action short films, documentary short films and animated short films are eligible to win Academy Awards® and other major awards, especially at film festivals. Also called a "film short" or "short." Related terms: pre-feature short film, short subject, cartoon, featurette, mini-movie, newsreel.

short-lived series Television series that is canceled before the end of its first season.

shot One continuous take. Related terms: scene, sequence.

shot and angle descriptions Following are examples of camera shots and angle descriptions that may be found in a script. Examples of shot types and camera angle descriptions: aerial (airplane, helicopter, balloon), air-to-air, angle on, angle favoring, angle tightens (dolly in/up to, move in, zoom in) angle widens (dolly out/back, pull back, zoom out), back to, binocular POV, blurred POV/view/vision, brief (quick shot of), cheat, chroma key, circle around (arc), circular pan, close on (tight on), closer (tighten), close-up, composite (glass, front-screen projection, matte, process, rear-screen projection), cover (insurance, protection, safety), day, day-for-night, day/night, defocus transition (focus out and then refocus to), dissolve to, door-crack POV, down angle (looking down), dream sequence (dream mode), drive-by, dry-for-wet, dutch angle (oblique/off-center/slanted angle), effects (special/visual effects, bluescreen, CCI, chroma key, composite, greenscreen, model miniature, orangescreen, split screen, etc.), elevator (straight up/down), establishing, establishing stock, extreme close-up (big/tight close-up, detail), extreme high angle (boom, crane, looking down from rooftop), extreme long-angle (distant), extreme low-angle (looking up), extreme wide-angle lens (fisheye lens), eye level, fast cut to (quick cut to), fast motion (accelerated motion), fast zoom in (crash zoom), fast zoom out, flashback (flashback sequence), flashforward (flash ahead in time), focus in, focus out (defocus), focus pull (shift focus to a nearby or distant subject), follow (track, move with), follow focus, full, freeze frame (still frame), ground level (floor level), group, handheld, head, head-on, high angle, hold, insert, intercut with, intercut series, into frame (into view), iris (iris effect), keyhole POV, knee level, long angle (far), low angle, master, matching, medium, mirror, montage (montage sequence), motion-stabilized (Glidecam, Panaglide, Steadicam, etc.), night, night filter (day-for-night), night-for-day, overhead (overhead looking down), over-the-shoulder, pan, passing, peephole POV, pickup, pit (below ground/drive-over POV), point-of-view (POV), POV through [fence, mask/hood, window, windshield, etc.], reaction, rear angle, reestablishing, registration, repeat (reprise), reveal (discover), reverse motion (backward motion), reverse angle, reverse POV, ripple dissolve to, run-by, running, search pan, series-of-shots, side angle, skyward, soft focus (diffusion lens), stock (library, newsreel), superimpose, swish pan, symbolic, tail-away, telescope POV, 360-degree pan, through window/windshield, tilt up, tilt down,, time-lapse, tracking (dollying, following, moving with), traveling (moving, trucking), trucking (moving vehicle), two-shot, underwater, upside-down, viewfinder POV, water tank, wide angle, wipe to, zoom-freeze, zoom in (angle tightens), and zoom out (angle widens).

shot area Ground and space within the shot. Also called the frame area, action area or action field. Related terms: camera's eye, director's viewfinder, field of view, safe action area, zone shot.

shot number In the screenplay, the number assigned to each shot by the first AD or production manager. Also called a scene number if it refers to a master-scene shot. Specialized shots, e.g., insert close-ups, reaction shots, which are part of a master scene, are numbered separately. Related terms: scene number, shooting out of sequence, shooting script.

shotgun mike Directional microphone able to pick up sound from a limited area, although the angle of acceptance is more limited than that of a directional mike. (A shotgun mike is to a directional mike what a telephoto camera lens is to a normal lens.)

show business (abbreviated as show-biz) Industries and professions involved with producing, promoting and performing entertainment shows. Also collectively called the entertainment industry, entertainment world or world of entertainment.

show cards See cue cards.

show curtain 1. Curtain that opens at the start of the first act of a stage play or other stage production. 2. Short for curtain time, as in a theater program.

show print Another name for a release print.

show tune Song used in a musical play or film.

showbiz jargon Language of show business. Also called show-biz lingo. Related term: filmspeak.

showcase production Theatrical stage production organized and presented to introduce new performers to invited agents, producers, directors, reviewers, etc. It also provides experience and a résumé credit for those involved. In the United States, 99-Seat theater productions are often used to showcase the talents of performers, writers, director and producer.

showman 1. Theatrical show producer. 2. Any producer. 3. Highly effective stage entertainer.

Showscan Trade name for a 65mm film camera that films at 60 frames per second and its 70mm theater projection system that projects at the same rate of speed. By comparison, standard 35mm film runs through a camera and projector at 24 frames per second. The faster Showscan speed produces sharper and and more realistic (almost three-dimensional) images. In recognition of the contribution of the Showscan CP-65 camera to filmmaking, its developers, Douglas Trumbull, Geoffrey H. Williamson, Robert D. Auguste and Edmund M. DiGiulio, were honored by the Academy of Motion Picture Arts and Sciences with 1992 Scientific and Engineering Awards. The Showscan camera-projection system is manufactured in the United States by the Showscan Film Corporation of Culver City, California. The projection part of the system is featured in numerous amusement attractions, including those found at the Luxor Hotel and Casino in Las Vegas, Nevada. Internet address: http://www.showscan.com

show-stopper Performance or special effect so well-received that audience applause brings a momentary halt to the show.

shrinkage Reduction in film size caused by loss of moisture during processing or by extended storage. The resulting image may be distorted; also, the film tends to tear due to stress during projection.

shtick (Yiddish for piece) Stage routine, act or performance, e.g., "The comedian went onstage, did his shtick and then left." Also called a bit.

shutter Device inside a camera; it is located behind the lens and controls how long (in seconds or fractions thereof) light is allowed to enter and strike the film or CCD imaging chip. Related terms: aperture, exposure, speed.

sidecar mount Also called a side car mount. Special attachment holding the camera onto the side of a vehicle; used during filming. Related terms: camera mount, car mount.

sidekick Assistant, ally or close friend. Related terms: comic sidekick, comic foil, straight man, buddy movie.

sidelight Light directed at a subject from one side. If two or more side-lights are used, it is also called a crosslight.

sides Audition script pages. Related term: copy sheet.

sight gag Joke based on visual comedy. The "hair gel" scene from *There's Something About Mary* (1998) is an example of a sight gag. Also called a visual joke or bit of visual humor. Related terms: gag, double-take, spit-take.

sight line Line of sight to the stage from a seat or area in the audience, e.g., "The audience's sight line is partially blocked by one of the studio television cameras." Related term: eye line.

signatory The representative of a company that has signed an agreement with a union or guild, obligating it to comply with the rules and regulations of that union or guild.

sign-in sheet Form to be filled in by talent upon arriving at a casting session or production set location. It requests information, such as performer's name, agent's name, union identification number, time of arrival, time of departure and the like. It is a union-required procedure. Related terms: audition report form, talent information form, time report.

sign-off Closing announcement, as on a radio show or TV news program. For example, "Thank you and good night."

silent bit Actor with no lines to deliver but who contributes to the action of a scene, for example, the waiter who spills hot soup on the principal actor (whereas the other waiters in the scene who wait on the tables are considered extras). There usually is an increased rate of pay for a silent bit. Related terms: silent part, bit part.

silent era Period in filmmaking history, beginning in 1893, with the public exhibition of a short film by Thomas Edison, featuring three blacksmiths working (they were Edison's actor-employees) in his just-patented Kinetoscope peephole viewing machine. Since that time, short and feature-length theatrical films without audible dialogue dominated the film industry. The first short "talkies" were demonstrated to fair-goers at the Paris Exposition in 1900; it was not until the late 1920s, however, that movies with audible dialogue began to move out of the experimentation stage. They increased greatly in number and running length as synchronized sound recording and playback systems improved and were installed in theaters. For North America and Europe, the silent era came to a slow end in 1931. Also called the silent film era or pre-talkie era. Related terms: silent film, talkie.

silent film Movie with no audible dialogue. Early silent films were accompanied by live music played in the theater; separate onscreen cards were used to present titles, credits, narration and dialogue. The opposite of a silent film is a talkie. Related terms: silent era, overlap dialogue.

silent part Nonspeaking performing role. Related terms: silent bit part, nonspeaking part.

silent print Processed film with a positive image but no sound track. Related term: picture print.

silent speed The proper rate of 16 to 18 frames per second is utilized for film not intended to be used with sound.

silhouette Backlit subject whose front shows little or no detail to the camera other than a general outline.

silk Large, rectangular cloth used to diffuse harsh light during shooting; it is principally used outdoors. Related terms: butterfly, diffuse, mask.

silking a set Placing white sailcloth or other fabric over various off-camera parts of a production set to lessen harsh light on it. Related terms: silk, diffused light.

silver card Large card covered or painted with a light-reflecting silver material; it is one type of reflector board that can be used to angle light onto a person or area. Used on a still photography, film or video production set.

silver screen 1. Nickname for the world of theatrical motion pictures. Related term: big screen. 2. Type of movie screen with a silvery reflective surface due to aluminum-particle coating or metallic paint. Movie screens in most theaters today are made of a finely perforated white material (to allow sound to pass through) stretched over a frame. Related terms: movie screen, screen.

simulcast 1. (n.) Program broadcast or cablecast on television and radio at the same time, so that viewers can utilize the superior sound system of their radios. A stereo simulcast is one featuring stereo sound. For example, local sporting events or performing arts shows are often simulcast. Often programs are simulcast in a foreign language on the radio. 2. (v.) To simulcast.

single Shot of a single person; filmed as part of the director's coverage of a scene. A single can be a close-up of the actor saying his key line and/or listening to spoken dialogue (a reaction shot); however, it can be any sort—close-up, medium shot, etc., as long as there is only one person in the shot. The opposite of a single shot is a double shot.

single broad See broad.

single card Individual onscreen credit billing; it is not shared with another individual. This may be a union requirement in some cases. Also called a separate card or single billing. The opposite is a shared card, also called shared billing.

single frame exposure Technique used in animation, stop motion and time lapse photography in which film is exposed frame by frame.

single system Method of recording sound and picture onto the same piece of film. Its use today is generally limited to news and documentary work, as the quality is inferior to the double system (which features separate picture and sound) and it can present problems (limitations) during the editing process.

single-lens reflex (abbreviated as SLR) Most popular film-camera viewfinder system in use for 35mm still-picture cameras. It consists of various optical components that cause the image entering the lens at the front of the camera to be reflected up to the viewfinder. What is seen through the viewfinder is what is recorded; there is no parallax. Single-lens reflex is also called through-the-lens viewing.

sister show Television show that is a spin-off from another.

"Sit into the shot." Direction from the director to an actor to sit down on a designated spot after "Action!" is called. The camera is angled on the chair and the actor's upper body descends into the shot as he sits down.

sitcom Sitcoms typically are produced as half-hour shows and are shot on film or videotape or performed live. Related term: situation comedy.

situation comedy Episodic comedy TV series having the same principal cast and setting in every episode and a new story to tell each week; based on a humorous dilemma or inter-esting set of circumstances facing one or more of the characters. Related terms: sitcom, TV series.

6mm Digital videotape six millime-ters wide.

16mm Camera and projection film 16 millimeters wide; it has perforations (sprocket holes) on one side only and space for an optical or magnetic soundtrack on the other (silent 16mm film has perforations on both sides). Introduced in 1923, standard 16mm film has a frame-size aspect ratio the same size as the screen on a standard television set—1.33:1 (4:3); it can also be masked for 1.66:1 or 1.85:1 wide-screen aspect ratios. Super 16mm, introduced in 1971, is a negative-only film with a widescreen film frame 40 percent larger than standard 16mm film. During processing, it is enlarged to a 35mm projection print. Both types of 16mm film have 40 frames per foot and one perforation next to

each frame. Sound 16mm film runs through a camera or projector at 24 frames per second, the same as 35mm movie film; silent 16mm film's run-ning speed is 16 frames per second. Before videotape and satellites became the standard methods of distribution in the television industry, filmed tele-vision programs and major commer-cials were downprinted from 35mm to 16mm and telecast by individual stations using their in-house telecine equipment. Syndicated old movies, reruns of classic TV series (the origi-nal *Star Trek* [1966], for example) and even televised coming attractions for theatrical films were distributed to television stations until the 1970s on 16mm black-and-white or color film with an optical soundtrack. The use of film meant that, occasionally, a bit of dust or lint would attach itself to the projection gate of the telecine and viewers at home would see a magnifi-cation of it, usually in one corner of the screen, until the telecine operator removed it using a short blast of com-pressed air. Today, old movies, reruns, non-network specials, etc., are distrib-uted and syndicated on videocassettes or by microwave satellite. Network, live and syndicated daily programs are distributed by means of a microwave satellite link between the network/dis-tributor and individual stations. Be-cause it costs less to use and can be shot with a lighter, less bulkier cam-era, 16mm film continues to be a popular choice with documentary, student and independent filmmakers. Related terms: film, flatbed editing machine, Kinescope, newsreel, wide-screen.

16mm-to-35mm blowup Motion pic-ture shot on 16mm film and enlarged to 35mm so it can be released theatrically. The 35mm size also allows for additional soundtracks.

65mm Camera film 65 millimeters wide with perforations (sprocket holes) on both sides. A movie shot on 65mm film stock can be transferred, retaining the exact same frame size, to the slightly wider 70mm projection print film. Related terms: downprint, IMAX theater, Panavision, perforation, 70mm, Showscan, VistaVision.

sked Short for schedule. Entertainment trade paper use.

skein Another name for a television series. Entertainment trade paper use.

sketch 1. Short theatrical performance. Related terms: comedy sketch, skit. 2. (n.) Rough drawing; artwork depicting an overall idea without showing a great amount of detail. Related terms: ad sketch, concept sketch. 3. Brief, written outline of information. 4. (v.) To prepare a sketch.

skill sheet List of a performer's skills or talents; it may be kept by an agency to aid casting personnel. Also called a skill card. Related term: talent information form.

skill test Check of a performer's claimed skill (as found on the actor's résumé). Also called a skill confirming test or skill demonstration. Related term: talent test.

skip framing Optical printing technique used to speed up action; every other or every third frame is printed. Double printing is the opposite of skip framing; it is used to slow down action by printing the same frame twice.

skit Short, theatrical performance. Related terms: blackout skit, sketch.

sky filter Graduated filter that, when shooting in black and white, darkens only the sky.

Skycam Trade name for an overhead camera-mount system consisting of a camera attached to a radio-controlled platform; it moves high over a shooting area, e.g., at an indoor sporting event, along a track of suspended cables.

SL 1. Abbreviation for "stage left." 2. Abbreviation for sign language; used in television program listings to indicate a program has an onscreen sign-language interpreter for the hearing impaired. Other services for the hearing impaired include closed-captioning (CC) and open-captioning (OC), both of which involve the use of onscreen subtitles.

slapstick Comedy based on physically aggressive, injurious or violent acts, e.g., slipping on a banana peel, being hit on the head by an object, being sprayed with a pressurized water hose, squeezing someone's nose or ear, or the like. For example, Jim Carrey often uses slapstick humor in his films. The term "slapstick" actually refers to a wooden stick used by circus clowns to create a loud slapping noise when one clown comically strikes another across the face. Related terms: cartoon violence, physical comedy.

slate 1. Hinged boards which, when clapped, provide a cue (used during editing) for synchronization of sound and picture. Information is written on the slate to identify the following: film title; director's name; cinematographer's name; roll number; scene number; take number; date. The call for action does not come until after the slate has sounded. Related terms: clapsticks, clapperboard. 2. In a video audition, orally stating an actor's name, agency representation and age (if a minor); this is done in front of a live camera at the beginning of the

audition. Related term: voice slate.
3. (v.) To schedule, e.g., "The movie is slated for release early next year." Entertainment trade paper use.

slate card Informal oncamera slate consisting of a nonglossy white cardboard sheet with handwritten scene and shot information on it. Also called a cardboard slate.

"Slate it." Direction to the assistant camera operator to display the slate or operate the clapboard in front of a running camera at the start of a shot. Also said: "Mark it," "Stick it."

sleeper Project that gets off to a slow start in sales or receives few reviews, but eventually finds success, either financially or with the critics. *The Blair Witch Project* (1999) is considered a huge sleeper hit. Also called a box-office sleeper or surprise hit.

Slingcam Trade name for a camera-carrying harness that slings over the shoulder of the camera operator. It is used for low-angle moving shots requiring a handheld effect. Related term: camera mount.

slogan Another name for a catchphrase, e.g., an advertising slogan.

slop print See scratch print.

slow motion Effect achieved by running the film through the camera at speeds greater than 24 frames per second; or through the projector at slower-than-normal speed (although, this is rarely done). Related term: slo-mo.

SLR Abbreviation for single-lens reflex.

slug Piece of leader or otherwise unusable film; it is temporarily inserted in a work print to replace damaged, unfinished or missing footage. Related term: fill.

small screen Another name for the medium of television.

smoke cloth Chemically treated cloth giving off wisps of smoke when burned at a smoldering rate.

smoke effect Appearance of smoke in a scene created by a fog or smoke machine, smoke pot, burning powder or fire from a burning fuel explosion. Related terms: A-B smoke, EZ Lite Smoke powder, fog/smoke machine, smoke cloth, smoke fluid, smoke pot, smoke tube, Spectrasmoke, Thermal Smoke, Z-Smoke tablets, fog effect, fire effect, Puff Powder, pyrotechnic effects.

smoke fluid Special liquid that produces a smoldering effect with wispy smoke when it burns; the effect appears after the liquid is applied to paper or cloth and allowed to dry. It can be used to simulate the aftereffects of a destructive indoor or outdoor fire. A source for smoke fluid (and smoke cloth) is the pyrotechnic special-effects company Tri-Ess Sciences, Inc., of Burbank, California.

smoke pot Metal container holding a quantity of smoke powder that emits smoke for a period of time; available in a variety of smoke colors. Two sources for smoke pots are Tri-Ess Sciences, Inc., of Burbank, California and Zeller International, Ltd., of Downsville, New York.

smoke tube Small, thin glass tube containing a quantity of nonpyrotechnic smoke-producing material; it is expelled by attaching a hose and rubber bulb or compressed-air container to one end. A second hose can be attached to the other end to control the direction of the smoke. Used for small smoke effects. Manufactured and sold by Zeller International, Ltd., of Downsville, New York.

SMPTE Abbreviation for Society of Motion Picture and Television Engineers.

sneak preview Advance showing of a film in a theater to a paying audience; conducted to test audience reaction or to generate word-of-mouth in the community. Changes are often made after a picture has been sneaked.

Sno-Foam Liquid foaming concentrate; when added to water, it produces a fluffy white biodegradable foam and can be applied to surfaces in large quantities via compressed air or as falling snow. Available, along with other snow and winter-season effects, from Tri-Ess Sciences, Inc., of Burbank, California.

snoot Conelike attachment fitted on the front of a light source; it is used to direct light to a certain area of the set.

snow bag or box Any of various perforated, overhead flexible containers filled with fake snow; they are shaken by pulling an attached cord offstage or offcamera. It can also be made to drop all of its snow at once. Related terms: drop box, snow effect.

snow effect Appearance of falling or surface snow; the snow is created by man-made artificial (water-based) snow, feathers, shredded plastic, dehydrated potato flakes, polyethylene fibers, polystyrene foam granules and chunks, paper mulch, gypsum, different grades of salt, baking soda, cotton, shaving cream (for small spots) or different types of sprayed-on liquid foam (for large areas). Depending on the type of scene and fake snow, it is applied by spraying, sprinkling or blowing (by dropping in front of a fan). To make cleanup easier, it can be placed on top of white muslin (cotton sheeting) spread on the ground or on artificially built-up areas. Related terms: Bio-Snow 2 Flake, snow bag, Sno-Foam, snow search, Crystasol, Frost Tex, Jetex, Zice.

snow search Location scouting trip to one or more winter-climate cities, recreational resorts or mountain wilderness areas in search of a shooting site with the amount of snow needed for the scenes.

soap Short for soap opera.

soap opera Nickname for an open-ended or continuing series on television, radio or the World Wide Web having the same principal cast and setting in every episode and a continuing storyline that follows the day-to-day personal and professional lives of its characters. It may be presented Monday through Friday or weekly and during the daytime or nighttime. The name originated as a result of the many early live serial dramas on both radio and television in the United States sponsored by national soap-product manufacturers (particularly Proctor & Gamble). The first television soap opera, *Faraway Hill*, a 30-minute romance drama, had a limited 11-week run in late 1946 on the DuMont Network in the United States. As television gradually became the dominant source of home entertainment, radio soap operas diminished. Related terms: soap, cybersoap, continuing series, cliffhanger, daytime serial, daytime TV, nighttime serial, sudser.

Soc. Sec. No. Abbreviation for Social Security Number. Also called a taxpayer ID number. Identification number generated in the United States and used on various employment forms (in some instances, a union identification number is used instead), work contracts, federal and state income-tax forms and informational records stored in agency and union files. Internet address: http://www.ssa.gov.

Society of Motion Picture and Television Engineers (abbreviated as SMPTE) In the United States, an organization founded in 1916, to advance and develop standards for filmmaking and, later, television technologies. Its members are film and television engineers and technicians. It also presents annual awards to recognize advancements in film and television production and processing technologies. The Society received a 1957 honorary Oscar® for its "contribution to the advancement of the motion picture industry." Internet address: http://www.smpte.org. Related term: universal leader.

Society of Stage Directors and Choreographers (abbreviated as SSDC) Union representing the interests of theater directors and choreographers in the United States. Founded in 1959 and based in New York City.

soft focus Fuzzy or unclear image; term is used when the camera lens is not focused properly by the focus puller or camera technician. This should not be confused with the process of shooting with a diffusion filter (or gauze or Vaseline) in front of the lens, which intentionally creates a romantic or hazy effect. Related term: diffused light.

soft light 1. Gentle glow on a set; it casts a minimum of shadows; created with the use of diffusers or gels.

soft wipe Optical effect; a wipe whose edges are blurred.

soliloquy 1. Speech or monologue by an actor who is alone onstage or oncamera; during such a speech, he makes reflective comments about personal issues or events in the story. Soliloquies are performed by actors in auditions and are common in daytime soap operas, where they are used to remind audiences of events that have occurred up to that point in the story. The Rodgers and Hammerstein musical *Carousel* (filmed and released in 1956) features a song entitled, "Soliloquy," sung by the lead male character, Billy Bigelow, as he stands alone on the stage. Related term: wild line. 2. Any character who talks to himself.

solo performance Presentation in which only one person performs, e.g., a solo acting performance or solo singing performance. Related term: one-man show.

songwriter Individual who writes lyrics and music. Related terms: lyricist, composer.

Songwriters Guild of America (abbreviated as SGA) Organization representing the interests of songwriters in industry contract and copyright issues. Founded in 1931 and based in Weehawken, New Jersey. Internet address: http://www.songwriters.org.

sound Audio portion of a film; it is recorded on magnetic tape or magnetic film. Several separate tracks (music, effects, dialogue) can be recorded and mixed later to create the composite sound track. A recent sound invention is Dolby, a noise-reducing system, that has greatly improved the fidelity of motion picture sound. Related terms: audience sounds, Dolby Sound, indigenous sound, live sound, overlap sound, wild sound, audio, background noise, DTS, HEAR, MOS, music, THX.

sound assistant Individual responsible for storing, maintaining and hooking up all audio cables and related sound equipment used on a production. The sound assistant also wires an actor or other person on-camera or onstage with a wireless radio microphone. Also called a soundperson, sound technician, sound engineer or a variety of other job-specific titles. Related terms: soundperson, cableman, cable puller, microphone operator.

sound bite Brief statement made by a journalist or his subject; typically, an edited section is cut out of a longer statement, hence, a "bite" of sound. Related term: sound clip.

sound camera Specially designed, blimped camera whose mechanical noise is sufficiently diminished so as not to be heard by the microphone during shooting. Related terms: barney, sound.

sound check Test for proper sound level, voice quality or sound equipment readiness. Also called a sound test, audio check or audio test. Related terms: mike check, countdown.

sound clip Brief sound recording or portion of an audiorecorded work. Related term: sound bite.

sound crew Typically, the sound crew consists of a production mixer, soundman/recordist (this individual should not be confused with the post-production mixer who mixes all the tracks when the picture is edited), the boom operator and the cable puller.

sound cue Signal received or given in the form of a sound.

sound designer 1. Sound-system designer for a building, room or

event. 2. Short for sound-effects designer.

sound editor Individual responsible for assembling and synchronizing ordinary and special sound effects. A sound editor may also create and record sounds. Related term: sound-effects mixer.

sound effects Third part of a sound track; on it are recorded all artificially-created or natural sounds (other than music or dialogue). These sounds, such as a door opening, a bird chirping, glass breaking, are recorded separately (wild sound) or transferred from a library of sound effects. Related term: foley.

sound effects designer Individual who specializes in planning and creating sound effects (oftentimes, they are highly unusual ones) for film and TV.

sound effects editor Individual who provides and edits sound effects. Related term: foley editor.

sound effects mixer Individual responsible for recording and combining a production's sound effects soundtracks. Related terms: foley mixer, sound mixer.

sound effects studio Sound studio where sound effects are created (electronically or manually) and recorded. Related term: foley studio.

sound mixer 1. Individual who combines recorded or live sound. Also used as a general job title, possibly referring to a production mixer, dialogue mixer, music mixer, sound effects mixer, rerecording mixer or a combination of any of these. Exact sound related job titles may depend on the size and complexity of the production and how many sound technicians are hired to work on it. Also called a mixer. Related term:

mixing. 2. Electronic device used to combine sounds from different input sources. Also called an audio mixer.

sound recordist One of the possible job titles for the individual operating the sound recording equipment on a production during shooting. Related terms: recordist, production mixer, soundperson, "Roll Sound," "Speed."

sound report Daily information sheet containing information about each shot; it is filed by a sound crew member (the sound recordist) and used as a reference in the synchronization of sound and picture elements. Also called a sound log.

sound speed Standard rate at which film or tape passes through the camera when it is being shot in sync with sound.

sound stage Large, soundproof building within a film production complex where scenes are shot on constructed sets and the sound is recorded under near-perfect conditions. Also called a soundproof stage, indoor shooting stage or film stage. Related terms: sound studio, scoring stage, stage no., studio set.

sound stripe Thin strip of ferromagnetic coating applied to the film's edge, on which the sound track is placed.

sound studio Room sealed from outside noises; in a sound studio, various types of sound can be created and recorded under controlled conditions. Also called a recording studio. Related terms: ADR studio, foley studio, sound-effects studio, sound stage, announcing booth.

sound test Another name for a sound check.

sound track 1. Audio portion of a film divided into three or four separate tracks or channels: dialogue, music, effects and a spillover track for additional sounds. An optical sound track is made from the mixed tracks before it is printed onto the side of the film in the lab. It is not uncommon for many separate units (there can be hundreds) to be individually edited and then mixed, to produce the final sound track. 2. Another term for the recorded version of a film's musical score, available to purchase on album, tape or compact disc.

soundperson Any individual with a sound-related job on a production. May also be called an audioperson, audio/sound engineer or audio/sound technician. Related terms: sound assistant, sound editor, sound mixer, sound recordist, boom operator, cableman, cable puller, microphone operator.

soup Slang for the chemicals (developer) in which film is developed.

SpaceCam Trade name for an Academy Award®-winning, gyroscopically stabilized camera system that can be mounted on a helicopter, boat or camera car. In recognition of the SpaceCam's contribution to filmmaking, its developers, Ronald Goodman, Attila Szalay, Stephen Sass and SpaceCam Systems, Inc., were honored by the Academy of Motion Picture Arts and Sciences with a 1995 Scientific and Engineering Award. Related terms: aerial shot, camera mount, helicopter shot.

spaghetti Western Nickname for a Western film; it is typically set in the southwestern part of North America during the late 1880s, but it actually is produced and filmed in Italy or its nearby countries (e.g., Spain or Yugoslavia). The term originated when describing a collection of such films that came to prominence in the 1960s. Popular examples include: *A Fistful of Dollars* (1964), *For a Few Dollars More* (1965), *The Good, the Bad, and the Ugly* (1966), *Hang 'Em High* (1968), *Once Upon a Time in the West* (1969), *They Call Me Trinity* (1971) and *My Name Is Nobody* (1974).

spark hit 1. Bullet-hit pyrotechnic charge producing a brief flash of sparks when detonated. 2. Plastic ball containing fine fish-tank gravel and a small amount of zirconium; it is shot at a hard surface from a Sweeney gun and a brief burst of sparks occurs upon impact. Also called a Zirk hit.

Sparkle Paste Two-part paste mix; it produces glittering sparks when it burns. Available from Tri-Ess Sciences, Inc., of Burbank, California.

speaking part Acting role in which the performer is heard and seen (except in the case of an off camera or offstage announcing or narrating part). Also called a speaking role.

spec 1. Short for speculatively done or on speculation, e.g., a spec script. 2. Short for TV special. Entertainment trade paper use.

spec script Screenplay was written on speculation. The writer spends his own time and money researching and writing the script, with hopes that a producer will buy it. If a writer sends a spec script directly to a producer who did not request it, it is also called an unsolicited script and may be returned unread. A spec script can also be used as a writing sample, especially by an unproduced or aspiring screenwriter; it also can be submitted in scriptwriting competitions.

special 1. Television program that is not part of an ongoing series and is shown as an important or out-of-the-ordinary event, e.g., a news special, entertainment special, variety special or comedy special. Also called a special television event or special presentation. 2. Out-of-the ordinary episode of a television series; it is promoted as a special. Also called a special episode or special presentation.

special blood effects Use of fake blood in a production. Fake blood (also called imitation blood, movie blood, stage blood or theatrical blood) is available or prepared in different nontoxic formulas and consistencies (e.g., light corn syrup and food coloring; light corn syrup, oatmeal and food coloring). In a blood knife, it is forced out through a small, concealed hose or sponge along the edge of the blade as the knife runs across the actor's skin. A-B blood comes in two liquid parts: one part is placed on the actor's skin and the other on the edge of a dull knife. When the two parts make contact, a chemical reaction occurs and simulated blood is created. In a scene involving bodily injury to a character, fake blood is forced through wounds by a concealed hose(s) or a concealed compressed-air supply on the body or by an off camera technician operating a hand pump or air-supply release valve; latex-bladder appliances with pinhole punctures can also used. (An example of this effect, often seen in horror films, is a scene in which a character's veins begin to bulge and leak blood.) Special blood effects requiring greater force, such as blood bursting forth from clothing, use small explosive charges called squibs. A squib, with attached electrical detonation wires, is placed alongside one or more small plastic bags or latex condoms filled with fake blood. These are taped to the front surface of a protective metal plate and fastened to the actor under his clothing. The squib's detonation wires run under the actor's clothing and off camera to a special-effects pyrotechnic operator, who operates a battery-connected switch. When the squib detonates with fake blood, it explodes outward, away from the metal plate, through the actor's clothing. The actor responds as if he was actually shot. Fake blood may also be applied by a special-effects makeup artist. Nontoxic, red-colored eye drops called eye blood are used to make the eyes appear to be bloodshot or bleeding. Special blood effects are used in varying degrees in scenes involving gunfights, knife fights, sword fights, fistfights and accidents and also various types of horror movie scenes. Related terms: A-B blood, blood capsule, blood hit, blood knife, squib, squib vest.

special business Out of ordinary and prominent activity by a performer. Related term: business.

special camera operator Member of the camera crew specializing in a particular kind of cinematography, such as underwater, handheld, aerial, etc. These operators typically are hired on a daily basis, depending upon the complexity and duration of the job.

special effects (abbreviated as FX, SFX) Unusual computer, mechanical, makeup, pyrotechnic, optical, lighting, weather, model miniature, etc., elements of a production. This can range from a practical (working) sink and garbage disposal to an intricate effect, such as those seen in the *Star Wars* films. All the elements of special effects (e.g., fire, air and water), in all their various forms (e.g., rain, mud, hurricanes, floods, fires) and their resulting damage (e.g., exploding buildings, mountain cave-ins, avalanches) are the responsibility of the special effects department. The first Academy Award® to be won in the newly created category of Special Effects (now called Visual Effects) was the 20th Century Fox film, *The Rains Came* (1939), set in India and starring Myrna Loy and Tyrone Power. Its footage of simulated monsoon floods, earthquakes, temples toppling, etc., successfully beat the other nominees, which included *The Wizard of Oz* and *Gone with the Wind.* Special effects are also called effects, movie (or big-screen/Hollywood effects/magic) or movie/Hollywood wizardry. Related terms: special blood effects, special eye effects, special makeup effects, special teeth effects; computer effects, optical effects, pyrotechnic effects, shock effects, visual effects; dust effect, fire effect, rain effect, smoke effect, snow effect, starfield effect; A-B foam, airbrush, animatronic, Audio-Animatronic, bluescreen process, camera trick, chroma key, cobweb spinner, drop box, explosion scene, fast motion, front projection, gag, gimbal stage, glass shot, greenscreen process, matte shot, model miniature, orangescreen process, paranormal phenomenon reenactment, picture-in-picture, puppet, rear-screen projection, registration shot, remote control, reverse motion, revolving stage, scrim, simulator ride, slow motion, suspension of disbelief, traveling matte, water tank, wire flying.

special eye effects Special effects with the eyes, such as contact lenses to change eye color or appearance. Eye color and appearance can also be changed using a frame-by-frame process using computer effects. Two sources for theatrical contact lenses are Studio Optix of New York City and VisionCare Associates of New York City and Sherman Oaks, California. Related terms: contact-lens special effects, sclera lenses, special blood effects, theatrical eyeglasses.

special guest star Type of guest-star credit for a television series, typically for a well-known performer. Related term: guest star.

special makeup effects Any makeup worn by a performer that radically changes his appearance, such as old-age makeup or monster makeup. Good examples are Robin Williams in *Mrs. Doubtfire* (1993) and Eddie Murphy in *The Nutty Professor* (1996). Special makeup effects also include eye, hair and teeth appliances and masks, costumes, dummies, puppets and body parts made of or covered with latex, urethane or silicone materials. An international source for special makeup effects and related supplies is Burman Industries, Inc., of Van Nuys, California, in the United States. Related terms: makeup, bladder-based makeup, proprietary makeup, alginate, Aqua Gel, bald cap, beard, cast, costume, dummy, facial lifts, foam latex, gross, latex, latex appliance, lifecast, monster part, mortician's wax, mustache, nose putty, puppet, special blood effects, special eye effects, special teeth effects, spirit gum, stubble, Super Goop, wig.

special portable camera Special handheld cameras mounted on body frames allowing fluid photography during motion; used for scenes that would be impossible to shoot with a standard camera on a tripod or dolly. Two brand names are Panaglide and Steadicam.

special teeth effects Unusual dental appliances, such as sharp fangs, broken or misshapen teeth, large or discolored gums, etc. Dental molds are made of the actor's upper and lower teeth using a material called alginate; from these, a special-effects makeup artist creates the desired appliance in a series of clay-sculpting and recasting steps. Teeth can also be discolored or blackened using a special brush-on liquid enamel. Related terms: alginate, flipper, tooth enamel.

special-ability extra Extra performer with a special skill or talent, such as horseback riding, sports playing, boat handling, skiing, ice-skating, roller-skating or a certain style of dancing.

special-effects artist Any individual involved in creating special effects (e.g., designing, drawing, sculpting, casting, building).

special-effects department That division of the production crew in charge of producing all the special effects on a production, from the elaborate (e.g., the *Star Wars* films) to the simple (e.g., a working sink). Also called a Special Effects Unit.

special-effects designer Individual specializing in planning the look, sound and action of special effects for film or stage productions; they are often highly complex or unusual effects.

special-effects shot Camera shot involving a special-effects process, method or device. Related term: visual-effects shot.

special-effects studio In-house workplace or commercial establishment that creates special effects. Related terms: digital-effects studio, visual-effects studio.

special-effects supervisor Individual responsible for overseeing a production's special effects; depending on the extent of duties, he may also be called a special-effects unit director. Related terms: CCI effects supervisor, visual-effects supervisor, pyrotechnic supervisor.

special-effects technician Member of the special-effects crew.

special-effects unit Another name for Special Effects Department; on some effects-heavy films, there may be several units within the Special Effects Department.

spectacle Major motion picture of epic proportions; it typically uses many wide scenic shots to create visually spectacular imagery.

Spectrasmoke Trade name for a special-effects smoke powder or solid that burns without flame. It is used in film productions as well as in theme parks and training simulations by fire and police departments and the military; it is also used to simulate fog. Available colors are white, gray, red, blue, green, yellow, yellow-green, violet, orange, pink and custom-blended colors. It is manufactured and sold by Tri-Ess Sciences, Inc., of Burbank, California. Related term: smoke effect.

speed 1. (n.) Rate that film travels through the camera, projector or printer, usually expressed in frames per second (fps) or in feet per minute. The normal speed for 35mm film is 24 fps (or 90 feet per minute). Related term: footage. 2. (adj.) Film's sensitivity to light as expressed in ASA, DIN or ISO numbers.

"Speed!" Cue from the soundman (production mixer) to the director, indicating the sound recorder is running at the proper speed for recording in sync with the picture.

spider Special metal device, used in slippery situations, to steady the camera on a tripod.

spider box Film industry term for a junction box, an electrical unit with outlets.

spill light Excessive and unwanted light falling on a subject or on a set.

spin 1. Creative, and sometimes fabricated, interpretation or explanation, e.g., "They put an interesting spin on the story." Related terms: spin doctor, spin team, damage control. 2. To interpret or explain creatively; to stretch the truth or weave a tale, e.g., to spin a yarn.

spin doctor Publicist whose actions are intended to correct or "heal" damage to a client's reputation or image caused by negative publicity.

spin team Group of professionals, such as publicists or attorneys, who work to correct negative publicity about a person, company or organization. Also called a spin crew or damage-control team. Related terms: spin, spin doctor.

spinning newspaper Early mechanical visual effect used onscreen to reveal the extent of interest or coverage of an important event by the news media. When the newspaper stops spinning, its headline can be read. The effect may include a succession of spinning newspapers and accompanying zoom-ins; newspapers and their headlines also can be shown using slow zoom-ins and moving close-ups. *Citizen Kane* (1941) used the spinning newspaper effect.

spin-off Television series featuring characters first introduced on another TV series. For example, *Buffy the*

Vampire Slayer (1997-) spawned *Angel* (1999-).

spirit gum Liquid adhesive used to attach makeup appliances, bald caps, wigs, beards, mustaches and sideburns. Other types of adhesives gentler to the skin are more widely used, such as a variety of surgical and prosthetic adhesives. All of these products use a separate liquid for thinning and removal. Related term: special makeup effects.

splice Two pieces of film joined together. The two types of splices are the hot or cement splice in which scraped ends of film are cemented together; and the dry or tape splice, in which the ends of film are joined together and taped without overlapping. Related terms: overlap splice, lap splice, butt splice, tape splice.

splicer Device used to join ends of film. There are three types of splicers: hot splicer, used for cement splices; hand splicer, a tape splicer operated by hand; machine splicer (aka Griswold), a hot splicer operated by the hands and feet.

split focus Technique for keeping two objects in focus, one in the background and one in the foreground, by focusing on a point in-between.

split reel Reel whose flanges screw together so that film on cores (rather than on reels) can be wound and rewound.

split screen Visual effect in which a movie or TV screen is divided into two, three, four, etc., sections to show separate images at the same time. For example, in *Pillow Talk* (1959), Rock Hudson and Doris Day talk to each other on the phone; he is on his phone on one side of the screen while she is on her phone on the other. Used more in the '60s and early '70s, this effect is achieved by masking one part of the frame and exposing the other, then reversing the process. Due to time and cost considerations, this is usually done optically.

sponsor 1. (n.) Individual, company or organization paying for all or part of the production, via advertising purchases or a grant. Also called a funding source or underwriter. Related terms: major sponsor, theater angel, commercial TV, promotional consideration. 2. Individual responsible for another or one who supports the other with money or efforts. Also called a backer, supporter, benefactor, angel or champion. 3. (v.) To provide funding or other services as a sponsor.

sponsor billboard Television still image advertising a sponsor's name or product/service, as during a commercial break or at the program's beginning or end. Related terms: billboard, TV still.

spoof Humorous parody. For example, *Airplane!* (1980) was a spoof of airplane disaster films.

spot 1. Broadcast of short duration. 2. Commercial or promo. Related terms: local spot, network spot, wild spot. 3. Short segment (information or entertainment) on a television or radio show. 4. Guest spot; cast spot. 5. Designated mark for a performer. 6. Any location, e.g., a nice spot for taking a photo. 7. To correct or improve a photographic image with a tiny spot of pigment or dye. Related term: retouch. 8. Short for spotlight.

spotlight 1. Type of directional light with a narrow, focused beam. Also called a spot lamp or spot. Related terms: ellipsoidal spot, junior spot, senior spot, limelight, lighting. 2. Circle of light produced by such a lamp. 3. To direct the beam of a spotlight. 4. Public attention or prominence. Related terms: in the spotlight, sharing the spotlight, thrust into the spotlight, limelight, center stage, public eye. 5. To call attention to.

spotting 1. Determining where music, sound effects or replacement dialogue is needed on a soundtrack. 2. Act or process of retouching a photograph using a finely tipped brush and pigment or dye to match the surrounding area.

spotting session Time during post-production when the director, composer, editor and music editor determine, or spot, where the music (score) for a film should be placed.

spousal/companion allowance Money provided to pay for the travel, lodging, and meal expenses of an actor's wife, husband, close friend, or relative while on location. Also called a spousal/travel-companion allowance or travel-companion allowance. Related terms: allowance, perk.

sprocket hole Rectangular hole with rounded corners on one or both edges of raw or developed photographic film. A sprocket is a wheel or cylinder with evenly spaced teeth that pushes film through a camera, projector or film processing machine. Related terms: perforations, pitch.

sprockets Small gears in the camera, projector or printer which advance the film. Related term: perforation.

spun Short for spun glass; it is used as a light diffuser. Because the glass can hurt hands or lungs, spun currently is made from synthetic material instead of from actual spun glass.

squeeze lens Another name for an anamorphic lens.

squib Small explosive charge detonated electrically by two attached wires connected to a remote switch and a direct-current power supply (battery); most often used to simulate a bullet hitting a target. A squib and its wires are always concealed from view when on a production set, as in a door or wall. If used on an actor, it is mounted on the underside of his shirt, on the front of a protective metal plate, and may be attached to a bag of fake blood that bursts when the squib is detonated. Because it is an explosive device, it requires a government-issued license to purchase, store and operate. Squibs are available in at least 24 different types, representing a variety of sizes, shapes, explosive strengths, flash, no flash, spark and no spark. Also called a squib hit or bullet hit (the latter can also refer to other related effects). Related term: gunfight scene.

squib vest Protective undergarment with attached metal plates, squibs and, possibly, blood bags.

squirrel cage 1. Electrical fan with a tubular slotted cylinder; it rotates to produce a current of air. Used in some special effects and stunt applications, e.g., to inflate and maintain pressure in an air bag. Also called a squirrel-cage fan or squirrel-cage blower. 2. Another name for a cylindrical revolving stage that allows a performer to appear to be walking or dancing on the walls and ceiling of a production set built inside it. Related term: revolving stage.

SR Abbreviation for stage right, as in a script.

SSDC Abbreviation for Society of Stage Directors and Choreographers.

ST On union forms, abbreviation for stunt performer.

stable Agency's clients, e.g., "The actor was added to the agency's stable of performers." Entertainment trade paper use. Related term: client list.

staccato 1. In speech, a manner of performing dialogue; uttering each word or syllable in an abrupt and distinct manner, as opposed to talking smoothly. A monotone staccato is one in which all words and syllables are spoken in a detached manner and in the same tone of voice. The voices of talking computers and robots in early science-fiction films and TV programs were often done this way. "Staccato," "monotone staccato" and "monotone" may appear in scripts as parenthetical directions. Related term: monotone. 2. In music, having each note separate and distinct.

stage 1. (n.) Indoor or outdoor area on which sets are constructed and filming takes place. 2. (n.) Structure, floor or area with a flat surface; it is used for performances, presentations, lectures or the like. Related terms: arena stage, elevator stage, floor-level stage, gimbal stage, portable stage, proscenium stage, puppet stage, revolving stage, thrust stage, "Exit, stage left," amphitheater, apron, backstage, curtain, curtain line, flat, fly loft, outdoor theater, proscenium, platform, runway, scene dock, theater-in-the-round, trap door, wing.

stage blood Fake blood; theatrical blood. Related term: special blood effects.

stage combat Theatrical fighting; make-believe fisticuffs, wrestling, martial arts, knife-fighting, swordplay or fencing. Also called theatrical combat. Related term: fight scene.

stage craft Effective production and/or performing techniques and devices.

stage credit Acknowledgment of having performed in or worked on a theatrical stage production. Also called a stage show credit, theater credit or play credit.

stage direction Instructions, orders or suggestions given by a stage director.

stage director Individual who directs stage productions (dramatic or comedic plays, musicals or other entertainment stage productions); individual whose creative medium is the stage, as opposed to film or video. Also called a theater director. Related term: play director.

stage door Doorway allowing entry to the backstage area of a theater. Also called a backstage door, backstage entrance, performers' entrance or actors' entrance. Related term: stage entrance.

stage electrician Individual responsible for setting up and maintaining the electrical elements of a stage production, including lighting. Related term: electrician.

stage entrance 1. Door outside a theater building that opens to the backstage area. Related term: stage door. 2. Entrance to the stage from either side (wing).

stage exit Departure point from the stage from either side (wing).

stage fright Sudden fear just before or during one's appearance in front of an audience or camera. Also called freezing or camera fright. Related terms: opening-night jitters, performance anxiety.

stage left (abbreviated as SL) Left side or section of a stage, from the point of view of a performer facing the audience. Stage left is different than house left or camera left. Related term: center line.

stage manager Individual responsible for supervising and monitoring the technical, design and performing activities of a stage production. The stage manager is in charge of scenery moves, prop changes, actor cues and directions to the actors from the director. A theater stage manager, besides the activities mentioned above, keeps track of the prompt-book, checks attendance and notifies performers of curtain and call times. A television stage manager also works closely with the director, who is in the control room, via a two-way radio communications link. An assistant stage manager may perform some of these duties, depending on the size of the production.

stage mother or father Mother of a child performer, a term often used in an unfavorable manner to refer to those mothers or fathers who pressure their children and make demands of and interfere unnecessarily with production personnel and processes. Also called a stage parent.

stage musical Comedy musical or musical play presented live on a stage, as opposed to a movie musical.

stage name Name a performer uses professionally to identify himself in the entertainment industry and public. It is not the individual's real full name; however, a stage name may retain part of the individual's real name. A stage name serves the same purpose a pseudonym, or pen name, does for an author. Also called a performing name. Related terms: acting name, professional name, name change.

stage no. Numerical digit assigned to a film or television sound stage building.

stage presence Individual's exhibited use of body movements, facial expressions and voice in presenting an onstage appearance and personality. Related term: presence.

stage production 1. Another name for a play. Also called a theater production or stage play. Related terms: stock production, 99-seat production, stage play. 2. Any show or entertainment presented on a stage. Also called a stage show. 3. Organization and presentation of such projects.

stage ready Ready for presentation on a stage; rehearsed.

stage right (abbreviated as SR) Right side or section of a stage, from the point of view of a performer facing the audience. Stage right is different than house right or camera right. Related term: center line.

stage version Representation or interpretation of a book, movie, TV program, song, news event, etc., on the stage. Related term: adaptation.

stage whisper Loud whisper, e.g., speaking in a whisper, but in a volume loud enough so the audience can hear what is said. A stage whisper can be used during a private conversation with another character or while making an aside comment to the audience.

staged reading Stage performance featuring a dramatic reading of a script's text by one or more actors, possibly with other performing elements included, such as music and dancing. Whatever lines are not memorized can be read from the script, making it an easier performance to produce. A staged reading can be presented in a variety of locations, from a regular indoor playhouse to a bookstore. Related term: reading.

stagehand Stage laborer; individual who moves stage props, scenery and the like. Related terms: backstage help, grip, roadie, scenery crew, set dresser.

stageworthy Having sufficient entertainment value or appropriateness for presentation on stage in front of an audience.

stair fall In stunt work, tumbling down a flight of steps by a stuntperson. Padding may be worn under the stuntperson's clothing, especially on the elbows, which are most susceptible to injury in this type of stunt.

stalkerazzi Nickname for picture-seeking media photographers who pursue celebrities in a harassing manner, e.g., by taunting them with insults, taking hidden-camera pictures of private moments or intentionally obstructing walkways. Related term: paparazzi.

"Stand by." Direction to prepare for or remain in readiness for an impending action, e.g., "Stand by . . . we're on the air in thirty seconds."

stand-alone theater Movie theater or playhouse not physically contained within another; it has its own entrance to the street or parking lot. For example, the Cinerama Dome Theater in Hollywood is a stand-alone theater; the AMC Theaters in the Century City shopping mall are not.

standard 1. Established principle, rule, guide or measure. 2. Song or instrumental composition that is familiar to a particular type of music; song or instrumental composition that is part of a repertoire, e.g., a jazz standard or Christmas standard. Also called a classic or favorite.

standard script format Preferred form in which screenplays are typed. If other formats are used, it can affect a production manager's estimates of how long it will take to shoot the screenplay.

standard stock Film stock most typically used, and therefore is known as the industry "standard," is 35mm.

standard-definition television Digital television system using less than 1,000 scanning lines to form pictures, as opposed to widescreen, high-definition television (HDTV). The exact number under 1,000 is determined by the system in use. Related term: SDTV.

stand-by Individual or object in a state of readiness. Also called a backup. Related terms: backup equipment, backup performer, on hold.

standee A large cardboard display of a movie's poster or star's likeness placed in certain high-traffic theatres.

stand-in Individual who substitutes for a star while the shot is set up and lit by the crew. Also called a stand-in extra. Related terms: double, second team.

stand-in doll Lifelike, life-size figure of a human baby used on a production as a stand-in for a real infant, as in a hospital delivery-room scene or a scene involving a physical stunt. Related terms: dummy, stunt dummy.

standing set 1. For film or television, a permanent outdoor or indoor set. For example, the back lot at 20th Century Fox Studios has a standing "New York" set. 2. For television, a production set (indoor or outdoor); that is permanently fixed in place for the run of the series. The structure and basic features of the set remain standing, as opposed to being disassembled (struck) and reassembled for the next episode. Typically, it is a key location, e.g., an office, living room or kitchen, that appears in every episode. Also called a permanent set.

stand-up 1. Performance consisting of a humorous monologue by a comedian in front of an audience. Related term: stand-up comedy. 2. News report by a television reporter standing in front of an active camera, e.g., "Several news stations had reporters doing live stand-ups at the snowed-in airport." 3. Free-standing, cardboard cut-out display, often of a celebrity; used to visually promote a product (e.g., in a grocery store) or a movie in a theater lobby. Related terms: life-size cut-out, store display.

Stanislavsky System Style of acting invented by Konstantin Stanislavsky (1863-1938). Also called the Stanislavsky Method. Related term: method acting.

star 1. (n.) Prominent, acclaimed, celebrated or distinguished performer. Often, a project will receive financing based solely on the star who accepts a role in it. Related terms: all-star cast, bankable star, Broadway star, CD-ROM star, movie star, superstar, celebrity. 2. Designation or title of a performer with a leading role in a production. Related terms: co-star, guest star, opening star, starring role, headliner, key cast member, lead. 3. (v.) To play a leading role or prominent part; to headline. 4. (n.) Anything prominent, acclaimed or special.

star commitment Oral or written agreement by a celebrity to be involved (under certain conditions) in a project.

star of stage and screen Famous actor who performs, or has performed, in both stage and screen productions.

star property Project suitable for a star's participation; strong script with a prominent starring role. Related term: property.

star quality Characteristic or attribute enabling a person to become a star. An individual may become a star due to talent, charisma, physical appearance, family relationship or a combination of these.

star system In early Hollywood, developing individual film performers as major celebrities, both on-screen and offscreen, as a means of promoting motion pictures to investors and the moviegoing public. Today, other talent, such as the director, writer, producer, etc., may instead be the major selling point of a film.

star treatment Special advantages, services, accommodations or protection provided to or traditionally associated with stars. Also called star fringe benefits, star frills, star perks, star needs. Related terms: superstar treatment, perk, red carpet, security.

star vehicle Entertainment project suitable for a top performer, for example, *Forrest Gump* (1994) was a star vehicle for Tom Hanks; in fact, his performance won him an Academy Award® or Best Actor.

Star Waggons A dressing room and production trailer rental company started by Lyle Waggoner. The trailers and dressing rooms are used widely on all sorts of productions in Hollywood.

starfield 1. Visual-effects shot in which a moving or stationary field of stars (represented as solid or twinkling points of light) are displayed on-screen. An approaching or receding starfield can be created electronically using a computer or by filming (via a computer-guided camera-tracking system) large glass sheets with stars painted on them. The term "starfield" may appear in scripts, especially those for science-fiction films set in space. 2. On a production set or theater stage, a painted nighttime sky or outer-space backdrop depicting a stationary field of stars; the stars may be painted or they may be tiny lights or lights projected from a light source. Related term: gobo.

starrer Motion picture having one or more prominent leading roles. Entertainment trade paper use.

starring credit Production credit designated for a leading actor in a film, TV program, video, play, or the like.

starring role Lead role or one of the lead roles, as opposed to a nonstarring or supporting role. A title role is a starring role. Related term: lead.

stars turned out Stars came to; stars showed up; e.g., "The stars turned out to celebrate one of their own" or "The stars turned out to greet the Queen." Entertainment media use.

start date Month and day a production is set to begin.

start mark Cue mark on the film leader and its sound track indicating the synchronization point; also used on composite prints to assist the projectionist in readying the film for projection. Related term: change-overs.

started Usually refers to an actor's first day of work. As there are many rules governing an actor once he begins work, the proper start date is very important. Related: drop and pick up, run of show.

starting fee Lowest hiring rate (on a graduated schedule of rates) for a particular type of work. Related terms: minimum fee, scale.

static marks Dark streaks on film due to friction in the camera or improper handling; they often occur in cold weather.

station 1. Radio or television transmitting and receiving facility or business. Related terms: radio station, TV station, call letters. 2. Place; office or base of operations.

station break Pause during a radio or television show during which a station identifies itself verbally or visually. Commercials or promos typically run before or after a station break. Related terms: commercial break, act break, station identification.

station identification Notification to listeners or viewers of a radio or TV station's identity. In the United States, stations are required by law to identify themselves at regular intervals. Related terms: station break, call letters.

Station 12 1. (n.) Office of the Screen Actors Guild in the United States used by casting directors and producers to inquire if an actor under consideration is a member in good standing of the union (dues paid, etc.). 2. (v.) To "Station 12" an actor or other type of SAG-jurisdiction performer, e.g., "The producer wants me to Station 12 this list of three actors who are up for the part."

statistics Numerical facts, such as sizes, amounts or measurements. Also called stats. Related terms: personal statistics, vital statistics.

Steadicam Trade name for an Oscar®- and Emmy-winning, motion-stabilizing camera mount that attaches to its user by means of an upper-body vestlike brace. The counterbalanced arm projecting from the front allows free and steady movement of the camera by the operator as he moves on an uneven surface. A small video monitor attached to the rig checks and maintains the framing of the shot. A Steadicam shot features stabilized moving camera images (no shaking, jerking or bumping). The film camera Steadicam was invented by (then) Philadelphia-based cinematographer Garrett Brown, who, along with Cinema Products Corporation of Los Angeles (the manufacturer), and under the supervision of John Jurgens, received a 1977 Scientific and Technical Oscar® from the Academy of Motion Picture Arts and Sciences. It was first used in the multiple Oscar®-winning film *Rocky* (1976) and gained even more fame as a spectacular cinematic technique in the theatrical film *The Shining* (1980). Various Steadicam designs are also available for professional and consumer video cameras. The hand-held Steadicam Jr., for consumer camcorders, was introduced in 1989.

steam chips Elemental calcium metal chips which produce a small quantity of simulated boiling and steam action when placed in water, soup, coffee or other water-based liquid; they leave a sludge residue. Also called calcium chips. Two sources for steam chips are Tri-Ess Sciences, Inc., of Burbank, California, and Zeller International, Ltd., of Downsville, New York.

Steenbeck Trade name for a product line of flatbed editing machines available in 16mm and 35mm film sizes. Related terms: editing, editing bench, Kem, Moviola.

step 1. (v.) To intrude or overlap, as to step on another actor's lines. 2. (n.) Point or level in a progression, e.g., the first step in becoming an actor. Related term: stepping stone.

step deal 1. Type of screenwriting contract in which the writer receives a payment for each step of the writing process, e.g., synopsis, treatment, first draft, polish, final screenplay. Con-

tinuation of the contract depends on fulfillment of each step of the contract's terms. 2. Any similar deal involving the director, producer or studio/distributor.

step outline See synopsis.

step printing Optical printing process in which the film is held with registration pins and is printed, frame by frame, to insure maximum steadiness. This process is used for projected backgrounds, traveling mattes, etc., when steadiness is a critical factor.

stepping into a role Assuming a part previously held by another actor. For example, Meryl Streep stepped into the lead role of *Music of the Heart* (1999) after Madonna left the picture. Related term: taking over a role.

stereo 1. Short for stereoscopic: of or related to seeing objects in three dimensions (height, width and depth), e.g., stereoscopic photography or a stereoscopic viewer. Related terms: 3D model, 3D CCI, 3D movie, 3D package, 3D scanner. 2. Short for stereophonic: of or related to sound that is recorded, received or transmitted on more than one track or channel using two or more microphones or speakers so a sense of depth is experienced by the listener.

stereo simulcast Radio-television simulcast featuring stereophonic sound.

stereophonic sound Method of audio reproduction; it adds fullness and realism to the sound and gives it a feeling of movement because the sound is recorded onto separate tracks through separate microphones. The tracks are then played back through separate speakers, corresponding to the placement of the microphones. Stereophonic sound quality is especially important for music and sound effects. It has been in use since the 1950s in most widescreen productions; currently, many standard format films are released in stereo.

stereoscopic cinema (aka 3-D) Technique of projecting film in such a way (and with the use of special 3-D viewing glasses) that an illusion of three-dimensional vision is achieved. Several different patented processes are used today.

stet Proofreader's mark meaning "Let it stand." For example, it may appear handwritten on a script page beside material that had been crossed out, indicating the crossed-out material should be reinstated when the script is reprinted as another draft.

sticks 1. Another name for clapsticks. 2. Another name for drumsticks. 3. Another name for a tripod.

Sticks Nix Hick Pix Famous headline that appeared in large block letters on the front cover of *Variety* (July 17, 1935), the New York City-based, entertainment-industry weekly trade newspaper. The eye-catching headline tongue-twister ran above an article describing how moviegoers in the midwestern United States (the Nebraska-Iowa-Illinois exhibition market area) were less interested in stories about rural and suburban life and instead wanted films with foreign and period society settings, as evidenced by the current top-grossing films for that area: *The Barretts of Wimpole Street* (1934), *House of Rothschild* (1934) and *The Scarlet Pimpernel* (1935). The subheadline for the article read: "Not Interested In Farm Drama." Almost 12 years later, the reverse situation existed, when on June 18, 1947, the front-page headline read: "Stix Still

Nix British Pix." Sixty years later, another similar headline appeared on the front cover of the July 24, 1995 issue: "Sticks Can't Nix Naughty Pix." In that instance, the headline referred to the increasing acceptance by some of the major U.S. studio-distributors and theater owners to release and exhibit prominent, sexually-themed "NC-17" rated films (e.g., *Showgirls* [1995] was mentioned).

still 1. Photograph shot with a still camera. 2. Glossy, 8" x 10" black-and-white or color photograph of an actor or scene from a film; typically, used for publicity purposes. Related term: headshot.

still frame Another name for a freeze frame from a film or video.

still photo Single photograph of an image. Related terms: production still, publicity still, action photo.

still photographer Individual responsible for taking still photographs on a movie set; such photos typically are used for matching and continuity purposes (e.g. hair, costumes, make-up, set decoration) or, they are used later, to for publicity purposes.

still video Television or computer onscreen image with no motion. Related term: video still.

still video camera Another name for a digital still camera. Also called a video still camera.

stock 1. Raw photographic film; unexposed negative film. Related term: film stock. 2. Commonly used, standard. Related term: stock footage.

stock character Type of character seen in many films of the same genre, e.g., a security guard in a spy thriller, bartender in a Western, or wife of a police officer in a crime drama. Also called a standard character or off-the-shelf character.

stock company Group of performers at one theater who perform a repertoire of plays. Also called a stock acting company. Related term: stock production.

stock footage Film footage of different eras, locations or things; it is duplicated and incorporated into a new production. Stock footage is used when certain shots would be too costly, difficult or impossible to recreate, for example, it can be of ships sinking, cars on highways in a certain city, aerial views, Times Square in 1945, etc. Stock footage is usually identifiable due to the difference in old and new film stock, and to the fact that the stock footage (which has been duped, then inserted into the film) has an extra generation and is therefore grainier. Related terms: library shot, newsreel footage.

stock photodisc Optical disc, as a CD-ROM, containing digitized photos that can be licensed for use by others. Also spelled stock-photo disc. Related term: Photo CD.

stock photograph Print or digitized photograph or slide transparency from an in-house library of stock shots or a stock-photo agency.

stock shot 1. Standard scenic, wildlife, historical, etc., shot taken from a library of such shots and used in a film or other work as a way to lessen production costs or to show historical accuracy, e.g., a stock shot of the pyramids in Egypt or of World War II military action. Related terms: establishing stock shot, stock footage, stock photograph. 2. Shot appearing in a TV series that is stored for use in future episodes, e.g., an establishing stock shot of the exterior of a char-acter's home that appears in every episode.

stop See aperture, f-stop, t-number.

stop down To reduce the size of the lens aperture so as to reduce the amount of light and increase the depth of field (by adjusting the diaphragm). Related term: astigmatism.

stop frame See freeze frame, hold frame.

stop motion Technique used in animation; in stop motion, the object to be animated is moved after the exposure of each frame or two. This process is widely used in television commercials, in which inanimate objects appear to move.

"Stop tape." Instruction to halt the recording or playback of audio or video tape. The opposite is "Roll tape."

stop-motion animation Process of creating movement in drawings, wire or mechanically jointed figures or other objects by filming the subject one or more frames at a time, making a small change in the subject's position, then recording another one or more frames and so on. This procedure is slowly and carefully repeated until the desired motion effect is achieved when the film is played back at normal speed. Also called stop-action animation. *The Nightmare Before Christmas* (1993) is an excellent example of stop-motion animation. Related terms: animation, animatics, foam latex, Go-Motion, movable miniature, puppet, time-lapse photography.

stopping point 1. Fixed or designated place where a moving camera stops. 2. Any location where an activity is supposed to stop.

story 1. Another name for an outline or treatment. 2. Any fiction or non-fiction tale with a beginning, middle and end. Related terms: back story, love story, moral of the story, story-line, adaptation, cliffhanger, climax, concept, conflict, discovery, dramatic irony, dramatic license, dramatic pause, ending, exposition, ironic moment, main plot, outline, plot, poetic justice, subplot, synopsis, treatment, trilogy. 3. News story.

story analyst Individual employed by a studio or production company to read and prepare reports on scripts, novels and the like. The coverage is given to a story editor for his decision as to whether or not the material should be considered by the exec-utive(s). Also called a reader. Related term: coverage.

story arc Specific storyline in a continuing TV series; it has a begin-ning and end and is played out over a number of episodes. Related term: arc.

story by Credit designated for the one or more individuals who provided the story upon which a script is based. If it is a union production, the Writers Guild governs what constitutes a "story" and who is eligible to receive the credit. Related term: written by.

story conference Meeting between the writer(s), story editor(s), producer(s) and director (or combination there-of) to discuss the development of a story or script and any revisions necessary.

storyboard 1. Series of drawings or photographs showing the progression of shots in a film sequence; typically, used to delineate an expensive action sequence but also could be used for an entire film. Director Alfred Hitchcock was famous for using complete storyboards, showing each shot in detail; in fact, he would not begin production without a complete storyboard. Used extensively in the production of commercials, story-boards are created by the advertising agency for sponsor approval, then are distributed to production companies for bids.

storyline What the story is about. Another name for the plot.

straight copy 1. Wording that is straightforward and to the point, e.g., straight news copy. 2. Script lines spoken plainly, without the use of voice characterization or other acting skills. Also known as straight-faced copy.

straight cut Sudden editing transition from one shot (or frame) to another. No dissolves, wipes or other optical or electronic effects are used. (The overwhelming majority of editing transitions made in films and TV programs are straight cuts.)

straight makeup Makeup application producing a beautifying enhance-ment or improvement to one's natural features. The opposite is character or old-age makeup.

straight man Partner to a comic who acts as the rational contrast to the comic's funny behavior; both are comedians. Male or female usage. For example, Bud Abbott was straight man to Lou Costello, and George Burns was straight man to Gracie Allen. The fully comic half of the team is also called a comic sidekick. Related terms: comic foil, sidekick.

straight time Standard working hours. Another name for a regular scale payment, as opposed to overtime or double time.

streamer Editing mark indicating to the optical house, re-recording mixer and foley artist where fades, dissolves effects, titles and other post-production effects are to be inserted.

Street of Dreams Nickname for Broadway in New York City. Variation: Avenue of Dreams.

street performer Individual who performs on the streets of a large city, usually for tips. Also called a street entertainer, sidewalk performer or sidewalk entertainer. Related term: street theater.

street shot Photograph or camera shot featuring a city, town or village street.

street theater Entertainment performed on a city street, including a plaza or park walkway. Such entertainment includes instrumental music, juggling, magic, etc. The performances are free, but onlookers may make a donation to the performer. Also called street entertainment, sidewalk theater or sidewalk entertainment. Related term: street performer.

stress marks Streaks occurring on a film print due to pressure or friction on the negative. Related terms: abrasions, scratches.

stretch 1. To lengthen; to make longer. As a direction to an oncamera or onstage performer, it means to slow down the pace or continue talking because there is time before the beginning of the commercial break or end of the program; typically, it is given in the form of a visual signal by pretending to stretch something (e.g., an imaginary piece of chewing gum) with the fingers and thumbs of both hands. Related terms: filler, padding. 2. To extend beyond one's usual or expected limit as a performer, e.g., to stretch into comedy acting after

having done only serious dramatic roles.

strike 1. To tear down a set after shooting has been completed; it is advisable not to strike any set until after the dailes have been approved. 2. To create a print from a negative (e.g., to strike a print). 3. To refuse to work due to a labor grievance.

strip Daily television series, especially one airing Monday through Friday. Typically, strip shows are syndicated and several episodes are recorded on the same day. Entertainment trade paper use.

stripe Band of magnetic coating applied to film. When making a magnetic composite print, the final sound track is transferred onto these magnetic stripes.

strobe Rapidly flashing light causing the subject in the film to appear to move in a jerky, disjointed manner. This effect is usually caused by an uneven relationship between the speed of the object being filmed and the intervals between exposures. Related terms: strobe lamp, stroboscopic lamp, stroboscope.

student film Fictional or documentary film, usually of short length, written, produced and directed by one or more students at a school. For example, George Lucas' student film, called *THX 1138*, was made while he attended the University of Southern California's School of Cinema/Television; an expanded version of it was released in 1971.

studio Room, hall, building or complex used for creative, instructional, manufacturing or transmission purposes. Also called a production facility. Examples of studio types include: acting, dance, film, foley, loft, photography, rehearsal, sound-effects, special-effects, TV, video and visual-effects. Related term: controlled studio conditions.

studio commissary Eating establishment located in, operated by and for employees of a film and/or television studio.

studio executive Policy-making or supervisory employee of a film and/or television studio. Related terms: development executive, executive in charge of production, production executive, network programmer.

studio floor manager Another name for a television stage manager.

studio guide Individual who guides visitors around a film and/or television studio. Also called a studio tour guide. Related terms: page, usher.

studio lighting Lighting equipment used in a production studio; some of it may be portable or adaptable for use on location. Related term: lighting.

studio (lot) Physical location and facilities (including offices, sound stages, etc.) used by in-house or independent production companies for development, production and post-production of motion pictures and television shows. A movie shot on a lot contains scenes filmed in specially built sets on sound stages or backlots, as opposed to scenes taking place on an actual location. For example, Martin Scorsese's film *New York, New York* [1977] was shot primarily on sound stages and backlots in Los Angeles while his film *Mean Streets* [1973] was principally shot on locations in New York.

studio (major) Organization that develops, produces and distributes motion pictures and television shows. In the old days of Hollywood, the studios were more powerful and self-sufficient than their modern-day counterparts: each kept under contract its own stable of producers, directors, actors and writers, as well as maintaining art, costume, makeup, publicity departments, etc. The studios had everything necessary for every phase of making movies, from concept to completion, including distribution, exploitation and exhibition. Today, studios hire personnel as needed and do not keep large numbers of employees on staff full-time. Some departments are maintained on an ongoing basis, e.g., legal, story, advertising, distribution.

studio producer 1. Producer who is a direct employee of a film or television studio. 2. Producer who chiefly works out of an office, as opposed to a field producer.

studio set Film or television production set located on a studio sound stage or on a studio back lot.

studio shot Photograph or camera shot taken at a studio, as opposed to one taken on location.

studio store Souvenir shop or studio-owned or -franchised retail store selling merchandise related to the studio or its entertainment productions. Related terms: movie memorabilia, movie merchandise.

studio system Operational structure of the Hollywood movie industry in which theatrical films were made on a highly efficient, mass-production basis and actors and directors were obligated to exclusive multi-picture or multi-year contracts and thus could not work on independent films; the system existed until the mid-'50s. The major studio not only was producer and distributor, but also acted as exhibitor, through ownership of national movie chains. In 1948, a decision by the United States Supreme

Court forced the studios to divest themselves of their movie theaters; this decision, along with the advent of television and actors demanding nonexclusive contracts, signaled the end of the studio system.

studio tank Large water tank at a film and/or TV studio complex used for various types of full-scale and small-scale water scenes involving actors or scale models of watercraft or marine life. Often, a wave machine will be used. For example, part of the mini-series *The Winds of War* (1983) was shot on the studio tank located at Paramount Studios in Hollywood. Related term: water tank.

studio teacher Instructor or tutor employed by a production company (studio-based, motion picture or television) to provide substitute elementary or secondary schooling on a temporary basis to one or more minor-aged performers working on a production; the studio teacher must teach for a certain number of hours per day (dictated by state law). Related terms: welfare worker, classroom trailer, schooling on a production.

studio tour Guided trip through the facilities at a film and/or TV studio or studio theme park, e.g., a studio tram tour or a studio walking tour. Related terms: production set tour, studio guide.

studio zone The radius around a studio considered to be a "local location." Any area outside of the studio zone (typically, a radius of 30 miles) is considered a "distant location" and the production is obligated to pay for the cast and crew to spend the night. If filming is at a local location, the cast and crew are compensated for mileage. In Los Angeles, the 30-mile radius is charted

from the old AMPTP headquarters at La Cienega and Beverly.

stunt Dangerous, or potentially dangerous, act or action performed by an actor or a specially trained stunt person. Related terms: gag, business.

stunt actor Another name for a stuntperson who performs a stunts in a film or television production.

stunt bag Bag holding equipment used by a stuntperson, e.g., a variety of safety padding attachments. Also called a war bag.

stunt coordinator Member of the crew responsible for the organization, implementation and safety of all stunts on a production.

stunt director Another name for a stunt coordinator. Related terms: fight director, second unit director.

stunt double Stuntperson who physically resembles or is made to physically resemble (with makeup, wig, clothing, etc.) an actor in a scene requiring a dangerous activity, e.g., jump through a window, fall off a building. Related terms: double, cyber-double, stuntperson, stunt photo double.

stunt driver Individual who is a specialist in performing stunts involving motorized, nonmotorized or horse-drawn (carriages, stagecoaches, etc.) vehicles. Examples of motorized vehicle stunts: crashing, high-speed driving, jumping, ramming a blockade, ramming the back of another vehicle (or being rammed), rolling over, skidding, sliding, spinning, taking evasive action and turning around. Related terms: bail out, car roll, car roll cannon, drag rig, hood ride, hood roll, pipe ramp, roof ride, stunt rider.

stunt dummy Representation of a person or animal substituting for a living person or animal during a stunt. Related terms: dummy, character mannequin, stand-in doll, puppet.

stunt gel Thick, nonburning liquid applied to a stuntperson' s skin and clothing prior to fire stunt scenes; it is also used to soak fire rescue blankets and towels. Some brand names are Zel-Jel, Hydrogel, and Water-Jel. Also called fireproof gel. Related terms: fire effect, Zel-Jel.

stunt horse Horse trained to perform stunts or to be in the vicinity of performed stunts, crowds, gunshots or pyrotechnic special effects. Related terms: trick horse, trick rider, stunt rider.

stunt mask In a fire stunt scene, a form-fitting covering for the face providing protection to the stuntperson from effects of heat and flames. A special two-part rubber used to create a stunt mask from a mold of the stuntperson's face is available from Zeller International, Ltd., of Downsville, New York. It was developed for the film *Scanners* (1981) by effects experts Gary Zeller and Dick Smith.

stunt padding Shock-absorbing body attachments worn by a stuntperson to protect against or to lessen physical injury. Stunt pads, e.g., for the knees, elbows, shoulders, back, hips, buttocks, shins (shin guards), hands and head (helmet) are identical to or adapted from safety padding used in professional sports and gymnastics. Elastic bandages are also used and may be incorporated into padding attachments. Related terms: padding, stunt bag.

stunt pilot Individual trained and licensed to operate an airplane or helicopter during an aerial stunt sequence. Related terms: pilot, aerial coordinator, bail out, hidden parachute.

stunt rider Stuntperson who performs stunts while riding a horse or motorcycle. Related terms: bulldog, drag rig, jerk harness, Pony Express mount, rodeo event, stunt horse, trick horse, trick rider.

stunt shot Photograph or camera shot in which a stunt occurs.

stunt unit Production unit responsible for the staging and filming of stunts.

stunt work Any activity involving one or more stunts. Related terms: explosion scene, fall, fight scene, fire effect, hazard pay, stuntperson.

Stuntmen's Association of Motion Pictures In the United States, an organization of male stunt performers and coordinators. It was founded in 1961 and is based in North Hollywood, California. Also called the Stuntmen's Association. Internet address: http://www.stuntmen.com.

stuntperson Individual trained to perform stunts in film or television productions, commercials, stage plays and various types of outdoor shows. A stunt double may be hired to take the place of an actor whose character is required to do a bit of dangerous action. Depending on the camera angle(s), shot distance, lighting and type of stunt, the stunt double may be required to resemble the actor to great degree. Stunt performers, male and female, undergo an extensive professional training course to learn their craft. Also called a stuntman or stuntwoman. Related terms: ND stunt performer, spotter, ST, stunt actor, stunt double, stunt driver, stunt pilot, stunt rider, utility stunt performer.

Stuntwomen's Association of Motion Pictures Organization in the United States, comprised of female stunt performers and coordinators. It was founded in 1967 and is based in Sherman Oaks, California. Internet address: http://www.stuntwomen.com.

stylist 1. Individual who is responsible for securing, placing, arranging, caring for and returning clothes, accessories and props used on a TV commercial or still-photo shoot. A stylist also makes sure that the set, actor(s), clothing or other items (such as client products and boxes or packages in which they are sold) look right for photographing or filming; he also makes adjustments as the session develops. Examples of stylists include clothing stylist and food stylist. 2. Any other type of styling artist, designer or consultant, such as a beauty or hair stylist.

subjective camera angle Camera angle from the point of view of a character in a story. Albert Brooks uses the subjective camera in comedic fashion in his film *Real Life* (1979), as he features cameramen wearing robotic-like camera-helmets to capture the typical American family and we see the results of their work. The opposite is an objective camera angle. Related term: point-of-view shot.

submerged printing See liquid gate.

subplot Second, third, etc., plot in a story, as opposed to the main plot. Also called a side story.

substitute performer Another name for an understudy or backup performer.

subtitle Word, phrase or sentence appearing as a caption at the bottom of the screen. A dialogue subtitle is one that translates a line of foreign dialogue into a recognizable language for the audience. Related terms: caption, intertitle, supertitle.

subtractive process Method used to achieve color in color photography by filtering out other colors from white light. Related terms: primary colors, additive process.

sudser Nickname for a television soap opera. Entertainment trade paper use.

sugar glass Brittle material (clear or colored) resembling glass; it is safer than real glass when used as a prop in a scene. Sugar glass is made from a precisely boiled (then cooled) sugar syrup consisting of white sugar, light corn syrup and water. (The recipe for sugar glass is similar to that for lollipops except that no flavoring is added). Although sugar glass is safer to use, it is hard to make clear with a minimum amount of bubbles, it becomes sticky when exposed to high humidity or heat and it can be unpleasant to sweep from the floor (which must be done because the pieces stick to the bottoms of shoes). Sugar glass was used mostly in the early decades of moviemaking; since then, brittle plastic resins were developed that do not have the problems of water-soluble sugar glass. These resins are now used by modernly-equipped, special-effects studios to make breakaway glass props and windows. Sugar glass, however, will always remain an alternative because of its easily obtainable, biodegradable ingredients. Related terms: breakaway glass, candy glass.

summer series 1. Limited-run television series shown during the summer months when regular series are on hiatus and in reruns. Related term: limited-run series. 2. Any organized schedule of events taking place during the summer months, e.g., a summer concert series.

summer stock Stock theater productions presented during the summer months. Related term: summer theater.

summer theater 1. Playhouse in operation only during the summer months, for example, a theater located in a vacation community with a large tourist population. "Summer theater" also includes productions presented on outdoor stages. Also called a summer stock theater. 2. World, field or profession of working in summer theater. Also called summer stock.

Sundance Film Festival Annual film festival held in Park City, Utah, in the United States; it showcases and bestows awards upon new, independent filmmakers in the categories of feature film, documentary, short film, American film and foreign film. The festival is sponsored by the Sundance Institute of Salt Lake City, Utah and Santa Monica, California. The Institute was founded in 1981, by actor-director Robert Redford. Internet address: http://www.sundancefilm.com/

sungun Portable, battery-powered, high-intensity light; used mostly for news or documentary work.

sunlight Light directly from the sun, as opposed to daylight (which includes skylight and reflected sunlight).

Sunset Boulevard (Los Angeles) Famous street in Los Angeles, California; it originates in the downtown area and travels west to the Pacific Ocean, where it intersects with the scenic Pacific Coast Highway. Sunset Boulevard traverses Hollywood, Beverly Hills, Bel Air, Brentwood and Pacific Palisades. The University of California at Los Angeles (UCLA) and many talent agencies are located along Sunset Boulevard. The "Sunset Strip" is an unincorporated section of the boulevard running through West Hollywood.

sunshade See matte box.

Super Goop Nontoxic gel; it is semi-transparent and used in special makeup effects to create a variety of gooey, slimy or oozing appearances, such as a chemical or oil spill, lava, alien body fluid or paranormal residue. Seen in such films as *Ghostbusters* (1984), *Poltergeist* (1982) and *Nightmare on Elm Street* (1984). It is available in different viscosities and can be colored to order. Manufactured and sold by Tri-Ess Sciences, Inc., of Burbank, California. Related term: Aqua Gel.

superimpose (abbreviated as super or SUPER:) To photgraph or print one or more images, one over the other, so they can all be seen at once. This effect can be achieved in the camera through multiple exposures of the same piece of film or by optically printing several images onto one piece of film.

supertitles In theater, such as in opera, narration and dialogue or lyric translations projected in large letters onto a wall over the stage; supertitles appear simultaneously with the performance. Some theaters may be equipped with small electronic screens on the backs of audience seats, on which translations appear in lighted letters.

supervising producer Television producer responsible for overseeing various production activities. The specifics of a supervising producer's job differ, according to the types of programs they produce and the number of producer-level positions within the company. Related terms: senior producer, producer.

supporting actor or actress Actor whose part in a production is secondary to the lead.

supporting cast Group of performers having supporting roles in a production.

supporting player Another name for a supporting actor.

supporting role Performing role secondary in nature to the lead. It is significant enough to be a prominent award category of the Academy Awards®, Emmy Awards, BAFTA Awards and many others. Also called a supporting character role or supporting part.

surrealistic Of or like a style of art or literature in which imagery of the human dream state or imagination is expressed in pictures or words. Examples of surrealistic images are those painted by artist Salvador Dali (warped, bent or melting images on barren landscapes) and settings in the fantasy film *What Dreams May Come* (1998), using dramatic landscapes painted by an artist who commits suicide in the film. Related terms: day/night, fantasy movie.

suspension of disbelief Temporary cessation or postponement of the audience's disbelief; putting aside real-life nature or logic for the sake of experiencing it as fictional entertainment, e.g., a movie about a talking pig and his talking barnyard animal friends requires a suspension of disbelief by the audience in order to enjoy the film as entertainment. Suspension of disbelief is an important factor in movies featuring many visual effects, such as science fiction, fantasy, horror and spy thriller films. The term was coined by English poet-essayist-critic Samuel Coleridge (1772-1834) in his book *Biographia Literaria*, published in 1817.

swashbuckler Dashing, flamboyant rogue. In older Hollywood films, a swashbuckler might have been portrayed by an actor such as Errol Flynn or John Barrymore; more recently, Harrison Ford portrayed a swashbuckler in the *Star Wars* and *Indiana Jones* trilogies. The swashbuckler film is an action/adventure film loaded with good humor and fun; there is always a dashing hero who saves a beautiful maiden in distress.

Sweeney gun Special-effects rifle using compressed air or nitrogen gas to shoot plastic or steel balls. It has fully automatic capability to simulate a machine gun. Related terms: blood hit, dust hit, glass hit, spark hit.

sweep To win many awards or award nominations.

sweeps period Another name for a ratings period.

sweeten 1. Adding musical sounds, audience sounds (applause, laughter, etc.), vocal sounds or sound effects to a soundtrack to improve its quality or effectiveness. 2. To increase or make more attractive, e.g., to sweeten the terms of a deal.

swing gang Individuals working under the set decorator and lead man; they dress and strike the set and, as such, they are the first to arrive at and the last to leave from the set or location.

swish pan Rapid movement of the camera, from right to left (or vice versa), causing a blurred image; it is mainly used for dramatic effect. Related terms: whip pan, zip pan.

sword-fight scene Scene in which characters engage in a battle of swordplay. The actors portraying the characters are trained in sword-fighting and the actual scene is choreographed and rehearsed carefully. A variety of fake (aluminum, wood, plastic, rubber, etc.) or real (blunt-tipped, sharp-tipped or retractible) blades may be used. To simulate a sword being thrust into and through a character, a visually effective and relatively safe illusion is used: at the climax of a swordfight, the victorious actor pushes his sword into the space between the arm and side of the losing actor, creating the illusion of the weapon penetrating the body. The effect is further enhanced by the losing character "acting" over the severe injury, either as the sword is pulled out or left in place. Fake blood may also be used in such a scene, usually in a reaction shot after a makeup artist has the chance to apply it to the character's costume or skin. Related terms: fight scene, knife, retractable.

sync See synchronization.

sync mark See start mark.

sync pulse 60-cycle pulse used to keep sound and picture in sync.

synchronization When the picture and sound coincide properly. Any other situation is considered out of sync.

synchronizer Editing device with interlocking sprocket wheels that allowing the editor to keep the sound and picture in sync.

synchronous sound 1. Sound in a motion picture that directly corresponds to the image, e.g., screeching brakes heard when we see a foot slamming down on the car's brake pedal. (In asynchronous sound, we might see the face of a woman looking on in horror as she hears the sound of the car's screeching brakes.)

2. Sound recorded in syncronization with the film.

syndicated 1. To describe TV shows and movies, being sold to individual television stations for broadcast in their geographical areas (markets). A TV series must have an acceptable number of episodes for a successful syndication deal to be achieved. 2. To describe articles, columns and comic strips, being sold through a syndicate to newspapers for simultaneous publication.

syndicated programming buyer TV station or cable network executive responsible for purchasing first-run and off-network syndicated television shows and movies from independent producers, independent distributors and network/studio syndication distribution divisions. A syndicated buyer attends a syndicated program convention to meet sellers and to decide whether available television series, movies and specials should be purchased for telecast during the coming year. Also called a syndicated program buyer or syndication buyer. Related terms: NATPE, NAB.

syndication Act of syndicating; state of being syndicated. Related terms: first-run syndication, off-network syndication, rerun syndication, evergreen, 16mm.

syndicator Production or distribution company or corporate division syndicating its series, movies or specials to television station and cable network buyers around the country and world. Related terms: syndicated programming buyer, television distributor.

syndie Short for syndication or syndicator. Entertainment trade paper use.

synopsis Brief summary or description of a project's plot. Its length may be anywhere from two sentences to many pages in length. A one-sentence description is called a log line; a longer report (including a log line, synopsis and critique of the work) is called "coverage" and concludes with the story analyst's opinion to "pass," "consider" or "recommend."

tabloid 1. Newspaper or magazine presenting a mix of sensational news, celebrity gossip, unusual human-interest stories, celebrity photos, health and diet tips, beauty and fashion tips, statistics and the like. Also called a gossip rag, scandal sheet. Collectively called the tabloid press. 2. Of, like or pertaining to a tabloid. 3. Any newspaper with pages that are about half the size of a standard full-size newspaper. Also called a tabloid-size newspaper.

tabloid journalism Sensationalized news gathering, reporting and content, for example, intrusive photos of celebrities or investigative reports and gossip on celebrities' private lives. Related term: news media.

tabloid TV Television news and informational programs featuring sensational news stories, similar to those found in tabloid papers. Related term: trash TV.

tachometer Device on a motion picture camera showing the speed at which it is running. It is read by the assistant cameraman to ensure the camera is running at the correct speed.

Taft-Hartley Act In the United States, another name for the Labor Management Relations Act of 1947, which states that a nonunion worker can be hired for a union job (e.g., a nonunion actor for a role in a movie) if the employer (producer) can justify in a waiver application to the union that no union member is equally qualified to perform the job ("She's going to have to be Taft-Hartley'ed if we want to hire her for the role."). Once employed under the Taft-Hartley waiver, the worker has 30 days to join the union; once a member of the union, he or she will be able to continue working with or seeking employment from union signatory companies as long as he or she remains a member in good standing, e.g., pays dues on time and follows union regulations. Related term: union member.

Taft-Hartley form In the U.S., a union form used for processing U.S. citizens and foreigners who are not union members and who have been offered employment with a U.S. producer. Besides the required information, a résumé and photo of the individual must be attached.

tag 1. Final or concluding part, as of a TV episode, play or speech. Also called a tag ending. Related term: epilogue. 2. Brief visual or voiceover location or sales announcement added to the end of a commercial. 3. To appoint someone to a job, e.g., "He was tagged to head the studio's new division." Same as to tap. Entertainment trade paper use.

tail End of a roll of film.

tail slate Another name for an end slate.

tail-away shot Camera shot in which the subject moves in a direct path away from the camera lens. The opposite of a tail-away shot is a head-on shot.

tails out Film wound backwards on the reel; roll of film with the end of the reel (tail) at the beginning. Tails-out prints must be rewound before being projected, as the first frames coming off the reel are the last frames of the picture.

take Single, continuous shot. The director may call for several takes of the same shot, until he gets what he wants from both the actors and the technical crew. (Luis Buñuel was renown for shooting only one take of each shot on many of his films.) Related terms: keep takes, outtakes, dailies, rushes.

take a meeting Slang meaning to have a meeting.

takeoff Another name for a parody. Also called a send-up.

take-up reel Reel that collects the viewed or projected film film. Related term: tails out.

taking over a role Assuming the performing responsibilities of an actor who has left a production (voluntarily or not). Same as stepping into a role.

talent All on-camera and off-camera performers, including animals.

talent agency Representational business whose clients are actors or other performers; such an agency works on a commission basis. "Talent agency" is a general term and implies the representation of individuals in any or a variety of fields of performing or creative work. Related terms: talent division, international agency, major agency, specialty agency, boutique agency, theatrical agency.

talent agent 1. Owner or employee of a talent agency who acts as a business representative for a performer; the agent obtains work for his or her client(s) and gets paid on a com-

mission basis. Related terms: animal agent, specialty agent, theatrical agent, TV commercial agent. 2. Talent agency and its operations, collectively. Also called a talent business or supplier of talent. Related terms: Association of Talent Agents, talent agency.

talent booking Engagement to act, sing, dance or otherwise perform. Also called a job or stint. Related terms: theatrical booking, gig.

talent division Section or department of an agency responsible for the representation of performing talent, usually actors. Related terms: talent agency division, television division, theatrical division, voiceover division.

talent information form 1. Form found at auditions or interview sessions; talent is asked to fill in such information as name, phone number, union memberships, personal statistics, clothing sizes and the like. Also called a talent information card/sheet, casting information form or talent size card. Related term: sign-in sheet. 2. Form that new representation clients may be required to fill out. Information contained on it may be entered into an agency's booking room computer. Also called an agency registration form/card/sheet. Related term: skill sheet.

talent payment company Business hired by another to manage its production or residual payrolls. Also called a production payroll service, payroll preparation service or payroll systems company. Related terms: paycheck, production accountant.

talent scout Employee or associate of a talent agency, movie studio, production company, television network, music company, sports organization or the like who seeks out and/or maintains an observance for new talent to represent. Such an individual usually has an official job title within the company and is referred to as a "talent scout" informally or in media stories. Also called a talent recruiter, talent spotter, new talent coordinator or director of new talent. Related term: new talent director.

talent search One or a series of activities conducted to find new talent. A talent search may be in the form of a casting search or talent contest.

talent test 1. Session conducted to find, select and verify one or more talented individuals. Another name for an audition. 2. Check of a performer's résumé-stated talent. Also called a talent confirming test or talent demonstration. Related term: skill test.

talk show Radio, television or computer interview program. If an audience is physically present, it is also called a studio-audience talk show. Also called a chat show (Great Britain). Related terms: computer online talk show, band, late-night TV.

talkie Nickname for an early motion picture having synchronized audible dialogue. Also called a talking picture. Related terms: Academy aperture, silent era.

talking head Nickname for an on-screen close-up or head-and-shoulders shot of a person who talks but does little else.

talk-show circuit Touring of television or radio talk shows to promote something, such as a movie, TV show or book. Related term: promotional tour.

talk-talk Another name for background voices in a scene.

tape 1. (n.) Short for audiotape or videotape. 2. Cartridge, cassette or reel of such tape. Related terms: master tape, magnetic tape. 3. (v.) To record sound or visuals on such tape. 4. (n.) Flat, flexible, narrow strip of adhesive material used to mark locations. 5. (v.) To measure the distance from a camera to a subject using a measuring tape attached to the front of the camera. Related term: camera-to-subject measurement.

tape booking A booking to appear in a production that will be shot on videotape for playing at a later time, as opposed to a live television booking. Also called a booking for taped television. Related terms: live-on-tape booking, videotape booking, video booking.

tape delay 1. Act of delaying the broadcast of a live-on-tape television program (e.g., an awards show or live talk show); the playback of the tape is telecast at a later time. Typically, a delayed broadcast is done to accommodate different time zones. Also called a videotape delay. Related term: delayed broadcast. 2. Momentary time delay on a live TV or radio program before it is broadcast to the public; typically, this is done so that any offensive language or unexpected nudity can be "bleeped" or edited out. Related terms: censor, live broadcast.

tape splice See splice.

taped music Music recorded on audiotape at an earlier time; it can be played back whenever needed, as opposed to live music, which is created at the time it is heard. Related terms: playback track, recorded music.

target Round screen that blocks light from wherever it is not wanted. Related terms: gobo, flag.

target audience Specific audience group at which a production, project or product is aimed, as opposed to a general, or mass, audience. Also called a target demographic audience or targeted buying group. Related terms: market research, narrowcast.

taxes Freelance professional performers and other talents generally are regarded as self-employed individuals and pay income taxes accordingly. Related terms: accountant, television earnings.

TBD Abbreviation for "To be determined." May appear on some union forms.

TCU Abbreviation for tight close-up. A tight close-up is also called an extreme close-up (ECU).

team coverage Reporting of a news story by various members of the journalism crew; a succession of reports by two or more journalists from the same station (radio or television) who present different aspects of an important news event. Related term: press coverage.

tear-jerker Film or other production causing causes the viewer to become moist-eyed or teary. A nickname. Related term: weepie.

tearsheet Page cut from a published work (e.g., magazine, newspaper, catalog, brochure, book). For a photographer, makeup artist, hairstylist, etc., a tearsheet is a visible example and proof of work done. Also called a clipping or cut-out. Related term: press clipping.

teaser 1. Short segment at the opening of a TV show or theatrical film; it attracts the audience's attention, making them to want to see more. Related terms: advance teaser campaign, hook, pre-credits sequence, prologue. 2. Similar oncamera or voiceover bit between the segments of any show. Also called a tease.

technical advisor Individual or company providing assistance in the form of specialized information on a particular topic to the producer(s), director, writer and others working on a film or television production. A technical advisor may be a law-enforcement expert, military expert, medical expert, historical consultant, author of a book being made into a movie or documentary, a living relative or other individual closely associated with the subject matter. A fee is usually paid for providing such advisory assistance. The terms "technical advisor," "technical consultant," "technical assistance provided by," "special consultant," "production consultant," "production advisor" or similar title may appear onscreen as a credit along with the individual's or company's name. Related terms: creative consultant, reenactor.

technical coordinator Individual responsible for assisting the director on a multi-camera project that is photographed continuously before a live audience or as if there was one present; his chief responsibility is supervising the movement of each camera throughout the show.

technical director Individual who supervises the technical aspects (e.g., mechanical, electrical) of a show.

technical rehearsal Performance to practice the physical movements, mechanical and electrical elements, special effects, etc., aspects of a production.

Technicolor Trademark color process invented during World War I by Herbert T. Kalmus and Daniel F. Comstock. Originally, it was a process that combined two colors (red and green) on the screen via a special projector. However, this process was expensive and unsatisfactory. In 1932, a more accurate and eye-pleasing Technicolor process was developed. The three stripe process uses three negatives; they are individually sensitive to the primary colors (red, green and blue) and printed onto a single strand of film in the lab. Internet address: http://www.technicolor.com. Related term: integral tripack.

teeth special effects Visual effects involving the teeth. Related term: special teeth effects.

telecast 1. To transmit signals over television airwaves or cable transmission lines. "Telecast" is a general term, while broadcast, cablecast and satellitecast are more specific with regard to the method of signal delivery. 2. One such television transmission, as of a TV program.

telecine Machine with electronic and mechanical features; it is used to transfer filmed images (e.g., from 35mm motion picture footage) into electronic signals which are then recorded on a master videotape or telecast directly. Modern telecines use digital processing technology. Related terms: film-to-video transfer, pan and scan, Rank Cintel, Kinescope, 16mm.

teleconference 1. Satellite-linked, audio-video meeting taking place at two or more locations between several participants. Also called a satellite conference. Related term: corporate television. 2. Multiple-participant conference using digital video-phone technology, either as separate units or over the Internet. Related term: video conference.

telefilm Television film. Another name for a TV movie.

telephone line-fed Sent over the worldwide telephone-line network, including ground-based, microwave-dish relay stations.

telephoto lens Lens with a focal length longer than normal; it is used mainly to photograph distant subjects as if they were close.

telepic Television movie. Entertainment trade paper use. Related term: vidpic.

teleplay 1. Script for a television movie or series episode. 2. The TV production itself; a television play.

teleplay by Production credit designated for the writer(s) of a television script. Related term: written by.

TelePrompTer Projection device allowing a speaker, performer or newsperson to read enlarged, continuous, vertically moving script lines from a slanted transparent glass or plastic plate (it's angled to reflect from a nearby TV monitor); the reader appears to be looking directly into the camera or out to the audience. The television studio version is mounted directly in front of the camera. The script wording is fed to the monitors by a separate, offstage delivery system, consisting of either a computer or conveyor-belt paper transport with an overhead-mounted video camera. The first TelePrompTers (original spelling) were manufactured in the United States by the TelePrompTer Corporation, a company no longer in business. Today, TelePrompTers are manufactured by numerous companies around the world. Also called a videoprompter. Internet address: http://www.teleprompter.com. Related terms: prompter, QTV, videoprompter.

telescope matte Black, light-blocking mask for a camera's lens; shooting through it gives the impression of a character looking through a telescope. It is similar to a binocular matte except that it has only one centered hole instead of two merging ones. Related term: microscope matte.

telescript Television script. Related term: teleplay.

telescripter Television scriptwriter; writer of scripts for television productions. Also called a telewriter.

telethon Television event taking place over many hours to raise funds, usually for a charity. One of the more well-known is Jerry Lewis' annual Labor Day Telethon for Muscular Dystrophy.

television 1. Medium by which light rays originating or reflecting from stationary or moving objects are converted into analog or digital electronic signals by a TV camera. Along with the audio signals, the electronic signals are converted into high frequency or ultrahigh frequency waves or digital signals for broadcasting, cablecasting or satellite-casting to television sets where the video signals are converted into onscreen pictures and the audio signals into sound. For color television, the video signals are converted into three different electron scanning beams projected at a regulated rate and number of lines per frame. The surface of the set's lightly curved glass is coated with tightly spaced vertical rows of colored phosphor rectangles, called pixels. Each vertical row consists of one color, red, green or blue and are arranged on the screen in consecutive groups of three: red-green-blue, red-green-blue, red-green-blue, etc., until the entire screen is filled. Each of the three electron beams is designed to scan the rows of only one color at a rate too quick to be noticed by the human eye. A picture is created by controlling the strength of each beam as it strikes a colored phosphor rectangle, causing it to light up. For example, a red apple is created by strengthening the electron beam that strikes an apple-shaped patch of red pixels and by weakening the green and blue scanning beams for that same area. Shadows and highlights are accomplished by regulating the strengths of all three beams where they correspond to the shadows and highlights on the real-life apple. The various combinations of red, green and blue are used to create all the colors seen on television. Related terms: cable TV, closed-circuit television, digital television, HDTV, satellite television, SDTV, television set, TV, ATV, DSS, electronic media, UHF, VHF, video. 2. Other means of creating television images on display screens, such as through the use of liquid-cystal display technology. Related term: LCD TV. 3. Television industry, world or profession. Related terms: children's television, corporate television, golden age of television, interactive television, long-form television, magic of television, television world, TV.

television campaign Ad campaign consisting of an organized airing of the same or related TV commercials.

television cutout board Black sheet with cutouts of television screens; the board is placed over a white sheet of artwork paper with television storyboard drawings on it. The drawings are positioned on the paper so they match the locations of the cutouts. Available in different sizes, the cutout boards are used mainly by advertising agencies as an effective way to present the story and action of a proposed television commercial to clients.

television distributor Company or division distributing completed television products, such as series and specials, to television exhibition markets. Also called a syndicator. Related term: exhibit.

television division Department of a studio or production company dealing with television-related projects.

television earnings Money earned from television employment, as determined by TV employer paycheck amounts. A performer must pay taxes on television earnings. Also called TV income or TV wages.

television industry Branch of business and service activities pertaining to the production, marketing and exhibition of television projects. Also called the TV industry, television business.

television magazine 1. Printed periodical featuring television programming information and articles about the television industry. 2. News or informational TV program presented in a format similar to print magazines of the same subject. Also called a TV magazine or videomagazine. Related terms: magazine, newsmagazine.

television schedule Timetable consisting of stations or channels, dates and exact times when television programs will be shown. Also called a TV schedule or television programming guide. Related terms: backup schedule, broadcast schedule, cable schedule, pulled from the schedule.

television version Theatrical film airing on television in a slightly edited version (e.g., offensive dialogue is dubbed over or shots involving violence or nudity are trimmed or deleted). Edits are made so the film can be shown on broadcast television in a country with government or voluntary industry guidelines. The original version of the film is called the "uncut" version.

television world Realm of activities, knowledge and interests associated with working in the television industry. Related term: television.

telly Nickname for television or television set (Great Britain).

tempo Speed and rhythm of the film's progression.

tenner Heavy-duty spotlight using a 10,000-watt lamp.

test audience Another name for a preview audience.

test deal Contract with an actor in a proposed television series or movie, contingent upon network or studio approval of said actor. A test deal is made so the network may have final cast approval and a firm idea of how much the production will cost; it is also used to prevent actors from renegotiating once they know the network is interested. Related term: deal.

test marketing Process of testing a proposed new product or the advertising to promote it; done to determine its sales potential, effectiveness or to see if any changes should be made before proceeding. In some instances, the product being test marketed may be released for sale or distributed for free in selected areas and the resultant sales figures or user comments analyzed. Related terms: exit poll, market research, preview audience.

test screening Trial exhibition of a film or TV program to evaluate audience reaction. Related terms: preview audience, trial run.

theater 1. Place where stage entertainment is presented to audiences, for example, amphitheater, Broadway, classical, commercial, community, dance, dinner, fringe, indoor, 99-seat, noncommercial, Off-Broadway, Off-Off-Broadway, outdoor, pub, stand-alone, summer and theater-in-the-round. Related terms: front office, house, out front, playhouse. 2. Theater industry, world, field or profession. Also called theaterdom, the stage or world of drama. Some types of theater include children's, educational, experimental, interactive, legitimate, live, musical, regional, repertory, resident and street. 3. Of or pertaining to theater.

theater angel Individual or organization providing financial backing, including sponsorship, donation or investment. Related terms: angel, backing.

theater community Group of persons working in or closely associated with the theater industry.

theater company 1. Another name for an acting company. Also called a theater acting company or resident theater company. 2. Business that owns and operates a playhouse.

theater director Another name for a play or stage director.

theater district Area within a city where numerous playhouses are located. Related terms: London Theatre District, New York City Theater District.

theater industry Branch of business and service activities pertaining to the production and marketing of stage plays. Also called the theater business or theater trade.

theater manager Manager of a movie theater or playhouse. Also called a house manager.

theater producer Producer of dramatic, comedic or musical plays for the theater. Also called a stage-play producer or Broadway producer (United States). Related term: stage-show producer.

theater program Published listing of participants and the scene breakdown for a theater production.

theater workshop Commercial (for profit) or noncommercial (nonprofit) group consisting of theater performers; it may be a general workshop or specialized one. Related term: acting workshop.

theater world Realm of activities, knowledge and interests associated with the theater industry.

theatergoer Individual who attends a theater performance. Also called a playgoer.

theater-in-the-round Theater consisting of a ground-level or raised stage completely or partially encircled by the audience. Also called a half-round stage or three-quarter-round stage. Related term: arena stage.

theatrical 1. Of or pertaining to theater or dramatic presentations. 2. Of or pertaining to motion pictures shown in movie theaters. 3. Artificial; showy. Related terms: theatrics, campy.

theatrical agency Representational business whose clients are actors or other stage performers. Also called an actors' agency, performers' agency, performing artists' agency or show-business agency. Related term: talent agency.

theatrical agent 1. Individual at a theatrical agency who represents a performer in the entertainment industry. The terms "theatrical agent" and "talent agent" are often used interchangeably. Also called a stage agent. 2. Theatrical agency and its operations collectively. Also called a theatrical agenting business or supplier of theatrical talent.

theatrical booking Engagement to act or perform. Also called a talent booking, acting job, dancing job or the like. Related terms: booking, gig.

theatrical business manager Business manager whose clients are actors and other types of stage performers.

theatrical division 1. Department of a studio responsible for theatrical feature films. 2. Department of an agency responsible for the representation of theatrical performers. (Other divisions may represent book authors, speakers, photographers, commercial artists or other professions.) Related term: talent division.

theatrical eyeglasses Eyeglasses with flat, clear pieces of glass or plastic instead of correction lenses that magnify or focus. Also called fake eyeglasses, stage eyeglasses or window eyeglasses. Related term: special eye effects.

theatrical film Motion picture shown in movie theaters, as opposed to a film broadcast on television or cable. Also called a theatrically exhibited film, theatrical motion picture, or bigscreener. Related terms: feature film, short film, big screen, release, remake, rerelease, revival.

theatrical screening Exhibition of a film in a movie theater.

theatrical use 1. Exhibiting or presenting in a theater or before a live audience. 2. Any use, e.g., photograph, news footage, product, other than in the electronic or print media.

theatrics Staged to achieve a desired effect; showy, e.g., "No theatrics. Just read the line straight, please."

theme Principal idea, concept or meaning of a production, exhibition, creative work or discussion.

theme act 1. Short, theme-based performance by performers, for example, a Wild-West shoot-out act at a fair. 2. Such a performance and the performer(s) collectively.

theme music Instrumental music identifying a film, TV series, play, setting, action sequence, character or performer (e.g., "My Heart Will Go On" from *Titanic* [1997], composed by James Horner). Related terms: theme song, main title theme.

theme park Combination working film and/or TV studio and entertainment theme park. Admission-paying visitors can see and experience various film-related exhibits, ride-through attractions and take a tram tour of the production facilities, including back lot streets. Universal Studios Hollywood was the first such studio theme park in the world. Also called a movie theme park or studio park. Related terms: Disney-MGM Studios, Universal Studios Florida, Universal Studios Hollywood, cast member, studio tour, theme park.

theme song Composition of words and music used to identify a production, character or performer. Favorite television theme songs include the title songs to "Gilligan's Island," "The Brady Bunch," "Flipper" and "The Patty Duke Show." Related terms: theme music, song.

Thermal Smoke Nonpyrotechnic white powder that produces smoke when it contacts with a hot surface. Formulated and sold by the special-effects company Zeller International, Ltd., of Downsville, New York, in the United States. Related term: smoke effect.

thesp Short for thespian. Entertainment trade paper use.

thespian 1. Another name for a dramatic actor. Derived from the name Thespis, a 6th century B.C. Greek poet considered to be the originator of Greek tragedy. Related term: synthespian. 2. Of or pertaining to dramatic acting.

thin negative Underexposed negative with little or no density.

third assistant director In Canada and the UK, second second assistant directors are called third assistant directors.

30-fps video Short for 30-frames-per-second video, the television standard used in the United States, Canada, Japan and other countries. (Europe is 25 frames per second.) Related terms: speed, video.

35mm Still camera, movie camera and projection film that is 35 millimeters wide, with perforations (sprocket holes) on both sides and, for movie film, space for a time-code track or other magnetic or optical soundtracks. Standard 35mm sound film has 16 frames per foot, 4 perforations per frame; it travels through a movie camera or projector at 24 frames per second. (The speed of early silent 35mm movie film was 16 frames per second.) Related terms: l6mm-to-35mm blowup, video-to-35mm transfer, Academy aperture, anamorphic lens, Arriflex, downprint, editing on tape, film-to-video transfer, flatbed editing machine, Panavision, perforation, slide, transparency, VistaVision, widescreen.

thread To place film over the sprockets and on through the gate and paths of the camera, projector or printer.

"Three... two ... one." Voice cue said to an individual about to appear in front of an active television camera.

Besides a cue, it also identifies the beginning of the footage, such as a news report. Related terms: In three ... countdown, cue, "Cue me."

three-camera (abbreviated as three-cam or 3-cam) Of or pertaining to three cameras (film or video), e.g., a three-camera shoot, three-camera production or three-camera coverage. Also called multiple-camera.

three-camera shoot Filming in which three cameras are positioned at different locations to record the same action, as a stunt or special-effects explosion. The best shots are edited together during post-production.

3D Short for three-dimensional film, in which the illusion of three dimensions is created. Height, width and depth. Also spelled 3-D. Related terms: 3D CGI, 3D movie, 3D package, 3D scanner, stereo, stereoscopic, 2D.

3D CCI Abbreviation for three-dimensional computer-generated imagery. Computer graphics and animation effects with a simulated 3D quality. Related terms: 3D, CGI.

3D model 1. Any form with height, width and depth, including model miniatures, clay sculptures, product prototypes and display mannequins. 2. Individual featured in a three-dimensional photograph, stereoscopic photograph, stereo drawing, hologram or 3D film, videorecording or computer image.

3D movie Film presented on a flat screen; it appears to be three-dimensional because it was shot using a special stereoscopic camera process and requires special viewing glasses to achieve the effect. A leading supplier of 3D film, video and print technologies, including being the world's largest manufacturer of 3D audience glasses (over 300 million to date), is

3D Video Corporation of Woodland Hills, California, in the United States. Related terms: IMAX 3D theater, IMAX Solido theater.

3D package Product package having embossed or vacuum-formed outer features which are three-dimensional.

3D scanner Position-coordinate plotting device used in CG-effects work; it circles an object or person with a laser beam to optically scan its surface outline in three dimensions. Also called a 3D laser scanner. Related terms: laser scanner, laser scanning session.

three-day player Performer hired on a production and paid to work a minimum of three days.

three-fold flat Structural background on a stage similar to a two-fold flat, except it has three hinged sides.

three-shot Photograph or camera shot featuring three subjects. Also called a group shot.

three-strip Original Technicolor process. Related terms: Technicolor, matrices, separation negatives.

three-wall set Production set with two side walls and one back wall. The camera(s) and audience are located in front of the open section.

thrill show Another name for a stunt show.

through-the-lens viewing Seeing what a camera lens will record on film by using a viewfinder system with internal optical elements (including a flip-up mirror in front of the film). Without through-the-lens viewing, a parallax situation may exist (the image recorded is slightly to one side because of the different line-of-sight angles for the viewfinder and lens). Related term: single-lens reflex.

throw Distance between the image on the screen and the lens of the projector.

thrust stage Stage with sufficient apron space (the stage area in front of the curtain) to allow a performance to be closer to the audience. Also called a projecting stage.

THX Trade name for sound technology systems licensed for use in movie theaters and home audio equipment by Lucasfilm, Ltd., Inc., of California. The system includes the quality and positioning of loudspeakers to take room acoustics into account so that the audience is provided with the most realistic sound possible.

tie-in 1. Of or pertaining to a connection between two or more things or events. 2. The connection itself, e.g., a film product tie-in. Related terms: cross-promo tie-in, merchandising tie-in, movie tie-in.

tight angle Close camera angle.

tight shot Shot in which the subject is the only image on the screen; the subject is framed tightly. Related term: close-up.

tighter angle Angle closer than the previous one.

tilt Up-and-down movement of a camera, as opposed to the sideways movement of a pan.

time 1. Duration; hours, minutes, seconds. Related terms: airtime, call time, camera time, clock time, compressed time, expanded time, overtime, real time, running time, stopwatch. 2. Year, century, or era, e.g., time period. Related terms: period drama, period movie, period wardrobe, setting.

time code 1. Onscreen numbering indicating elapsed hours, minutes, seconds and frames per second; used in editing to indicate duration and to locate specific frames on videotape or film. 2. Pattern or signal used to synchronize projected film images with a separately played audio CD. Related terms: time-code track, DTS.

time cue card Small, handheld cue card displaying the minutes or seconds remaining until a commercial break occurs. It may be one of many cards (contained in a spiral-hinged, flip-the-card format) showing different times.

time report On a production set, chart on which times of arrival, meal breaks and departure are recorded to determine and to keep track of overtime, to avoid meal penalties and the like. Actors' signatures may also be required. Filing a time report is a union-required procedure (United States). Also called a time sheet. Related term: production time report.

time slot Position or place on a schedule, e.g., "The network gave the TV series an 8:30 p.m. Monday time slot." Also called a weekly time period or spot on a network's schedule. Related terms: bad time slot, doomed time slot, good time slot, bumped, network programmer, network shuffling, new day and time.

time-and-a-half Another name for overtime.

time-code slate Electronically controlled clapboard featuring a large (approximately one inch), red, light-emitting diode (LED), digital-counter display; it appears on the upper section of the board, below the clapstick and the space where the project's title appears. The display reads hours, minutes, seconds and frame numbers in frames per second (there is a battery pack in back). Bringing the clapstick down operates

a display function switch. A time-code slate reads and displays a selected industry time code provided by a time-code generator mounted on the back. The time code allows for accurate and easier synchronization of picture and sound. In 1991, an Emmy Award was bestowed upon its inventor and manufacturer, Denecke, Inc., of North Hollywood, California. Also called an electronic slate or electronic clapboard.

time-code track Encoded pattern or series of electronic signals used to identify individual film or video frames during editing or to synchronize images and sound. Related terms: Academy aperture, DTS.

time-lapse Method of exposing frames at a single time or at preset intervals. When the film is projected at normal speed, it the action appears to have been speeded up (e.g., small plants emerging from the ground, a spider spinning its web). *Koyaanisqatsi* (1983) is an example of such time-lapse photography.

timer Laboratory technician evaluating the color balance of each shot; he then orders any necessary color corrections.

timing 1. Actor's ability to create the proper tempo in a scene through the rhythm and flow of his performance. 2. Lab technician's evaluation of the density and color balance of each shot of the film, to achieve the desired contrast and color balance. 3. Actual running time of a project, the script timing is usually performed by the script supervisor and is a detailed analysis of exactly how long (to the second) each scene will run. Timing a script early in the project can save money because scenes that appear too long can be cut in the writing process instead of waiting until the film is being edited.

Tinseltown Nickname for Hollywood, especially as a place of glamour.

title role Acting part which comprises the title of the project, e.g., one of the two title roles in William Shakespeare's *Romeo and Juliet,* Julia Roberts' title role in *Pretty Woman* (1990) or Denzel Washington's in *The Hurricane* (1999). If the role is played by an actor (as opposed to an animal, special-effects creature, etc.), it is almost always a starring role.

title song Theme song named after the title of the movie or TV series in which it is heard.

titles Words and credits appearing at the beginning and end of the film. The name of the film at the beginning is called the main title; the others credits are referred to simply as front credits or end credits (or the end crawl). Subtitles appear at the bottom of the screen and translate dialogue from a different language.

t-number See t-stop.

tonal key Range of light and dark tones in an image. High key signifies a bright scene with mainly light tones and no heavy shadows; low key signifies a scene with heavy shadows and few light tones.

tongue-in-cheek Humorously pretending or teasing; fooling or joking around.

toning Chemical process that turns black-and-white film to sepia.

'toon Short for cartoon.

'toon tune Musical composition used in a cartoon, including a feature-length animated film.

tooth enamel Special tooth coloring applied by brush to an actor's front teeth to give them the appearance of missing or discolored teeth. It is available in different colors and washes off when the scene is finished. Related terms: black tooth enamel, special teeth effects.

top actor or actress 1. Actor at the top of the acting profession in roles, income or recognition. 2. Actor with top billing in a production. Also called a topliner or headliner.

top banana 1. Lead comedian in a comedy act. Originally used in burlesque. The next comedian after the lead is the second banana. Related terms: banana, comedian. 2. Lead or most important person in any group.

top billing Credit(s) placed in the most advantageous position vis-a-vis the main title of the picture on the screen and in the paid advertising for the picture (e.g., above the title and centered if there is one name; or above the title and to the left if there are two names). In the event there are two stars of equal stature, it is not unusual to see the credit on the right placed higher than the credit on the left so as to impart equal importance. Although, typically, top billing is a concern of the director, producer and actors, it is not unusual to see a cinematographer, editor, costume designer and/or production designer also negotiate for preferred billing.

top hat See high hat.

top sheet Summary sheet; the first page of the budget form; it provides the subtotals for each budget category listed and includes the bottom line costs of the project.

top-grossing film Movie ranking above others in income received from box-office ticket sales and other distribution outlets. Currently, the top-grossing film of all time is *Titanic* (1997). Also called a top-grosser, top money-earner, top money-maker, one of the top-grossing films of the season/year, one of the top five films, box-office champ, or box-office champion. Related terms: all-time box-office champ, B.O. champ, blockbuster, megahit, smash hit.

torch fluid Long-burning flammable liquid formulated to be used as a smokeless fuel for stationary or hand-carried, cotton-wicked torches. Two sources for torch fluid are Tri-Ess Sciences, Inc., of Burbank, California (which custom designs and builds ceremonial torches) and Zeller International, Ltd., of Downsville, New York. Also called torch fuel. Related term: fire effect.

Toronto International Film Festival Annual festival in Canada, held in September in the port city of Toronto; it features new Canadian and world films.

tour 1. Performing tour. 2. Press tour. 3. Studio tour. 4. Production set tour.

touring company Acting company that travels on a scheduled basis from theater to theater to perform. Also called a traveling theater company. Related terms: road company, troupe, comedy troupe.

track 1. (n.) See sound track. 2. Wooden or metal rails laid on the ground; the dolly moves smoothly on them in tracking shots (aka dolly shots). 2. (v.) To move the camera on tracks so as to smoothly follow the action in a scene.

tracking shot Moving shot in which the camera follows the action in a scene. The camera is placed on a dolly which moves on tracks; or, it is placed on a camera car or other moving vehicle. In *Love Story* (1970), director Arthur Hiller uses tracking shots when Jenny Cavilleri (Ali MacGraw) and Oliver Barrett IV (Ryan O'Neal)

walk through the Harvard campus throughout the course of their courtship. Related terms: dolly shot, traveling shot, trucking shot.

trade paper Industry newspaper. Related terms: *Amusement Business, Back Stage, Back Stage West/Drama-Logue, Billboard, Daily Variety, Hollywood Reporter, Playbill, Stage, Variety.*

trade-paper announcement Advertisement in a trade newspaper intended to dispense important or noteworthy information to the industry, such as a new film project or a business merger.

trades Published material (e.g., newspaper, magazine or newsletter) reporting on a particular industry or profession. Related term: trade paper.

tragedy 1. One of the two main forms of drama, the other being comedy. Tragedy is more commonly called serious drama, hard drama or hard-hitting drama. 2. Production whose story is based on a serious theme.

trailer 1. Short advertisement of a feature film; it is shown to movie theater audiences before the main feature or is aired on television as a commercial. Typically, it consists of selected scene segments with dialogue, music and narration. A trailer's structure does not necessarily correspond to that of the film. Teaser trailers run less than 90 seconds; regular trailers may be of any length but are typically less than two minutes. Like films, trailers are rated by the MPAA (Related term: rating). Today, trailers are considered an art form in their own right and reflect highly sophisticated aesthetic techniques combined with carefully determined marketing strategy. The term originated in the 1920s, when short entertainment and coming attractions trailed the main feature in movie houses. Related terms: coming attractions, movie commercial. 2. Short, promotional video clip for a television program or series. Also called a video trailer. Related terms: promo, sneak preview.

training video Instructional videotape that teaches the viewer how to do something. Related term: instructional video.

transfer Any magnetic duplication of picture or sound, e.g., to record a sound track from the original 1/4" tape to magnetic film or to record a film onto videotape. Transferring from one size of videotape to another is called dubbing.

transit poster Advertising wall or display stand poster found in areas of or on forms of transportation. Also called a transit card, transit sheet, transit billboard or vehicle advertising panel. Related term: bus advertising.

transitional effects See dissolve, fade, wipe.

transitional scene 1. Scene that changes the story's location or time of day. 2. Scene in which there is a temporary shift of setting. Related terms: dream sequence, flashback.

translite Lighted backing; it gives the illusion of being outdoors.

transparency Image on a transparent substance such as glass, film, etc.; it is suitable for viewing or projecting. Still transparencies (slides) are often used in process shots, to project a background for a scene.

transportation Department responsible for transporting the crew and all necessary equipment and vehicles to and from the production. Cars used in front of the camera (called picture cars) are sometimes the responsibility of the prop department.

transportation captain Individual responsible for the various transport, service and storage vehicles used behind the scenes and in front of the cameras on a production. Depending on the type and size of a production, there may also be one or more transportation co-captains, picture car coordinators, drivers and technical personnel. Also called a transportation manager.

trash TV Nickname for television shows (principally, talk and news shows) presenting a regular diet of sensational, controversial, strange or sexually suggestive topics. Also called exploitation TV or extreme tabloid TV.

travel allowance Money paid to a performer to compensate for traveling to a nonstudio location booking; rate is based on distance. Related terms: allowance, travel-time fee, studio zone.

travel day Day scheduled for traveling to a distant shooting location. For location shooting, a travel day is considered work time, therefore cast and crew must be paid for their travel time.

travel-companion allowance Money provided to cover the costs of transportation, lodging and meals for a performer's friend or relative while on location. Related terms: spousal/companion allowance, allowance.

traveling matte Visual-effects film process in which moving images, such as those of an actor or spaceship, are combined (frame by frame) with other action or with a still background. The process necessitates an optical printer to perfectly insert the moving images on one length of film footage into unexposed areas of the identical space size on a second length of film footage (containing the new background action or still picture). The images in the traveling matte are obtained by filming with the bluescreen, greenscreen or orangescreen process. Related term: matte.

traveling shot Shot in which the camera moves on a dolly, a camera car or other moving vehicle. Related terms: dolly shot, tracking shot.

travel-time fee Payment to a union (or, nonunion) actor for traveling to a location, such as one outside a major city's studio zone (according to conditions specified in a union contract). Related term: travel allowance.

treatment Detailed story outline or synopsis; it usually includes sample dialogue and narrative. A treatment is typically 15 to 45 pages long and serves as a guide for the script when it is written. Related term: outline.

trial run 1. One or more test performances of a play or showings of a film. Also called a tryout (for a play) or a test screening (for a film). 2. Test performance of an acting scene, stunt sequence or other event. Also called a run-through or rehearsal.

triangle Collapsible, three-legged device designed to hold the legs of a tripod; it prevents them from slipping apart. Related term: spider.

trick Stunt, feat or ability. Related terms: camera trick, trick camera shot, trick horse, trick line, trick rider, animal trainer.

trick horse Horse trained to perform stunts or amusing acts on cue. Related term: stunt horse.

trick line Another name for a breakaway line. The breaking or snapping point on a breakaway prop, created by cutting and then spot-gluing the pieces or by scoring an indented line (as on a piece of balsa wood). Also

called a precut breaking line or score line.

trick photography See special effects.

trick rider Horseback rider who performs tricks, such as jumping on a horse from the rear or standing on the backs of two moving horses, etc. Related term: stunt rider.

trilogy Series of three related literary, musical or dramatic works. For example, the *Indiana Jones* trilogy (*Raiders of the Lost Ark* [1981], *Indiana Jones and the Temple of Doom* [1984] and *Indiana Jones and the Last Crusade* [1989]) all featured archaeologist/adventurer Indiana Jones (portrayed by Harrison Ford); all three were directed by Steven Spielberg. Related term: film series.

trim 1. (n.) Unused sections of film; they are cut from the scene by the editor during post-production. 2. (v.) To cut or shorten a scene during editing. 3. "Trimming a light" means adding a scrim to knock down the brightness.

trim bin Receptacle used for storing lengths of cut film during the editing process; it is mounted on wheels and has an open box or bag section, above which is a metal frame with a row of hooks from which the lengths of film are hung. The trims placed there are inventoried in case any have to be reedited into the film. Scrap film (that which is unusable, such as clapboard shots) may be thrown into a separate bin for disposal or it could be stored by the producer for some other purpose. Related term: bin

trim prop Anything hung on the wall of a production set, such as a curtain, painting, sign or other decoration.

trim tabs See cinetabs.

trip gear Automatic timing device (an intervalometer) allowing a camera to expose single or multiple frames at a pre-arranged time or at a steady speed. Related term: time lapse photography.

tripack Color film composed of three layers of emulsion, each one sensitive to one of the three primary colors. Related term: integral tripack.

triple threat Expression referring to an individual who can do the work of three, for example, an actor-singer-dancer. Orson Welles and Woody Allen are two of the more well-known triple threats. Related term: hyphenate.

tripod Three-legged stand made of metal or wood on which a camera or other equipment is mounted. Adjustable, three-legged stand to which a camera can be attached (with use of a tripod head). There are many sizes and kinds of tripod heads, including: friction head, gyro head and fluid head. Related terms: VISTA Telescoping Tripod, camera mount, Duopod, MegaCrane, Mini-Crane, monopod, QuickLift, rain effect, sticks.

trombone Extendable clamp used when hanging lights on the walls of the set.

troupe Traveling group of performers. Related terms: comedy troupe, touring company.

trucking shot See dolly shot, tracking shot.

tryout notice Another name for a casting notice.

t-stop Calibrated for the individual lens, the t-shop shows the amount of light transmitted through the lens. It is similar to an f-stop, but more precise, as f-stops show only the amount of light entering the lens.

turnaround Negotiated right of a writer or producer to submit a project to another studio or network, if the company that developed the property elects not to proceed with production. Typically, the right is subject to the condition that the developing company's investment is repaid; it also may require the developing company to retain an interest in the film's earnings.

turnaround time Minimum and specific number of free time that must be given to a cast or crew member before that person may return to work without incurring a penalty. The time is established by that individual's union contract. For example, an actor must be given 58 hours of non-work time between completion of work Friday and beginning work on Monday. Related term: forced call.

turret Revolving lens mount used before the invention of the zoom lens (especially on television cameras and 16mm cameras). Lenses mounted on a turret are swung rapidly into position by rotating the mount. Related term: rack.

TV commercial foreign-use fee Additional payment to a principal commercial actor when the advertisement is designated for airing in a foreign country; it is a union-required payment.

TV commercial rate 1. Fee for television commercial acting, voiceover or production work. Also called a TV commercial scale payment. 2. Fee charged for airing a television commercial; a TV advertising rate.

TV commercial residual Residual paid for acting or voiceover work performed in a television commercial that has aired. Also called a commercial use payment.

TV movie Motion picture produced for television. This is opposed to a theatrical movie, which is produced for distribution in theaters and later is shown on television. Related terms: made-for-TV movie, TV-movie, movie-of-the-week, MOW, long-form television, miniseries, telefilm, telepic.

TV network 1. Group of affiliated television stations. 2. The stations and corporation managing the network collectively. Related term: network.

TV residual Payment to a television performer for a repeat showing of a program in which he has appeared. TV residuals, which are union-required payments from the producer, end after a certain number of additional (rerun) airings. Related terms: residual, film residual.

TV station 1. Place where television broadcasts originate, including the buildings and equipment used (e.g., numerous large, outdoor satellite dishes). Related term: bug. 2. Business or organization operating such a place. Related terms: independent TV station, network affiliate, TV network.

TV station call letters Combination of alphabet letters officially identifying a television station. Related term: call letters.

TV studio camera Large, professional-grade, broadcast-quality television camera that shoots studio-based images and feeds them to the master control room and video recorder and, on live productions, also to the transmission equipment. It is mounted on a wheeled dolly and may have a TelePrompTer attached to its front.

TV version Television representation or interpretation of a news story, book, song or other work. Related term: adaptation.

TV-14 Rating for television programming that may not be appropriate for children under 14; the program may contain mature themes, strong language and some sexual content. Related term: rating.

TV-G Television rating for programming suitable for general audience viewing; it contains no strong language, little or no violence and little or no sexual dialogue or situations. The TV-"G" rating was first used in the United States in January 1997. Related term: rating.

TV-MA Television rating for programming intended for mature audiences (adults) only; it may be unsuitable for viewers under age 17 because it may contain profane language, graphic violence and explicit sexual content. Related terms: "M," rating.

TV-PG Television rating for programming that may contain some strong language, limited violence and some suggestive sexual dialogue and situations. The TV-"PG" rating in the United States, along with TV-"Y," TV-"Y7," TV-"G," TV-"14," and TV-"MA," was unveiled on December 19, 1996, by industry spokesperson Jack Valenti, head of the Motion Picture Association of America, and first used onscreen and in print as a program classification in January, 1997. The rating is decided by the program's producer, network, syndicator or cable or satellite channel but a local television station can reclassify it to meet their community's standards. Sports and news programs are not rated. Related terms: "PG"-rating, rating.

TVQ In the United States, a rating given to individuals and products (e.g., actors, TV series, performers, newspeople, cartoon and puppet characters, authors, doctors, consumer products) to gauge how familiar and popular each is with a surveyed segment of the national television-viewing public. About 2,000 Americans take part in each survey by mail, eight times per year. Entertainment companies may purchase a single TVQ rating or the entire package of all TVQs. The TVQ survey is conducted by Marketing Evaluations of Port Washington, New York. Also called a Q rating or Q score.

TV-series movie Any TV movie based on a television series, including a pilot movie, TV-reunion movie or special two-hour episode. *Cagney and Lacey*, which began as a television series, found new life as recurring telefilms.

TV-Y Rating for children's programming; it is suitable for youths of all ages. The rating was first used, along with other TV ratings, in the United States in January, 1997. Related term: rating.

TV-Y7 Children's television rating for programming appropriate for youths age seven and up. The show's content is suited for children who can make a distinction between make-believe and reality; it may contain mild violence and some scenes may frighten children under the age of seven. Related terms: TV-"Y," rating.

12-classification Rating issued for films and videos by the British Board of Film Classification. Full wording: "'12'—Suitable only for persons of 12 years and over. Not to be supplied to any person below that age." Also called a "12" certificate. Related term: rating.

two-camera Of or pertaining to two film or television cameras, e.g., a two-camera shoot, two-camera production or two-camera rehearsal.

two-camera shoot Filming session using two cameras positioned at different angles.

2D Abbreviation for two dimensions or two dimensional; having height and width but no depth.

two-fold flat Structural background on a performing stage with two sides hinged together so it can be folded like a book and easily stored. Also called a double flat. Related terms: book flat, flat.

two-hour episode Episode of a television series (typically, 30 or 60 minutes), expanded to two hours in length. May also be called a special two-hour movie episode. Related term: TV-series movie.

two-part episode TV-series episode twice its normal length and presented in two parts on two different days. Related terms: cliffhanger, conclusion, "To be continued."

two-person audition 1. One in which a performer (who has been cast) participates in the audition of a potential castmate. 2. Any audition involving two people. Talent unions in the United States prohibit mass auditioning of actors; each audition must be held in a private setting, as opposed to a public one. Related term: audition.

two-person interview Interview session between one interviewer and one interviewee. If it is for television or radio, a number of technical crew people are present but they are out of sight. The interviewee may also have people present in the same room, such as a publicist, manager or friend. A two-person interview may also be conducted remotely using satellite, telephone or computer technology.

Also called a one-on-one interview. Related term: interview.

two-shot Close camera shot just wide enough to keep two people inside the frame.

two-wall set Production set with two walls joined to form a corner.

Tyler mount Device used to attach a camera to a helicopter or camera plane; it is equipped with a gyro to eliminate vibration.

type classification Role-playing or physical-feature category designation of an actor. Related term: character type.

typecast 1. To cast a performing role according to a particular physical or image type. The opposite is to cast against type. Related terms: acting stereotype, look the part. 2. To have been cast continually according to one's physical or image type rather than for the ability to assume different performing roles, e.g., "Once you've been typecast, it is difficult, but not impossible, to break the mold and be seen as a viable choice for a variety of acting roles."

typed out Deleted from further casting consideration. Related term: made the cut.

U-classification Film and video rating used in Great Britain by the British Board of Film Classification; it corresponds to the "G" rating in the United States and the "Family" rating in Canada. Full Wording: "Universal"—suitable for all. Also called a "U" certificate. Related term: rating.

UC-classification Rating issued by the British Board of Film Classification for videos offered for sale or rental in Great Britain. Full wording: " 'UC'— Universal. Particularly suitable for young children." Also called a "UC" certificate. Related term: rating.

ugly-up To make oneself less attractive; this is done by removing or adding makeup or by dressing down or by changing one's hairstyle. For example, a celebrity may put on such a disguise so as not to be recognized by fans and photographers when in public. Related terms: dress down, celebrity.

Uher Trade name for a small, sensitive audio tape recorder used on location shooting; somewhat obsolete by today's standards. Related term: Nagra.

UHF Abbreviation for ultrahigh frequency. Television broadcast band covering 300 to 3,000 megahertz and channels 14 to 83. Related term: TV channel.

ultraviolet Light that cannot be seen but which causes a bluish cast on photographic film. Related term: haze filter.

umbrella Type of collapsible reflector resembling and operating like an outdoor rain umbrella; it is mounted on an adjustable pole stand and has an attached lamp that continually shines or flashes as it bounces light onto a set or subject. Related term: bounce board.

unaired episode Episode of a TV series that has not been (and possibly may never be) televised. Related term: lost episode.

unbilled 1. Actor who does not receive theatrical billing; actor whose work is not visibly credited. Wesley Snipes appears uncredited in *Waiting to Exhale* (1995). Related term: uncredited.

uncast Not cast, e.g., "That role is still uncast." Also referred to as being unfilled, available or up for grabs.

uncredited Not given visible credit. Related term: unbilled.

uncut Not cut; not changed or altered; intact.

uncut version 1. Original version of a film, seen as it was exhibited in theaters and before any editing for television. Related terms: foreign version, television version. 2. Version of a film before any shots or scenes are deleted (to meet a time restriction or to comply with a film rating board's guidelines). Related term: director's cut.

under budget 1. Below the cost allotted. 2. Insufficiently funded.

undercrank To shoot a scene at slower than normal speed to produce accelerated motion; the term originated in the days before sound when motion picture cameras were cranked by hand.

underdeveloped Negative film that has been given too little time in the developer; or, it has been processed in solutions at the wrong temperature thus producing a thin negative.

underexposed Film that has been subjected to too little light; or, it has been subjected to light for too short a time. The result is a thin negative.

under-five 1. Acting part in which the player speaks between one to five lines (up to 50 words). 2. Actor cast to play such a part.

underground film Term used in the late '50s through early '70s, describing films produced independently of studios or without major financial support; typically the subject matter was experimental, subversive bohemian or of interest to only a limited, special group. Related term: independent film

underline See script breakdown.

underplay To perform a role in a restrained and subtle manner. Underplaying may be done purposely, to achieve a particular effect, or unintentionally, due to poor acting skills (in which case, it may be interpreted as giving a weak performance). The opposite is to overplay.

underscore 1. (n.) Music heard during action and dialogue scenes. 2. (v.) To compose or provide an underscore.

undershoot To shoot insufficient footage for adequate coverage of a scene. Although the tendency today is to overshoot (budget willing), undershooting can be more disastrous: the lack of necessary footage typically isn't noticed until post-production, when it may be impossible, or prohibitively expensive, to return to

production for pick up shots to cover the missing material. A knowledgable script supervisor, working in conjunction with the editor, should be able to avoid this situation.

understudy Substitute performer who is prepared to perform a lead role on stage should the regular actor be unable to perform. Actress Shirley MacLaine became a star when she was the understudy for Carol Haney, the lead in the Broadway production of *Pajama Game* and was pressed into service when Haney broke her leg.

underwater bluescreen Visual-effects bluescreen positioned on one submerged side of a water tank. The largest underwater bluescreen in history was used in the production of *Waterworld* (1995).

underwater housing Special waterproof container for a camera; it allows for safe shooting in and under the water.

underwater photography Branch of photography, using special cameras, lights, lenses and housings, which permits shooting in and under the water.

underwater unit Production unit responsible for filming underwater scenes. Related terms: dry-for-wet, wet-for-wet.

union Labor organization determining work standards, wages, hours, credits, etc., on behalf of its members. Depending on how strong and well-organized the union or guild is, it may also offer legal advice, health and pension benefits, dental plan, have an internship program, a film society, etc. Related term: guild.

union card Identification slip issued to each dues-paying member in good standing; every member should be able to produce his card when working on a production. Related terms: Equity card, SAG card.

union contract 1. Agreement between a labor organization and signatory producer; it details wages, working conditions, etc., for the union's members. The contract is for a specified number of years. Before it expires, the terms of a new contract are negotiated and then approved or rejected by the union's members. (A strike may be called if the old contract expires and a new one cannot be agreed upon.) 2. Standardized contract form created by a union for use by an employer in the hiring of its members, e.g., a day-player (daily) contract, three-day contract, freelance weekly contract, etc.

union dues Payments made at regular intervals to a union by each of its full members and, in the United States, those in the financial-core status category; dues are used to fund the union's administrative operation and various benefit programs. Related terms: paying your dues, financial-core status.

union fee scale Schedule of graduated minimum payments for jobs done within a union's jurisdiction. Also called a union rate scale, union pay scale, theatrical compensation scale or union payment table. Related term: scale.

union initiation fee One-time payment to a union required from its new members upon joining. In the United States, for SAG, the initiation fee is approximately $1,100; for AFTRA and AEA (Equity), the fee is just under $1,000 for each (all amounts subject to change).

union member Individual who is officially in the ranks of union membership. In the United States, the Labor-Management Relations Act of 1947, also known as the Taft-Hartley Act (named after its sponsors in Congress), banned unions from having "closed shops," a situation in which employers were only allowed to hire union members. The Taft-Hartley Act allows states to choose whether employer-union contracts are required to contain a union security clause stating that if the employee hires a nonunion employee, that employee must join the union within 30 days or face employment termination by the employer. If the nonunion employee fails to join the union within the prescribed period during which first employment occurs, he cannot be hired by any other signatory employer until union membership is acquired. Signatory employers are required to report to the union the names, Social Security numbers, etc., of all nonunion employees, usually within 15 days of the date of being hired. Once the employee becomes a union member, he is able to work with and seek employment from union-contracted signatory companies as long as the employee remains a member in good standing (e.g., pays membership dues and follows union rules). Another clause usually found in union contracts is one detailing preference of employment. For actors, this means that producers are required to try casting a part from among qualified union actors; if none is available, the producer must inform the union in writing using a Taft-Hartley form, stating why a particular nonunion actor must be hired instead. In right-to-work states, an individual is not required to join a union within 30 days after being employed. In Florida, a right-to-work state, Article 11, Section 6 of the State Constitution reads as follows: "The right of persons to work shall not be denied or abridged on account of membership or non-membership in any labor union or labor organization." California and New York, two other states high in film and television production, are not right-to-work states; these states do not have laws or constitutional provisions prohibiting unions from making agreements with various industries requiring workers to become dues-paying members once employed. Related terms: financial core status, right-to-work state, Station 12, Taft-Hartley, Taft-Hartley Act, Taft-Hartley form.

union representative Union employee who represents the interests of its membership. Also called a union official, union leader, union spokesperson or union contract negotiator.

union rule book Printed material detailing union regulations, including union-employer industry contracts covering specific areas of work within the union's jurisdiction.

union signatory list List of talent agencies or production companies that have agreed to the terms of a union-employer contract (also called a union-management contract) or other union agreement. Related terms: signatory, franchised agency.

unit 1. Film or video crew or team. Also called a company. Related term: production unit. 2. Mobile production unit. 3. One of a number of things, products, or people, e.g., a TV-audience population unit. 4. Investment share in a project or production. Also called an investment unit.

unit director 1. First unit director; the overall director of a production whose name appears on the opening credits. 2. Second unit director; the individual who guides the unit shooting scenes other than those assigned to the first, or principal, unit. The second unit may be involved with the preparation and shooting of one or more stunts, special effects or location footage. Related term: second unit director.

unit director of photography 1. First unit director of photography; principal cinematographer on a production. 2. Second unit director of photography; second cinematographer, typically responsible for shooting of aerial shots, difficult stunts, special effects, or distant-location footage. Related term: second unit director of photography.

unit manager Individual on a production assigned to act as local business and production head of a particular film unit (e.g., second unit while shooting on location). Also called unit production manager or UPM. Related term: unit production manager.

unit production manager (abbreviated as UPM) Executive assigned to the production by the producer; he is responsible for coordinating and supervising all administrative, financial and technical details of the production and overseeing the activities of the entire crew. Related term: production manager.

United Scenic Artists U.S. labor union representing scenic designers, scenic artists, costume designers, costume painters, lighting designers and display workers in the fields of film, television and theater. Founded in 1918 and based in New York City.

Internet address: http://www.usa879. org.

universal leader Film leader attached to the beginning and end of each reel of the release print; it corresponds to cue marks in the picture just before the end of each reel to assist the projectionist in making changeovers. It is replacing academy leader.

unlimited use cycle Cycle of use (typically, 13 weeks) in which a client pays a principal performer a single calculated fee for the right to air a commercial as many times as it wishes during the cycle; there are no residuals in such a use cycle. In the United States, compensation for wild-spot use is computed this way.

unrated version Movie that has not been submitted to a motion picture rating board for issuance of a rating. Typically, the term is used when referring to a video movie. Related term: NR.

unshot Not filmed or videorecorded; existing only in script form or as an idea.

unsolicited script Unrequested script; one sent or delivered without first being requested. Large production companies and major studios typically will return unsolicited scripts, unopened. Companies that do accept unsolicited scripts may require the writer to sign a standard or company release form, protecting the company from being sued if it has a similar idea already in development. Typically, an unsolicited script is also a spec script.

unspooling Another name for screening.

unsqeeze A film that has been shot with an anamorphic lens must be projected with another anamorphic lens so that it can be viewed properly. Related term: wide screen.

up front Describing that period before production begins, e.g., a producer makes a deal to receive money up front from a studio.

upgrade To raise the status of a performer to a greater role or pay level. Related terms: bumped, downgrade.

upped 1. To be increased, e.g., "They upped the offer for my script." 2. To be promoted, e.g., "The exec was upped to a new post." Entertainment trade paper use.

upside-down clapboard Clapboard held upside-down, indicating the last scripted shot in a scene. Related term: end slate.

upstage 1. (n.) Background portion of a set (or stage); the part that is farthest away from the camera (or audience). 2. (v.) Intentional or unintentional blocking of one actor by another from the camera; or an actor making a distracting gesture or facial expression causing the audience's attention to focus on that actor. To steal a scene. (Children and animals are notorious upstagers.)

upstage foot Foot positioned closest to or moving toward the back of the stage.

uptempo Fast-paced tempo; quick moving.

use cycle Period of use (typically, 13 weeks). The term is found in union contracts for television performers. Related terms: unlimited use cycle, cycle.

use payment Money paid for the use of something; a union contract term for "residual." Not all film and TV productions require use payments to performers.

utility person Member of the crew who assists on the set; he provides assistance to a variety of departments.

This position is typically found on videotape productions.

utility stunt performer Union designation in the United States for a stunt performer hired on a weekly contract basis; he is allowed to double for more than one lead actor in a production and may perform any general stunt work.

V Television rating for programs containing violence. The rating may be accompanied by a numerical level, such as 1, 2 or 3. Related terms: "FV," rating.

variable focus lens See Zoom lens.

variable shutter Special shutter, expressed in degrees of opening, used to control exposure of film to light; it can be used in making fades and dissolves in the camera as it has two aperture plates, one stationary and one movable.

variable-area sound track Optical sound track in which the impulses are recorded as horizontal bars; they vary in density from black to light grey. Related term: optical sound track.

variable-speed motor Camera motor capable of running from 4 fps to 5O fps; used in shooting slow motion or accelerated motion. Related terms: wild motor, overcrank, undercrank.

Variety Los Angeles-based entertainment industry trade newspaper with offices worldwide. Founded in 1905 and published weekly (the first issue was published on December 16, 1905). Published by Cahners Publishing Company, a division of Reed Publishing USA. Internet address: http://www.variety.com. Related terms: *Daily Variety*, Stix Nix Hick Pix.

variety agency Another name for a talent or theatrical agency.

variety series Television series based on the variety show format. *The Ed Sullivan Show*, which aired on CBS from 1948-71, was television's longest-running variety series.

variety show Television, radio or stage show featuring a number of unrelated comedy, singing, dancing and skill-related entertainment acts. Related terms: variety series, talent show, "Take a bow," vaudeville.

vaudeville Early form of stage entertainment presented as a varied collection of short acts, such as song and dance routines, comedy sketches, acrobatic and animal acts, etc. When television came into existence, vaudeville shows evolved into what are now called television variety shows. Related terms: burlesque, variety show.

vault Fireproof storage area whose temperature and humidity levels are controlled; film (typically, negatives, but sometimes prints) or videotape are stored here for safe-keeping.

V-chip Small integrated circuit (IC) required by U.S. federal law to be included in new television sets beginning in 1999. When activated by the set's owner, it allows a parent or guardian to block television shows that have been rated inappropriate for children. Also required in Canada. Related term: rating.

VCR Abbreviation for videocassette recorder.

veepee Vice-president of a corporation or organization. Entertainment trade paper use.

vehicle 1. Any automobile, truck, portable trailer, etc., used on a production. Related terms: location vehicle, camera car, car hit, car roll, crane, honey wagon, location dressing room, picture car, star's motorhome, star's trailer, stunt driver, transportation captain. 2. Entertainment project, script or role that propels an individual to his career goal. Related term: stepping stone.

vehicle camera mount Attachment or place for a camera on a vehicle. Related term: camera mount.

Velcro shirt Garment with Velcro strips instead of the typical buttons or snaps, so a performer can quickly remove the shirt during a quick costume change. On such a shirt, buttons are sewn permanently in place and the button holes are sewn shut, so the shirt does not look different; only its method of closing and opening is different. Velcro is a product trade name and is derived from a combination of two French words: "velours" ("velvet") and "crochet" ("hook"); it has been available commercially since the 1950s and is widely used on theatrical costumes. Its first prominent oncamera appearance was in the original *Star Trek* (1966-69) television series, when it was used to hold phaser handguns and communicators in place on the sides and backs of the actors' costumes.

velocilator Camera support made to lift a camera, camera operator and focus puller in the air (to a maximum of six feet); some are powered while others are moved by hand. Related terms: dolly, crane.

venue 1. Locale; place where something happens. 2. Theater; playhouse; place where a performance occurs. Entertainment trade paper use.

verbal cue Another name for a voice cue.

VHF Abbreviation for very high frequency. VHF is the television broadcast band covering 30 to 300 megahertz and channels 2 to 13 (there is no Channel One in television broadcasting). The frequency band below Channel Two is reserved for other uses. Related term: UHF.

VHS Abbreviation for Video Home System. VHS is a logo trademark owned by JVC (Victor Company of Japan, Limited), which created and developed the system for home videocassette recorder-playback machines (VCRs); the VHS format offers 240 lines of horizontal resolution while Super VHS (S-VHS) has a higher resolution version, offering 400 lines. VHS was introduced to the consumer marketplace in 1977. Use of the logo must be licensed.

vid Short for video. Entertainment trade paper use. Related terms: homevid, kidvid.

vid exec Executive of a video-related company. Entertainment trade paper use.

vidbiz Short for video business; the video industry. Entertainment trade paper use.

vidclip Short for video clip. Entertainment trade paper use.

video 1. Electronic image-making system recorded on magnetic tape; typically used in television, commercials, music videos and in home use. 2. Visual part of a tape. Related term: audio.

video assist Use of a video camera, monitor and recorder-playback machine in conjunction with a motion-picture film camera so the shot can be viewed on a TV screen simultaneously or immediately afterward by the director, director of photography and others (actors, stunt supervisor, visual-effects supervisor, etc.). In recognition of video assist's contribution to filmmaking, the developer of the technique, Paul A. Roos, was honored by the Academy of Motion Picture Arts and Sciences with a 1988 Technical Achievement Award. Related term: playback.

video audition Audition in which the performers are videorecorded for later viewing during the casting decision-making process. A video audition is done to check an individual's television screen presence, performing talent, recorded voice and role suitability. Because it is less expensive and faster, it can be done in place of a filmed screen test. Also called a videorecorded audition, video screen test or video test.

video camera Handheld, shoulder-mounted or structurally attached camera using electronic components (as opposed to film) to record or transmit pictures and (depending on camera type) sound. Related terms: digital video camera, microvideo camera, camera, camcorder, CCD.

video clip 1. Brief videorecording or portion of a videorecorded work. Related terms: digital video clip, vidclip, preview clip, video promo. 2. Portion of a filmed work that has been transferred to video. Related term: film clip.

video clip clearance Permission to use a segment of a videorecorded work on a television program or in a home video or motion picture. Related term: clip clearance.

video conference 1. (n.) Audio-video meeting via video phones, the Internet or a satellite link. Related term: teleconference. 2. (v.) To video conference.

video dailies Video footage from a day's work on a production; by using advanced digital technology, full-

motion video dailies can be transmitted over phone lines from one remote location to another. For example, for *Jurassic Park* (1993), filmed scenes on videotape were transmitted via fiberoptics using Vynex to Steven Spielberg in Poland, where he was filming *Schindler's List* (1993).

video dropout Momentary white speck or horizontal streak on the screen of a television set or video monitor during playback of a videotape; caused by an imperfection of the tape coating, such as dust or a spot lacking magnetic particles.

video editing Process of selecting and electronically assembling video-recorded material onto a master tape or master disc. Related terms: video-tape editing, A and B editing, editing, off-line editing, linear editing, non-linear editing, on-line editing, video dailies.

video head drum Spinning cylindrical drum inside a VCR or camcorder housing its two or more video heads. Also called a video head cylinder.

video heads Tiny electromagnets positioned opposite each other on the head drum in a VCR or video camcorder; they convert the picture portion of an incoming television or live camera signal into magnetic patterns on the metal particle coating of videotape. A videocassette recorder (VCR) may have two to six heads; a videodisc recorder has no video heads because it uses laser technology to record and play back images and sound.

video master Another name for a master videotape or master videodisc.

video matchback Process of matching edited video images to the corresponding images on unedited film-negative footage when a filmed production is edited on video. Also called matchback from video. Related terms: editing on tape, video-to-35mm transfer.

video mixer Electronic device used to combine video shots from two or more sources. Depending on the type of mixer, it can also be used to add a variety of transitional and special effects, such as fades, dissolves, wipes, zooms, freeze frames and chroma key. Related term: A and B editing.

video phone Special telephone incorporating a small video camera into its transmission and reception circuitry; each phone also includes a built-in viewing screen. Computers connected to the Internet may also be outfitted to function as video phones. Related terms: teleconference, video conference.

video piracy Illegal duplication and sale of copyrighted videos or theatrical films transferred to video. Related term: piracy.

video prerelease Release of a movie or other production to the home video market before it airs on television.

video press kit Press kit in the form of a videorecording distributed to members of the news media. Also called an electronic press kit or EPK. Related term: sneak preview.

video printer Electronic device that produces selected still color photographs from a video source connected to it. Related term: photograph.

video projector Electronic device that casts images from a video source onto a remote screen. Video projectors are available in various sizes and designs and can be mounted from the ceiling, wall or on a tabletop. Related term: projector.

video sleeve Videocassette cover; typically, it is made of cardboard and has one end open so the video may slide in. Also called a video slipcase.

video still 1. Frozen television or computer screen image. Related terms: still video, TV still, freeze frame, video printer. 2. Picture produced by a digital still camera.

videocassette Rectangular plastic case containing two reels and a supply of videotape. Videocassettes are available in eight millimeter (8mm), one-half inch (12.7mm) and three-quarter inch (19.05mm) sizes (measuring the width of the tape). New types of cassettes feature four millimeter (4mm) and six millimeter (6mm) tape. Videocassettes are inserted into VCRs or camcorders. Also called a videotape, tape or video. Related terms: vidcassette, prerecorded video.

videocassette recorder (abbreviated as VCR) Machine having electronic and mechanical components which record and play back images and sound on videotape. Also called a videocassette recorder-playback machine. Related terms: camcorder, VTR, video head drum, video heads.

videodisc Thin, plastic disc with digitally encoded pictures and sound; these elements are optically recorded using a powerful laser light as a sequence of pits, in between which are shiny surfaces which reflect a less powerful laser light during playback. A videodisc can be the size of a compact disc or laserdisc; smaller sizes are also possible as miniaturization of the technology improves. Related terms: digital videodisc, CD-ROM, digital versatile disc, DVD, ETOM disc, laserdisc, videorecording.

videodisc recorder Machine that records pictures and sound on a videodisc. Related terms: digital videodisc recorder, DVD recorder.

videoprompter Video prompting device; any device using an off camera or offstage video monitor to display script lines and directions to an individual oncamera or onstage. Related terms: prompter, Tele-PrompTer.

videotape 1. (n.) Flexible plastic tape containing a coating of minutely sized iron-oxide particles; designed for recording and playing back color images and sound through magnetic alignment and reading of the coating's sensitive particles. Available width sizes include: 4mm, 6mm, 8mm, one-half inch (12.7mm), three-quarter inch (19.05mm) and one inch (25.4mm). All are manufactured in cassette form except the one-inch size, which is supplied on a single reel. Related terms: audiotape, base side, videocassette, video dropout. 2. (v.) To record images with or without sound on such tape. Related terms: videorecord, tape, "Roll tape," "Stop tape." 3. Another name for a videocassette. Related term: videorecording.

videotape editing Process of cataloging, selecting, arranging and rerecording videotaped shots and scenes onto a single master tape. Related terms: video editing, A and B editing, editing on tape, worktape.

video-to-35mm transfer Process of transferring images shot or created (as by a computer) on videotape, videodisc, etc., to 35mm motion-picture film so they can be exhibited theatrically. The opposite is a film-to-video transfer.

Videotronic Trade name for an animatronic character featuring patented, internal video-projection technology; invented by American Jeff Machtig of PeopleVision, a company located in Nutley, New Jersey. Videotronic characters can be seen at the MGM Grand Hotel in Las Vegas, Nevada (the "Wicked Witch") and at the Foxwood Casino in Ledyard, Connecticut (a trio of historical characters).

vidgamer Video game manufacturer. Entertainment trade paper use.

vidpic Video motion picture, e.g., a TV movie. Entertainment trade paper use. Related term: telepic.

vidstore Video store; video rental store. Entertainment trade paper use. Related terms: vidderies, sell-through, Video Software Dealers Association Convention.

viewer Device for looking at film. Related terms: Moviola, Kem, Steenbeck, editing bench.

viewer discretion advised Cautionary statement alerting television viewers that portions of the program (e.g., language, violence, graphic depictions or nudity) may be unsuitable, disturbing or offensive to some viewers.

viewfinder Part of the camera used to compose the image. Some viewfinders are separate from the picture-taking lens; most cameras used today combine the viewfinder and lens. Related terms: rackover, parallax.

vignette 1. Image with a clear central area and blurred or shaded borders. Antique photographs often utilize this effect. 2. Short performance or segment. Related term: cameo lighting.

virtual actor Another name for a computer-generated (CG) actor.

virtual image 1. In optics, the reflected image seen in a mirror. Related term: mirror shot. 2. In computer-generated effects, a scene or element that is part of a virtual-reality environment.

virtual reality (abbreviated as VR) Computer-generated, three-dimensional depiction of an area (room, building or landscape) that, by a variety of methods, can be "walked around" and "walked through" in real time. Related term: cyberspace.

virtual-reality set design Virtual-reality representation of a proposed production set. Also called a VR set design, VR set, VR set model or VR storyboard.

Vista Telescoping Tripod Trade name for a camera mount consisting of a sectional aluminum pole that telescopes upward from the center of a tripod base; it features a variety of remote-controlled capabilities and is available in different heights. Often used with a video camera. Manufactured and sold by Luska Instruments of Mississauga, Ontario, Canada. Related term: tripod.

VistaVision Trade name for an Academy Award®-winning, motion picture camera and projection system using standard 35mm film running horizontally (as opposed to vertically) through its machinery. This creates a frame size that has twice the image area of 35mm film shot in traditional cameras. From 1954 to 1961, Vista-Vision was used to shoot over 70 feature films, including *White Christmas* (1954; its first use), *Artists and Models* (1955), *The Colossus of New York* (1956), *High Society* (1956), *The Man Who Knew Too Much* (1956), *The Searchers* (1956), *The Ten Commandments* (1956), *Funny Face* (1957), *Gunfight at the O.K. Corral* (1957), *Houseboat* (1958), *North By Northwest* (1959) and *One-Eyed Jacks* (1961; its last feature film use). Today, it is used mostly to film visual-effects specialty short films. In recognition of Vista-Vision's contribution to filmmaking, the Technical Departments of Paramount Pictures Corporation were honored by the Academy of Motion Picture Arts and Sciences with a 1956 Class III Scientific and Technical Award for "the engineering and development of the Paramount lightweight horizontal-movement Vista-Vision camera." Related terms: IMAX Ridefilm theater, perforation.

visual cue Cue given by visual means, e.g., by a light or hand gesture. Related terms: "Cue me," hand cue, light cue, "You're on!"

visual-effects Term generally used to mean special effects; it also can include special lab work, lighting, sets, filters and pushed film, all of which contribute to the film achieving a certain look. Many times, on large budget productions, there is a Visual (Effects) Consultant or Director.

visual-effects designer Individual who devises the specific details and procedural requirements needed to achieve one or more visual effects. Related term: special-effects designer.

visual-effects producer Individual or company that creates visual effects for film, television and computer-software clients.

visual-effects shot Advanced special-effects shot, such as a bluescreen shot; typically, it requires completion during post-production via optical or computer technologies.

visual-effects studio Commercial or in-house studio that creates visual effects. Related term: digital-effects studio.

visual-effects supervisor Individual responsible for overseeing the planning and creation of one or more visual effects. Related terms: CCI effects supervisor, special-effects supervisor.

VO Abbreviation for voiceover.

vocal 1. Spoken or uttered by the voice; oral. 2. Song's accompanying lyric.

vocalist Another name for a singer.

voice actor Actor portraying a character only by speech or other vocalized sounds, such as a cartoon character or a character in a radio drama. Related term: voice over artist.

voice cameo Small, speaking-only acting role in an animated or live-action film, television program or videogame. *The Simpsons* (1989) is known for using famous actors in voice cameo roles. Related term: guest voice.

voice coach Individual who helps a performer in the areas of accents or dialects, improving enunciation or projection of words, etc. A voice coach may also specialize in a particular field, such as singing. Also called a voice teacher, voice instructor, voice trainer, voice specialist, accent/dialect teacher or speech coach. Related terms: dialect coach, dialogue director, voice/speech lessons.

voice cue Word, phrase or vocal sound that acts as a cue. Also called a verbal cue or verbal signal. Related terms: cue, countdown, "And . . . Action!"

voice exercise Physical training activity involving a specific type or degree of speaking, singing or sound vocalization; done to help maintain or improve one's voice. Related terms: exercise, voice/speech lessons.

Voice of God Nickname for an announcer who has a deep voice or a voice that has been electronically enhanced.

voice over Dialogue or narration coming from off-screen, the source of which is not seen. Related terms: cartoon voice over, TV commercial voice over, wild line.

voice over artist Individual, unseen when performing, hired for or specializing in doing voiceover work, as in TV or radio commercials. Also called an offscreen announcer, offscreen narrator or (as a vocalist) commercial background singer/jingles singer. Related terms: announcer, narrator, voice actor, voice over talent.

voice over talent 1. Special ability to perform voice overs, such as a distinctive announcing voice, impressionist voice or cartoon character voice. 2. Individual who does voice overs or such individuals collectively.

voice slate Vocalized slate at the beginning of a shot, as opposed to a visual slate (done with a clapboard). Also called an oral slate or verbal slate.

voice test Demonstration or check to determine quality, suitability or sound level of a performer's voice (recorded, amplified or live) before or during a performance or audition. Related term: mike check.

VR Abbreviation for virtual reality.

VTR Abbreviation for videotape recorder. A VTR is a cassette recorder or a reel-to-reel videotape recorder. A VCR (videocassette recorder) is a VTR using cassettes only.

WA Abbreviation for wide angle.

waiver To waive one's right; typically, giving up something that is contractually called for.

walkie-talkie Two-way communication device. Generally, these are used on the set by assistant directors to transmit information and requests quickly.

walk-on 1. Small, nonspeaking acting part in which the performer walks onstage or on the set. Related terms: bit part, silent bit, business.

walkout 1. An audience walkout. 2. Another name for a strike; work stoppage.

walk-through See run-through.

walla Noise from the background, typically, indistinguishable voices. Related terms: talk-talk, omnis, wild sound, background sound.

wardrobe Collection or supply of clothes, costumes and accessories worn by an actor in a film, play or television show. Related terms: audition wardrobe, character wardrobe, interview wardrobe, period wardrobe, personal wardrobe, accessory, costume, dancewear, fashion, pregnancy prosthesis, outfit.

wardrobe allowance Additional payment to an actor as compensation for wearing his own clothing on a job; this is a union-required payment. The amount of payment depends on what type of clothing is involved (e.g., evening or nonevening wear). Also called a cleaning allowance. Related terms: TV commercial wardrobe allowance, allowance.

wardrobe assistant Individual assisting in the handling and caring of the wardrobe used on a production. Related terms: dresser, costumer.

wardrobe call Request or notice to an individual to arrive at a particular time and place for a theatrical or fashion fitting. Also called a costume call.

wardrobe department Section of a film studio or theater responsible for storing, caring for and/or creating different types of production wardrobes. Also called a Costume Department.

wardrobe fitting Session in which a performer tries on the costumes for a production; typically, there are several fittings for each actor on the production. Also called a theatrical wardrobe fitting. Related terms: costume fitting, fitting, wardrobe test.

wardrobe mistress (or master) See costumer.

wardrobe supervisor Individual responsible for supervising all wardrobe-related activities on a production. The wardrobe supervisor may perform the same duties as a costumer; on larger productions, a wardrobe supervisor may oversee the work of one or more costumers/dressers. Also called a wardrobe master or mistress. Related term: costumer.

wardrobe test Live, videorecorded or filmed test, conducted prior to the performance, to see how a costume looks on a performer.

warm-up 1. Short period of stretching one's muscles prior to strenuous physical activity. 2. Short practice period before proceeding with a skilled activity. 3. Short period of entertainment or discussion with an audience to put them in the proper mood (e.g., laughing or applauding) for the upcoming main performance. Also called a warm-up act or warm-up routine.

warm-up comedian Stand-up comedian hired to entertain an audience before the start of a stage or television show.

warning bell 1. Signal to those on the production that the film is about to roll. One ring means shooting is about to commence and "Quiet on the set" is required; two rings is "all clear" because shooting has stopped. 2. Signal alerting the projectionist that a changeover is approaching.

warning light 1. Revolving, flashing or steady bright light warning those nearby of impending or current filming, broadcasting or screening; it is typically located outside the entrance door of a studio or screening room. Also called a stand-by light, filming-in-progress light or taping-in-progress light. Related terms: red warning light, on-the-air light, screening-in-progress light, wigwag light, closed set. 2. Light indicating damage or trouble, as on an electronic instrument or system control panel. 3. Glowing light on a camera indicating the unit is operating. Also called a camera cue light or power-on light.

wash Water-bath removing all developer and fixer from film that has just been processed.

water tank Any large receptacle, located in a studio, used for holding water. Some special-effects film processes use an indoor water tank, as in the creation of unusual cloud formations (paint is poured into the tank water and the action is filmed in slow motion) and other sky phenomena that are part of composited shots. An outdoor water tank (pond or pool) is used when a larger water setting is required. Related terms: dump tank, studio tank, underwater bluescreen.

Watersculpt Snow Batting Thick, white spun-fiber batting (fluffy or wadded sheets or roll of natural or synthetic fibrous material) rolled or placed on surfaces to create the effect of fallen snow. Water can be sprayed on it to further create a naturally sculpted appearance. Available in different widths and thicknesses from Sturm's Special Effects International, Inc., of Lake Geneva, Wisconsin, in the United States. Internet address: http://www.wisenet.net/users/Sturm SFX/. Related term: snow effect.

wave machine Large, powered device with a cylindrical container (drum) revolving off center while sitting in water; it creates a wave with each revolution. Another type of wave machine has a large wedge that can be raised and lowered as desired to create waves of different sizes and strengths. Also called a wavemaker or wave generator. Related term: studio tank.

waxing Wax applied to the edging of new films so they run through the projector smoothly.

weapons master Individual responsible for supplying, maintaining and securing firearms, knives, swords and related accessories used on a production. Some types of firearms, such as machine guns, require a special government license to possess. The weapons master may also be the property master (the general title), the individual ultimately responsible for all props, including weapons and blank ammunition. Also called a weapons expert or weapons specialist.

weather day Alternate day of shooting for which an individual may be booked in case the primary day is canceled due to bad weather; a weather-day booking may also be called an alternate booking.

weather delay Postponement or period of waiting caused by inclement weather.

weave Unwanted sideways movement of the film in the projector or camera.

web Slang for network. "Weblet" is slang for a new or up-and-coming network.

web exec Television network executive. Entertainment trade paper use.

weblet Small TV network. When the Fox channel was first created, it was referred to as a weblet. Entertainment trade paper use.

wedge Test strip provided by the lab; it arrives with the dailies and indicates the range of densities possible for that negative, thus enabling the cameraman to see the accuracy of the exposure. Related term: cinex strip.

weekly player Performer hired and paid at a weekly rate; he or she receives a weekly salary according to a union pay scale (if applicable). There are also day players, three-day players and contract players.

weekly ratings Network program ratings compiled by a ratings company on a weekly basis and listed in order of ratings size and share.

welfare worker Licensed individual who supervises school children on a production set, according to estab-

lished laws and regulations. In California, it is a union job. Also called a studio teacher. Related terms: studio teacher, classroom trailer, schooling on a production.

"We're clear." Announcement by a television director, assistant director or stage manager informing everyone on the set that all TV cameras are currently not transmitting or recording (e.g., during a commercial break or at the end of the program). Also said: "We're out," "We're in commercial," "We're in the break."

Wescam Trade name for a remote-controlled and motion-stabilized 35mm camera system that can be mounted on nearly any moving vehicle. In recognition of Wescam's contribution to filmmaking, its inventor, J. Noxon Leavitt, and Istec Incorporated, received a Scientific and Technical Award from the Academy of Motion Picture Arts and Sciences in 1989. Full name: Wescam Stabilized Camera System.

Western dolly Camera platform with large rubber wheels allowing for smooth, guided movement over rough, bumpy surfaces.

wet gate See liquid gate.

wet-for-wet Actually filming underwater when the script requires such a shot; the opposite is dry-for-wet. Related terms: underwater bluescreen, underwater movie, underwater unit.

wetting down Spraying, sprinkling, sponging or rubbing water, oil or other liquid on the skin or hair of an actor before filming to create a variety of wet looks, such as sweating from physical exercise or wetness from a rainstorm.

WGA Abbreviation for Writers Guild of America.

whip shot See swish pan.

whirly See crane.

wide angle shot encompassing and area of 60 to 65 degrees or more; this is more than a normal lens would capture and requires the use of a wide angle lens. In *Giant* (1956), the picture of James Dean sitting in his car with the oil wells in the background was a wide angle shot.

wide angle lens Convex lens emphasizing the convergence of parallel lines in the distance and, therefore, the sense of depth. Standard lenses usually cover a range of between 45 to 50 degrees; wide angles cover from 60 to 65 degrees and up. A 35mm lens is the standard wide angle (without too much distortion) used for anamorphic systems (there is not too much distortion), while 24mm lenses are used for regular spherical systems that shoot in 1.85:1; fisheye lenses start at 17mm and go down to 10mm, or even 8mm, with increasing distortion. With a wide angle lens, objects in the foreground appear disproportionately large when the lens is an extremely wide angle while objects in the background appear disproportionately small.

wide release Release of a product, such as a film or video, to a large number of exhibition or marketing outlets. Also called a wide-scale release or broad release. Related terms: general release, release.

widescreen Screen or frame image with an aspect ratio (width-to-height relationship) greater than 1.33:1 (also called 4:3), which is the aspect ratio of early black-and-white films, standard 16mm films and standard television-set screens. Most 35mm motion pictures are shot in the widescreen aspect ratio of 1.85:1 (Academy standard). Examples of widescreen aspect ratios (in which the width is greater than height) are 1.66:1 (35mm film), 1.78:1 (HDTV; also called 16:9), 1.85:1 (35mm film), 2.05:1 (70mm film), 2.2:1 (70mm film) and 2.35:1 (35mm film using an anamorphic "squeeze" lens). Related terms: Academy aperture, Academy standard flat, anamorphic lens, anamorphic print, aspect ratio, HDTV, letterboxed movie, letterbox format.

widescreen format Shape and size characteristic of a wide screen. Related term: letterbox format.

widescreen processes Filming and projection systems producing a broader-than-normal image. Related terms: aspect ratio, cinemascope, anamorphic, screen, Panavision 70.

wig Covering of artificial or real hair designed to be worn over existing hair or on a bald or partially bald scalp. The first movie to use a special-effects "hair-raising" wig was the silent haunted-house film *Haunted Spooks* (1920), which starred comedy actor Harold Lloyd (1893-1971): upon seeing a man's pair of pants walking around without a body, the hair on top of Lloyd's head raised upward, matching the fear on his face. Related terms: matching wig, hairdress, hairpiece, hairstyle, toupee.

wigwag Light outside a sound stage; when it is lit, it's an indication that cameras are rolling and no one is allowed onto the set. Related term: warning light.

wild line Word, phrase or sentence recorded later and not when the scene is actually shot; this may be done when an actor's line is changed (improved or corrected), when a character is thinking to himself in a scene and the audience hears his thoughts over the onscreen action (a soliloquy voiceover) or when a character is off screen and narrating the action onscreen (a narration voiceover).

wild motor See variable speed motor.

wild picture Film shot without sound. Related term: MOS.

wild shooting Shooting a scene without sound; MOS shooting.

wild sound or wild recording Any sound recorded independently (or out of sync) from a live camera; this may include wild lines, background noises, sound effects and music. Also called nonsynchronous or nonsync sound. Usually, these are natural sounds (wallah, room tone, off-camera dialogue) which make the scene more real when later mixed with the sound track. Related terms: wild track, sound effects.

wild spot Television commercial for a national product or service; the spot is shown across the country, in different market cities by individual network-affiliated or independent stations, at different times selected and paid for by the advertiser. The actual playing of the spot is generated at the local station and is not part of the programming and commercials fed to the station by the national network (if the station is an affiliate). Also called a locally aired national product/service commercial.

wild spot payment scale Union pay scale of money to be paid to television commercial actors who perform in wild spots. Also called a wild spot payment table.

wild track Soundtrack containing wild sound. Also called a wild recording.

wild wall Movable wall on a production set. Related term: flat.

wind machine Turbine engine or fan used to produce the effects of wind. Related terms: Ritter, special effects, stunt coordinator.

wind, specifically A-wind or B-wind Refers to the way the film is wound onto the core (emulsion side up or emulsion side down). In 35mm film, the winds are standardized because there are two sets of sprocket holes: A-wind (emulsion down) is used for printing while B-wind is used in the camera for shooting. When going through multiple generations between negative and release print, each generation is the opposite wind from the previous. Sixteen millimeter film has sprocket holes only on one side of the film and reversal film is used for shooting. The concept of winds is intricate with 16mm; for more information, consult a film laboratory.

winding Moving film or tape from one reel to another or back onto its original reel or core. Related term: rewind.

windscreen 1. Any object or structure that blocks the effects of fast-moving air currents on a production set. 2. Foam rubber or artificial fur covering for the outside of a microphone; it helps eliminate unwanted wind, speech and breathing sounds, especially when used outdoors. Also called a microphone cover, microphone shield, microphone sleeve or wind gag. Available in different colors and sizes. A voice screen, also called a pop filter, is a circular screen that helps reduce the hard-sounding "p" words and sibilant speech sounds ("s," "z," "sh," "zh," "ch," and "j"). It also helps protect the microphone elements from moisture contained in the singer's or speaker's breath. An industry source for both windscreens and voice screens is Markertek Video Supply of Saugerties, New York. Internet address: http://www.markertek.com. Related terms: gobo, Popper-Stopper.

wing it To improvise or do something without rehearsal or planning. Related term: ad-lib.

wipe Optical effect achieved in post-production. One image is replaced by another and it's made to look as if the first was actually being wiped off the screen by the second. The manner in which the two images interface is virtually unlimited. Related term: optical printer.

wire flying Lifting a performer and suspending him through the air over a production set, stage or audience by thin wires (wire-stranded cables) attached to a specially designed body harness worn under the costume. Two wires (cables) offer more stability and aerial maneuverability than a single one. Wire flying may be used as part of a special-effects process or stunt sequence. If used as part of a stunt, it may be to protect the stuntperson (or principal actor) during a dangerous, above-the-ground stunt. Wire flying outdoors uses a crane to control the flyer's lift-off, flight, descent and landing. In a theater or studio, off-stage pulleys and counterweights allow a specially trained offstage crew to raise and lower the flyer with ease. Multistrand aircraft cable or construction cable is used to fly performers or heavy objects. Piano wire or monofilament (fishing) line is used to fly or levitate medium-to-light objects. Scenes and stage effects involving wire flying are rehearsed carefully. According to talent union

contracts, this is considered a dangerous activity, thereby making the wire-flying performer eligible for hazard pay. Also called wire work. Related term: wire-flying scene.

wire removal Post-production technical process in which a computer is used to remove the wires holding up a person or object in a wire-flying scene. The pixels on the screen depicting the image of the wires are located and are electronically retouched. For example, a pair of gray wires shown against a blue sky are electronically colored blue in every frame so they become invisible in the completed footage. (To make the wires easier to locate, they may be physically painted a bright color, such as orange.) After each frame is retouched, the wires (and anything else needing correction or elimination, such as shadows caused by the wires) are no longer visible and the person or object appears to be suspended or flying independently. Related term: digital retouching.

wire-flying scene Special-effects or stunt scene (including computer visual effects) in which an actor is lifted, suspended, moved horizontally or diagonally through the air, or lowered to the ground. The actor must wear a concealed body harness with attached, thin metal cables. In film and television productions, the supporting wires are electronically edited out during post-production by a computer retouching process. In some scenes, hooking an actor to a pair of thin wire cables to achieve the illusion of flight or levitation is not possible; in these instances, the actor is positioned at the end of a metal boom or on a table mount and composited with a desired background using a blue (or green or orange) screen, chroma key, front projection or other type of visual-effects process. Related terms: flying scene, wire flying, wire removal, decelerator, descender, safety harness.

wireframe 1. Internal metal-wire support skeleton base, used in the construction of some types of special-effects clay sculptures and animation puppets. Related term: armature. 2. In computer animation, a three-dimensional, digital outline drawing of an object or character; it can be moved onscreen to view its various sides and its surface or skin can be generated to make it appear solid or made of liquid. Related term: laser scanner.

wireless microphone Small, portable microphone with an accompanying mini-transmitter; it sends audio signals over a selected radio frequency to a receiving unit. In the most common system, a small, clip-on microphone is attached to an individual; it is connected to a rectangular battery-powered audio pack (the mini-transmitter) with a wire that runs up through the individual's clothing. Speech and other transmitted sounds are picked up by a matching frequency receiving unit and are recorded or amplified and retransmitted to one or more speakers. Wireless handheld microphones have the same technology and are used by stage performers and as a backup if the wireless microphone fails. A headset wireless microphone features a swivel boom that positions the microphone at the individual's mouth. It also has an earphone and additional circuitry housed in a mini-transceiver battery pack, permitting two-way communication between the

wearer and others connected to the system. A wireless microphone is also called a wireless mike, radio mike, cordless mike or body mike. Related terms: microphone, dropout, ear-prompter, headset, walkie-talkie.

Witch's Fire Special-effects pyrotechnic powder that burns with flames and crackling sparks. Formulated and sold by Zeller International, Ltd., of Downsville, New York, in the United States. Related term: pyrotechnic effects.

word-of-mouth Dissemination of information by members of the public, e.g., word-of-mouth advertising. For example, "The film's box-office success was based largely on word-of-mouth." Many times, word-of-mouth can make or break a film. Part of the surprising success of *The Blair Witch Project* (1999) was due to its positive word-of-mouth. Related terms: advance teaser campaign, buzz, sleeper.

work permit 1. Official document issued by a government agency allowing a minor to work under certain conditions. A work permit is not required everywhere. Also called a child's working papers. 2. Official document issued by a government agency permitting and regulating the employment of a foreigner; usually included as part of a work-oriented travel visa. A tax may be deducted from income earned while working in a foreign country. Related term: Taft-Hartley form.

work print Untimed print assembled from dailies with tape splices. When the work print reaches the final cut stage, the negative is conformed to it. Also called a picture workprint or cutting copy. In addition to the picture workprint, there may also be a sound workprint (also called a magnetic film worktrack) used in the synchronized editing of sound. Related terms: rough cut, negative cutter.

workday Day during which work is scheduled to be done on a production. A shooting day is a workday.

working title Temporary name given to a film until a final name is selected. Sometimes, working titles are used up to the film's release so as to preserve the film's secrecy and to prevent piracy. For example, *E.T. the Extra-Terrestrial* (1982) had as its working title, *A Boy's Life*, until just before its release; most of Woody Allen's films have working titles such as *Woody Allen Fall Project*, with the year at the end.

worktape Videotape containing assembled selected shots and scenes in a desired tentative sequence; used by the director, producer or client to determine if additional editing needs to be done before a master tape is made.

world premiere First showing of a work anywhere in the world. A world broadcast premiere is the first showing on broadcast television. Theatrical films and made-for-TV movies may have world broadcast premieres.

worldwide box office Total domestic and foreign box-office receipts; all the money a theatrical film or stage show takes in at theaters or performing halls.

wow bow Fantastic opening in terms of its significant first day, weekend or first week box-office receipts. Entertainment trade paper use.

WP Abbreviation for "weather permitting."

wrangler 1. Individual responsible for the selection and total care of livestock on the set. Wranglers transport, corral, feed, etc., any type of animal, such as horses, mules, cattle, sheep, goats, llamas, ostriches, pigs, chickens, or the like. A wrangler also helps actors handle and mount the animals. Also called a livestock handler, livestock person, livestock provider or animal specialist. Related terms: animal handler, animal trainer. 2. Also used for other types of wildlife providers and handlers, e.g., an insect wrangler, spider wrangler, snake wrangler or rodent wrangler.

wrap 1. Completion of a day's shooting; it can also refer to the completion of a particular assignment or location or to the end of principal photography. Related terms: "That's a wrap," wrap party, wrap time, wrap up, last day of shooting.

wrap party Party for the cast and crew of a production, typically held at the end of production.

wrap time Period of time on a set or in a studio just after a production completes filming for the day. Related term: clean-up.

wraparounds Verbal introductions (by the host) to various segments of a TV or radio show. Related term: bumper.

writer approval Approval by an actor, director, etc., of a scriptwriter as a condition for becoming involved with the project. Related term: approval.

Writers Guild of America (abbreviated as WGA) In the United States, the union for film, television and radio scriptwriters. Writers Guild of America, East, headquartered in New York City, represents scriptwriters east of the Mississippi River; Writers Guild of America, West, headquartered in Los Angeles, represents scriptwriters west of the Mississippi River. The two are affiliated; each offers a script registration service to members and nonmember writers. Internet address: http://www.wga.org. Related term: WGA Award.

writing sample Example of an individual's writing ability. An aspiring screenwriter's writing sample is usually a spec script and demonstrates his creative talent.

written by Writers Guild of America designation meaning original story and screenplay has been written by the named author.

X 1. Abbreviation for a single frame. 2. Number of times, e.g., "Transfer this track 3X."

X-copy First duplicate transferred sound master.

XCU Abbreviation for extreme close-up.

X-dissolve Abbreviation for cross-dissolve.

XFR/XFER Abbreviation for transfer.

XLS Abbreviation for extreme long shot.

X-rating 1. Rating issued to projects that contain extremely violent or explicitly sexual content; age limits for the X-rating vary. Some countries no longer use the "X"-rating for commercially released theatrical films. For example, the Motion Picture Association of America in the United States replaced the "X"-rating with the "NC-17" rating on September 27, 1990. In Great Britain, the "X"-rating was replaced in 1982, with the classification numbers "18" and "R-18" in 1982. Abbreviated as "X." Related terms: motion picture rating board, rating. 2. Rating issued by a producer of sexually oriented adult material (adult videos, CD-ROMs, magazines, etc.) alerting and warning exhibitors, store owners, employees and the public that the material is subject to legal restrictions and cannot be shown to or purchased by individuals under a specified age, such as 18 or 21. The "X"-rating is not a registered trademark and exists in the public domain. The "X"-rating on packaging and covers of sexually oriented material is not as common as it once was. Instead, the phrases, "Adults Only," "Not for sale to minors," "Not for sale to anyone under [age]," etc., may appear. The exact wording of the cautionary statement may be controlled by law. Related terms: XXX, adult video, blue movie, R18-classification.

y-cable/y-joint Two-pronged electrical connecting unit with plugs or connectors at all three ends.

yearly ratings Ratings for network and syndicated programs; compiled on a yearly basis by a ratings company and listed in order of rating size and share. Related terms: rating, ratings period.

"Your back is to the camera." Director's verbal notice to an actor that his back is mistakenly positioned toward the camera. The actor should turn around to an appropriate angle so the camera can get a clear shot. Also said:

"Your back is facing the camera," "Turn around so that the camera can get a clear shot of you."

"You're on!" 1. Direction to a TV performer or newsperson that he will be in front of an active camera in a matter of seconds; may also be given in a visual cue (pointing the forefinger at the person) preceded by a verbal countdown. Related terms: "Cue me," "Three . . . two . . . one." If used in radio, it may be said as, "You're on the air." 2. Direction to a stage performer that it is his turn to go onstage and perform.

ZB Abbreviation for zoom back. Variation: ZO (zoom out.)

Zed card Another name for the composite card used by a TV commercial actor or model; named after its originator, Mr. Zed from Germany.

Zel-Jel 1. (n.) The trade name for an Academy Award®-winning, fire-protection stunt gel manufactured and sold by Zeller International, Ltd., of Downsville, New York. Zel-Jel is a clear, water-soluble, nonflammable coating that insulates the skin or clothing from heat or direct flames for up to three minutes. When spread directly on the skin, it allows a flammable substance placed on top of it to burn without causing injury to the performer. Zel-Jel was introduced in 1975, and has been used in many films, including *Firestarter* (1984*)*, *Indiana Jones and the Temple of Doom* (1984) and *Scanners* (1981). In recognition of Zel-Jel's contribution to filmmaking, its inventor, Gary Zeller, was honored by the Academy of Motion Picture Arts and Sciences with a 1988 Technical Achievement Award. Related terms: stunt gel, fire effect. 2. (v.) To apply Zel-gel, e.g., "The stuntperson's clothing has been Zel-Jelled."

Zellene Fuel Clean-burning, gelled fuel that is one type of flammable liquid available to special-effects crews; can be applied directly to a stuntperson over stunt gel without the dripping or runoff associated with thin fuels. Formulated and sold by Zeller International, Ltd., of Downsville, New York.

Zellene Powder Powdered additive used to thicken fuels when staging fire and explosive scenes. Formulated and sold by Zeller International, Ltd., of Downsville, New York.

zeppelin Tube with perforations; it is attached to a shotgun microphone to limit wind noise. Related term: zeppelin windscreen.

ZI Abbreviation for zoom in.

Zice Trade name for a nontoxic, granulated powder; when combined with water, it forms simulated crushed ice. It is used in television commercials, advertising photography and theatrical productions. A related product, Crystal Zice, produces larger simulated ice pieces. Available from Zeller International, Ltd. (inventor), of Downsville, New York and Burman Industries of Van Nuys, California. Related term: snow effect.

zip pan See swish pan.

Zirk hit Another name for a spark hit.

ZO Abbreviation for zoom out. Variation: ZB (zoom back).

zoetrope Turning, circular device which gives the illusion of motion; used for viewing a series of pictures before the days of motion pictures.

zone shot Camera shot that records one specific section of a production set. A zone shot is usually done to process a composited-image visual effect, such as a split-screen or one involving a matte. An actor in a zone shot should not stray out of the designated performing area. For example, if an actor is being shot using a keyhole matte, he can move only within the small zone within the shot or he will not be seen in the final shot.

zoom Method of changing the size of the subject in an image by changing its focal length (when using a zoom lens); this is accompanied by a change in the depth of field. When the camera zooms in, the subject appears to become larger and the depth of field is lessened; when the camera zooms out, the subject becomes smaller and the depth of field increases; when the camera moves in and out on a dolly, the depth of field remains the same.

zoom lens Camera lens having a focal length that can be changed continuously without loss of focus. A zoom lens offers the ability to magnify and demagnify images without having to change lenses or reposition the camera. Also called a variable-focal-length lens. Related terms: digital zoom, telephoto lens, wide-angle lens.

zoom shot Film or video camera shot in which a zoom lens is used. In it, magnification of the subject can be varied by controlling the lens to bring the subject closer or farther away while remaining in focus. Related term: zoom lens.

Zoptic Front Projection System Trade name for an Academy Award® winning, front-projection system named after its inventor, Zoran Perisic. It is used to achieve certain types of visual effects not possible with standard front projection systems. For example, an actor to be filmed is placed above the ground on a custom support structure attached to the end of a sturdy metal pole. The pole protrudes perpendicularly from a hole in the highly reflective movie screen from an area directly behind the actor, who now appears to be suspended in mid-air in front of the screen. The camera and projector are positioned to shoot the screen straight on, keeping the pole from being seen in the completed footage. Desired background images are projected on and only picked up by the screen. Zoom lenses on both the camera and projector are operated to achieve an enhanced effect of movement within the scene. The Zoptic Front Projection System first achieved fame through its use in the series of *Superman* movie series starring Christopher Reeve. Related term: front projection.

Z-Smoke tablet Compressed powder in a large tablet shape that produces dense white smoke when burning; it can be broken into pieces or used whole. Formulated and sold by Zeller International, Ltd., of Downsville, New York, in the United States. Related term: smoke effect.

About the Authors

Ralph S. Singleton is the author of four books from Lone Eagle Publishing: *Film Scheduling, Film Budgeting, Film Scheduling/Film Budgeting Workbook* and *Movie Production and Budget Forms . . . Instantly!*

Those titles give first indication of what makes Ralph Singleton such a worthy author for the new second edition of his **Filmmaker's Dictionary**. In 21 years of motion picture experience, he has risen through the ranks to the head of his class in production knowledge and experience. Beginning as a production assistant, he segued on an upward scale to assistant location manager, location manager, DGA trainee, second assistant director, first assistant director, production manager, associate producer, producer, executive producer and director.

Singleton has had ample opportunity to learn the filmmaker's craft while working side-by-side during the 1970s with such experts as William Friedkin on *The French Connection,* Alan J. Pakula on *Klute,* Sidney Lumet on *Network* and Martin Scorsese on *Taxi Driver.* Singleton devoted much of the '80s to the mammoth Dan Curtis mini-series, *The Winds of War,* working with Francis Coppola at Zoetrope Studios, and then the popular *Cagney and Lacey*—producing 98 episodes and winning an Emmy in the process. Returning to features, he co-produced *Harlem Nights* and co-executive produced *Another 48 Hrs* starring Eddie Murphy. Singleton's producer credits continued to impress in the '90s. He produced *Leap of Faith* starring Steve Martin, *Clear and Present Danger* starring Harrison Ford, *Last Man Standing* with Bruce Willis, *Murder at 1600* with Wesley Snipes and the sci-fi epic *Supernova.* Singleton is a frequent lecturer at universities and colleges across the country. He lives in Los Angeles.

James A. Conrad is the owner and founder of a Florida-based research company and the author of a highly respected dictionary for the Performing Arts community.